D1103030

Macro Command	Page

Computer users are not all alike.
Neither are SYBEX books.

We know our customers have a variety of needs. They've told us so. And because we've listened, we've developed several distinct types of books to meet the needs of each of our customers. What are you looking for in computer help?

If you're looking for the basics, try the **ABC's** series. You'll find short, unintimidating tutorials and helpful illustrations. For a more visual approach, select **Teach Yourself**, featuring screen-by-screen illustrations of how to use your latest software purchase.

Mastering and **Understanding** titles offer you a step-by-step introduction, plus an in-depth examination of intermediate-level features, to use as you progress.

Our **Up & Running** series is designed for computer-literate consumers who want a no-nonsense overview of new programs. Just 20 basic lessons, and you're on your way.

We also publish two types of reference books. Our **Instant References** provide quick access to each of a program's commands and functions. SYBEX **Encyclopedias** provide a *comprehensive reference* and explanation of all of the commands, features and functions of the subject software.

Sometimes a subject requires a special treatment that our standard series doesn't provide. So you'll find we have titles like **Advanced Techniques, Handbooks, Tips & Tricks**, and others that are specifically tailored to satisfy a unique need.

We carefully select our authors for their in-depth understanding of the software they're writing about, as well as their ability to write clearly and communicate effectively. Each manuscript is thoroughly reviewed by our technical staff to ensure its complete accuracy. Our production department makes sure it's easy to use. All of this adds up to the highest quality books available, consistently appearing on best seller charts worldwide.

You'll find SYBEX publishes a variety of books on every popular software package. Looking for computer help? Help Yourself to SYBEX.

For a complete catalog of our publications:

SYBEX Inc.
2021 Challenger Drive, Alameda, CA 94501
Tel: (415) 523-8233/(800) 227-2346 Telex: 336311
SYBEX   Fax: (415) 523-2373

Mastering
Quattro Pro 3

Mastering
Quattro® Pro 3

Third Edition

Gene Weisskopf

SYBEX® San Francisco • Paris • Düsseldorf • Soest

Acknowledgments

As much as I would like to take complete credit for everything in this book, I would also like to keep it a work of nonfiction. Just as with any other endeavor, its success is due to a diverse group of people who contributed to it both directly and indirectly.

For helping to keep the computer revolution alive and well, I extend my appreciation to the members of the Sacramento PC Users Group, especially to those in the Davis Chapter.

Tony Barcellos once again gets my thanks and admiration. His razor-sharp understanding of mathematics helped me to distill the matrix and optimization examples in this book to their essential levels. Even he must find it difficult to be humble.

I would like to thank Nan Borreson at Borland for serving as my interface when I needed information. Special appreciation goes to Greg Joy for keeping me in touch with Borland and Quattro Pro, and for his continuing support of user groups.

This book was developed and written in GrandView 2.0, and I offer my greatest respect and appreciation to John Friend, its developer.

I must thank Jim Savercool at the phone company, who has been more than patient with my deferred consulting schedule (see, there really was a book). My warm respect goes to Peter Dyson, my cohort in SYBEX books, whose perspective is of the highest calibre.

Marilyn Smith, the editor of this and the previous editions, did a wonderful job on the editing while keeping me on my toes. Her suggestions were clear and practical, and added much to the quality (but not the quantity) of this book. My thanks to Dianne King, acquisitions editor, for her pleasant and helpful assistance. And thanks also to Brendan Fletcher for his role as project editor.

Finally, my thanks and appreciation to all of you who made the previous editions a success and whose input helped shape this edition.

Contents
at a Glance

Table of Contents

3 Making Cell Entries

51

7 Printing Your Spreadsheets   195

8   Managing Your Files   **231**

9 Navigating Your Disks with the File Manager   269

13 Adding Sizzle to Your Graphs with the Graph Annotator

Introduction

When Borland International released Quattro Pro in the final months of 1989, it was immediately evident that it had hit the bull's-eye in the spreadsheet market. Where the original Quattro scored high in 1987, Quattro Pro continued in that tradition by addressing the primary needs of spreadsheet users at the beginning of the new decade:

- Ability to work with multiple spreadsheets, and link data among them
- Presentation-quality spreadsheet output
- Enhanced graphs and highly advanced graphing tools
- Realistic memory requirements
- Normal text-mode display to provide high speed and efficiency on the millions of existing DOS computers
- Graphics mode display so that graphs can be inserted into the spreadsheet and viewed with spreadsheet data
- Complete Lotus 1-2-3 version 2.01 file and command compatibility, including a "soft" interface with Lotus 1-2-3 and Quattro menus

This very impressive list of enhancements placed Quattro Pro at a level of power, sophistication, and ease of use that surpassed any other spreadsheet program.

By the time Quattro Pro version 2 was introduced in the fall of 1990, Quattro Pro had already established itself as one of the top contenders in the spreadsheet market. A tremendously successful first year brought it industry-wide praise and numerous awards. Some of the new features in version 2 were:

- Support for Lotus 1-2-3 release 2.2 files and linking formulas
- Three-dimensional graphs

- Graph buttons that let you control the progress of the slides in a graphics slide show
- Exportation of graphs in the PCX file format
- Importation of clip art in the CGM file format
- Capability to copy a named graph's settings from one spreadsheet to another
- The Paradox Access, which allows you to run both Paradox and Quattro Pro at the same time, integrating the power of each without sacrifice
- The Solve For command, which lets you solve for an unknown after you have already set up the mathematical relationship
- More choices for video display modes

And now, Quattro Pro version 3 has added a wealth of new features, enhancements, and items from the "wish list" of Quattro Pro users:

- A true WYSIWYG display (for an EGA or a VGA system) that shows all fonts and spreadsheet enhancements, lets you adjust row heights, display or hide the spreadsheet grid lines, and scale the size of the display
- A command to save all open files
- More printing enhancements, including faster printing, a Print to Fit command, banner-mode layout, print scaling, multiple copies, and a wider right margin (up to 511 characters)
- An improved DOS Shell command, which lets you write Quattro Pro macros that run other programs from DOS and then return to Quattro Pro
- More graph enhancements, including sound and transition effects for slide shows and graph buttons, sculpted graph boxes, drop shadows for graph text, and a command to automatically save your named

graphs

- Improvements in the Graph Annotator, which let you automatically align objects and create a background graph button for more control of your slide shows

- The option of designating either the left or right mouse button to be the active one

- More memory information on the Options–Hardware menu

- The ability to limit the amount of expanded memory that Quattro Pro utilizes

- A Values command on the Print and Options menus, which shows the current status of the settings on those menus

Continuing in the tradition of its predecessor, Quattro Pro version 3 is both an enhancement to the original program and an affirmation that Quattro Pro has become the spreadsheet that the competition has to match.

WHO SHOULD READ THIS BOOK

Mastering Quattro Pro 3 will serve a variety of readers. You don't have to be an expert to understand this book; every attempt was made to present the material in a clear and jargon-free style. If you are new to spreadsheets, this book will be your guide as you learn the fundamentals of the program. All examples and exercises are concise and easy to follow, so that you won't waste time trying to figure out the purpose of the spreadsheet under discussion.

If you are familiar with spreadsheets, you will go farther and faster with *Mastering Quattro Pro 3*. It covers every aspect of Quattro Pro, and it will therefore be a handy reference as well as a tutorial for those features and techniques with which you are not familiar.

WHAT THIS BOOK COVERS

The 18 chapters of this book were written with the assumption that the reader would start at the beginning and work through to the end. Therefore, the earlier chapters make fewer assumptions about how much the reader knows, and the later chapters rely to some extent on the material in earlier chapters.

If you are new to spreadsheets, start with Chapter 1 and continue through the book. If you have experience with other spreadsheet programs, such as Quattro or Lotus 1-2-3, you may want to read the first two chapters as a way of introduction, and then turn to the topics that interest you.

If you have not yet installed the program, read Appendix A first. It explains the installation process and offers tips that may be helpful when you install the program.

FEATURES OF THIS BOOK

Every command in Quattro Pro is discussed in *Mastering Quattro Pro 3*. Menu commands are shown with a dash between choices, and if the command has a shortcut key, that key is shown in parentheses. For example, you may read "Use the Edit–Copy command (Ctrl-C)." This refers to the Copy command on the Edit menu, whose shortcut is invoked by pressing and holding down the Ctrl key while pressing the letter C.

You will find margin notes throughout the book. They serve as adjuncts to the body of the text, as follows:

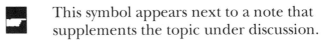 This symbol appears next to a note that supplements the topic under discussion.

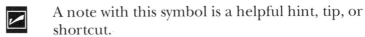 A note with this symbol is a helpful hint, tip, or shortcut.

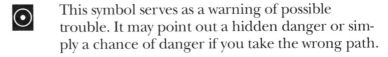 This symbol serves as a warning of possible trouble. It may point out a hidden danger or simply a chance of danger if you take the wrong path.

Most of the figures in this book were captured on a computer using a Hercules monochrome graphics card. Your screens may not appear exactly the same if you are using a different video adapter, but those differences should be slight.

TIPS FOR USERS OF QUATTRO AND LOTUS 1-2-3

If you are already a user of Quattro or Lotus 1-2-3, you should find the transition to Quattro Pro to be an effortless one. Everything you have learned in either of those programs can be transferred to the new one. The first day you install Quattro Pro, you can retrieve a spreadsheet you have created in 1-2-3, for example, and continue working with it in Quattro Pro. In fact, you can simultaneously work on half a dozen Lotus spreadsheets and another dozen Quattro spreadsheets, and really begin to take advantage of Quattro Pro.

The commands in Quattro Pro include just about all those found in both Quattro and Lotus 1-2-3. In general, unless any differences are noted, you should assume that any feature in Quattro Pro that is similar to one in Quattro or Lotus 1-2-3 behaves in the same manner. For example, block names (or range names in 1-2-3) behave in the same way in all three programs, although the commands are worded somewhat differently in each.

Instead of using Quattro Pro's default menus, you can change to either a Quattro or Lotus 1-2-3 menu tree with the Options–Startup–Menu Tree command. Although your first inclination may be to switch to a more familiar menu system, it is really not necessary. The default menu tree is laid out in a logical format that makes the command structure very accessible. Within the first half hour of browsing through Quattro Pro, you should be able to recognize all the commands that are the equivalents to those in Quattro or 1-2-3.

Another benefit to staying with the default menus is that those commands that are unique to Quattro Pro will be readily available in a logical location. In the Quattro or 1-2-3 menu tree, those commands are of necessity placed within the context of

Due to the continuing litigation between the Lotus Development Corporation and Borland International, the fate of the 1-2-3 menu tree is tenuous. The available menu trees will be listed on the menu.

the menus, and they may not be easy to find. For example, the Quattro Pro command Options–Startup–Menu Tree is called the Worksheet–Global–Default–Files–Startup–Menu Tree command in the 1-2-3 menu tree.

Keep the alternate menus in reserve for those times when they are truly needed:

- You may need to refer temporarily to a more familiar menu during the early stages of learning Quattro Pro.

- When a person who is familiar with another spreadsheet needs to use your computer.

- When you retrieve a Quattro worksheet and want to run its macros, you will need to load the Quattro menu tree.

HARDWARE REQUIREMENTS

Quattro Pro will run on any IBM or compatible computer, including those using the 8088, 8086, 80286, 80386, and 80486 processors. The machine must have a minimum of 512 kilobytes of system memory (RAM) and a hard disk.

If you want to use the Paradox Access to run both Paradox and Quattro Pro at the same time, you will need a computer that has an 80286 or higher processor and 2 megabytes of RAM (see Chapter 14 for more about the Paradox Access).

Normal installation will use almost 4 megabytes of disk space, but you should have a minimum of 4.5 megabytes available so that there will be room for Quattro Pro to create soft font files as it needs them.

Your computer needs DOS version 2 or higher, so if for some strange reason you are still using DOS 1.0, it's time to buy a newer version!

A graphics video adapter card is needed if you want to display graphs or preview your printouts on the screen. Many graphic standards are supported, including CGA, EGA, VGA, Hercules, AT&T, and Compaq. In order to run Quattro Pro version 3 in graphics (WYSIWYG) mode, however, you need either an EGA or a VGA display.

If your computer has expanded (EMS) memory, Quattro Pro will be able to store much larger spreadsheets in memory, and it will run a little faster as well. You don't have to tell the program what your memory configuration is; it will automatically detect that each time you run it.

Quattro Pro works very well with a mouse, although you must install the mouse and mouse software before you run Quattro Pro. Refer to Appendix A if you have not already installed your mouse.

1

Getting to Work
in Quattro Pro

Fast
Track

THIS CHAPTER PRESENTS AN OVERVIEW OF QUATTRO PRO. It describes how to start the program and introduces the spreadsheet screen and its components. The essentials of using the keyboard and the mouse come next, followed by the highlights of the Quattro Pro menus and Help screens.

STARTING QUATTRO PRO

Before you can start Quattro Pro, you must run the Install program (on the first Quattro Pro disk). Refer to Appendix A for installation instructions. With the program installed, follow these steps to start up:

Substitute the drive and path you have used during installation if they are different than C:\QPRO.

1. From the DOS prompt, type **C:** and press ↵ to make the drive on which the program is installed the default drive.

2. Type **CD \QPRO** and press ↵ to make the Quattro Pro subdirectory the default.

3. Type **Q** and press ↵ to start the program.

The Quattro Pro spreadsheet will appear on the screen, and you will be ready to get to work.

If your computer has expanded (EMS) memory, and you don't specify otherwise when you start Quattro Pro, the program will allocate all of that memory for its own use. This not only lets you create larger spreadsheets, but it also speeds up many of the Quattro Pro program routines.

If you are running one of the few other programs that use extended memory, Quattro Pro may not recognize it, and you could experience conflicts over the extended memory. Use the /X parameter, but then experiment to see how your system performs.

If you wish to limit the amount of EMS memory allocated, use the /E*n* command-line parameter when you start the program. Replace the *n* with the number of 16-kilobyte (K) blocks of EMS memory that you want Quattro Pro to take. For example, to tell Quattro Pro to use no EMS memory, start the program with the command **Q /E0**. To give Quattro Pro 64K of EMS memory, use the command **Q /E4**. Remember, you only need to specify the amount of memory when you do not want Quattro Pro to take whatever EMS memory is available.

If your computer has extended memory, you can use another command-line parameter when you start Quattro Pro to make it run a little faster. For example, if your computer came with 1 megabyte of memory, it probably has 384K of extended memory. When you start Quattro Pro, use the /X parameter: **Q /X**. That way, it will store its program swap files in the very fast extended memory instead of on your slower hard disk.

MAPPING THE SCREEN

The Quattro Pro spreadsheet should look familiar if you have used other spreadsheet programs. Even so, you may not recognize a few of its features. Figure 1.1 shows the basic Quattro Pro screen.

Note that several areas of the screen are reserved for use with the mouse. These areas are covered later in the chapter, in the discussion of using the mouse. The menu bar across the top of the screen is described in the section about navigating the menus. The other screen elements are discussed in the following sections.

THE WORK AREA

The *spreadsheet*, or *worksheet*, is made up of rows and columns. The *rows* are identified by numbers, and are labeled down the left side of the screen. In Figure 1.1, rows 1 through 20 are visible but there is a total of 8192 rows in a Quattro Pro spreadsheet.

The *columns* are identified by letters, and are labeled along the top of the screen. There are 256 columns in a Quattro Pro spreadsheet, labeled A through IV (column AA follows column Z, column BA follows column AZ, and so on). Columns A through H can be seen in Figure 1.1.

At the junction of any row or column is a *cell* (in a bit, we'll calculate how many cells there are in a spreadsheet). Each cell is identified by its column and row, so that the *address* of the cell at the junction of column E and row 9 is referred to as E9. In Figure 1.1, cell E9 has a text entry in it that says *Cell-E9*.

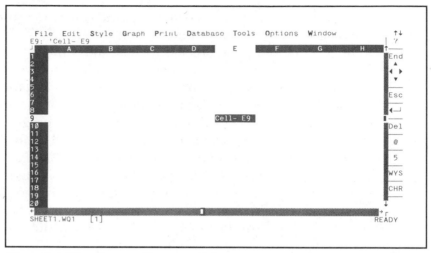

Figure 1.1: The Quattro Pro spreadsheet

CELL ENTRIES AND OPERATIONS

You enter data into the cells of the spreadsheet. Each cell is separate and unique from all the other cells, and it can hold a maximum of 254 characters. You can move from cell to cell in a number of ways, but the most common means is by using the arrow keys on your keyboard: ←, →, ↑, and ↓.

The *cell selector* is the highlighted bar that shows which cell is the *current,* or *active,* cell. Whenever you start a new spreadsheet, the cell selector is always on cell A1, in the upper-left corner of the spreadsheet.

When you type an entry for the current cell, the results of your keystrokes first appear on the *input line,* which is on the second row of the screen. When you press ↵, or move the cell selector to a different cell, the data on the input line is placed into the current cell. When you create or edit an entry that is longer than the input line (76 characters), the line will expand up to four lines so that you can see the entire entry.

As you move the cell selector around the worksheet, information about the current cell (the one that is highlighted by the cell selector) appears in the input line. In Figure 1.1, the cell

The cell selector's current column letter is highlighted at the top of the spreadsheet, and its row number is highlighted to the left of the spreadsheet. This tells you at a glance exactly where the cell selector is in the spreadsheet.

selector is on cell E9, and you can see the contents of that cell on the input line.

The other information on the input line, preceding the current cell contents, includes the cell address, followed by the numeric format, column width, and font. These other attributes will be discussed later in the book.

Let's begin working with the program by making a cell entry that calculates the number of cells in the Quattro Pro spreadsheet. This is simple. Since there are 8192 rows and 256 columns in the spreadsheet, just enter the following formula in any cell, using an asterisk to denote multiplication (don't include any commas, spaces, or other stray characters): **8192*256**. Press ↵ to insert the formula into the cell. On the screen, you should see the result of the formula: 2097152.

That's a lot of cells—probably a couple of million more than you will ever need in a single spreadsheet.

THE STATUS LINE

The bottom line of the screen is the *status line*, where information about the current spreadsheet file is displayed.

In Figure 1.1, you can see the file name of the current spreadsheet at the left of the status line. In this case, the spreadsheet is named SHEET1.WQ1, which is the default name that Quattro Pro uses for the first spreadsheet you open until you save the spreadsheet under another name.

The window number, [1], next to the name identifies the current window. Each new window that you open in Quattro Pro is assigned a unique number in consecutive order, so that the next window to be opened would be 2, the next 3, and so on (note that the default file name, such as SHEET1, and the window number, such as [2], are not directly related).

At the far right on the status line is the mode indicator, where the current mode of the spreadsheet is shown. In Figure 1.1, the spreadsheet is in Ready mode.

There are quite a few mode indicators that may appear in place of the Ready indicator. For example, you will see the Edit

⊙ Even though there are over 2 million cells in the spreadsheet, the number you can actually use is strictly limited by the amount of RAM (random access memory) in your computer.

▨ When in doubt, be sure to take a look at the mode indicator. A common mistake is to try to perform an operation without being in the correct mode, such as trying to access the menus while in Label mode.

indicator when you are editing a cell. The Help indicator will appear when you're using the Help function. Table 1.1 lists the mode indicators that can appear on the status line.

On the status line, between the file name and the mode indicator, is space for other status indicators. For example, when you press the Caps Lock key, the Caps indicator will appear, reminding you that this key is now toggled on. The other indicators that you may see on the status line are listed in Table 1.2.

Note that these other status line indicators are replaced by the current cell contents when you edit a cell. When you are finished editing, the status line returns to its usual display.

Table 1.1: Mode Indicators

INDICATOR	MEANING
CALC	Manual recalculation is on and one or more formulas has changed since the last recalculation.
EDIT	You are editing a cell.
ERROR	An error has occurred.
FIND	You are using the Database–Query–Locate command.
FRMT	You are editing the format line with the Tools–Parse–Edit command.
HELP	You are in the Help system.
INPUT	You are using the Database–Restrict Input command.
LABEL	You are entering a label (text).
MACRO	A macro is being executed and has control of the system.

Table 1.1: Mode Indicators (continued)

INDICATOR	MEANING
MENU	You are making a choice from a menu.
OVLY	A program overlay file is being accessed.
POINT	You are pointing to a block of cells during a command or formula.
READY	All other activity has stopped; you are free to perform any command or function.
VALUE	You are entering a value (number).
WAIT	System is in use for printing, file activity, and so on.

Table 1.2: Other Indicators on the Status Line

INDICATOR	MEANING
BKGD	Background recalculation is in progress.
CAP	Caps Lock is on.
CIRC	There is a circular formula somewhere in the spreadsheet (use the Options–Recalculation command to find the exact cell).
DEBUG	The macro debugger is toggled on, and executing a macro occurs one step at a time as you press the spacebar.
END	You have pressed the End key.

Table 1.2: Other Indicators on the Status Line (continued)

INDICATOR	MEANING
NUM	The Num Lock function is toggled on; using the number keypad will now produce numbers.
OVR	The Insert key has been pressed, putting the spreadsheet in Overwrite mode.
REC	The Tools–Macro–Record command is on, and your keystrokes are being recorded as a macro.
SCR	You have pressed the Scroll Lock key; moving the cell selector will now scroll the window.

USING THE KEYBOARD

Along with being your means of typing data into cells, the keyboard provides access to many of the program's features. The following sections explain how to enter data, move the cell selector, cancel commands, and use the function keys.

ENTERING DATA

When you are typing from the keyboard in a word processor, your text is simply one long string of characters. You may edit those characters and move them to new locations, but it is still one coherent string. In a spreadsheet, however, the only structure is the grid of rows and columns; how you make use of the 2 million cells is completely up to you.

All the data in the spreadsheet is built from the usual keyboard letters and numbers and some punctuation characters.

You might type text that consists of letters, numerals, and punctuation, or you might type a formula that has numbers, numeric operators, and parentheses.

Some special keys are available while you are typing your data into a cell or editing the characters in an existing entry. For example, you can press the Backspace key to delete the character to the left of the current cursor position. Table 1.3 lists the keys you can use for entering and editing data.

MOVING THE CELL SELECTOR

Remember, the spreadsheet that you see on your screen is really just a tiny window onto a very large matrix of rows and columns. The only way to enter, view, or edit cells in another portion of the spreadsheet is to move the cell selector to the area you want, thereby moving the window.

Depending on the style of keyboard you are using, you may have one or two sets of arrow keys. One set is on the number keypad on the right side of your keyboard; the other will be separate, dedicated arrow keys.

The Num Lock key toggles the function of the number keypad. When the Num indicator is not visible on the screen, the keypad can be used for moving the cell selector. If the Num indicator is on, the number keypad can be used for entering numbers.

The arrow keys are also used to move the selector through menus or options screens.

Each time you press one of the arrow keys, the cell selector moves one cell in the arrow's direction. If the cell selector is in cell C5, pressing → moves it to D5; pressing ↓ would move it to C6.

If the cell selector is in column A, pressing ← will simply provoke Quattro Pro into issuing a small beep (because it can't move any farther to the left). The same is true when you press ↑ while the cell selector is in row 1.

When you move the cell selector below row 20 or to the right of column H, the screen will *scroll*; you are moving the viewing window over a new portion of the spreadsheet.

Table 1.3: Cell Entry and Editing Keys

KEY	FUNCTION
Caps Lock	Forces all letters you type to be uppercase; the Cap indicator will appear on the status line. Note that this is not the same as holding down the Shift key; it affects only uppercase and lowercase letters.
Ins	Toggles between Insert and Overwrite modes, so that characters you type will either push any existing characters to the right, or will overwrite them. The Ovr indicator will appear on the status line when the program is in Overwrite mode.
Escape	When typing a new entry, erases all characters and returns to Ready mode.
Del	Erases the character at the cursor's position; can also be used from Ready mode to erase the contents of the current cell.
Backspace	Erases the character to the left of the cursor.
Ctrl-\	Erases all characters from the cursor to the end of the line.
Ctrl-Backspace	Same as Escape.
Tab or Ctrl-→	Moves the cursor five characters to the right.
Shift-Tab or Ctrl-←	Moves the cursor five characters to the left.
Home	Moves the cursor to the beginning of the entry.
End	Moves the cursor to the end of the entry.

Table 1.3: Cell Entry and Editing Keys (continued)

KEY	FUNCTION
← or →	When used with a new entry (from Ready mode), enters the data into the cell, moves the cell selector left (or right), and returns the spreadsheet to Ready mode. When used in editing an existing entry (from Edit mode), the keys move the cursor left (or right) on the input line (remaining in Edit mode).
↑ or ↓	Enters the data into the cell, moves the cell selector up (or down), and returns the spreadsheet to Ready mode. However, when you are entering a formula and the cursor is at the end of the line and after a valid operator (such as + or *), the spreadsheet will be placed into Point mode. You can then point to the cell or block that you want referenced in your formula (see Chapter 4 for details on pointing and using formulas).
PgUp or PgDn	Same as ↑ or ↓, only the cell selector will move a screen's worth of rows.

MOVING SCREEN BY SCREEN

The size of the current window determines how many rows or columns the cell selector jumps when you press any of the keys that move the cell selector a screen at a time.

Instead of moving the cell selector row by row or column by column, you can move it an entire screen at a time with any of the following keys:

- PgUp: Moves the cell selector up one full screen.
- PgDn: Moves the cell selector down one full screen.

- Tab or Ctrl-→: Moves the cell selector right one full screen.
- Shift-Tab or Ctrl-←: Moves the cell selector left one full screen.

You can scroll the window without moving the cell selector by toggling on the Scroll Lock key. You will see the Scr indicator on the status line. Now when you press an arrow key to move the cell selector, it will remain in the same cell while the rows or columns of the spreadsheet scroll through the window.

MOVING IN LARGE JUMPS

In a spreadsheet as large as Quattro Pro, moving the cell selector to a distant location by moving it cell by cell or even screen by screen can be far from satisfactory. Instead, there are several ways to move in large jumps:

- Press function key F5, type the cell address to which you want to go, and then press ↵. The cell selector will jump to that address. Note that if the cell you chose was not visible on the screen when you pressed F5, the window will be arranged so that the cell you selected will be in the upper-left corner of the screen.
- Press End, and the End indicator will appear at the bottom of the screen. Now press any of the arrow keys, ←, →, ↑, or ↓, and the cell selector will move as far as it can in that direction, based on the rules given in Figure 1.2. The figure also gives examples of using this method.
- Press Home to move the cell selector to cell A1, no matter where it was in the spreadsheet. When you press End-Home, the cell selector jumps to the last occupied row and column in the spreadsheet. In Figure 1.2, that would be cell D15. But if there were an entry in cell G3, for example, then pressing End-Home would jump the cell selector to G15, because column G would be the last occupied column.

- If you are working with more than one window at a time and know the number of the window that you want, you can jump to it by pressing Alt and the number, such as Alt-3 to jump to window number 3. You

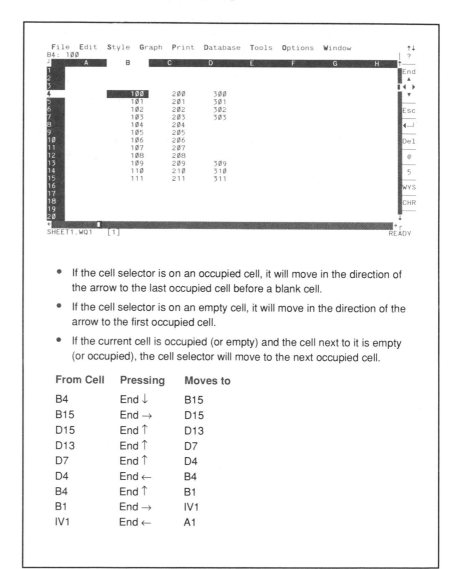

- If the cell selector is on an occupied cell, it will move in the direction of the arrow to the last occupied cell before a blank cell.

- If the cell selector is on an empty cell, it will move in the direction of the arrow to the first occupied cell.

- If the current cell is occupied (or empty) and the cell next to it is empty (or occupied), the cell selector will move to the next occupied cell.

From Cell	Pressing	Moves to
B4	End ↓	B15
B15	End →	D15
D15	End ↑	D13
D13	End ↑	D7
D7	End ↑	D4
D4	End ←	B4
B4	End ↑	B1
B1	End →	IV1
IV1	End ←	A1

Figure 1.2: Using the End key to move the cell selector

can also use the Window–Pick command (pull down the Window menu and select Pick), which displays a menu of all the windows that are open. Simply choose the one you want, and the cell selector will jump there.

HOLD EVERYTHING!

There are two important keys that you will need on a regular basis. The first is the Escape key. Whenever you are in the process of entering data or executing a command, you can use Escape to back you out of what you are doing, one step at a time.

For example, type a few characters, but don't press ↲. To cancel the entry you are making and return to Ready mode, just press Escape. Or, if you are three levels deep into a menu command, you can press Escape three times (once for each menu level) to return the spreadsheet to Ready mode.

To cancel a command completely with one keystroke, use Ctrl-Break; hold down the Ctrl key, and then press Break (located near the upper-right corner of your keyboard). So if you are many levels down in a menu, one press of Ctrl-Break will return the spreadsheet to Ready mode. The Ctrl-Break key will also cancel a print routine or an executing macro. When in doubt, press Ctrl-Break to hold everything.

ACCESSING FEATURES WITH FUNCTION KEYS

The function keys fulfill two purposes in Quattro Pro. First, they serve as shortcuts for commands on the menus. For example, function key F10, the Graph key, is a shortcut for the command Graph–View. You can use either the function key or the menu to execute the same command.

Some function keys have no corresponding menu command. For example, function key F2, the Edit key, lets you edit the contents of the current cell, and there is no similar menu command.

You will find a complete list of all the function keys on the inside cover of this book. The following function keys are the ones you will probably use the most:

- F1 (Help): Calls up the Quattro Pro Help screens.

- F2 (Edit): Puts the spreadsheet into Edit mode, allowing you to edit the contents of the current cell.

- F5 (GoTo): Prompts you for a cell address, and then jumps the cell selector to the cell you specified.

- F9 (Calc): Recalculates all formulas in the spreadsheet.

USING THE MOUSE

Whether or not you use a mouse with Quattro Pro is your own choice. If you are fast with the keyboard, you may find little or no advantage to using a mouse. On the other hand, if the keyboard is foreign terrain to you, the mouse may prove to be a very practical ally.

You can put a mouse to work in a variety of ways in Quattro Pro, but all of its tasks really fall into two distinct categories: moving the cell selector about the spreadsheet or invoking Quattro Pro commands. Keep in mind that all the functions of the mouse can be duplicated from the keyboard.

Whether your mouse has one, two, three, or more buttons, Quattro Pro uses only one button, by default, the one on the left. There are three different actions you can perform with the mouse:

You can use the Options–Hardware–Mouse Button command to specify either the left or right mouse button as the active one.

- Pointing: Moving the mouse pointer to any part of the screen. For example, point to relocate the cell selector or choose an item from the menus.

- Dragging: Holding down the mouse button and moving the mouse. For example, drag to highlight a block of cells in the spreadsheet.

- Clicking: Giving the mouse button a quick click, generally to select an item to which you are pointing.

Try these quick exercises to get a feel for the mouse actions:

1. Point to cell C6 by moving the mouse until the mouse pointer is over that cell.

2. Now click on that cell by quickly pressing and releasing the left mouse button. The cell selector should be highlighting cell C6.

3. To select the cells in the block C6..E14 (cell C6 through cell E14), hold down the mouse button and move the mouse pointer to the right and down (dragging). As you move, the cells will be highlighted. Release the mouse button when you have highlighted the block C6..E14.

4. There is no action to perform on this block at this time, so point to any other cell, such as B1, and click the mouse. This will remove the highlighting and move the cell selector to cell B1.

USING THE TOOLS ON THE MOUSE PALETTE

Down the right side of the screen is a series of boxes that make up the *mouse palette* (see Figure 1.1). This menu is simply an aid for mouse users; it can be accessed only by a mouse. The first item in the palette is a question mark (?). Pointing at the ? and clicking your mouse brings up the Quattro Pro Help screens, as though you had pressed F1.

The next box, with the word End and the four arrows, moves the cell selector in the direction of the arrow on which you click, as though you had first pressed the End key. Clicking on the right arrow is the same as pressing End-→ on the keyboard.

The next four mouse palette boxes perform the same function as the Escape, ↵, Delete, and Alt-F3 (@ functions list) keys, respectively. The box labeled 5 has no action assigned to it. The box beneath it, labeled WYS (for WYSIWYG) switches the display to graphics mode. The last box, CHR (for character) changes the display to text mode.

Together, these seven boxes make up the *programmable* items of the mouse palette. You can change the definition of each of these to suit your own needs, using the Options–Mouse Palette command (which is discussed in Chapter 18).

MOVING THE CELL SELECTOR WITH THE MOUSE

Anytime that you have more than one window open at a time, you can easily move from one window to another simply by clicking inside the window that you want; just point and then click.

Just to the left of the mouse palette is a vertical shaded bar called the *scroll bar*. When you click on any portion of this bar, the cell selector is moved vertically in the spreadsheet. Another scroll bar is located along the bottom of the spreadsheet. It is used to move the cell selector horizontally.

There is a small *scroll box* within each scroll bar. You can move the cell selector by pointing at the scroll box and then dragging it.

At either end of each scroll bar is a *scroll arrow*. Clicking on a scroll arrow moves the cell selector one cell at a time in the arrow's direction.

Don't confuse the two arrows in the zoom box with the upward-pointing scroll arrow above the vertical scroll bar.

MOVING AND SIZING THE WINDOW

In the upper-right corner of the screen, above the mouse palette, is a box that contains two arrows, ↑ and ↓. This is the *zoom box* (it actually belongs to the menu bar that runs across the top of the screen). It is used to expand or shrink the current (active) window. Try pointing at the zoom box (at either of the arrows), and then clicking. The window should shrink to about half of its original size. Click again to return the window to its previous size.

In the lower-right corner of the screen, just above the mode indicator, is a tiny inverted L that is the *resize box*. To change the size of the window, simply point at the resize box and then drag it to a new location. The lower-right corner of the window will move accordingly, thereby resizing the screen.

When a window is not full-screen size, it will be enclosed in a double-lined box. The window's path and file name will appear in the upper-left corner of the box, which helps you to identify each window if there are several on the screen. You can move the window to a new location on the screen by pointing to any of its borders and dragging the window to its new position (see Chapter 10 for more information about working with windows).

Finally, you can click on the *close box* to remove the current spreadsheet window from memory. This is the same as choosing the File–Close command. The close box is in the upper-left corner of the spreadsheet (not the screen), at the junction of the column and row labels.

NAVIGATING THE MENUS

The menus in Quattro Pro contain the commands for performing practically all the operations that are available in the program. You can use menu commands to open a file, save a file, print your spreadsheet, run a macro, and so on.

The menus are in the menu bar across the top of the screen. These are called *pull-down menus* because they "pull down" from the menu bar.

Selecting a menu item may either execute the desired command or simply call another menu with more choices. Some Quattro Pro menus are many layers deep; you keep making the appropriate choice until you finally reach the actual command or option you wish to invoke.

The menus are logically laid out and easy to find, whether you are using the keyboard or a mouse.

MAKING CHOICES FROM THE MENUS

To invoke commands or options from the menus, from Ready mode, first open, or access, the menu bar. There are two different ways to do this:

- From the keyboard, just press the slash key (/). The first item on the menu bar, File, will be highlighted, meaning the menu bar is now active and waiting for you to make a choice from it.

- With a mouse, just point to the desired item on the menu bar and click the mouse button. That item's menu will appear, ready for you to make a selection.

After you have activated the menu bar, you can use one of these methods to select an item:

- Using the arrow keys, move the highlighting left or right to the command you want to choose, and then press ↵.

- Simply type the highlighted letter of the command (usually the first letter), such as F for File or P for Print.

- With a mouse, point to the item and click the mouse button.

Remember, the Escape key is used to back out of the menus. When you have opened the menus, just press Escape one or more times to back out of each menu level and return to Ready mode.

Using the first or third method is great when you are new to Quattro Pro and its menus are still unfamiliar. It's easy to move the highlighting (either by using the arrow keys or pointing with the mouse) through the menus, looking for the command you want; and as you highlight a command, a description of it appears in the status line at the bottom of the screen.

If you are new to Quattro Pro, start making menu selections by using the highlighting method. Besides being easier, it also gives you a chance to become familiar with the menus.

The second method provides split-second access to any commands on the menu and is the expert's choice. To invoke a rather long command, such as Graph–X-Axis–Mode–Log, all you need to do is type the letters GXML, and you've executed the command.

USING SHORTCUTS

Quattro Pro provides an even quicker way to execute menu commands. By using a menu *shortcut,* you can choose a command with a single keystroke, no matter how far down the menu tree that command may be. There are two types of shortcut keys in Quattro Pro: function keys and Ctrl-key combinations.

FUNCTION-KEY SHORTCUTS

A function key can either provide a unique command, such as F2 for Edit, or can serve as a single-keystroke substitute for a menu command. For example, the F10 key is equivalent to the Graph–View command, and Shift-F2 is the same as the Tools–Macro–Debugger–Yes (or No) command.

CTRL-KEY SHORTCUTS

Unlike function-key shortcuts, Ctrl-key shortcuts are defined by the user. You can assign a Ctrl-key shortcut to any item on the Quattro Pro menus. Some commands already have shortcuts assigned to them (although you can change them if you like), and you can see those shortcuts next to the command on the menu. For example, bring up the Edit menu by typing / **E**. Your screen should look similar to Figure 1.3.

Remember, the program must be in Ready mode before you can use either the menus or a shortcut.

Notice that Ctrl-C is listed next to the Copy command, Ctrl-M is next to Move, and Ctrl-E is next to Erase Block. These are the Ctrl-key shortcuts for the commands. Notice also that the Undo command has the shortcut Alt-F5; this command has a dedicated function key.

To erase one or more cells in the spreadsheet, you can use Ctrl-E as a shortcut for the Edit–Erase Block command: From Ready mode, hold down the Ctrl key and press E (uppercase or lowercase), and then specify a block of cells to erase.

To assign a Ctrl-key shortcut to a menu item, you must first activate the menu bar and highlight the command for which you want the shortcut. For example, the command File–Utilities–DOS Shell temporarily returns you to the DOS prompt, while leaving Quattro Pro and your worksheet still in memory. If this

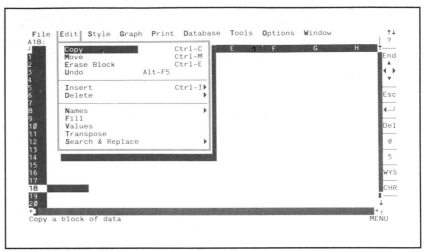

Figure 1.3: The Edit menu and its shortcuts

were a command you frequently needed, having a shortcut could be a real benefit. As an example, we'll create the short-cut Ctrl-B for that command. Follow these steps:

1. From Ready mode, activate the menu bar by pressing /.

2. Choose the File command.

3. Choose the Utilities command.

4. With the highlighting on the DOS Shell command, press Ctrl-⏎ (hold down the Ctrl key and press ⏎). At the bottom of the screen you will see the prompt

   Hold down the Ctrl key and press any Letter, or <DEL>

5. Hold down the Ctrl key and press B. The prompt will disappear, and you should see the phrase Ctrl-B next to the DOS Shell command.

6. Press Escape twice to return to Ready mode.

7. From Ready mode, press Ctrl-B and then press ⏎. You will be returned to the DOS prompt, having executed the File–Utilities–DOS Shell command with a single keystroke.

◉ One drawback to menu shortcuts is that there are only 26 of them available: Ctrl-A through Ctrl-Z. If you want to leave Quattro Pro's 15 predefined shortcuts alone, only the following letters are available: B, H, J, K, L, O, Q, U, V, Y, Z.

8. Type **exit** to return to Quattro Pro.

DELETING A SHORTCUT

If you try to create a Ctrl-key shortcut that is already used by another command, you will see the error message

Shortcut key is already in use

Press Escape to clear the error message, and then press Escape one or more times to return to Ready mode. You will then have to delete the shortcut before you can assign it to another command. Let's delete the shortcut we just assigned, as follows:

1. Bring up the File–Utilities menu.
2. With the highlighting on the DOS Shell command, press Ctrl-↵.
3. Press the Del key once.
4. Press Del again to confirm that you want to delete the shortcut for this command.

The Ctrl-B next to the command should disappear, meaning that there is no longer a shortcut assigned to this command. Now you could use Ctrl-B as the shortcut for some other command.

SHRINKING OR EXPANDING THE MENUS

Menus in Quattro Pro show not only the shortcut key for each command (if a command has one), they also show the default setting currently in effect, where relevant. For example, next to the File–Directory command is the current default drive and sub-directory, which may be something like C:\QPRO on your menu.

But showing the option settings or shortcut keys makes the menus rather wide, and this can sometimes block your view of the underlying spreadsheet. Quattro Pro lets you shrink the width of the menus, thereby hiding the options or shortcuts.

To shrink a menu, just press the gray − key on the numeric keypad. To expand it back again, press the gray + key on the numeric keypad.

FINDING ANSWERS ON THE HELP SCREENS

The Quattro Pro Help system is a very valuable, built-in resource. It is a series of information screens that explain the program's commands and features. The file that holds these screens is about 400K in size, so you can imagine how extensive they are.

No matter where you are in Quattro Pro, help is always available by simply pressing F1 or by clicking on the ? with your mouse. Help is *context sensitive*, so whether you are editing the contents of a cell or moving through the menus, a press of the F1 key will bring up a Help screen that gives you relevant information about your position in the program.

> To return to the worksheet from the Help system, just press Escape.

For example, bring up the Edit–Names menu and highlight the Create command. Then press F1. Your screen should look like the one shown in Figure 1.4.

Most of the Help screen in Figure 1.4 consists of useful information about the Edit–Names–Create command. Near the bottom of the text, the word *Labels* is highlighted. If you were to press ↵, another Help screen would appear with information about the Edit–Names–Label command. A Help screen may have several of these keywords (each is in bold or a different color typeface), and you can simply move the highlighting to one of them and press ↵ to get more information.

At the bottom of the screen in Figure 1.4 are three index keywords: Menu Commands, Edit Commands, and Block Names. You can highlight any of one of these, press ↵, and see another screen of information related to the keyword.

There are just a few keys you will need within the Help system:

- ←, →, ↑, or ↓: Moves between the keywords.
- Home: Moves to the first keyword on screen.
- End: Moves to the last keyword on screen.
- F1: Brings up a Help screen for the Help system.
- Backspace: Shows the previous screen.
- Escape: Returns to the spreadsheet.

If there is more information than will fit on one screen, one of the options at the bottom of the screen will be Next. Choose it to view the next screen. That screen will also have a Next choice if there is yet one more screen, as well as a Previous choice that lets you return to the previous one.

There is a topical index for the Help system that is always close at hand. Press F1 while in the Help system, and a Help screen titled Using the Quattro Help System (1/2) will appear. Not only does this screen give you some information about using the

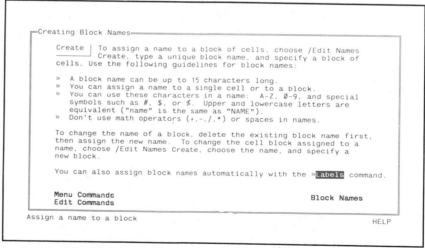

Figure 1.4: The Help screen for the Edit–Names–Create command

Help system, but it also has a Help Topics choice at the bottom of the screen. This item brings up the table of contents for the Help system, which is the top level of all the Help screens; from it, you can branch down to any other screen.

This chapter has introduced you to the basic tools of Quattro Pro, the ones that will help you get to work quickly and with assurance. The next chapter will present you with a nutshell tour of the process of building a spreadsheet.

2

Building
a Spreadsheet

Fast
Track

BEFORE LEARNING ABOUT THE DETAILS OF THE MANY features in Quattro Pro, you should get more familiar with how the program works. This chapter provides a quick introduction to the process of building a spreadsheet.

AN OVERVIEW

We will create a simple spreadsheet that calculates a car's mileage for a given set of gas fill-ups. You may be surprised at the number of steps involved for such a small project. In this example, you will perform the following tasks:

- Enter both text and numeric data
- Use label prefixes when entering text
- Write formulas
- Copy a cell to a block of cells
- Save a file to disk
- Work with multiple files in memory
- Apply formats to numeric cells
- Print your work

This exercise will give you a good idea of the powers of Quattro Pro. Some of the spreadsheet tools that are called into play may seem foreign at this early stage, but they all will be discussed in detail in other chapters.

Figure 2.1 shows how the spreadsheet will appear when finished. In the five columns, you will make the following entries and calculations:

- Enter the odometer reading at the time of the gas fill-up
- Calculate the miles driven between fill-ups
- Enter the number of gallons purchased
- Calculate the mileage

• Compare each entry's mileage to another mileage figure for a mythical "national average" for this model car

One of the best features of a spreadsheet program is that you can start a project in any part of the spreadsheet and begin with any part of your data, formulas, or text. But it is always easier to start from the simple and work to the complex. For this project, that means starting the work in cell A1, and beginning with the structure of the spreadsheet, then working up to the data, formulas, and cell enhancements (or formats).

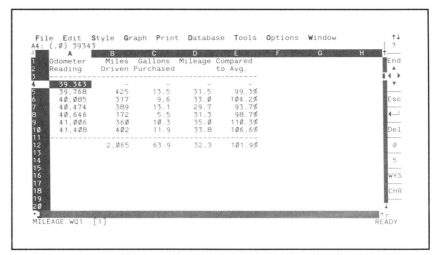

Figure 2.1: The completed Mileage spreadsheet

CREATING THE SHELL

The shell of the spreadsheet is its basic structure, without the data. Now we will enter the column titles and lines to separate the titles from the dates. But first, you should be in Quattro Pro with a blank spreadsheet on the screen. If your current spreadsheet is not empty, use the File–Erase command to erase its contents.

ENTERING THE COLUMN TITLES

With the cell selector in cell A1, begin entering the column titles that are in Figure 2.1. Type each cell entry, press ↵, and then move to the next cell, as shown in the following list:

CELL	ENTRY
A1	**Odometer**
B1	**Miles**
C1	**Gallons**
D1	**Mileage**
E1	**Compared**

Now, move to cell A2 and continue with the column titles for that row:

CELL	ENTRY
A2	**Reading**
B2	**Driven**
C2	**Purchased**
D2	(no entry in this cell)
E2	**to Avg.**

ENTERING THE DASHED LINES

See Chapter 3 for more information about label prefixes. Refer to Chapter 5 for the details of using the Edit–Copy command.

Below the column titles, in row 3, we will add a horizontal line to separate the titles from the data. To create the line we will enter a backslash (\), followed by a hyphen, in each cell in the row. The backslash is a repeating label prefix. We'll type the first one in cell A3, and then use the Edit–Copy command to copy it to the other four cells in that row. Follow these steps:

1. In cell A3, type \– (that's a backslash followed by a hyphen) and press ↵. You should see a dashed line in cell A3 that is exactly as long as column A is wide.

2. Press / to activate the menu bar.

3. Select the Edit–Copy command.

4. Press ↵ to accept the current cell, A3, as the source block.

5. Move the cell selector right to B3, the first cell of the destination block.

6. Press the period key (.) to anchor this cell as the beginning of the block.

7. Specify the destination cells by moving right three more cells to E3.

8. Press ↵ to complete the Copy command.

You should now see a dashed line extending across all five columns.

COPYING THE LINE TO THE LAST ROW

Since we know how many rows of data will be in this small spreadsheet, you can copy the dashed line to the row at the bottom of the data, which is row 11. Here is the procedure:

1. With the cell selector still in cell A3, press / to activate the menu bar.

2. Select the command Edit–Copy.

3. You want to copy the entire row, so move the cell selector right to column E. The cells in row 3 will be highlighted as the source block.

4. Press ↵ to accept the block A3..E3 as the source cells.

5. Move the cell selector down to cell A11, the beginning of the destination block of cells. Because you are copying a row of five cells, you only have to specify the left corner of the destination block of cells, cell A11.

If you are using a mouse, you can click and drag to highlight the source and destination blocks.

6. Press ⏎ to accept cell A11 as the destination and complete the Copy command.

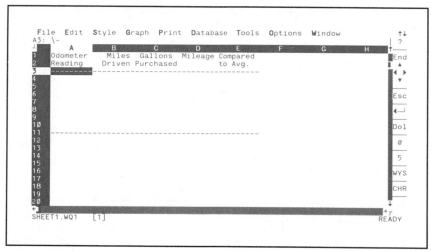

Chapter 6 covers the use of the Style–Line Drawing command.

You should now see the same dashed line from row 3 duplicated in row 11. Figure 2.2 shows the spreadsheet at this stage. Note that we could have used Quattro Pro's Style–Line Drawing command to create the lines, but for now, it's more practical to use the repeating label prefix to draw a horizontal line.

*Figure 2.2:*The spreadsheet after entering the column titles and dashed lines

ENTERING THE DATA

Now you are ready to enter the data. Start with the odometer readings in column A and the gallons in column C. Note that cells B4, C4, D4, and E4 contain only a hyphen, which signifies that there will be no mileage calculation for the very first entry. You must precede the hyphen with a quotation mark, which is a label prefix that makes the hyphen appear right justified in the cell.

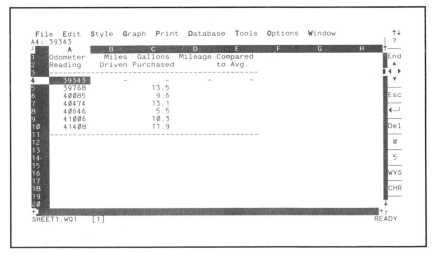

The rules for entering numbers and using label prefixes are discussed in Chapter 3; the use of cell formats is covered in Chapter 6.

When entering numbers in a spreadsheet, you never include commas. Use only numerals and a decimal point (if required). Later, you can apply a numeric format that displays commas.

Enter the following data in our spreadsheet:

CELL	ENTRY	CELL	ENTRY
A4	39343	B4 to E4	"–
A5	39768	C5	13.5
A6	40085	C6	9.6
A7	40474	C7	13.1
A8	40646	C8	5.5
A9	41006	C9	10.3
A10	41408	C10	11.9

Now, your spreadsheet should look like the one shown in Figure 2.3.

Figure 2.3: The spreadsheet after entering the data

SAVING YOUR WORK

With this much completed, now is a good time to save your work to disk. Having a recently saved file is the only insurance you have against power failures, mistyped commands, or any of the other possible disasters than can befall your computer work.

Follow these steps to save your spreadsheet under the name Mileage:

1. Type / to activate the menu bar.

2. Select the File–Save command.

3. If you want to specify a different drive or subdirectory than the one Quattro Pro offers, press Escape twice and type in the new drive or path.

4. Type the file name **MILEAGE** and press ↵.

You will be back in Ready mode with your work safely stored on disk. Note that the file name now appears on the left side of the status line at the bottom of the screen.

ENTERING THE FORMULAS

Formulas are covered in Chapter 4.

Now we will create formulas to calculate the miles driven and the gas mileage (columns B and D). The data for column E will be handled differently a little later on in the chapter.

CALCULATING THE MILES DRIVEN

Follow these steps to create the first formula:

1. Place the cell selector in cell B5 to write the first formula, which calculates the miles driven between fill-ups by subtracting the previous odometer reading in cell A4 from the current reading in cell A5.

2. In cell B5, type the formula **+A5–A4**.

3. Press ↵ to complete the formula. You should see the result of 425 displayed for that cell. If Quattro Pro beeps or displays an error message, press Escape and type the formula again.

You could type this formula into each cell in column B, so that in cell B6 you would enter +A6−A5, and so on down column B. But it's much easier, and also ensures complete accuracy, if you copy the current formula to the other cells.

4. With the cell selector still on the completed formula in cell B5, activate the Quattro Pro menu bar by pressing /.

5. Select the Edit–Copy command.

6. Press ↵ to accept the current cell, B5, as the source block.

7. Move the cell selector down to cell B6, the first cell of the destination block.

8. Press the period key to anchor this cell as the beginning of the block.

9. Specify the destination cells by moving down four more cells to cell B10.

10. Press ↵ to complete the Copy command.

You now have the proper formula in each cell in column B. Move the cell selector to each one and look at the formula on the input line for that cell. When you copy a formula in Quattro Pro, cell addresses are automatically adjusted to their new location.

CALCULATING THE MILEAGE

Enter the formulas in column D by following these steps:

1. Move the cell selector to cell D5 to create the mileage formula, which will divide the miles driven (column B) by the number of gallons used (column C).

2. In cell D5, type the formula **+B5/C5**.

3. Press ↵ to complete the formula. You should see the result of 31.48148 displayed for that cell (you may see more or fewer decimal places displayed on your own system).

4. Copy this formula to the other cells in column D by following the procedure we just used to copy the miles-driven formula, marking D5 as the source cell and cells D6 through D10 as the destination cells. Your screen should now look like the one shown in Figure 2.4. Once again, it's a good time to save your work.

5. Activate the menu bar and select the File–Save command. Since the file already exists on disk, Quattro Pro asks if you want to Cancel the command, Replace the file on disk with the one in memory, or Backup the file on disk.

6. Choose Replace to save the current spreadsheet to disk, replacing the previous version of it. The changes you have made to your worksheet are now safe on disk.

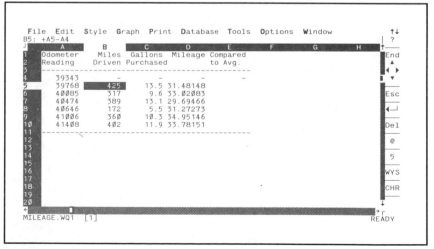

Figure 2.4: The spreadsheet after entering the formulas

CREATING A SECOND FILE

The File commands are discussed in Chapter 8.

Now we will open a new file to hold information for column E of our Mileage spreadsheet. This will illustrate how easy it is to work with multiple spreadsheet files in Quattro Pro. You will open a second window and enter a value that will later be used to perform more calculations in the Mileage spreadsheet. The second spreadsheet will be designed to contain a completely separate set of data that can be quickly linked to your first spreadsheet.

Follow these steps to create the second spreadsheet:

1. Open a new spreadsheet by issuing the File–New command.

There are two items that tell you this is a different spreadsheet from the Mileage spreadsheet: the file name at the bottom of the screen says SHEET2.WQ1, not MILEAGE.WQ1, and the number [2] next to the file name indicates that this is the second active window.

To jump to another active spreadsheet in one quick step, press Alt and the number of the window. Pressing Alt-1 will take you to the Mileage spreadsheet, and pressing Alt-2 moves to this newly opened, blank spreadsheet. With a mouse, if several windows are on the screen, simply click within a window to make it the current one.

2. In the new, blank spreadsheet, enter the following text:

CELL	ENTRY
A1	**National average**
A2	**mileage for this**
A3	**model car –>**

3. Move the cell selector to cell C3 and enter the value **31.7**, which represents the mythical average mileage for all cars of a certain model. This small spreadsheet is shown in Figure 2.5.

4. To save the spreadsheet, use the command File–Save and specify the name **NATLAVG** (for national average).

You now have two spreadsheets saved to disk.

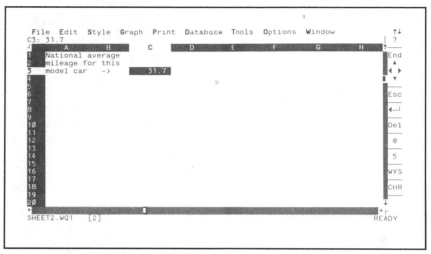

Figure 2.5: The secondary worksheet

LINKING THE SPREADSHEETS

Now we will return to the Mileage spreadsheet and write a formula that compares (by percent) each of the mileage figures (in the first spreadsheet) with the national average (in the second spreadsheet). Follow these steps:

Manipulating windows is covered in Chapter 10.

1. In order to see both spreadsheets on the screen at the same time, invoke the Windows–Tile command, and Quattro Pro will automatically size both of the windows so that each is visible on the screen.

2. Press Alt-1 to return to the Mileage spreadsheet.

3. Move the cell selector to cell E5, in the column labeled Compared to Avg.

4. Type **+D5/** to start the formula, but don't press ↵ yet.

5. Press Alt-2 to jump the cell selector to the second spreadsheet.

6. Move the cell selector to cell C3 (the cell containing 31.7).

◾ The difference be-
tween absolute
and relative cell addres-
ses in formulas is dis-
cussed in Chapter 4.

7. Press function key F4 once (which makes the cell reference an absolute one).

8. Press ↵ to complete the formula.

The cell selector will return to cell E5 in the Mileage spreadsheet, where the result of the formula should be 0.993107 and
a few more trailing decimal places. The cell contains this
formula:

+D5/[NATLAVG]$C$3

The formula takes the value in cell D5 and divides it by the
value in cell C3 in the worksheet named Natlavg. The dollar
signs next to the column and row address of C3 make it an absolute reference, as opposed to the relative cell address used in
the other formulas. Now you can copy this formula to the
remaining cells in the column.

9. With the cell selector on cell E5, invoke the Edit–Copy
   command.

10. Press ↵ to accept cell E5 as the source block.

11. Move the cell selector down to cell E6, the first cell of
    the destination block.

12. Press the period key to anchor this cell as the begin-
    ning of the block.

13. Specify the destination cells by moving down four
    more cells to cell E10.

14. Press ↵ to complete the Copy command. You now
    have the proper formula in each cell in column E.
    Your screen should look like the one shown in
    Figure 2.6.

15. Before continuing, expand the Mileage spreadsheet to
    full size by using the command Window–Zoom. Now
    all the columns of the spreadsheet are visible on the
    screen at the same time.

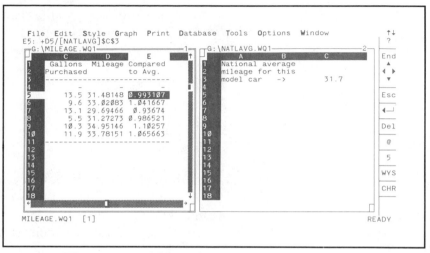

Figure 2.6: The two spreadsheets sharing the screen

CALCULATING TOTALS

The arithmetic shortcuts, @ functions, are covered in Chapter 4.

Now we will calculate the sums for columns B (Miles Driven) and C (Gallons Purchased) using one of the built-in functions of Quattro Pro. With these figures, we will be able to calculate the overall mileage in column D and the overall percentage in column E. Follow the procedure below to calculate the totals:

1. Position the cell selector at the bottom of column B, on cell B12.

2. Type **@SUM(** to begin the formula, but don't press ↵.

3. Move the cell selector up to cell B10.

4. Press the period key to anchor the beginning of the block of cells we will be summing.

5. Move the cell selector up to cell B4.

6. Type the closing parenthesis,), and press ↵. The cell selector will return to cell B12.

Your formula should return the result 2065, the sum of all the miles driven. Now you can copy this formula to C12 to sum the total gallons used.

7. Issue the command Edit–Copy.

8. Press ↵ to specify the current cell as the source block.

9. Move right to cell C12, the destination block, and press ↵.

The result of the formula in C12 should be 63.9. With these totals, you can now calculate the overall average and percent. The formulas are already written in the cells in columns D and E; you just need to copy them to cells D12 and E12.

10. Move the cell selector to cell D12.

11. Issue the Edit–Copy command.

12. Press Escape to "unanchor" the source block.

13. Move up two cells to cell D10 and press the period key to anchor the source block at this cell.

14. Move right to cell E10 and press ↵ to specify D10..E10 as the source block. The cell selector will return to cell D12.

15. Press ↵ to specify D12 as the destination block.

The two formulas in cells D10 and E10 will be copied to cells D12 and E12, with the results of 32.31612 and 1.019436, respectively.

The last phase of constructing the spreadsheet is to enhance the display of the numbers in the Mileage spreadsheet.

ENHANCING THE DISPLAY WITH NUMERIC FORMATS

One of the primary things to remember when working in Quattro Pro (and most other spreadsheet programs) is that there is a distinct difference between the contents of a cell and its display.

In the Mileage spreadsheet, you have been entering numbers and formulas into cells, but you have not controlled the way the numbers appear on the screen. For example, the formulas you just created to compare the mileage figures do not align along their decimal points and do not form a nice straight column.

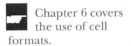

Chapter 6 covers the use of cell formats.

Through the use of *cell formats*, we will now make the display more attractive and easier to read. We are not going to change the contents of the cells, just their display.

ADDING PERCENT SIGNS

The results in column E are supposed to be percentages, so it would be nice if each had a percent sign after it and appeared as a whole percent, such as 99% instead of 0.993107. Follow these steps to format the percentages:

1. With the cell selector on cell E5, issue the command Style–Numeric Format.

2. From the Numeric Format menu, choose Percent.

3. When prompted for the number of decimal places, type **0** and press ↵. You will now be prompted to specify the block of cells that you want to modify with a format.

4. Move the cell selector down seven more cells to highlight all of the formulas in column E, including the one below the dashed line, and then press ↵ to complete the command.

The column should now show all whole numbers followed by a percent sign. But look on the input line, and you will see that the contents of each of the cells is exactly the same as it was before; only the display has been changed.

DISPLAYING ONE DECIMAL PLACE

Next, we will format the numbers in column D (Mileage) to show each number with just one decimal place. Follow these steps:

1. Move the cell selector to cell D5.

2. Issue the command Style–Numeric Format.

3. Choose Fixed.

4. When prompted for the number of decimal places, type **1** and press ↵.

5. Move the cell selector down seven more cells to highlight all of the formulas in column D as the cells to be modified.

6. Press ↵ to complete the command.

Now the display for each of the mileage figures will show just one decimal place, and the numbers will be nicely aligned along their decimal points.

ADDING COMMAS TO THE DISPLAY

Finally, format the first two columns (A and B) to display commas before thousands and no decimal places.

Move to cell A4, under Odometer Reading, and format the cells in that column, and those in column B as well. Follow the steps you used to format the other columns, but choose the format style that is signified by a comma on the menu, and choose 0 decimal places. To specify the block to be modified, include the cells in columns A and B, so that you highlight the block A4..B12.

Notice that the display of the numbers in column B does not change with the new format. This is because they are all less than 1000, so no comma is needed, and they have no decimal places to display.

Your finished worksheet should look like Figure 2.1. It is now ready to be printed.

PRINTING YOUR WORK

Chapter 7 covers the ins and outs of printing in Quattro Pro. If you need help installing your printer, refer to Chapter 18.

It's easy to print a simple spreadsheet like the one we have built here. However, before you print, make sure you have specified the proper printer during Quattro Pro's initial setup. To verify that you have installed the correct printer, invoke the command Options–Hardware–Printers–1st Printer. You should see the name of your printer in the command's menu box. If not, use the commands on this menu to select your printer from the list.

You should also check to be sure that the Device setting is correct for your system. More than likely, your printer is connected either to Parallel-1 or Serial-1.

Make sure your printer is turned on and, if it uses continuous feed paper, that the paper in it is aligned at the top of the form. Then follow these steps to print the spreadsheet:

1. Press Home to move the cell selector to cell A1 (starting at the upper-left corner of the work area is simply a convenience).

2. Issue the command Print.

3. Choose Block from the Print menu.

4. Press the period key to anchor the corner of the block to be printed at cell A1.

5. Press End-Home, and the cell selector should jump to cell E12, the lower-right cell in the work area. If your spreadsheet has extraneous data in it, the cell selector could jump somewhere else. In that case, just press Escape and specify the block as A1..E12.

6. Press ↵ to accept the block A1..E12.

7. We will accept the default values for all the other print settings, such as margins and page length. Select Spreadsheet Print from the menu, and the printing will begin.

A laser printer will not eject the page until the page is filled or until you instruct the printer to eject it. That is why the Form Feed command must be given.

8. Issue the command Adjust Printer–Form Feed to tell the printer to eject the rest of the page that was just printed.

You now have a printout of the current spreadsheet, but it needs to be saved to disk one more time, so that the completed work will be available for further use in future sessions. Once again, issue the File–Save command, and then choose to Replace the version on disk with the one that is in memory.

If you want to return to the DOS prompt, you can now exit Quattro Pro. To do so, issue the File–Exit command. Since no changes have been made to either of the open files since they were each saved to disk, you should return to the DOS prompt immediately. If you had made changes without saving the file, Quattro Pro would have asked you if you want to save your work before leaving the program.

This tour of the building process in Quattro Pro has introduced you to many of the essentials of the spreadsheet, including entering text, numbers, and formulas; copying cells; applying numeric formats to cells; saving your work; and printing your spreadsheet. The next chapter covers the many aspects of entering data.

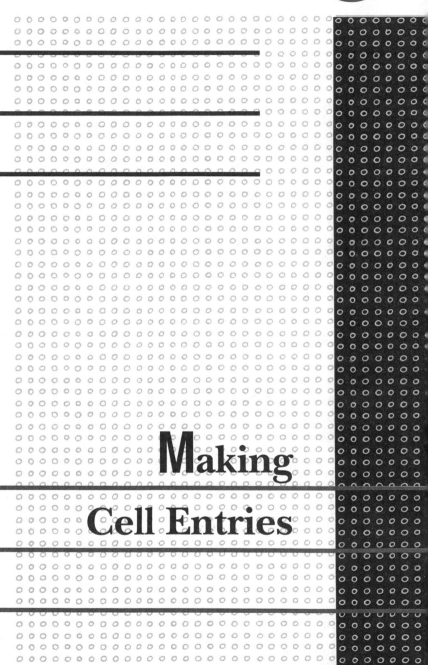

3

Making
Cell Entries

Fast
Track

EACH CELL IN A QUATTRO PRO IS A SEPARATE ENTITY from the other 2,097,151 cells, and what you enter in a cell is equally unique. This chapter covers the process of entering data into those cells.

You will find discussions of the different types of text and numeric entries, including formulas and dates, the Undo command, cell protection, and the built-in Quattro Pro tools that help with data input.

TEXT VERSUS VALUES

The most important rule to remember about entering data in Quattro Pro (and most other spreadsheets, as well) is that an entry is either text or a value, but never both. A value can be either a number or a formula that produces a result. Remember this rule:

- Cell entries are either text or values.

This rule is important simply because Quattro Pro is designed to perform arithmetic, and it can do this only with numbers.

That may sound pretty obvious, but remember that computers are very literal creatures. If you do not specify precisely what you mean, the results will at best be unpredictable, and at worst will give you the wrong answers without your realizing it. Numbers have numeric value in Quattro Pro, but text has no value at all (a numeric value of zero).

In general, if you ever want to perform any kind of calculation with a cell entry, that data should be a valid number, not text. Numeric entries might include dollars, age, temperature, height, weight, area, or date, for example. Problems can arise when you enter data as text when it should be a number.

Why would a date need to be numeric? If you enter dates as numbers in Quattro Pro, you can perform date arithmetic with them. For example, you might want to calculate how many days there are between two dates, or what the date will be 45 days from today's date. The manner in which you enter dates in Quattro Pro will be covered later in this chapter (and in Chapter 4 as well).

A text entry, on the other hand, is one you would never intentionally include in a calculation, for example, a name, title, address, zip code, or phone number. It may be confusing at first, but when you enter a phone number in Quattro Pro, you must enter it as text, not as a number.

CREATING AND EDITING CELL ENTRIES

Remember, the cell entry, or contents, is a separate entity that should not be confused with the display of the cell on the spreadsheet screen.

When you enter data into a cell, you are either creating a new entry for that cell or editing its contents. There's really only one way to edit, or modify, an existing cell entry, but there are many ways to enter new data into a cell. You can use any of the following methods to make a new entry:

- Type it in directly
- Copy data from another cell
- Move data from another cell
- Bring in data from another worksheet's cell
- Import data from a text file
- Use a Quattro Pro command, such as Edit–Fill or Tools–Parse

You can create a new entry for a cell at any time. If the cell was previously empty, it will now contain the new data. If the cell already contained data, your new entry will replace it.

To modify the contents of a cell, you must edit that cell. Place the cell selector on the cell you want to change and press function key F2, the Edit key.

The input line above the spreadsheet will contain the contents of the current cell. The cursor will be positioned at the end of the data on the input line, ready for you to make your changes. The various editing techniques and keys were discussed in Chapter 1.

ENTERING TEXT

In the broadest terms, a *text* entry (or *label* or *string*) is anything that is not a value. A numeric entry or formula must follow a few strict rules in order to be accepted, but a text entry is anything outside those rules.

WATCHING THE MODE INDICATOR

The key factor that determines whether an entry is text or a value is the very first character that you type to begin the entry. In order for Quattro Pro to consider your entry as a number, the first character must be one of the following:

- A number, from 0 to 9
- A decimal point (a period)
- Any of the signs +, −, $, #, @, or (

If you start an entry with any other character, Quattro Pro will consider it to be text, and it will display Label as the mode indicator. As you continue typing, the other characters will be considered part of your text entry, whether they are letters, numbers, arithmetic signs, or any other characters. Type the following and then press ↵:

The count was 7, 8, 9.

You will see your entry on the screen, but the input line actually shows

'The count was 7, 8, 9.

The entry begins with an apostrophe. This special character is a label prefix, and all text in Quattro Pro begins with one.

But what do you do if you want to create a text entry that happens to begin with a number, such as a street address? Type the following address:

789 Main St.

As soon as you typed the 7, the mode indicator changed to Value, meaning that Quattro Pro considers your entry to be numeric or a formula. Now press ↵.

Quattro Pro beeps and displays the error message

Invalid cell or block address

Your numeric entry is invalid because you tried to mix text with it. Notice that the cursor on the input line is positioned on the space between the *9* and the *M*. This is Quattro Pro's way of indicating the first offending character it finds in this numeric entry.

You have two choices at this point. You can either eliminate the text or, in this case, force your entry to be text, not a value. You make it a text entry by simply starting the entry with a nonnumeric character. For example, if you pressed the spacebar first, Quattro Pro would immediately be in Label mode, and you could continue with the address. But there is a better way, and that is to use a label prefix.

USING LABEL PREFIXES

A *label prefix* is simply a special character that signifies that the cell entry is text, not a number. A label prefix can perform two functions: it defines a cell entry as being text, and it can also signify how the text entry will appear within the cell.

There are five label prefixes in Quattro Pro:

- ' (apostrophe): Aligns the text with the cell's left edge.
- ^ (caret): Centers the text in the cell.

- " (quotation mark): Aligns the text with the cell's right edge.

- \ (backslash): Repeats to the width of the column whatever characters follow it.

- ¦ (broken vertical bar): Indicates the text is nonprinting; used for printer control.

You will use the broken vertical bar label prefix only rarely. It will be discussed later in the book.

A label prefix does not appear on the screen; it is strictly for internal use within the cell. When you are entering text (while the mode indicator says Label), Quattro Pro will automatically assign a label prefix to it after you press ↵ to enter it into the cell. But you can also begin an entry by typing a label prefix, which will force the entry to be taken as text.

The label prefix is the first character of the cell entry and is actually a part of the text in the cell. It will appear on the input line when you edit the cell, and it can be changed just as any other character can.

If you see a label prefix on the screen, you have probably entered two of them: the first one acts as a label prefix, but the second is just another character in your label. Or, you may have used the single-quotation mark character instead of an apostrophe.

CHANGING AN ENTRY'S LABEL PREFIX

You may have noticed that the label prefix Quattro Pro automatically gives text entries is an apostrophe, which indicates left alignment. If you want the text to be centered or right justified, you must specifically say so by starting the entry with a caret or quotation mark. For example, type **^Text**. Because you typed the caret, your text will be centered within the cell.

If you have an existing numeric entry that you want to be text, press F2 to edit that cell, press Home, type the label prefix that you want, and press ↵. The cell will now contain a text entry.

This command also aligns numeric entries, although it doesn't preface them with a label prefix (which would make them text entries). Unless you want them aligned as well, do not inadvertently include numeric cells when changing the alignment of a block of text cells.

To change the alignment of an existing text entry, press F2 to edit the cell, press Home, press Del to delete the label prefix, type in the new label prefix, and then press ↵.

However, when you need to change the alignment in a block of cells, it is easier to use the Style–Alignment command. Choose the alignment you prefer from its menu, specify the block of cells you want to change, and the job is done. Quattro Pro will change the label prefix for any occupied cells in that block. If you later enter a numeric value in a blank cell that was in the realigned block, it will also have the new alignment; however, if you enter text, it will still have the default alignment.

MAKING LONG TEXT ENTRIES

A cell in Quattro Pro can hold as many as 254 characters (including the label prefix). However, each column in the spreadsheet is by default only 9 characters wide. When you type a text entry that is longer than the column is wide, the text will overhang the cell. Even though the display of the text extends beyond the boundary of the cell on the screen, the text entry is still contained within that single cell.

Overhanging text will extend as far to the right as necessary. If the text is longer than 72 characters (the width of the Quattro Pro screen), you will have to scroll the screen to the right to see more of the text.

However, the overhanging text will be cut off in the display if there is another cell entry to its right. Figure 3.1 shows an example.

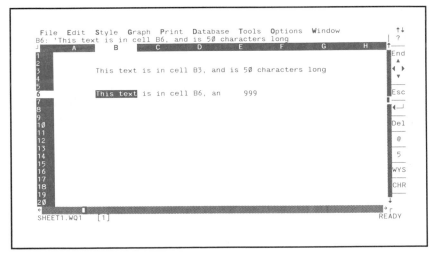

*Figure 3.1:*Overhanging text in Quattro Pro

A text entry of 50 characters is in cell B3, and it extends to the right a good portion of the screen. In cell B6 is an entry that is also 50 characters long. But in this row, there is also an entry in E6 (the number 999), which effectively cuts off the long text in cell B6.

Again, the actual entry in cell B6 is not affected by the entry in cell E6; only the display is changed. If you were to erase the entry in cell E6, the text in cell B6 would overhang, as does the text in cell B3.

ENTERING VALUES

When you enter *values*, which are formulas or numbers, you must exercise care in how you make the entry. Whereas text entries can include any characters after the preceding label prefix, a numeric entry or formula must contain only valid numeric characters.

RULES FOR ENTERING VALUES

A value in Quattro Pro can be either one of the following:

- A number, such as 1, 2, or 999.78
- A formula, such as 2+2, 32.7*B1, or @SUM(D9..E12)

As stated earlier, a value in Quattro Pro must begin with one of the following characters: +, −, $, #, @, or (. The symbols $, #, and @ are special characters that must be used in specific ways. The # sign is used only with logical operators within formulas, such as #NOT#. The $ sign is used in cell references in formulas to denote an absolute row or column address. The @ sign is used only to begin an @ function. All of these are discussed in detail in Chapter 4.

After you have begun to enter a value, you must be precise and exclude any invalid characters from it. A value cannot contain the following characters:

- Commas (as you might want to use in the number 12,123)
- Two or more decimal points
- Any spaces or other text characters
- Unbalanced parentheses (an opening parenthesis must always have a closing one)
- Any of the characters +, −, $, #, @, or (if used in an invalid way

Keep in mind that the number you enter into a cell and the way it is displayed on the screen are almost separate issues. You can make the display of a number appear in one of many different styles by applying a format to the cell with the Style–Numeric Format command. Cell formats are discussed in detail in Chapter 6.

There is one other character that can be included in a numeric entry, and that is the percent sign (%). You can use it to simplify the process of entering a percent. When you type % after a number, it divides the number by 100, making it a percent. Here are some examples of how the % sign affects numeric entries. Notice that the symbol must be placed directly after a number in order for it to be valid.

ENTRY	*RESULT*
17%	0.17
101%	1.01
25+4%	25.04
10%+16	16.1
28%−12%	0.16

ENTERING FORMULAS

A *formula* is a combination of data and operators that produces a result. The data may consist of numbers, text values, or cell addresses. The operators may include any of the valid Quattro Pro operators, such as +, −, *, and / (Chapter 4 covers the details of entering formulas).

Quattro Pro calculates the result of the formula automatically when you press the ↵ key to insert the formula into a cell. For example, type the number **5** into cell A1. Now type the formula **7+A1** into cell A2. You will see the result of 12 displayed for cell A2, although the cell still actually contains the formula as you typed it. Now move to cell A1 and change the 5 to a **50**. The formula in cell A2 immediately updates itself and returns the result of 57.

Because a formula is simply a type of value, it must follow the rules in order to be taken as a value by Quattro Pro: it must begin with a valid numeric character and must not contain invalid or misplaced characters.

For example, suppose you wanted to enter the formula above, only in reverse order, A1+7. Unfortunately, as soon as you type the letter A, Quattro Pro goes into Label mode and assumes you are making a text entry. The way around this is to begin the entry with a valid numeric character: +A1+7 or (A1+7).

As soon as you type the +, Quattro Pro goes into Value mode, and it will accept the rest of the entry as a valid formula.

The + has no effect on the sign of the entry. A number or cell address is assumed to be positive unless you specify otherwise, and a + sign would not change a negative value to a positive one.

USING TEXT VALUES

There is another type of value entry that is text, not numeric. A *text* (or *string*) *value* is the result of a formula, and is never preceded by a label prefix. The text value produced by a formula is in all respects the same as text that you type directly into the spreadsheet. The advantage of text values is that they can be manipulated to produce some very worthwhile results, much in the way that numbers can be manipulated.

All the text within a formula for a text value must be enclosed in quotation marks. You can *concatenate*, or combine, two text

items into one by using an ampersand (&). All of the following
produce text values (assume that A1 contains your name):

- +"This is a text value"
- +A1
- +"My name is"&A1
- +A1&" is not your name"

Text values can be very powerful tools in Quattro Pro, and
their use will be covered in more detail in Chapter 4.

ALIGNING NUMBERS

By default, all numbers are right justified in their cells. Whatever you do, don't preface a number with a label prefix in order
to change its justification, or that number will become a text
entry that cannot be used for calculations.

You can use the Style–Alignment command to choose left,
centered, or right alignment for numbers. Unlike text alignment, however, there are no label prefixes involved.

Before you realign numbers in your spreadsheet, consider the
effect this will have on their display. Figure 3.2 contains three
columns of data that are identical in content but not in their display. Together, they demonstrate some number-alignment
problems and solutions.

Column A has been widened to 21 characters so that its long
column titles could be centered within the column. The year in
cell A3 is a number that has been centered, which aligns it nicely
below the other two title cells. But the numbers in the column below the titles have also been centered, which means that they are
not aligned along their decimal points and are almost impossible to read.

The second column of data shows a better, if not perfect, solution. The column width and titles are the same as in the first
column (the year is a formula that increments the year in column A by 1), but the numbers have not been aligned; they are

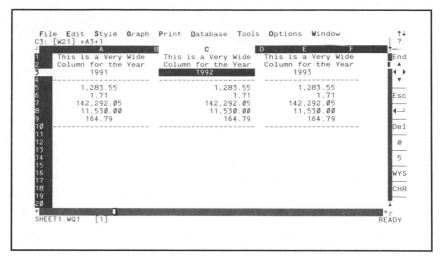

Figure 3.2: Aligning numbers

in their default, right-justified position. Even though the numbers appear a little cramped on the right side of the wide column, they are aligned along their decimal points.

The third column provides the best solution, but it is actually two columns. Columns E and F are 16 and 4 characters wide, respectively. The long titles are in column E and overhang into F. The numbers in column E are right aligned, but still reasonably centered below the titles, and they still align along their decimal points.

ENTERING LARGE NUMBERS

Unlike a long text entry, which will overhang the cell on the display, a numeric entry with too many digits to fit in the cell will be changed to another style. If even a style change wouldn't make the number fit, the value won't be displayed at all.

For example, enter the number **123456789** into cell D1. If your Quattro Pro is using its factory default settings, you should see this result on the screen:

1.23E+08

Quattro Pro always reserves the last space in a cell for a percent sign or closing parenthesis. Since the default width of a cell is 9 characters, all the digits in this number could not be displayed. Therefore, Quattro Pro simply chose another style in which to display this number: scientific (or exponential) notation.

If you want all the digits of the entry to be displayed on the screen, you must widen column D by using the Style–Column Width command. Follow these steps to widen column D to 10 characters:

1. Activate the menu bar and select the Style–Column Width command.

2. When prompted for the width of the column, enter the number **10**.

3. Press ↵ to complete the command. Column D is now 10 characters wide, and the number 123456789 should appear in its entirety.

4. Using the Style–Column Width command again, press ← five times to shrink column D to only 5 characters wide. As you shrink the column, your cell entry will once again be displayed in exponential notation, but when it gets to 5 characters, even that style will not fit. Without a means for displaying your number, Quattro Pro simply shows asterisks across the width of the column:

    *****

Asterisks across a column are a signal that you must provide more room for the display by widening the column or by using a different format. Note that if you have applied a specific format to a cell, Quattro Pro will not automatically change the entry to exponential notation if the column is not wide enough. Instead, it will display asterisks. Chapter 6 discusses numeric formats in detail.

ENTERING DATES

A date is simply our way of noting a specific moment in time. You can easily convey a date by writing it in one of many styles, such as the following:

- January 1, 1992
- Jan. 1, '92
- 1/1/92
- 1.1.92
- 01-Jan-92

All of these are valid dates to us humans, but they are not to Quattro Pro. Here is the rule to remember when dealing with dates:

- If you ever plan to perform any sort of arithmetic with dates that you are entering, make sure you enter them as numbers, not as text.

Quattro 1 and Lotus 1-2-3 both use January 1, 1900, as day 1. Both also make the mistake of counting the year 1900 as a leap year. See Chapter 4 for cautions on calculating dates in both of these programs.

Quattro Pro has a built-in system for dealing with dates. Essentially, it is based on the date December 31, 1899, which is considered day 1. All dates after that are assigned a consecutive number, so that January 1, 1900 is 2, January 2 is 3, and so on. The date number of January 1, 1992, is 33604.

If you follow Quattro Pro's rules for entering dates, you will be able to perform many types of operations with dates in the spreadsheet:

- Determine how many days there are between two dates by subtracting one date from another.
- Find the date 45 days in the future by adding 45 to the current date.
- In a database, find all records with a date greater than a specified date.
- Fill a column of cells with dates that are all one week apart.

However, if you are entering a date and you know that you will *never* need to perform any of these operations with it, then you can type that date in any style you like.

WORKING WITH A NET: THE UNDO COMMAND

If you make a change to your spreadsheet, and then wish you hadn't, you can take advantage of the Edit–Undo command. This command simply cancels your last operation and returns the spreadsheet to its state before that operation.

For example, if you make a cell entry that replaces the contents of a cell, invoking the Edit–Undo command will return that cell to its prior condition. Or if you use the Edit–Erase command to erase a block of cells, you can restore the deleted entries by using Edit–Undo.

Before you can access this command, however, you must first enable it with the command Options–Other–Undo–Enable (by default, this command is disabled).

Try it on your system:

After enabling Undo, you can choose to have it always enabled by selecting the Update command from the Options menu. Otherwise, the next time you run Quattro Pro, Undo will again be disabled.

1. Issue the command Options–Other–Undo–Enable.

2. Choose Quit from the Options menu to return to Ready mode.

3. Type the number **1234** in cell A1 and press ↵.

4. Enter the word **NEW** in that same cell.

5. Issue the Edit–Undo command, or press the shortcut key Alt-F5. The number 1234 should now be back in cell A1.

6. From Ready mode, press Del once to delete the contents of cell A1.

7. Press Alt-F5, and the number should reappear in the cell.

Another command, Tools–Macro–Transcript, cancels some or all changes you have made to your spreadsheet since retrieving it. This command is discussed in Chapter 17.

There are a few disadvantages to the Undo command. First, it will slow down your system a little because it must keep track of the changes you make in order to be able to undo them.

There are also some routines that cannot be undone. These include applying a cell format, deleting a file from disk, adding line drawing or shading to cells, and changing any command settings (such as a print header).

PREVENTING CHANGES WITH CELL PROTECTION

When you are working in a spreadsheet with many hundreds or thousands of occupied cells, it is all too easy to inadvertently erase, overwrite, or otherwise change a cell.

Quattro Pro provides a tool by which you can *protect* cells, thereby preventing them from being changed. For example, you might want to protect a block of formulas, because once you have written them correctly, you certainly don't want them being changed. Or you might want to protect cells that contain numbers that are key to many formulas in your worksheet; if those cells were changed, your entire spreadsheet would produce invalid results.

All cells in the spreadsheet are by default protected. With the command Style–Protection–Unprotect, you can selectively unprotect blocks of cells. There are two ways to determine whether or not a cell is unprotected:

- You will see a U on the input line for that cell.

- Unprotected cells are assigned a different color than protected ones, so that any occupied, unprotected cells will stand out from the others. On a monochrome system, unprotected cells will be in bold type.

Cell protection, like cell formats and fonts, is included with the contents of the cell when you copy or move that cell to another location.

Protecting cells is a two-step process, much like using the Undo command. Whether a cell is protected or unprotected makes no difference if *global protection* is not enabled. To activate

Don't be overly extravagant with unprotecting cells that may not need it. Each blank cell that you unprotect requires 4 bytes of memory.

the protection status of all cells in the worksheet, use the command Options–Protection–Enable.

When you now try to change a protected cell when protection is enabled, Quattro Pro will beep and issue the message

Protected cell or block

You will have to press Escape to return to Ready mode. Only unprotected cells can be changed at this point.

Once you have enabled global protection, if you decide that you really need to enter data into a protected cell, you have two choices available:

- You can simply unprotect that one cell with the Style–Protection–Unprotect command.

- You can choose to disable protection on a global basis with the Options–Protection–Disable command.

Whether or not you use protection in your spreadsheets depends on who will be using them and what kind of luck you have had in the past. Protection can easily be a last-minute decision because all you need do is enable global protection and every cell will be locked tight. Then you can simply unprotect the cells you feel must be accessed.

Realize, however, that protection is not a foolproof system. Anyone can choose to disable global protection and make changes to the spreadsheet.

You can password-protect your spreadsheets so that only authorized users can retrieve them. This is discussed in Chapter 8.

DIRECTING DATA ENTRY WITH THE RESTRICT INPUT COMMAND

If you are using cell protection, you can invoke the Database–Restrict Input command to have the cell selector move only to unprotected cells in a block you specify. Protected cells will be off limits, and the person behind the keyboard can spend less time worrying about which cells are valid data-entry cells.

The spreadsheet in Figure 3.3 shows an example of how this command works. The 12 cells that contain the word *Data* have each been unprotected with the command Style–Protection– Unprotect. All the other cells around them are protected (the default state). The unprotected cells are the ones in which you enter data. The protected ones are those that should not be changed, such as formulas, text that serves as titles or identifiers, or numbers that serve as the basis for further calculations.

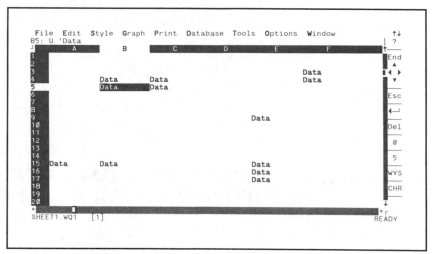

Figure 3.3: Accessing only the unprotected cells in a spreadsheet with the Database–Restrict Input command

It does not matter whether or not you have enabled protection with the Option–Protection– Enable command. The Database–Restrict Input command will operate the same with protection enabled or disabled.

To take advantage of the protected status of the cells in the spreadsheet shown in Figure 3.3, you would issue the Database– Restrict Input command and specify A4..F17 as the block of unprotected cells. This would have the following effects:

- The mode indicator Ready will be replaced by Input. The Quattro Pro menus are disabled while in Input mode.

- When you move the cell selector, it will jump only to the next unprotected cell. When you have moved it to the last unprotected cell in a row or column, it jumps to the next unprotected cell in the next row or column. The PgUp and PgDn keys are disabled. Pressing Home jumps to the unprotected cell closest to the upper-left corner of the block, and pressing End takes it to the lower-right corner.

- The first cell in the block you specified becomes the upper-left corner of the screen. For this reason, you might want to specify a larger block of cells, so that row and column titles are included in the block, for example. Even though those cells are protected, they will be incorporated in the screen during the command.

The Input mode indicator will remain on and cell selector movement will be restricted, until you either press Escape or ↵. When you return the spreadsheet to Ready mode, the cell selector jumps back to the cell it occupied before you issued the Database–Restrict Input command.

SIMPLIFYING DATA ENTRY WITH THE DATA ENTRY COMMAND

You may often encounter problems when entering data because of the black-and-white difference between text and numbers in Quattro Pro. For example, you may forget to preface a street address or phone number with a label prefix or inadvertently enter a date as text.

To circumvent these frequent stumbling blocks, Quattro Pro provides the command Database–Data Entry. With it, you specify a block of cells, and then choose the type of data that you want to limit to those cells. You have three choices:

- General: Returns the block of cells to the default state; any data can be entered.

- Labels Only: Forces all new entries in the block to be text (a label prefix is automatically placed in front of any entry you make).

- Dates Only: Forces all new entries in the block to be dates; entries must be typed as valid dates.

Valid dates and times are determined by the styles that are available on the Style–Numeric Format–Date (or Time) command. Only the following are valid date entries (available for date calculations) in Quattro Pro:

- 01-Jan-92
- 01-Jan
- Jan-92
- 01/01/92
- 01/01

The valid date entries depend on the option–International–Date command's settings. The ones shown here are valid per the default settings in effect when the program is installed.

To reset a block of cells to their default, use the Database–Data Entry–General command. Note that once you have entered dates into Dates Only cells, resetting those cells with the General command will turn all the entries into standard, numeric date entries.

MINI-WORD PROCESSING WITH THE TOOLS–REFORMAT COMMAND

When you are utilizing the spreadsheet to its fullest capacity, you will enter a lot of text. Most of your text entries will be short column titles or one- or two-word identifiers. But every now and then, you will want to enter a short paragraph of text, and that is when the Tools–Reformat command will be of great value.

Quattro Pro reformats all rows of text within the block you specify or until it encounters a blank, or nontext, cell.

Much as a word processor automatically breaks each line of text at the right margin, the Tools–Reformat command simply reformats one or more cells of text entries in a column so that their right margins all fall in the same column. Figure 3.4 shows a simple example. Column B in the upper window of the figure contains long labels in each of the cells B2 through B5. Those lines are supposed to constitute a single paragraph. Unfortunately, when entering text into several cells to form a paragraph, it is next to impossible to have each line end up about the same length. In the lower window in the figure, the same text was formatted using the Tools–Reformat command, as follows:

1. For convenience before starting the command, place the cell selector on the first label, B2.

2. Issue the command Tools–Reformat, and you will be prompted to specify the blocks to be modified.

3. Move the cell selector to highlight the block B2..F8, which signifies column F as the right margin limit.

4. Press ↵, and the text will be reformatted so that no line extends beyond column F.

Note that it is always safer to specify a few more rows than you think necessary for this command. In the example, the block included row 8, even though the reformatted text only went to row 7.

If you do not specify enough rows for the given number of columns (the width), Quattro Pro will not be able to reformat

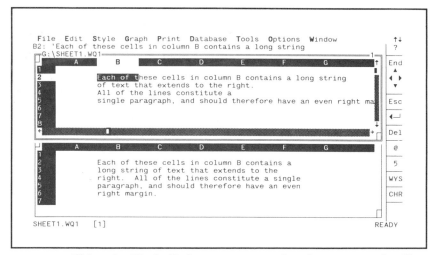

Figure 3.4: Using the Tools–Reformat command to format several cells of long labels

the text within the limited space. It will instead issue the error message

    Reformat block is full

It will reformat the text as best it can, but one or more lines at the bottom of the block will overhang to the right of the columns you specified.

On the other hand, you can instead specify just the top row of the reformat block, such as cells B2..F2 in Figure 3.4. Quattro Pro will then reformat the text to the given width, using as many rows as required. The problem with this method is that all the rows beneath the reformatted column of text entries will be affected by the shift in rows.

In Figure 3.4, all the cells in column B below cell B2, the reformat row, would shift up (or down) as the text is reformatted. Entries in all other columns, however, would not be affected, so that those in column B may no longer be aligned with cells to their left and right. This does not happen when you specifically include all the rows in the reformat block.

This chapter has laid the ground rules for entering data into Quattro Pro. In the next chapter, you will learn how to create and use formula entries in a variety of ways.

4

Creating
Formulas

Fast
Track

EACH CELL IN A QUATTRO PRO SPREADSHEET CAN HOLD only 254 characters. But there are over 2 million cells in the spreadsheet, and each spreadsheet can link to as many as 63 others. That's over 134 million cells! The tool that ties all these cells together is formulas.

In this chapter, you will learn how to build formulas, recalculate your spreadsheet data, and avoid common errors.

CONSTRUCTING A FORMULA

A formula in Quattro Pro can be as long as 254 characters and may consist of any of the following parts:

- Value: Numeric (19.5) or string ("hello")
- Cell address: B5, A3..D12, or a block name (THIS_CELL)
- Function: @SUM, @STD, @COUNT, and so on
- Operator: +, −, *, >, =, and so on
- File name: Such as [MYFILE.WQ1], to create links
- Comments: Optional, to add a comment at the end of the formula

Creating linking formulas, with references to other spreadsheet files, is covered in Chapter 11.

Together, the parts of a formula produce a result, and it is that result which Quattro Pro retains as the value for the formula's cell. For example, if you enter the formula 5*2 into cell A2, Quattro Pro automatically calculates and displays the result of 10. Whenever you refer to this cell in another formula, such as +A2, or a command, such as Edit–Value, the result, 10, will be used in the calculation.

You have already learned that a cell's contents are not the same as the cell's display. Now you have an intermediate rule to remember:

- If the cell contains a formula, its result is the final contents of the cell.

In the example above, the result of 10 is, in this sense, the contents of cell A2.

INCLUDING VALUES

The formula 2+3 contains two numeric values, 2 and 3, and an operator, +. The result, 5, is numeric. You can include any numeric values in a formula. Just remember to include only valid characters, which are limited to the decimal point and a trailing percent sign if you want to enter a number as a percent.

A value may also be a string value. The simplest string formula consists of a single string value, such as:

+"Hello, I'm"

The beginning + signifies a value or formula, and the text is enclosed in quotation marks.

It is important to remember that numeric and string values can never exist as such in the same formula, just as you cannot mix text and numbers in a cell entry.

You can, however, convert text that looks like a number into an actual number, and then use that in a numeric formula. You can also convert a number into a string and use that in a string formula. Either way, the result of a formula can be either numeric or string, not both.

INCLUDING CELL ADDRESSES

A formula can refer to other cells in the current spreadsheet, as well as to cells in any other spreadsheet in memory or on disk. It is this expansive capability that gives Quattro Pro its real power.

There are several ways to refer to one or more cells in a formula: type the address, point to the cell, or use a block name.

TYPING THE CELL ADDRESS

You can use upper-case or lowercase letters in the address. After you have entered the formula into a cell, all the letters in it are made uppercase.

You can refer to a cell in a formula simply by typing its address. For example, you could enter the formula:

25+A3–B2+12

If the values 10 and 6 were in cells A3 and B2, respectively, the result of the formula would be 41. Remember that if the formula begins with a cell address, you must preface the address with a +, −, or an opening parenthesis:

+A3+25−B2+12

(A3+25−B2+12)

POINTING TO THE ADDRESS

An easier method of including an address in a formula is *pointing*. You can simply move the cell selector to the cell you want, and its address will be entered into your formula. To use the pointing method, the cursor must be at the end of the input line and follow a valid formula operator.

As an example, let's enter a formula using this technique. Follow these steps:

1. Enter the value **10** in cell A3.

2. Enter **6** in cell B2.

3. Move the cell selector to cell A1, and type **25+** to begin the formula. Note that the mode indicator displays Value.

4. Move the cell selector down two rows to cell A3. Notice that the mode indicator now shows that the spreadsheet is in Point mode, and that your formula on the input line now looks like this:

   25+A3

   If you have a mouse, you can simply click on the cell you want, and its address will be placed in your formula.

5. Your cell selector is still on cell A3. Type − (minus) to continue the formula.

6. The cell selector returns to cell A1, and the mode indicator displays Value again.

7. Point to cell B2.

8. Type + to continue the formula.

9. Type **12**, and then press ⏎ to complete the formula. The input line shows

   25+A3–B2+12

The result of 41 appears on the display.

REFERRING TO A BLOCK OF CELLS

A *block* of cells is any rectangular set of contiguous cells. You will frequently refer to blocks of cells when using various Quattro Pro commands, such as Print, Copy, or Fill, and also when you are working with functions in formulas.

You describe a block by specifying two of its diagonally opposite corner addresses, most typically its upper-left and lower-right corners. When specifying a block, you include two periods between the two addresses.

For example, the reference

   B3..D7

refers to the block of cells that has cell B3 at its upper-left corner and D7 at its lower-right. The block contains 15 cells, 5 cells in each of the columns B, C, and D.

You could also refer to this block with any of the three other pairs of corners: D7..B3, D3..B7, or B7..D3. However, the upper-left and lower-right corners are the standard frame of reference.

Just as you point to a single-cell address when writing a formula, you can also point to a block of cells. Move the cell selector to one corner of the block, press the period key, and then point to the remaining cells in the block. If you are using a mouse, you can just point and drag to highlight the block of cells.

You can try this method now, using the Mileage spreadsheet we created in Chapter 2. We'll use the @SUM function to total a group of numbers (this function is discussed along with the others later in the chapter).

1. Recall the Mileage spreadsheet.

2. Move the cell selector to the bottom of the numbers in column B (Miles Driven), cell B12.

3. Type **@SUM(** to begin the formula (be sure to include the opening parenthesis). The mode indicator will display Value.

4. Point to the cells you want to sum by moving the cell selector to the top of the column, cell B5. The mode indicator will display Point, and your formula will look like this:

    @SUM(B5

You can specify the block using any of the other references, such as B10..B5, and the result will be the same.

5. Press the period key once to *anchor* the corner of the block at cell B5. This is the beginning of the block, and you will extend the block from this cell. The formula in the input line will now look like this:

    @SUM(B5..B5

If you pointed to the wrong cell by mistake, you can press Escape to unanchor the block. Then move the cell selector to the cell you want and press the period key to anchor the block there.

6. Point to the remaining cells in the column until you have highlighted the block B5..B10. The formula will now include this newly defined block:

    @SUM(B5..B10

7. Type) (a closing parenthesis) to finish the formula, and then press ↵. The result of the formula in cell B12 is 2065.

8. Repeat these steps to create this formula in cell C10:

    @SUM(C5..C10)

    The result is 63.9.

Along with typing the address or pointing to the cells, another way to specify a cell within a formula is by using a block

When you want a formula to refer to a block name, instead of typing the name, you can select it from the Names menu, displayed by pressing F3.

name. A block name is simply a name you specify to describe the address of a single cell or block of cells.

For example, using the Edit–Names–Create command, you could specify the name MYCELL for cell B19. Thereafter, whenever you need to refer to cell B19, you could use the name MYCELL. The following formulas would be equivalent:

20*B19

20*MYCELL

Formulas are easier to write when you use block names because you don't have to remember the exact cell address. They are also easier to read because the block name appears in the formula in place of the address it represents.

Using block names can be very helpful for many spreadsheet operations. They can be used in any Quattro Pro command that requests a block of cells, for printing, copying, moving, data input, and so on. The use of block names is described in detail in the next chapter.

REFERENCING ABSOLUTE AND RELATIVE CELL ADDRESSES

In Chapter 2, you saw that when you copy a formula using the Edit–Copy command, cell references in it adjust their addresses to the copied formula's new location in the spreadsheet. Cell references that adjust are called *relative* addresses—the cells to which they point are only relative to the formula's position in the spreadsheet. You can also use absolute addresses to prevent the formula from adjusting, and mix references to make only the row or column absolute.

RELATIVE ADDRESSES ADJUST

In a relative address, such as in the formula +B3 in cell A1, the address does not really refer to that specific cell, but rather to the cell that is "one column to the right and two rows down." If you copy the formula from cell A1 to cell C15, the cell reference will adjust relative to its new position, so it still refers to the cell that is "one column to the right and two rows down," and will now read +D17.

ABSOLUTE ADDRESSES DO NOT ADJUST

When you don't want a cell reference to adjust, you can use a reference that is *absolute,* which will not change when the formula is copied.

To make a cell reference absolute, you simply preface its column letter, row number, or both with a dollar sign:

+$B$3

You can copy this formula to any cell in the spreadsheet and it will still refer absolutely to cell B3.

Figure 4.1, which shows the pair of spreadsheets we created in Chapter 2, illustrates the use of an absolute address. The formula in column E of the Mileage spreadsheet calculates the percentage by referring to two cells:

+D5/[NATLAVG]$C$3

The formula divides the contents of the cell in column D by the contents of cell C3 in the Natlavg spreadsheet. When you copied that formula to the rest of the cells in column E, you were intending that it should "divide the value in the cell one column to the left by the value in cell C3 in the Natlavg spreadsheet." In other words, you wanted the cell reference to column D to be relative, but the reference to C3 to be absolute.

Cell references behave the same whether they refer to a cell in the current spreadsheet or to one in another spreadsheet.

MIXED ADDRESSES GO BOTH WAYS

A mixed cell reference is one in which you make either the column or row absolute, but not both, as in

+$A1

+A$1

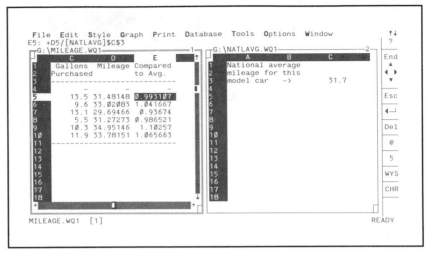

Figure 4.1: An absolute cell reference does not adjust when the formula is copied

Deciding just what type of reference is needed may not always be crystal clear, but it's really not too complex. Make both the column and row absolute when you want to refer to only one specific cell, no matter where you might copy the formula.

Generally, you might make only the column reference absolute (such as $A1) when you are copying formulas across a row. You could make only the row reference absolute (A$1) when you are copying the formula down a column.

The need for relative and absolute references also applies to block addresses in your formulas. If you want to copy a formula but maintain its reference to a specific block, you must make the reference absolute:

   @SUM($A$1..$G$20)

You can create a mixed reference to a block (although you rarely want to do so), as in

   @SUM($A1..$G20)

USING FUNCTION KEY F4 FOR ABSOLUTE REFERENCES

You can take advantage of function key F4 to create absolute cell references in formulas. This key is available when you are creating a new formula or editing an existing one. The F4 key can also be used when you are referring to a block.

As you type an address into a formula, press F4 once, and the reference will become absolute ($A$1, for example). Press it again to make only the row absolute (A$1). You can press it a third time to make just the column absolute ($A1). A fourth press of the F4 key returns the address to a relative one (A1).

USING OPERATORS

The glue that joins the numbers, text values, functions, and cell addresses in a formula is the *operators*. Besides the most frequently used operators, such as +, −, *, and /, there are quite a few others in Quattro Pro.

There are three factors ruling the order in which each operation is performed in a formula: its rank in the order of precedence, the use of parentheses, and its position within the formula. The third factor is the simplest. If the other two factors are equivalent (and do not come into play), a formula is evaluated from the left to the right.

THE ORDER OF PRECEDENCE

By convention, all operators are assigned a rank in the order of precedence. When a formula contains more than one operator, the rank of each one determines which operation is performed before the others.

At the highest rank are the parentheses, in that the calculation order is strictly ruled by their presence. If there are no parentheses involved, the order is governed by the ranking shown in the Table 4.1 (a higher rank is evaluated before a lower rank), which lists all the Quattro Pro operators.

Here are a few examples to help illustrate the importance of the rankings:

$$2+3\wedge2 = 11$$

$$3*4+1 = 13$$

$$4+1*3 = 7$$

$$10-8/2 = 6$$

Table 4.1: Quattro Pro Operators and Their Order of Precedence

OPERATOR	DESCRIPTION	PRECEDENCE
()	Parentheses	8
^	Exponentiation	7
+ −	Positive and negative	6
* /	Multiplication and division	5
+ −	Addition and subtraction	4
=	Equal	3
>	Greater than	3
<	Less than	3
>=	Greater than or equal to	3
<=	Less than or equal to	3
<>	Not equal to	3
#NOT#	Logical NOT	2
#AND#	Logical AND	1
#OR#	Logical OR	1
&	String concatenation	1

There is an easy way around these rules, however, and it's as simple as a pair of parentheses.

INCLUDING PARENTHESES

You can direct the flow of calculations by enclosing sections of a formula within parentheses. This overrides both the left-to-right priority and the order of precedence. The flow of calculation halts when it encounters an opening parenthesis, so that the formula within the parentheses can first be evaluated. The result is then included as the flow continues. Think of a pair of parentheses as a minicell; the formula within them produces a result, which is then used in the rest of the formula.

Using the examples from the previous section, you can see how parentheses change the result of a formula:

$$(2+3)^2 = 25$$

$$3*(4+1) = 15$$

$$(4+1)*3 = 15$$

$$(10-8)/2 = 1$$

Each of the following formulas contains the same pieces as the others, but parentheses have been included to direct the result (the first two formulas are equivalent):

$$5+3*6-4 = 19$$

$$5+(3*6)-4 = 19$$

$$(5+3)*(6-4) = 16$$

$$5+3*(6-4) = 11$$

$$(5+3)*6-4 = 44$$

Even when parentheses are not needed to direct the flow of calculation, you may find them helpful in clarifying the intent of your formula. By grouping sections of a formula within parentheses, you can document the intended flow of that formula.

CALCULATING WITH FUNCTIONS

A Quattro Pro *function* is a shortcut for a longer series of calculations. There are 113 functions in Quattro Pro, and each of them begins with the @ symbol and contains a keyword, such as SUM, AVG, or VLOOKUP.

As soon as you type the @ symbol, the mode indicator will display Value. You must spell the function keyword exactly, or Quattro Pro will display an error message, and you will not be able to enter the formula into the cell. But there is help available at your fingertips.

Alt-F3 is the Functions key. It brings up a menu of all the functions, arranged in alphabetical order. You can scroll through the list until you find the one you want. Highlight that function, press ↵, and it will be placed on the input line as though you had typed it.

In most functions, the keyword is followed by a pair of parentheses. Within the parentheses are one or more parameters; some are required and some are optional.

In Quattro 1, when you are selecting a function from the Functions menu (Alt-F3), you can expand the menu in order to see each function's syntax and parameters. This feature is not available in Quattro Pro.

FUNCTION PARAMETERS

The parameters for a function fall into these categories:

- Numeric values
- Text values
- Special keyword attributes

You can substitute either a single-cell address, block of cells, or a block name for any of these parameters. Multiple parameters are always separated by a comma; do not include any spaces.

A very common function that you have already used sums a block of cells, as in

@SUM(C4..E30)

In this case, the function sums all the cells shown in its parameter, the block C4..E30. Parameters for this function can include numbers, a single-cell address, a block, a block name, or another function that returns a number.

Functions like @SUM that deal with blocks can generally accept more than one block (or value), for example

@SUM(C4..E30,A19,55,1143,G5..G7)

This formula simply sums all the blocks and values shown.

Other functions deal with text and take as their parameters a text string, a cell address, or the name of a block that contains text. For example, the @LENGTH function returns the number of characters in a string, so that

@LENGTH("Some text")

results in 9.

Still other functions require a special attribute as part of their parameter. For example, the @CELL function returns certain information about a cell, so that

@CELL("format",A1)

returns the type of numeric format that is currently applied to cell A1.

The following sections briefly summarize the functions by category. Refer to the tables on the inside covers of the book for an alphabetical listing of all the functions. For detailed descriptions of functions, see the Quattro Pro *@ Functions and Macros* reference manual.

USING MATHEMATICAL FUNCTIONS

Mathematical functions that take parameters use only numeric values (or cell addresses that contain numeric values). All the functions return numeric values as their results.

Note that the trigonometric functions, such as the @SIN and @COS functions, deal with radians, not degrees. You can use the @DEGREES function to convert from radians to degrees. It is equivalent to the formula

(DEGREES)*@PI/180

The @PI function returns the value of pi. The @RADIANS function converts from radians to degrees, and it is equivalent to

(RADIANS)*180/@PI

Therefore, in order to find the tangent of 45 degrees, you could write the formula this way:

@TAN(@RADIANS(45))

Table 4.2 lists the Quattro Pro mathematical functions.

Table 4.2: Mathematical Functions

FUNCTION	RETURNS
@ABS(n)	Absolute value of n.
@ACOS(n)	Angle that is the arc cosine of n.
@ASIN(n)	Angle that is the arc sine of n.
@ATAN(n)	Angle that is the arc tangent of n.
@ATAN2($n,n1$)	Arc tangent of the angle determined by the coordinates ($n,n1$)
@COS(n)	Cosine of n.
@DEGREES(n)	Converts from radians, n, to degrees.

Table 4.2: Mathematical Functions (continued)

FUNCTION	RETURNS
@EXP(*n*)	Value of *e* (the mathematical constant) raised to the *n*th power.
@INT(*n*)	Truncates any decimal portion from *n*, leaving only the integer portion.
@LN(*n*)	Natural logarithm of *n*.
@LOG(*n*)	Logarithm of *n*.
@MOD(*n,n1*)	Remainder of *n* divided by *n1* (the modulus).
@PI	Value of pi.
@RADIANS(*n*)	Converts from degrees, *n*, to radians.
@RAND	A random number between 0 and 1.
@ROUND(*n,n1*)	Rounds off *n* to *n1* decimal places.
@SIN(*n*)	Sine of *n*.
@SQRT(*n*)	Square root of *n*.
@TAN(*n*)	Tangent of angle *n*.

Avoid including extra cells at either end of the block when using functions that count, such as @COUNT, @AVG, and @STD. If you do and those cells are occupied, they will be counted and included in the calculations.

USING STATISTICAL FUNCTIONS

Statistical functions all perform some type of statistics. Each takes a list of numbers or cell addresses as its parameter. For example, the @AVG function averages the numbers or cells in its list, and it can be written in any of the following forms:

@AVG(B3..D12)

@AVG(B3..D12,C6..C9,F23..I100)

@AVG(16,5,B3..D12)

Another statistical function, which we have used in several examples, is @SUM. In many spreadsheets, your @SUM formulas can be written to include an extra cell at the beginning and end of the range. This provides two benefits: it allows you to insert rows within your data and have those rows stay within the sum range, and it lets you delete rows of data without deleting the first or last cells of your sum range. Both of these points will be discussed further in the next chapter, which covers the aspects of handling blocks in Quattro Pro.

Table 4.3 summarizes the statistical functions.

USING TABLE LOOKUP FUNCTIONS

Table lookup functions return the value of a cell that is found within a block of cells (such as A5..G30) or a list of cells or values (such as B3,C9,6,50,F10) in one of its parameters.

It is important to remember that the columns of the block are referred to in terms of their *offset* from the first column. Therefore, the first column is column 0, the second is 1, and so on.

Table 4.4 lists the table lookup functions.

USING SPREADSHEET INFORMATION FUNCTIONS

The spreadsheet information functions return some type of information about a cell or block of cells. The @CELL, @CELL-POINTER, and @CELLINDEX functions take an *attribute* (enclosed in quotation marks) as part of their parameters.

The following attributes can be included:

- *Address*: Cell address
- *Col*: Column number of the cell
- *Contents*: Contents of the cell
- *Format*: Cell's numeric format

- *Prefix*: Label prefix of a text entry
- *Protect*: Cell's protection status
- *Rwidth*: Width, in characters, of a block of cells
- *Row*: Row number of the cell
- *Type*: Type of cell entry
- *Width*: Width of cell's column

Table 4.3: Statistical Functions

FUNCTION	RETURNS
@AVG(*list*)	Average of the numeric values in the *list*.
@COUNT(*list*)	Number of nonblank cells.
@MAX(*list*)	Largest numeric value.
@MIN(*list*)	Smallest numeric value.
@STD(*list*)	Population standard deviation of the numeric values.
@STDS(*list*)	Sample standard deviation of the numeric values.
@SUM(*list*)	Total of the numeric values.
@SUMPRODUCT(*block1*,*block2*)	Multiplies each cell in *block1* by the corresponding cell in *block2*, and then sums all the resulting products.
@VAR(*list*)	Population variance of the numeric values in the list.
@VARS(*list*)	Sample variance of the numeric values.

Table 4.4: Table Lookup Functions

FUNCTION	RETURNS
@CHOOSE(*n,list*)	The item from the list in position *n* (the first item in the list is in position 0).
@HLOOKUP(*x,block,offset*)	Looks for *x* (closest numeric match or exact string match) in the first row of *block* and returns the value found in the cell below *x* in the row specified by *offset*.
@INDEX(*block,col,row*)	Returns the value found in *block* at the junction of *col* and *row*.
@VLOOKUP(*x,block,offset*)	Looks for *x* (closest numeric match or exact string match) in the first column of *block* and returns the value found in the cell to the right of *x* in the column specified by *offset*.

For example, the formula

@CELLPOINTER("address")

returns the cell address at the cell selector's location.

Table 4.5 summarizes the spreadsheet information functions.

USING STRING FUNCTIONS

You can't add one string of text to another, but you can *concatenate* them, or join them together. Performing this type of operation is known as *string arithmetic.*

The ampersand, &, is the operator you use to join two text strings. Because you are creating a formula, the text you join must be text values, not just plain text. In other words, no label prefixes are involved.

Table 4.5: Spreadsheet Information Functions

FUNCTION	RETURNS
@@(*cell*)	Contents of the cell whose address is specified in *cell*.
@CELL(*attribute,block*)	Status for the given *attribute* of a cell or upper-left cell in *block*.
@CELLINDEX(*attribute,block,col,row*)	Status for the given *attribute* of the cell found in *block* at the junction of the column and row.
@CELLPOINTER(*attribute*)	The status for the given *attribute* of the cell at the cell selector's location.
@COLS(*block*)	Number of columns in *block*.
@ROWS(*block*)	Number of rows in *block*.

As you saw in Chapter 3, text within a string formula must be enclosed in quotation marks, as in

+"This is a simple text value"

The formula can also reference a cell that contains text (either a text value or plain text). For example, if the first name, Pat, is in cell A1, and the last name, Pilz, is in cell B1, then

+A1&B1 returns PatPilz

+A1&" "&B1 returns Pat Pilz

+A1&" E. "&B1 returns Pat. E. Pilz

+B1&", "&A1&" E." returns Pilz, Pat E.

There are quite a few functions that allow you to manipulate strings. Some functions, such as @LEFT and @MID, extract pieces from a text string. Other functions, such as @LENGTH and @FIND, return a number based on the contents of a text string.

Just remember that all text must be enclosed in quotation marks, and you are not allowed to mix numeric and text values in the same formula. The @STRING and @VALUE functions are provided so that a formula can either be all text or all numeric. For example, if a name were in cell A5 and that person's age were in cell G16, you could combine the two into one text formula in this way:

> +"Did you know that "&A5&" was "&@STRING(G16,0)&" years old?"

String formulas can grow quite long and complex. Always test your formula as it grows, instead of writing the whole thing and then trying to figure out why it doesn't work. Or, as recommended for long logical expressions, split the formula among several cells.

Although the formula shown above is not very long or complex, it can serve as an example of how you can break down long string formulas. You could enter the various pieces in separate cells, and then concatenate them all together in one formula.

You could lay out the pieces this way:

> D1: 'Did you know that
>
> D2: ' was
>
> D3: @STRING(G16,0)
>
> D4: ' years old?

Then, in another cell, you could write the formula that ties all the pieces together, such as this:

> +D1&A5&D2&D3&D4

Table 4.6 summarizes the string functions.

Table 4.6: String Functions

FUNCTION	RETURNS
@CHAR(*n*)	The ASCII character corresponding to the value of *n*.
@CLEAN(*s*)	Removes all nonstandard ASCII codes from string *s*.
@CODE(*s*)	The ASCII code of the first character in string *s*.
@EXACT(*s1,s2*)	Compares string *s1* with string *s2* and returns 1 if they are exactly alike. Unlike the expression *s1≠s2*, this function is case sensitive.
@FIND(*s1,s2,n*)	Position number of the first occurrence of *s1* within *s2*, starting from position *n* in *s2*.
@HEXTONUM(*s*)	Converts to a decimal value the string *s*, which looks like a hexadecimal value.
@LEFT(*s,n*)	First *n* characters in string *s*.
@LENGTH(*s*)	Length of string *s*.
@LOWER(*s*)	Forces all letters in string *s* to lowercase.
@MID(*s,n,n1*)	Returns *n1* characters from string *s*, starting with character number *n* (the first character is number 0).
@N(*block*)	Numeric value in the cell at the upper-left corner of *block*.
@NUMTOHEX(*n*)	Converts the numeric value *n* to a string that looks like the hexadecimal equivalent of *n*.
@PROPER(*s*)	Forces all words in string *s* to initial capitals.
@REPEAT(*s,n*)	A string value made by repeating *n* times the string *s*.

Table 4.6: String Functions (continued)

FUNCTION	RETURNS
@REPLACE(*s1,n1,n2,s2*)	Puts string *s2* into string *s1*, replacing *n2* characters, starting at position *n1*.
@RIGHT(*s,n*)	The last *n* characters in string *s*.
@S(*block*)	The string value in the cell at the upper-left corner of *block*.
@STRING(*n1,n2*)	Converts the numeric value *n1* into a string, and rounds it to *n2* decimal places.
@TRIM(*s*)	Trims all leading or trailing spaces and any multiple internal spaces from string *s*.
@UPPER(*s*)	Forces all letters in string *s* to uppercase.
@VALUE(*s*)	The numeric value of string *s*, which looks like a number.

USING DATE AND TIME FUNCTIONS

To perform date arithmetic in Quattro Pro, you must enter the dates in a form that Quattro Pro can interpret. There are three basic steps involved:

1. Determine the correct date number.
2. Enter that number into a cell.
3. Give that cell a format that makes the number appear as a date.

The date and time functions are described in Table 4.7.

Table 4.7: Date and Time Functions

FUNCTION	RETURNS
@DATE(*y,m,d*)	Date value for the specified year *y*, month *m*, and day *d*.
@DATEVALUE(*s*)	Date value for string *s* that looks like a valid Quattro Pro date.
@DAY(*n*)	Day of the month for the date value *n*.
@HOUR(*n*)	Hour for the time value *n*.
@MINUTE(*n*)	The number of minutes past the hour for the time value *n*.
@MONTH(*n*)	Month as a number for the date value *n*.
@NOW	Current date and time value as determined by your computer's built-in clock.
@SECOND(*n*)	Number of seconds past the minute for the time value *n*.
@TIME(*h,m,s*)	Time value for the specified hour *h*, minute *m*, and second *s*.
@TIMEVALUE(*s*)	Time value for string *s* that looks like a valid Quattro Pro time.
@TODAY	Current date value as determined by your computer's built-in clock.
@YEAR(*n*)	The year for the date value *n*.

DETERMINING THE CORRECT DATE NUMBER

As mentioned in Chapter 3, Quattro Pro's system of keeping dates is based on a starting date of December 31, 1899. Quattro Pro counts this day as day 1, and numbers each day consecutively after that.

Therefore, to enter the date December 15, 1991, you need to count to that date and enter the corresponding number, 33587, into a cell. Are you expected to count from 1 to 3300-and-something every time you want to enter a date? You could, but Quattro Pro provides functions that can calculate the number for you.

The @DATE function takes as its parameters a year, month, and day and calculates the correct date number. The year is always expressed as the number of years since 1900, so that 1991 would be entered as 91. The month is just the number of the month, so that January is 1. To calculate the date number for December 15, 1991, just enter this formula:

@DATE(91,12,15)

The result is 33587. The function calculated the correct date number and placed it in the cell for you.

The formula to determine the number of days between January 1 and December 15 is:

@DATE(91,12,15)−@DATE(91,1,1)

To calculate the date that is 161 days after December 15, 1991, you would enter:

@DATE(91,12,15)+161

Another function, @NOW, returns the current date and time, as reported by your computer's built-in clock. This function, which does not take a parameter, updates the time on screen whenever the spreadsheet is recalculated.

After the date number is in the cell, you need to format it as a recognizable date.

Although Quattro Pro uses December 31, 1899, as its starting date, it is still compatible with Lotus 1-2-3, which uses January 1, 1900. This is because Quattro Pro knows that there was no February 29, 1900, which Lotus does not. Therefore, the two programs will use the same date number for all dates on or after March 1, 1900.

You can perform date arithmetic that produces dates before 1900, because Quattro Pro can format a date as far back as March 1, 1800 (although the @DATE function cannot produce these dates). Dates prior to December 30, 1899, are negative numbers, so that March 1, 1800, is the date number −36463.

APPLYING DATE FORMATS

All you really need to do is make the display of the number look like a date. You don't want to change the number itself because Quattro Pro works only with date numbers. Instead, just pick one of the date formats from the Style–Numeric Format–Date menu.

For example, the first format on the Date menu would make the number 33587 appear like this on the display:

15–Dec–91

When you have subtracted one date from another to determine the number of days between the two, you do not format the result as a date. The answer is simply an integer number that represents the number of days, not a date.

Note that this style creates a date that is too wide for the normal column width of 9 characters. You will have to expand the column width to 10 or use a shorter date format.

The four other date styles format the cell as follows:

15–Dec
Dec–91
12/15/91
12/15

TAKING A SHORTCUT WITH DATES

It can be time consuming to enter a date function and then apply the format, as well as a little confusing at first. But Quattro Pro provides yet another tool that rolls both operations into one.

When you want to enter a date, just press Ctrl-D, and then type the date in the style in which you want it to be formatted. For example, press Ctrl-D, and the mode indicator will change to Date, indicating that you are now entering a date. Then type **12/15/91** and press ↵. The display will show the date as you typed it:

12/15/91

but the cell contents will contain the value 33587. Ctrl-D takes care of both entering the date number and applying the format.

The only hitch to using Ctrl-D is that the date you enter must look like one of the Quattro Pro date formats; otherwise, Quattro Pro won't be able to interpret it correctly.

WORKING WITH TIME

The Quattro Pro system for handling dates also lends itself to dealing with time. The system divides a day into fractions.

Midnight is the starting point, and is therefore 0. The time 6:00 AM is one-fourth of the day, and is denoted by 0.25. Noon is 0.50, 6:00 PM is 0.75, and 11:59 PM is 0.999.

Therefore, in order to describe a precise date and time, you specify a whole number that represents the date and a decimal fraction that represents the time. The time of 6:00 PM on December 15, 1991, looks like this:

33587.75

The @NOW function returns just such a number—a whole number for the date and a decimal fraction for the time.

The @TIME function corresponds to the @DATE function. Its parameters are hours, minutes, and seconds, so that a function to return the time 6:15 AM and 30 seconds looks like this:

@TIME(6,15,30)

Note that Quattro Pro uses 24-hour time, just as your computer does. So in order to calculate the time value for 6:30 PM, you would enter this function:

@TIME(18,30,0)

USING FINANCIAL FUNCTIONS

When you are working with one of the financial functions, keep in mind that interest is always expressed as its actual value. Use 0.12, not 12 to represent 12 percent. Also, the values for the interest rate and term should always be expressed in relation to the same units. If you are making deposits each month, then your yearly interest rate should be divided by 12 to produce a monthly rate. The term would be the total number of deposits, or 12 in this case.

For example, the @FV function calculates the future value based on regular deposits over a given term at a given interest rate:

@FV(*pmt, int, term*)

If you are making a monthly deposit of $100 for five years, at an annual rate of 11 percent, the formula would look like this:

@FV(100,0.11/12,60)

The result is $7,951.81. If you were making quarterly payments of $300 over five years, the formula would look like this:

@FV(300,0.11/4,20)

Table 4.8 lists the financial functions.

Table 4.8: Financial Functions

FUNCTION	RETURNS
@CTERM(*int, fv, pv*)	Given the interest rate *int* and present value *pv*, returns the number of compounding time periods needed to reach the specified future value *fv*.
@DDB(*cost, salvage, term, per*)	The double-declining balance depreciation of an asset over the number of periods in *term*, its useful life.
@FV(*pmt, int, term*)	Given regular payments *pmt* and interest rate *int*, returns the future value of an investment at the end of *term*.

CH. 4

*Table 4.8:*Financial Functions (continued)

FUNCTION	RETURNS
@FVAL(*int,term,pmt,[pv],[type]*)	An updated version of @FV; *pv* and *type* are optional.
@IPAYMT(*int,per,term,pv,[fv],[term]*)	The portion of a payment that is interest, not principal.
@IRATE(*term,pmt,pv,[fv],[type]*)	An updated version of @RATE.
@IRR(*guess,block*)	The internal rate of return of an investment, as specified by the numeric values found in *block*, which represent periodic cash flow. The preliminary guess, *guess*, serves as a seed for the calculations.
@NPER(*int,pmt,pv,[fv],[type]*)	An updated version of @CTERM and @TERM.
@NPV(*int,block*)	The net present value of a future cash flow, as specified by the numeric values found in *block*.
@PAYMT(*int,per,prin,[fv],[type]*)	An updated version of @PMT.
@PMT(*prin,int,term*)	Amount of payment due.
@PPAYMT(*int,per,term,pv,[fv],[type]*)	The portion of a payment that is principal, not interest.
@PV(*pmt,int,term*)	Returns the present value of regular payments *pmt* and interest rate *int* over the period of *term*.
@PVAL(*int,term,pmt,[fv],[type]*)	An updated version of @PV.
@RATE(*fv,pv,term*)	Interest rate needed to produce *fv* from *pv* over the period in *term*.
@SLN(*cost,salvage,term*)	The straight-line depreciation of an asset over the number of periods in *term*, its useful life.

Table 4.8: Financial Functions (continued)

FUNCTION	RETURNS
@SYD (*cost,salvage,term,per*)	The accelerated depreciation of an asset over the number of periods in *term*, its useful life.
@TERM (*pmt,int,fv*)	Number of payment periods needed to produce *fv* from payments *pmt*, given rate *int*.

USING LOGICAL FUNCTIONS

Logical formulas can evaluate a complex relationship and return a short answer. The result is either a Yes or a No, a True or a False, or in computer talk, a 1 or a 0.

Is the following formula true?

16=99

No, of course not, but it does represent a logical formula. If you type that formula into a cell in Quattro Pro, the result will be 0, because it is false.

There are many ways to write logical expressions in Quattro Pro, but all of them are based on a set of statements that are either true or false.

The most common logical expression is built around the @IF function, which looks at a statement and returns one result if it is true, and another if it is false:

@IF (*statement,true,false*)

This function is frequently used to compare two values in two cells, and return an appropriate value as a result:

@IF(A5=M169,B1,D19)

This example decides whether or not the contents of cell A5 are equal to that of cell M169. If it decides that they are equal, then

When you are manipulating a Quattro Pro database and using a formula in your criteria block, that formula is always a logical one. It may not itself return a 1 or a 0, but it will be looked at in that sense. During a Locate command, for example, the formula is checked for each record. If the result is True, that record is selected.

it returns whatever is in cell B1. If the statement is false, it returns whatever is in cell D19.

The logical operators (see Table 4.1) provide further tools for making logical decisions. You can use the less-than operator, for example, to see if one cell is less than another:

> @IF(C12<C20,F5,G5)

This formula means if the value in cell C12 is less than that in cell C20, return whatever is in cell F5. If cell C12 is not less than cell C20, return the contents of cell G5.

There is no limit to the kinds of testing your logical formulas can do, and they can grow to be rather complex formulas that are difficult to decipher. It is frequently a good idea to split one long formula into several adjacent cells, as in the formula shown above, where the true result was placed in one cell and the false result in another.

Table 4.9 summarizes the logical functions.

USING DATABASE FUNCTIONS

The database functions are enhanced versions of their statistical functions counterparts. You won't get much use from them unless you know something about the workings of a database in Quattro Pro.

Each of these functions simply performs a different statistical operation on the given data, and all require the same type of parameters, as follows:

- *Block*: A block of cells that can serve as a database input block, and therefore must include a unique title over each column.

- *Offset*: The column on which the function will perform its operation. Columns are counted from the left column of *block*, so that the first column has an offset of 0, the second column is 1, and so on.

Table 4.9: Logical Functions

FUNCTION	RETURNS
@ERR	Simply returns the value ERR (same result as dividing a value by 0).
@FALSE	Returns 0.
@FILEEXISTS(*filename*)	Returns 1 if the named file is on disk, and 0 if it is not.
@IF(*cond,true,false*)	If condition *cond* is true, returns *true* statement; otherwise, returns *false*.
@ISERR(*x*)	If *x* results in ERR, returns 1; otherwise, it returns 0.
@ISNA(*x*)	If *x* results in NA, returns 1; otherwise, it returns 0.
@ISNUMBER(*x*)	If *x* is a number, returns 1; otherwise, it returns 0.
@ISSTRING(*x*)	If *x* is a string, returns 1; otherwise, it returns 0.
@NA	Always returns NA (not available).
@TRUE	Returns 1.

- *Crit*. The criteria block that will be used to determine which records in *block* will be included in the calculation.

We'll discuss the use of database functions for spreadsheet databases in Chapter 14. These functions are summarized in Table 4.10.

Table 4.10: Database Functions

FUNCTION	RETURNS
@DAVG (*block, offset, crit*)	Average of the numeric values in the column.
@DCOUNT (*block, offset, crit*)	Number of nonblank cells.
@DMAX (*block, offset, crit*)	Largest numeric value.
@DMIN (*block, offset, crit*)	Smallest numeric value.
@DSTD (*block, offset, crit*)	Population standard deviation of the numeric values.
@DSTDS (*block, offset, crit*)	Sample standard deviation of the numeric values.
@DSUM (*block, offset, crit*)	Total of all numeric values.
@DVAR (*block, offset, crit*)	Population variance of the numeric values.
@DVARS (*block, offset, crit*)	Sample variance of the numeric values.

USING SYSTEM FUNCTIONS

The system functions provide information about the current session of Quattro Pro. They are particularly helpful in macros which cannot, for example, look at the Options–Hardware menu to see how much memory is available.

Table 4.11 lists the system functions.

Table 4.11: System Functions

FUNCTION	RETURNS
@CURVALUE (*menu,item*)	Current value for a Quattro Pro menu command setting.
@MEMAVAIL	Amount of conventional memory that is available.
@MEMEMSAVAIL	Amount of expanded memory that is available.
@VERSION	Version number of Quattro Pro.

ADDING COMMENTS

You can append a comment to any formula simply by finishing the formula with a semicolon, and then writing the comment. For example, you could add a comment in this manner:

@SUM(C8..L8)/B19*100; result will be a percent whole number

Your comment can be as long as you like, as long as the number of characters in it and the formula do not exceed the 254-character maximum.

SPREADSHEET RECALCULATION

Whenever you make a new cell entry, Quattro Pro will recalculate and update the results of any formulas that reference your entry. Quattro Pro is smart enough to ignore formulas that are not affected by your new entry. This is known as *intelligent recalculation.*

CHOOSING A RECALCULATION MODE

You can choose from the three different modes of recalculation listed on the Options–Recalculation–Mode menu: Automatic, Manual, or Background.

By default, Quattro Pro recalculates the spreadsheet every time you make an entry, but performs the recalculation in the *background*. This allows you to keep working; Quattro Pro will recalculate the formulas during pauses between your keystrokes. You will see the Bkgd indicator on the status line. Generally, background recalculation is the most practical choice.

But there may be times when there is no need for formulas to be evaluated every time you make an entry, or when the constant updating is distracting. In those cases, you can set recalculation to manual. In manual mode, changing one cell in the spreadsheet does not start a recalculation, but it does cause the Calc indicator to appear on the status line. This notifies you that no calculations have been performed since a change was made to the spreadsheet. Quattro Pro will not recalculate the formulas until you press function key F9, the Calc key. Then the mode indicator will change to Wait, and you will not be able to continue working until the recalculation process is finished. All formulas in the spreadsheet will be up to date when the Ready mode indicator reappears.

You can also choose automatic recalculation. This mode is almost the same as background, except that you must wait while the recalculations are performed. The advantage to this mode is that when the mode indicator goes from Wait to Ready, every formula in the spreadsheet is current.

RECALCULATING WITH F9, THE CALC KEY

The Calc key, F9, can be very useful when you are working with formulas. When you are writing or editing a formula, pressing F9 performs a local recalculation of just the formula, and the formula's result will appear on the input line. You can press ↵

Formulas always require more memory than values. If you write a formula and later realize it will never need to be updated, you can turn it into a value. Simply edit the formula, press F9, and then press ↲. You can also turn a block of formulas into their corresponding values using the Edit–Value command, as discussed in Chapter 5.

to place that result into the cell (replacing the formula), or press Escape to cancel the operation.

The F9 key can also be used as a quick way to combine several numbers or cell addresses into one value, and then place that value into a cell. For example, suppose that in the Mileage spreadsheet, one of the fill-ups actually consisted of three smaller purchases of 5, 3, and 9 gallons over a few days, and only the last one actually filled up the gas tank. To calculate the total number of gallons, you would enter 5+3+9. Then you could press ↲ at this point, and simply leave this formula as the cell entry. However, it would be more practical to type the formula and press F9, leaving the value 17 on the input line. Then you can press ↲ to place that result into the cell.

SOLUTIONS TO COMMON PROBLEMS IN FORMULAS

The ease with which you can create formulas in Quattro Pro can sometimes lull you into carelessness. Your haste or inattention can leave your formula vulnerable to errors.

Once you have written a formula, you can leave it alone and let it perform its task, with no attention required on your part. In other words, once a mistake appears in a formula, it will most likely remain there for all eternity. And, because formulas serve as the connection among all the cells in the spreadsheet (as well as among cells in other linked spreadsheets), errors in formulas can invalidate the entire purpose of your spreadsheet.

Perhaps the easiest and most devastating error you can make is to type a number into a cell that is supposed to contain a formula. Instead of a "soft" formula that will produce a new result as data in the spreadsheet is changed, you will have a "hard" number that is unchanging.

Another common problem occurs because it is all too easy to write a formula that references the wrong cell. You can mistype the column or row of the address or point to the wrong cell.

Sometimes an address will be duplicated, so it is referred to twice. The solutions to these and other common problems are discussed in the following sections.

USING SIMPLE TEST DATA

Here is the first safety rule to use when writing formulas:

- Use simple test data.

For example, if you have a block of numbers with @SUM functions at the bottom of each column, you can enter a 1 into each cell of the block, and then verify that all the @SUM functions produce the same, correct result. If you had accidentally typed a number instead of one of the functions, that number would stand out in glaring contrast to the others.

Figure 4.2 illustrates how important it is to verify your formulas with simple test data. There are @SUM formulas in row 15 that total each column, and similar formulas in column H that total each row. One of the @SUM formulas in row 15 is actually a value, not a formula. Can you tell which one it is?

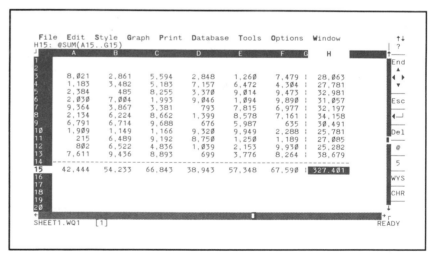

Figure 4.2: Can you tell which total is incorrect?

Figure 4.3 shows how simple test data can prevent errors from getting out the door. Each cell in the block of data has been replaced with a 1. Each column of 11 cells should then add up to 11, as each row should total 6. As you can see, all the formulas display the correct result, except for the one at the bottom of column D. It contains a hard number, not a formula.

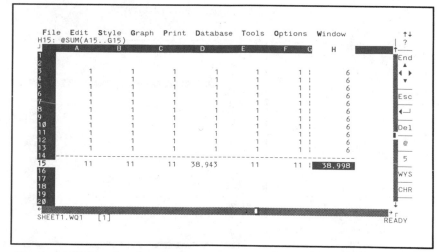

*Figure 4.3:*Using simple test data can expose formula errors

DISPLAYING YOUR FORMULAS AS TEXT

Normally, only the result of a formula is displayed on the screen, which is why it was so difficult to detect the error in Figure 4.2. To view the actual contents of a cell, you must move the cell selector to the address in question and look at the cell's contents on the status line.

But there is another way to see the contents of not just one cell, but many cells, and right on the display. You do this by using the Style–Numeric Format command and choosing the format called Text. A formula cell that has this format displays the actual cell contents (the formula) on the screen instead of the result of the formula.

If you suspect that a formula in a block of formulas has been replaced by a number, just format the block as Text. Any nonformula cells will immediately stand out from the others. After you've checked the block of formulas in question, you can change the format back to its original style.

Figure 4.4 is the same spreadsheet as shown in Figure 4.2, but this time all the cells have been formatted as Text. Even though the columns are not wide enough to display the entire formula in each cell, the value that was mistakenly entered into cell D15 stands out very clearly.

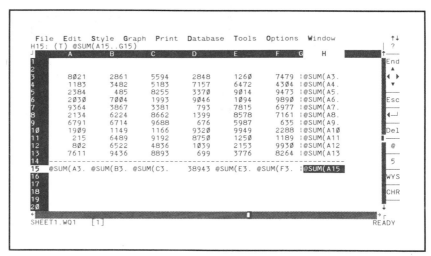

Figure 4.4: Format a block of formulas as Text to reveal any nonformula cells

An equally efficient means of finding nonformula cells is with the Window–Options–Map View command. It affects the entire spreadsheet, and has the added benefit of not changing any cell attributes, as the Text format does. In a block of cells that is supposed to contain only formulas, a cell of a different type will stand out distinctly.

Figure 4.5 shows the spreadsheet from Figure 4.2 while Map View is enabled. All the columns are narrowed to a 1-character width. Formula cells are noted with a +, numeric cells with an n, and text cells with an l (as in *label*). Once again, notice how clearly the number in cell D15 stands out from the formulas that surround it.

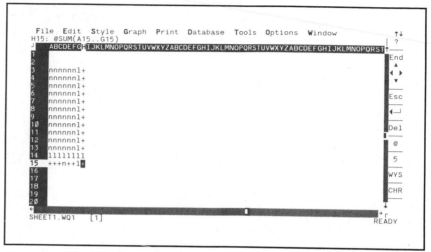

Figure 4.5: The Windows–Options–Map View command provides a bird's-eye view of your spreadsheet data

USING CELL VARIABLES

Suppose that you have many formulas that calculate a sales tax on given items in the spreadsheet. The sales tax rate is 6.5 percent, so a formula to find the sales tax for an entry in cell B16 looks like this:

+B16*0.065

This will work fine, but you'll have a job in front of you the next time your local sales tax is increased. Not only will you have to track down every formula in the spreadsheet that uses 0.065, but you will have to be sure that each occurrence really represents sales tax, and not some other purpose.

The simple and all around better solution is to use a *cell variable*. In a separate cell, for example, B5, enter the value 0.065. To the left of that cell, in A5, enter the title Sales Tax to indicate that B5 contains the sales tax amount. Now your sales tax formulas can refer to cell B5:

+B16*$B$5

Notice that the reference to cell B5 is absolute, so that if you were to copy the sales tax formula, the reference to that cell would not adjust.

When the sales tax is increased to 7 percent, you only need to enter the new value in cell B5, and the job is done. All formulas that refer to that cell will now refer to the new amount.

Including a cell variable in a formula is a classic reason for using a block name. As you will see in Chapter 5, block names are one of the most helpful tools in Quattro Pro. You are never required to use them, but you will be amazed at the number of ways they will assist you. For example, if you gave the name SALES_TAX to cell B5 (using the Edit–Names–Create command), the sample formula would look like this:

    +B16*$SALES_TAX

Not only do you not need to know the precise cell address of the sales tax cell, you can also tell at a glance if a formula refers to the correct cell.

WRITING FORMULAS THAT CROSS-FOOT

You can write a *cross-foot* formula that compares two totals and displays an appropriate message if the two do not match. You perform the checking with an @IF function. For example, in Figure 4.2, the formula in cell H15 sums up row 15 to produce a grand total. Because it is in the lower-right corner of the spreadsheet, it could logically have summed column H to produce the same grand total. Notice that the result it is displaying, 327401, is the correct total for row 15, but it is not correct for the figures in column H.

You could catch this error by placing the following cross-foot formula in cell H15:

    @IF(@SUM(A15..G15)<>@SUM(H3..H14),"Imbalance",
    @SUM(A15..G15))

This formula reads "if the sum of row 15 does not match the sum for column H, then display the text *Imbalance*. Otherwise, display the total for row 15." In Figure 4.2, the formula would display the imbalance message even before test data was entered.

ROUNDING RESULTS

You will sometimes encounter minor discrepancies in the results of two formulas that should, in theory, produce the same result. The problem may be an exasperating one when you have written a cross-foot formula that refuses to admit that two totals are the same, even though they appear to be.

The reason is that some calculations do not produce exact results; the square root of 2 and pi divided by 3 are two such examples. When you are comparing sums for columns and rows that contain such calculations, there may be differences between the two totals. These differences may only be in the fifteenth decimal place, but they are nonetheless not exactly the same, and the cross-foot formula would dutifully report that.

The way to circumvent this problem is by first *rounding* the totals, and then comparing the rounded results. You round numbers in Quattro Pro with the @ROUND function. Here is how you would write the cross-foot formula shown earlier, so that it compares the two totals only to the second decimal place (note that this is just one formula, but is shown in three pieces for clarity):

@IF(@ROUND(@SUM(A15..G15),2)<>

@ROUND(@SUM(H3..H14),2),"Imbalance",
@SUM(A15..G15))

The result will be rounded to the second decimal place, and any numbers past that will not be shown. Notice that the last @SUM, the true statement of the @IF function, was not rounded. There was no need to do so because this total is displayed, not compared.

However, problems can quickly arise when you round the number's display, but not the contents of a cell. As you have learned, it is all too easy to confuse the contents of a cell with its display. A very common problem arises when a cell is given a format that makes it appear different from its contents.

Figure 4.6 shows the result of this problem. In column B, there are ten cell entries, each displaying the number 10. A sum formula at the bottom of the column somehow comes up with the seemingly bizarre result of 96. Something is wrong, but it's not because the formula is in error.

By looking at the input line at the top of the screen, you can see that cell B1 does not actually contain 10, but 9.6. As it turns out, all the data cells contain 9.6, but each has been given a numeric format of Fixed with 0 decimals, as shown by the (F0) on the input line. The format rounds the display to the specified number of decimals, resulting in the display of 10. The formula sums up the values and arrives at the correct answer of 96. As always, you can't have your cake and eat it, too.

If you want your numbers displayed without any decimals, enter them that way. Or, if you are referring to numbers in another location, use the @ROUND function to round those

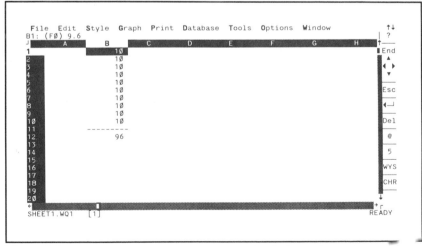

Figure 4.6: When numeric formats are involved, formulas may appear to give the wrong results

values, such as @ROUND (M23,0). Either way, the total will then be correct.

AVOIDING INCORRECT ABSOLUTE OR RELATIVE REFERENCING

Another way to include an error in a formula is by the incorrect use of absolute or relative cell addressing. For example, you might correctly create a cell variable for the sales tax amount in the earlier example, but later forget to refer to that cell with an absolute reference when including it in a formula. That formula will produce the correct result, but if you were to copy it to another location, the reference to the sales tax cell would adjust, and the new formula would be incorrect.

There's no simple way to prevent this from happening, although the use of a block name would help. If a formula does not include that name, you know that it is not referring to the correct cell.

AVOIDING CIRCULAR REFERENCES

Another common problem results from writing a formula which somehow includes itself within the calculation, thereby creating a *circular reference.*

For example, suppose you were revising one of the @SUM functions in the Mileage spreadsheet, and you anchored the top of the sum range at cell B5 and then simply pressed End-↓ to quickly highlight the entire column of data. That's a very useful trick to move rapidly through a block of cells, but it would cause trouble in this case.

This is because End-↓ would place the cell selector at the very bottom of the column, on cell B12. That cell just happens to be the same cell that contains the @SUM function, so if you didn't move the cell selector up a row, the function would be including itself:

@SUM(B5..B12)

⊙ If you see the Circ
indicator, investi-
gate the problem and, if
it is not justified, correct
the circular reference.

To see the problem with circular references for yourself, just change the @SUM function in the spreadsheet so it includes itself. Then press F9, the Calc key, and watch that formula take off to new highs as it includes itself in every recalculation. Fortunately, there's an easy way to find and correct the problem.

First of all, you will see the Circ indicator at the bottom of the screen whenever Quattro Pro finds a circular reference. As soon as it appears, you should stop what you're doing and correct the problem. Invoke the command Options–Recalculation, and then look at the address next to Circular Reference on the menu. It will point to the cell with the problem.

There may be times when a circular reference is justified, but you should definitely be aware of the situation and know just where the reference is occurring. For example, you might use a circular reference in a calculation to produce a gross profit by subtracting expenses from income. The circular reference arises when one of the expenses, such as overhead, is a formula that is calculated as a percent of the gross profit. Each time the spreadsheet is recalculated, the overhead expense evaluates to a new, slightly different figure that in turn affects the profit, which in turn affects the overhead, and so on. The profit and overhead amounts become a little more accurate each time.

AVOIDING DIVISION BY ZERO

A formula that divides a number by zero produces the result ERR because such an operation is mathematically invalid. For example, if cell B14 has the value 0 (either because it is blank or contains a zero, a formula that results in zero, or text), this formula would result in ERR:

A5/B14

There's nothing wrong with getting that result (after all, it is the correct result), but it may interfere with other formulas that refer to it. This is because a formula that references a cell that contains ERR will also result in ERR, so that one error cell will propagate throughout the spreadsheet.

When a cell will be used as the divisor in a formula, try to be sure that the cell never equates to 0. When that is not possible (which is frequently the case), use an @IF function in your division formula to check the divisor cell:

@IF(B14=0,0,A5/B14)

If cell B14 contains 0, the formula results in 0, which is usually an acceptable solution in such a case. Otherwise, the division is performed.

Now that you know how to make more complex cell entries using formulas, we will move on to more efficient ways to work with the cells on your spreadsheets. Chapter 5 covers techniques for manipulating cell blocks.

5

Manipulating Cells and Blocks

Fast
Track

THE COMMANDS AND TECHNIQUES COVERED IN THIS chapter will help you in the frequent task of working with blocks of cells. You will learn how to copy, move, and delete cells, as well as how to take advantage of block names, one of the most powerful, and underutilized, features in Quattro Pro.

Other techniques for manipulating blocks discussed in this chapter include transposing rows and columns, filling blocks of cells with consecutive numbers, inserting and deleting rows and columns, and searching for specific characters within a block of cells.

COPYING BLOCKS

Duplicating cells in Quattro Pro allows you to build your spreadsheet rapidly and with precise accuracy (by eliminating errors due to repetitive typing). As you saw in the last chapter, when you copy a formula, any cell references in it automatically adjust to their new location in the spreadsheet (unless you make those addresses absolute by prefacing them with a $). This means that you can write one formula and use it in many locations. For example, you can write a formula to sum a column of numbers, and then copy that formula to a dozen similar columns to sum them as well.

The command Edit–Copy (shortcut Ctrl-C) requires two specifications: a *source* block of cells and a *destination* block. The destination cells can be in another active worksheet, which greatly expands the power of the command.

When you copy a cell, everything in that cell is duplicated, including the following:

- Cell contents
- Specified data type
- Numeric format
- Alignment status for values
- Protection status

The Edit–Copy command will overwrite any existing data in the destination block. Be careful when you specify both blocks. Remember to keep a recently saved copy of your spreadsheet on disk as insurance against disaster.

- Font
- Shading
- Line drawing

For example, suppose you want to copy cell A5 to cell D10. Cell A5 contains the label *Some text*, and the input line for that cell shows

Label A5: (C0) U [15] [F7] 'Some text

Along with the left-justified text, the other information attached to that cell will be copied:

- Label: Anything entered in this cell will be treated as text, set by the Database–Data Entry–Labels Only command.
- (C0): The numeric format is Currency, with 0 decimal places, set by the Style–Numeric Format–Currency command.
- U: The cell is unprotected, set by the Style–Protection–Unprotect command.
- [F7]: The font number is 7, set by the Style–Font–7 command.

The width of column A, [15], is also indicated on the input line for cell A5. But that is one attribute that is not attached to a cell, so it will not be copied. In the example, the width of column D will not be affected by the copied cell.

On the other hand, shading and line-drawing attributes are not shown in the status line, but are nonetheless copied along with the cell contents.

Although the source and destination cells will be exact duplicates, any formulas that referred to the source cell will not in any way relate to the copied cell. As far as the rest of the spreadsheet is concerned, the two cells are completely unrelated—they just look the same.

You can copy one cell to another cell, a single cell to a block, a block to a single cell, or a block to a block. The effects of the Copy command are a little different in each case.

COPYING A SINGLE CELL TO A SINGLE CELL

The simplest copy operation is that of copying one cell, such as A5, to another, such as D10. You can use one of the standard methods to specify each cell: type the address, point to the cell, or use a block name (more on block names later in the chapter).

Let's copy a single cell by typing the addresses.

1. Enter the phrase **Some text** into cell A5.

2. For this example, press Home to move the cell selector to cell A1.

3. Press / to activate the menu bar.

4. Select the Edit–Copy command.

5. Type **A5** and press ⏎ when prompted for the source block.

6. Type **D10** and press ⏎ when prompted for the destination block.

The job is done, and the cell selector was never moved. Typing the address may be the best choice when you know the exact addresses of the source and destination cells, and it would be inconvenient to point. Now erase cell D10.

7. With the cell selector still on cell A1, invoke the command Edit–Erase Block.

8. Type **D10** and press ⏎ when prompted for the block to be modified.

Cell D10 should be blank. Now you will copy the same cell, but this time you will use a shortcut key and point to the source and destination cells.

It is generally more convenient to position the cell selector on the source or destination cell before using the Copy command.

9. With the cell selector still on cell A1, press Ctrl-C to invoke the Edit–Copy command (hold down the Ctrl key and then press C).

10. Press Escape to erase the default block that is offered, A1..A1, so that the input line shows only the address A1.

11. Press End-↓ to move the cell selector to cell A5.

12. Press ↵ to select this cell as the source cell.

13. Press → three times, then ↓ nine times to move the cell selector to cell D10.

14. Press ↵ to specify cell D10 as the destination cell for the copy.

The cell selector will return to cell A1 after the cell is copied.

COPYING A SINGLE CELL TO A BLOCK OF CELLS

In the Mileage spreadsheet we created in Chapter 2, you copied a single cell to create the dashed lines across the columns, and you wrote a single formula to calculate the miles driven and copied it to the rest of the cells in that column. Other formulas were created and copied in the same manner.

The only difference between this type of copy operation and the one discussed in the previous section is that you must specify a block of cells as the destination. We will continue with our simple example and copy the contents of cell A5 to the block D10..F15.

1. It doesn't matter where the cell selector is before you begin, so just press Ctrl-C to issue the Copy command.

2. Type **A5** and press ↵ to designate the source cell.

3. Type **D10..F15** and press ↵ to specify the destination block.

Each cell in the block D10..F15 should be filled with the label from cell A5. Now you will use the pointing method to erase some of the copied cells. Pointing to the destination block requires that you first anchor the corner of the block.

4. The cell selector should still be on cell A1. If it is not, press Home to move it there.

5. Press Ctrl-E to invoke the Edit–Erase Block command.

6. You don't want to erase the block A1..A1, so press Escape to unanchor the block that is offered.

7. Move the cell selector to cell E10 and press the period key to anchor the block at this cell.

8. Press →, then End-↓ to move to cell F15.

9. Press ↵ to erase that block.

As you can see, the process of pointing to a block to copy or erase is the same.

COPYING A BLOCK OF CELLS TO A SINGLE CELL

When you specify a block as the source and a single cell as the destination, the copied block will begin at the destination cell and fill the same number of cells as the original block. Now we will copy once more, but this time from a block, D10..D15, to a single cell, F7.

1. Move the cell selector to cell D10, the first cell of our source block.

2. Press Ctrl-C. The prompt offers you the block D10..D10.

3. Press End-↓ to highlight the rest of the column, D10..D15, and then press ↵ to accept the block as the source block.

4. The cell selector will be back on cell D10; press → twice, then ↑ three times to move to cell F7.

5. Press ↵ to accept F7 as the destination block.

The cell selector will go back to its original cell, D10, and the block F7..F12 will be an exact duplicate of the block D10..D15.

COPYING A BLOCK OF CELLS TO A BLOCK OF CELLS

It is easy to copy a block of cells to another block of cells if you follow this simple rule of thumb:

- Copy a single column to a single row, or a single row to a single column.

If the source block is a column of cells, such as F5..F10, you can duplicate that column across many cells in the same row, such as B2..G2. If the source is a row of cells (C22..H22), you can copy that row to many cells down a column (A100..A150). As a final example of copying, we'll copy the block from the previous example, D10..D15, to B1..E1.

1. With the cell selector on cell D10, press Ctrl-C.
2. Press End-↓ to highlight the source block D10..D15 and press ↵.
3. Press End-↑ to move the cell selector to the top of column D, and then press ← twice to move to cell B1.
4. Press the period key to anchor the destination block at cell B1.
5. Press → three times to highlight the block B1..E1, and then press ↵ to specify it as the destination block.

The cells in the source block, D10..D15, will be duplicated in columns B through E.

TIPS ON HIGHLIGHTING BLOCKS

You will spend plenty of time working with blocks in Quattro Pro. This section provides some tips that will make the process easier and faster.

USING THE SELECT KEY, SHIFT-F7

You can highlight a block before you invoke a command by using the Select key, Shift-F7. Place the cell selector on one of the corner cells of the block you want to select, and then press Shift-F7. You will see the Ext indicator at the bottom of the screen, which means that you can extend the highlighting by moving the cell selector. Highlight the block, and then invoke the command.

The command will use your highlighted block for its first input. For example, if you chose Edit–Erase, the block would be erased. If you chose Edit–Copy, the block would be used as the source block of cells.

You can also use your mouse to highlight a block before invoking a command.

UNANCHORING CELLS

You can unanchor a highlighted block by pressing either Escape or Backspace. When you press Escape, the cell selector remains at the corner that had been the anchor cell. Pressing Backspace unanchors the block and also returns the cell selector to the cell on which it resided before you issued the command.

Use the key that places the cell selector in the best position for what you want to do once the block is unanchored.

ROTATING THE ANCHOR

When you are pointing to a block, you can expand the highlighting either to the right of or down from the anchor cell. The corner of the highlighting that you are moving is called the *active* corner.

If you now try to expand the block to the left of the anchor by moving the active corner left, the block will just shrink or move past the anchor column. However, there is a simple way to expand a block in both directions.

Whenever you are pointing to a block, you can *rotate* the anchor cell to another corner of the highlight by pressing the period key. Each press will move the anchor, and therefore the active corner, to the next corner in a clockwise rotation. The blinking cursor will show you which corner is the active one, and you will see the block address change on the input line.

For example, suppose you have highlighted B10..F20 as the source block for the Copy command (the anchor cell is currently B10, and the active cell is F20). But now you want to include column A and rows 8 and 9 in the block. Just press the period key twice to move the active corner to B10, the upper-left cell of the block. The input line will show that the command is now referring to the block F20..B10. Now you can use the cursor-control keys to expand the highlighting from the active cell to include column A and rows 8 and 9.

The best tip for selecting blocks is to use block names, as discussed later in the chapter.

> When you are highlighting a block that is so large that one (or more) of its corners is off the screen, you can rotate the active cell to view any of its corners.

MOVING A BLOCK TO A NEW LOCATION

Whereas the Edit–Copy command creates a duplicate of the source block, the Edit–Move command actually moves the source cells to the new location. It prompts you for the source block and the destination block, and as always, you can type the addresses, point, or use block names.

MOVING VERSUS COPYING CELLS

Just as with the Copy command, when you move a cell, everything that is connected with that cell moves with it: cell contents, protection status, shading, format, and so on. Unlike the Copy command, however, formula cell references do not change. When you move a cell, the addresses in a formula remain the same, no matter if they were relative or absolute.

Another difference between the Copy and Move commands is the way that formulas in other cells in the spreadsheet are affected when a cell to which they refer is moved. When you copy a cell, formulas will still refer to the original cell. When a cell is moved, however, any references to it are reset to the new location. The following exercise demonstrates this significant difference.

1. Enter **10** in cell A1 of a blank spreadsheet.

2. Enter **5+A1** into both cells B6 and B7, so that each returns a result of 15.

3. In cell C3, type the formula **+B6+B7**. This simply adds both of the other formulas to produce a total of 30.

4. Use the Style–Numeric Format–Text command to give the three formula cells a Text format. The actual cell contents (the formula), not the result, are displayed on the screen. Your spreadsheet should look like Figure 5.1.

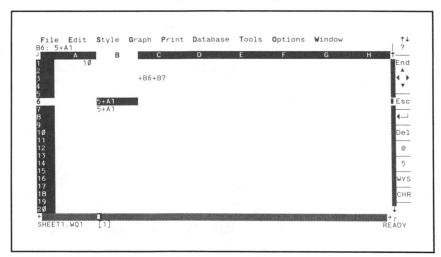

Figure 5.1: A spreadsheet to demonstrate the effects of the Copy and Move commands

5. Invoke the Edit–Move command and designate B6 as the source block and E6 as the destination block.

6. Invoke the Edit–Copy command and designate B7 as the source block and E7 as the destination block. The resulting spreadsheet appears as shown in Figure 5.2.

Look at the formulas in their new destinations in column E. The formula in cell E6 was moved, and it still refers to cell A1. But the formula that was copied to cell E7 now refers to cell D1; it has adjusted its reference relative to its new location. The result of this formula is different from the original formula that referred to cell A1 (5 versus 15).

Also note the formula in cell C3. Its original reference to cell B6 followed that cell when it was moved to its new location, so that it now refers to cell E6. However, its reference to the copied cell in B7 has not changed; it still refers to the original in B7. The formula does not know or care about that cell being copied.

MOVING A CELL TO A BLOCK CORNER

Because you can destroy a block or block name by moving a cell onto its upper-left or lower-right corner cells, you should always

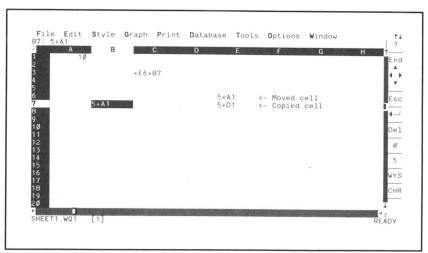

Figure 5.2: The results of copying and moving two cells

use caution when moving cells about the spreadsheet. However, there is a way to move a cell onto a sensitive corner cell. Instead of using the Move command, just copy the cell to the destination, and then erase the original cell. If the original is a formula, you can prevent its cell references from changing by turning the formula into a label. Follow this basic procedure:

1. Before you copy the formula, press F2 to edit it. Then press Home and type a label prefix (such as an apostrophe) and press ↵.

2. Use the Edit–Copy command to copy the formula, as text, to its new location.

3. Edit the duplicate and remove the label prefix. The formula will return.

4. Erase the original cell, and the job is done.

Be aware that you should never "move" a cell in this manner if there are other formulas in the spreadsheet that are supposed to reference it. Their references will not follow the duplicate to the new location; they will continue to refer to the original.

ERASING THE CELL CONTENTS IN A BLOCK

We've used the Edit–Erase Block command (Ctrl-E) several times already. To erase a cell or block of cells, you simply invoke the command and indicate the cell or cells you want to erase.

You should use a little caution when you erase a cell because once its contents are gone, they are gone forever. That is, unless you have a little insurance.

The best protection against accidental erasures is to have a recently saved copy of the spreadsheet on disk. There is also the Undo command, which can undo an erasure as long as you press the Undo key (Alt-F5) before making any other changes to the spreadsheet.

Don't forget that the Undo command must first be enabled with the Options–Other–Undo–Enable commmand. You can then use the Options–Update command if you want Undo enabled for every session in Quattro Pro.

Another way to erase a cell when the spreadsheet is in Ready mode is to simply press the Del key. This erases the current cell. If you first highlight a block with the Select key, Shift-F7, you can erase the entire block simply by pressing Del.

Of all the components of a cell, it is only the contents that are actually erased. A cell retains its protection status, shading, line drawing, format, font, data type specification, and alignment status for values. When you erase a cell, you are not really creating a blank cell, you are just emptying it of its contents. To create a truly blank cell, you must either delete its row or column or also reset all its other attributes with the appropriate commands (such as Style–Numeric Format–Reset).

USING BLOCK NAMES FOR PINPOINT ACCURACY

One of the problems of dealing with blocks is that it can be very difficult to remember their cell coordinates. Every time you insert or delete a row or column, the addresses of all the blocks that are below or to the right of the insertion or deletion will change. But there is a simple but elegant way of dealing with this that will enhance just about every spreadsheet you will ever create.

A block name is a name you assign to a block in a spreadsheet by using one of the commands on the Edit–Names menu. The name can be as long as 15 characters and can include any characters. However, there are a few rules of style that should govern your names, as discussed shortly. Once you have named a block, you can use that name in any command or formula that refers to that block.

Try this quick example:

1. Erase the entire contents of your current spreadsheet by issuing the File–Erase command.

2. Select the Edit–Names–Create command.

3. In response to the command's prompt for a name, type **MYCELL** (uppercase or lowercase does not matter), and then press ⏎.

4. Type **B5** as the cell you want to name, and then press ⏎.

Cell B5 now has the name MYCELL assigned to it, but nothing in the spreadsheet has changed. Let's continue with the example to see how convenient it can be to have a named block.

5. Press End–→, then End–↓ to move to the bottom-right corner of the spreadsheet, miles from anywhere.

Suppose you now want to return to the cell you just named, but you can't remember its exact cell address. Since it is named, that's not a problem.

6. Press the Goto key, F5.

7. When prompted for the address to go to, type **MYCELL** and press ⏎.

8. Now that you are back at MYCELL, type the number **29** into it (we will use this cell later).

No matter how many rows or columns you insert or delete in the spreadsheet, or where you might move your named block, you will still be able to reference it by its name.

You can also use the Edit–Names–Create command to redefine the address of an existing name as well as assign new names. The Create command always offers you a list of the current names in the spreadsheet, so that you can pick the name you want to redefine and specify its new coordinates. Any formulas that refer to that name will reference the new coordinates.

BLOCK NAMING CONVENTIONS

In general, you do not need to name a block or cell if you are only going to work with it a single time. The more frequently you refer to a specific area of the spreadsheet, however, the more important it is to have a name assigned to it. You should certainly consider names for any of the following if you regularly refer to them:

- Blocks that you frequently need to access for entering data or viewing
- Variable cells that are referred to in formulas
- Blocks that are used as tables in formulas
- Blocks that are printed
- Blocks that are sorted
- Blocks that are part of a spreadsheet database
- Any cells that are referred to in macros

You can display a list of block names in the current spreadsheet by using the Choices key, F3, or the Edit–Names command. Quattro Pro sorts the list alphabetically, so that names that begin with the same character will appear together in the list. You can take advantage of this by assigning similar names to certain types of cells.

For example, you may frequently have 10 or 20 cells that serve as variable cells for formulas or macros. If you name each of them so that they all begin with the letter V (for variable), all those cells will be together on the list of names:

```
V_INFLATION
V_INTEREST
V_RATE_FACTOR
```

Formulas that use any of the lookup functions, such as @VLOOKUP or @INDEX, refer to a block of cells as one of their parameters. Generally, those blocks should be named, and if their only purpose is to serve as a table for those formulas, you could begin all their names with the word TABLE:

```
TABLE_EMP_NUM
TABLE_MONTHS
TABLE_RATES
```

Quattro Pro allows you to use any characters you want in a block name, but the following guidelines should govern your choices:

- Avoid spaces so that the name does not appear to be two names in a formula. For example, this formula is hard to interpret: +B19*YEARLY TOTAL+J66. If you want a name to appear as two words, use an underline instead of a space: +B19*YEARLY_TOTAL+J66.

- Avoid arithmetic operators (any of the characters shown in Table 4.1). Because names are used so frequently in formulas, you certainly don't want to disguise a name as a formula. For example, if a formula referred to a cell named +FIRST(QTR)+, it might look like Y143++FIRST(QTR)+*B150.

- Don't use a name that could also be interpreted as a cell address, such as A1, GO91, IQ100, or GW1991. Not only would these names be lost in a formula (they would look like addresses), but Quattro Pro will treat them as the actual cell addresses. The formula's result would not be what you wanted, and the error might be difficult to track down later.

FINDING NAMES FAST WITH THE CHOICES KEY, F3

When you have dozens or hundreds of block names in a large spreadsheet, you may not remember how names are spelled or how many variations of a particular name you have (such as QTR1, QTR2, QTRLAST, and so on). Help is no farther away than your function keys.

Anytime you need to insert a block name into a Quattro Pro command (such as Edit–Copy) or formula you are writing, simply press function key F3, the Choices key. An alphabetized list of all the block names in the spreadsheet will appear.

Simply highlight the name you want in the three-across list, press ↵, and that name will be entered into the command or formula, as though you had typed it.

If you want to see the cell address that each name covers, just press the plus key. The list will change to a single column of names with their addresses to the right. Press the hyphen key, or minus sign, to return the list to its original state. You can also press the F3 key a second time to expand the list to full-screen size.

If your list has dozens or hundreds of names in it, you may find it cumbersome to page through the screens of names, looking for the one you want. In this case, you can have Quattro Pro help you search. While the list is displayed, press the F2 key. You will see the prompt

> Search for: *

The Choices key can also prove valuable when block names aren't involved. For example, when you have invoked a file command that requires a file name (such as File–Open), you can press F3 to expand the list of files to full-screen size. This not only makes it easier to find the file you want, but it also shows you the date, time, and size of each file.

Just type the first character of the name for which you are searching, and the cursor will jump to the first name on the list that begins with that character. Type a second character, and the name that begins with those two characters will be highlighted. Continue to type characters to narrow the search to the specific name you want.

USING NAMES TO MAKE YOUR FORMULAS SIMPLE AND ACCURATE

You have already given the name MYCELL to cell B5 in your spreadsheet, and you have also entered the value 29 into it. Here's a quick way to see how block names can simplify formulas: Move the cell selector to cell A3 (or any cell besides B5) and type the formula **5+MYCELL**. The result of 34 will appear on the screen, and the input line should show the formula as the contents of the cell.

If you edit this formula (press F2), you will find that the name is replaced by the cell address, B5. This allows you to see the actual cell address and also to edit it.

In this short exercise, you have actually seen two of the biggest advantages of block names:

- You can refer to a named cell just by typing its name into the formula.

- The name, not the address of the named cell, will appear in the formula.

By referencing a cell's name instead of its actual address, you are less likely to refer to the wrong cell. If you use the Choices key (F3) and select the name to use in the formula from the list, your chances of making a mistake are negligible.

Names can also point out referencing errors. When a formula is supposed to refer to a block name, it will be quite obvious that something is amiss when that name no longer appears in the formula. Suppose you had a column of formulas in column K, each of which multiplied the cell to its left, in column J, by the cell named MYCELL. If you moved the cell selector to each one and viewed its contents on the input line, you would know something was wrong if the formulas looked like this:

```
+J19*$MYCELL
+J20*$MYCELL
+J21*$C$19
+J22*$MYCELL
```

Another benefit of using names is that they make it easier to interpret the purpose of a formula that refers to them. For example, if you saw a formula that looked like this:

```
@SUM(BUDGET91)*$INFLATION
```

you could probably guess that it takes your 1991 budget and multiplies it by an inflation factor that is in the cell named INFLATION.

Note that you can make an absolute reference to a name in a formula by prefacing the name with a $, as in the formula above. However, if you want to make only the row or column absolute when you refer to a named block, you must specify the cell address, not the block name.

NAMING SEVERAL CELLS WITH ONE COMMAND

The Edit–Names–Label command lets you name many cells with one step. For example, if you are creating names for cell variables that will be used by financial functions, you know you will need several single-cell names in one area of the spreadsheet.

Figure 5.3 shows how this command works. In cells A2, A4, and A6 are text entries that identify the cells to their right, B2, B4, and B6. For example, the label V_INTEREST in cell A2 identifies cell B2 as a variable cell that holds an interest rate. The labels not only serve to identify these cells, but they can also be used to name each of the cells, B2 through B6, in one operation. Place the cell selector on cell A2, invoke the Edit–Names–Labels command, and choose Right from the list of choices for label placment (Right, Down, Left, and Up). When you are prompted

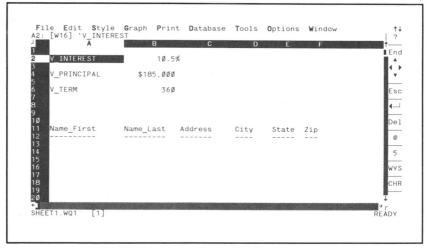

Figure 5.3: Assigning block names by using labels

for the label block, either type the address or point to the block A2..A6, and then press ↵ to complete the command. The names V_INTEREST, V_PRINCIPAL, and V_TERM would be assigned to cells B2, B4, and B6, respectively.

In row 11 of Figure 5.3 is another set of text entries that will be the column titles for a spreadsheet database of names and addresses. When working with a database, naming the first row of data below each column title can be a great help. To use the column titles as the source of the names, simply issue the Edit–Names–Labels–Down command and specify the block A11..F11. Each of the cells in row 12 will be given the name that appears above it in row 11.

Here are a few guidelines for using the Labels command:

- Be sure to follow the same naming conventions that you would if you were creating the name with the Edit–Names–Create command. Avoid spaces, arithmetic operators, and so on, as explained earlier in the chapter.

- Make sure that the name in each cell is spelled precisely as you intended.

- Avoid any blank spaces before or after the label.

- Only the specific text that you want for the name of each cell should be in the label block. For example, you may want to include a note or comment in the cells below each of the labels in A2..A6 in Figure 5.3. But don't do this until after you have used the Labels command. Otherwise, you will name cells that you do not need named.

DELETING BLOCK NAMES

You can delete any name you have created by using the Edit–Names–Delete command. You can either pick the name you want to delete from the list displayed or type the name at the prompt.

Quattro Pro's optional Lotus-compatible menus, like those in Lotus 1-2-3, do not offer the Yes/No menu for the Range–Name–Reset command. As soon as you invoke the command, every name in the spread-sheet is gone.

Deleting a name will not harm any data or formulas in the spreadsheet. It simply means that you will no longer be able to refer to the block by the name you had given it. Formulas that had referred to the name will now show the actual cell address that the name had defined. For example, the formula @SUM(TOTAL) might become @SUM(M244..Z305).

Note that the Undo command, if it has been enabled, can be used to restore one or all block names.

To remove every name in the spreadsheet at one time, use the Edit–Names–Reset command. This is a pretty drastic thing to do, so the command offers a second, affirmation menu. You can choose Yes to reset all the names, or No to cancel the command and leave the names alone.

MAKING A TABLE OF BLOCK NAMES

The Edit–Names–Make Table command simply produces a two-column table in the spreadsheet that lists all the block names in one column and the addresses they define in the second column. This is the same list you see when you invoke the Edit–Names–Create command or use the F3 key.

The list is actually written into the cells in two columns of your spreadsheet, starting from the cell selector's position. Be sure there are plenty of empty rows below the cell selector so that the list won't overwrite any important data.

You can sort the block name table by using the address column as the sort key to find all names in a given area of the spreadsheet. When you have many names in the table, you can use the Edit–Search & Replace command to search for a specific address, row number, ERR cell, and so on.

Figure 5.4 shows the table of block names as it would appear in the spreadsheet in Figure 5.3. The Edit–Names–Make Table command was invoked while the cell selector was on cell A22. Because names can be up to 15 characters long, column A has been expanded to 16 characters wide with the Style–Column Width command.

CAUTIONS WHEN USING BLOCK NAMES

You should avoid assigning two names to the same block. Besides being redundant, duplicate names can cause a real problem if you decide to redefine the address of one of the names.

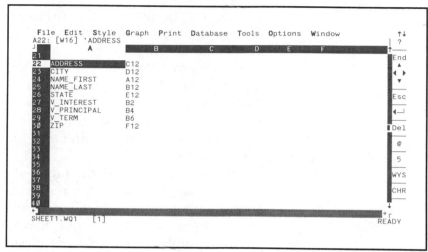

Figure 5.4: The table created by the Edit–Names–Make Table command

By changing the definition of one name, the other name's definition will also be changed, and you may not realize this has happened.

You should also be aware that you can "destroy" a block name if you "damage" either its upper-left or lower-right corner cells. There are really only two operations that can destroy a block corner cell: moving a cell onto it or deleting its row or column.

For example, if the name DATA covers the block B5..E10, and you move a cell onto cell E10, you will "pop" the block, and the name DATA will no longer be valid. The name will still exist in the list of names, but its address will simply be ERR. Any formulas that referred to the name DATA will now refer only to ERR. For example, @SUM(DATA) would become @SUM(ERR). You will have to either erase or rewrite each of those formulas.

Even if a block is not named, moving a cell onto its corner cell would cause any formulas that referred to that block to show ERR instead of the address.

COPYING FORMULAS AS VALUES

The Edit–Values command is virtually identical to the Edit–Copy command, except for the effect it has on formulas. It copies only the value of the formula to the new location. This freezes the results of formulas, saves memory, and shortens recalculation times.

You may have formulas in a block that perform calculations on a block of data. If you want to retain the results of the formulas for future use, you can use the Edit–Values command and copy the formulas as values to another location. There, the values will remain static while the formulas can produce new results for new data.

Another reason to use the Edit–Values command is to get rid of a formula that you no longer need. If you know that no further calculations will ever be performed and only the current result is important, you should change the formula into a value.

For example, you might enter dates by using the @DATE function. The formula produces a date number, but that is all you need. You will never be changing the date, so the formula is excess baggage. That is the time to invoke the Edit–Values command and turn all the @DATE formulas into actual numbers.

Suppose you had entered a column of dates in the block B1..B100, and you were now ready to turn the formulas into values. You would invoke the Edit–Values command and specify the block B1..B100 as the source and B1 as the destination. By specifying the same block for the source and destination, the formula values will be copied back on top of the formulas and replace them. When you retain only the values, your spreadsheet will require less RAM, and recalculation speeds will be faster.

Don't forget that the values are actually replacing the formulas, so this could have potentially destructive results if you need to retain the formulas. As with any major change to the spreadsheet, a recently saved copy of your work is your best insurance.

Remember that you can also change a formula into a value by pressing F2 to edit the formula cell, then pressing F9.

The Undo command will also undo the results of the Edit–Values command.

TRANSPOSING COLUMNS TO ROWS AND ROWS TO COLUMNS

The Edit–Transpose command behaves very much like the Copy command; it duplicates cells in another location, and formulas will adjust their references in the process. The only difference is that it transposes the rows and columns of the source block when it copies them into the destination block.

Transposing blocks can be a real convenience when, for example, your data is laid out in a wide format that uses many columns but not too many rows. If you later decide that you would like to print your work within the width of a single page, you can use the Edit–Transpose command to reorient the spreadsheet so that it uses a few columns and many rows.

The only problem with this command is that transposed formulas will adjust to their new locations, but their new location will be totally unrelated to their original one, and their results will therefore be irrelevant. For this reason, you will generally transpose data but not formulas.

Figure 5.5 shows a small spreadsheet that has one column for each month of the year and six rows of data. As you can see, the columns extend off the right side of the screen. To reorient the spreadsheet, you would invoke the Edit–Transpose command and specify the block A3..N10 as the source and cell A22 as the destination.

The block will be duplicated at cell A22, and the result will appear as shown in Figure 5.6. The data has been neatly transposed so that the rows are now columns and the columns are rows. However, you will have to recreate the dashed horizontal and vertical border lines, which are now oriented in the wrong direction.

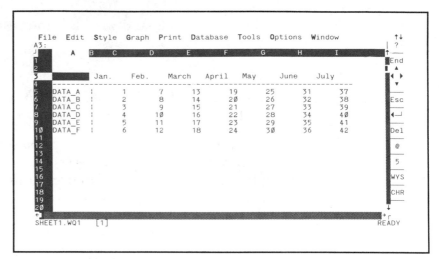

Figure 5.5: A block of data before being transposed

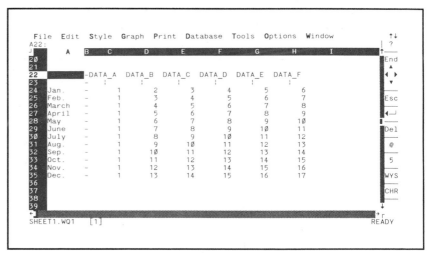

Figure 5.6: The block of data after being transposed with the Edit–
Transpose command

FILLING A BLOCK WITH NUMBERS

There are three methods for filling a block of cells with consecutive numbers. The first method is simple: just type the numbers into each cell in the block. But that's too much work, so it really doesn't count. The other methods involve using a formula or invoking the Edit–Fill command.

USING A FORMULA TO FILL CELLS

You can write a formula and then copy it to the rest of the cells in the block to fill the cells with numbers. For example, suppose you wanted to fill a column of cells, beginning at B1, with numbers that start at 10, increment by 10 in each cell, and go up to 150. You may not know how many cells will be used, you just want the highest value to be 150. Here is the procedure you could use:

1. In cell B1, enter the starting value, **10**.

2. In cell B2, enter the formula **+B1+10**, which will result in 20.

3. Copy the formula in cell B2 to enough cells in the column so that the maximum attained is 150 (in this case, it is easy to figure you will need 15 cells in all). The result of 150 should appear in cell B15.

4. Turn these formulas into actual values with the Edit–Values command. Specify the block B1..B15 as the source and B1 as the destination.

USING THE EDIT–FILL COMMAND

Quattro Pro provides a third method for filling a block of cells with consecutive values that is even easier than using formulas: the Edit–Fill command. This command, however, requires four responses from you:

- The destination block that will receive the numbers. It can be any block of cells. The cells will be filled column by column. The values will overwrite any data already in those cells, so be sure that the block you are filling does not have any existing cells that you don't want to lose.

- A start value (the number from which to begin incrementing). This value can be any number or formula that returns a number as a result, or a cell address that contains a number (positive or negative, with or without decimals). This number will be placed in the first cell of the destination block.

- A step value (the number by which to increase each cell). This value can also be any number, formula, or cell address. Each cell will be this much greater (if the step value is positive) or less (if the step value is negative) than the cell before it in the block.

- A stop value (the number at which to stop incrementing). This value is the highest number you want in the filled block, or the lowest one if you are incrementing with a negative step value.

Here are the steps to follow to fill the same block as in the previous example:

1. Invoke the Edit–Fill command.
2. Type in the address **B1..B1000** as the destination block and press ↵ (that's right, 1000).
3. Enter **10** for the start value and press ↵.
4. Type **10** for the step value and press ↵.
5. Enter **150** for the stop value and press ↵.

As soon as you press the final ↵, the block of cells will be filled as you specified.

Why was such a large destination block chosen? In this case, you didn't care how many cells were in the block. The criteria was simply that the block should start in cell B1, and that the numbers should start at 10, step by 10, and stop at 150. As soon as that value was reached, the command stopped filling, and the excess cells in the destination block were simply ignored.

There will be other times, however, when the size of the destination block is more important that the stop value. For example, if you have entered a column of data and now you want to number the rows from 1 to whatever the final row value would be. In this case, you would specify the precise destination block, such as the cells in the column to the left of your data. The start value would be 1, as would the step value. But you may not really know what the stop value should be, nor do you care. It is the size of the block that will limit the fill. Simply specify an overly large stop value, such as 99999, or accept the default stop value of 8192 (which happens to be the number of rows in the spreadsheet). Your block will be filled to the last cell, but no farther, no matter what the final ending value is.

Here is a very convenient way to fill a block of cells with the dates that coincide with the first Monday of each week in the year. We'll use 1991 as the sample year and fill column A.

1. Invoke the Edit–Fill command.

2. Specify the block by typing in the address **A1..A1000**.

3. The start value will be the first Monday of 1991, which happens to be January 7. Enter the formula **@DATE(91,1,7)**.

4. Enter **7** for the step value, which represents 7 days in a week.

5. The stop value will be the last day of the year. Enter **@DATE(91,12,31)**.

The block will be filled, starting with the number 33245 in cell A1 and ending with 33602 in cell A52. You could now format these numbers as dates with the Style–Numeric Format–Date command.

EXPANDING AND CONTRACTING THE SPREADSHEET

Even though there will always be a fixed number of columns and rows in the spreadsheet, you are free to delete them or insert new ones as your designs require. The commands Edit–Insert (shortcut Ctrl-I) and Edit–Delete offer you two choices: Rows and Columns.

When you insert one or more rows, all rows at and below the insertion are pushed down. When you insert one or more columns, all columns at and to the right of the insertion are pushed to the right. You can never lose data "off the edge of the Earth" due to an insertion. For example, if there is data in row 8192 (an unlikely possibility) and you try to insert a row into the spreadsheet, your command will be thwarted and you will see the error message

    Out of spreadsheet boundary

The same would be true if there were data in column IV and you tried to insert a column.

When you delete one or more columns (or rows) by using the Edit–Delete command, the columns to the right (or the rows below) are all moved to the left (or up) to fill in the gap.

When you invoke either the Edit–Insert or Delete command, you are prompted to specify the block in which you want to insert or delete rows or columns. You must enter a valid Quattro Pro address for these commands, although it is only the row numbers in the address that are important for the Insert or Delete Rows command. For example, to insert three rows at row 2, you could respond with the block address A2..A4, D2..D4, or L2..AB4. When you insert or delete columns, be sure to

Remember that deleting the upper-left or lower-right corner cell of a block will destroy any name associated with that block, as well as any formulas that refer to the block.

specify the exact columns; the row numbers are not important.

As you insert or delete rows or columns, all formula cell references are adjusted. However, you may have to plan ahead when you write your formulas so that rows or columns can be inserted or deleted within the formula's block reference.

For example, suppose we want to add three new rows to the Mileage spreadsheet from Chapter 2, so that new data can be entered. With the new rows and data, the formulas in columns B, C, and D can be copied to the appropriate rows. Let's add the three rows to the bottom of the work area, just above the formulas.

1. Move the cell selector to cell A11 and invoke the Edit–Insert–Rows command. The command prompt offers the block A11..A11.

2. Leave the anchor cell at A11 and extend the highlighting down to row 13, so the prompt displays the block coordinates A11..A13.

3. Press ↲. The new rows will be inserted, as shown in Figure 5.7.

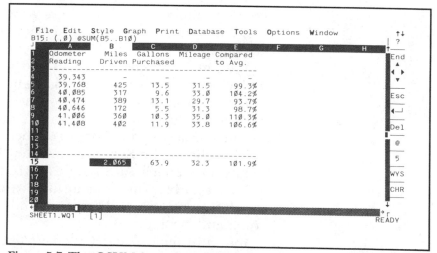

Figure 5.7: The @SUM formulas in the Mileage spreadsheet did not adjust after three new rows were inserted

4. Move the cell selector to the @SUM formula that is now in cell B15. The input line shows this cell's contents as

@SUM(B5..B10)

The formula has not included the new rows within its block, and if data were added to the new rows, it would produce invalid results if we did not stop to correct it. To correct the formula now, we will edit it to include both of the dashed lines at the top and bottom of the rows of data (as it should have been written originally).

5. Change the formula in cell B5 to **@SUM(B3..B14)**.

Now you can insert rows anywhere between the dashed lines, and the formulas will automatically expand to the lower limit of their block as the dashed line on the bottom is moved down.

FINDING DATA IN YOUR SPREADSHEET

Spreadsheets can easily grow to sizes you never imagined possible, and it's easy to lose your way in the forest of rows and columns. Block names are one way to tame this wild environment, and the Edit–Search & Replace command is yet another vital ally.

You can use this command to find specific characters within a block of cells. It can search for them in text or value cells, as well as in formulas. For example, you can locate any cell that has a numeric value that is greater than 1000, or you can find all the formulas that contain a specified block name.

First, choose the Edit–Search & Replace–Block command to define the search area. Specify a block as you always do, and you will see that block address in the Search & Replace menu (if you don't, press the plus key to expand that menu to expose the command parameters).

You must then specify the characters for which you want to search, using the Search String option on the menu. Just type the exact characters you want to find (we'll come back to this option in a moment).

The Replace String option can remain blank unless you want to replace any or all occurrences of your search string with the characters you specify here.

You have three choices under the Look In option:

- Formula: Searches the actual cell contents of the cells in the block. The number 4 will be found when it is part of a value (149) or part of a formula (4*3). But the result 4 of the formula 2+2 will not be found.

- Value: Searches the results of any formulas, as well as any numeric or text entries. The number 4 would be found when it is the result of a formula (2+2) or part of a number (149) or text string (44 Main St.).

- Condition: Allows you to specify a logical formula for the search string, which will be used as the search criterion. Use the formula A1>=100, for example, to find all cells with a value greater than or equal to 100. For the address, you can use either the current cell or a ? to represent the current cell.

When you set the Look In option to Condition, you can perform some very powerful searches that rival just about any search you can perform with the Database–Query commands. Here are some examples:

- To search for any negative numbers, use the formula ?<0.

- To find all numbers in a block of cells that are equal to January 1, 1991, enter ?=@DATE(91,1,1).

- To search for cells that equal the number or the result of the formula in cell B15, enter ?=$B$15.

- To locate any cells that are greater than 10 but less than 20, enter ?>10#and#?<20.

The Direction option lets you direct the search through the block either by rows (the default) or by columns.

The Match option, by default, looks for the search string in any group of characters, so that searching for SUM will find both @SUM and SUMMARY. You can instead choose Whole, which forces the search to look for only complete character strings that match your search string. Using this option, only the separate word SUM would be found in the previous example.

The option called Case Sensitive lets you choose Any Case, the default, so that the search string will be found in either uppercase or lowercase letters. Choosing Exact Case forces the search to find only those letters that also match the case of the search string.

Finally, the Options Reset command returns all the settings on the Search & Replace menu to their defaults.

To actually begin the search, choose the Next (or Previous) command from the menu. The cell selector will jump to the next (or previous) cell in the block that matches the search criteria. Once you have set your various search parameters, you can use the shortcuts Ctrl-N for Next and Ctrl-P for previous (in Ready mode).

In this chapter, you have been introduced to the essential block commands. In the next chapter, you will work with the commands that affect the display of your spreadsheet, not the cell contents themselves.

6

Enhancing Your
Spreadsheet's Display

Fast
Track

THIS CHAPTER DESCRIBES HOW TO ENHANCE YOUR spreadsheet by manipulating the display, while leaving the cell contents untouched. The following features will be covered here:

- Applying numeric formats
- Adjusting column widths and row heights
- Adding lines and shading
- Forcing page breaks
- Printing bullets (for lists)
- Hiding zeros
- Using fonts and displaying them on the screen

None of these features affects the results of any calculations in the spreadsheet; they change only the way those results are displayed.

THE PRICE OF ENHANCEMENTS

There is one important point to make before continuing. When you apply almost any of the display enhancements to an otherwise empty cell, a certain amount of your computer's RAM will be required. Therefore, you should not enhance your spreadsheet any more than necessary.

Don't format a thousand cells in a column just because you might need them formatted someday. Not only does this require RAM, but when you save the spreadsheet to disk, those thousand empty cells will have to be flagged as formatted, and disk space will be required to hold that information. It's all right to preformat a few dozen rows or columns, but be somewhat conservative as you build your spreadsheets.

LOCAL, GLOBAL, AND SYSTEM SETTINGS

The differences between *local, global,* and *system* settings are just as important as those between text and numbers, and a cell's contents and its display. You can change the alignment of text in the cells in a block by using the Style–Alignment command, which has a *local* effect; it changes only the block you specify.

If you don't specify otherwise, all text entries will be left justified. By default, this is the *global* style for the entire spreadsheet. You can change the global (default) style for all text entries by using the Options–Formats–Align Labels command. For example, if you invoke this command and choose Center, all text that you later enter into the spreadsheet will be prefaced with the ^ label prefix and centered in the cell. However, the label prefixes (and, therefore, alignment) for existing text entries will not be affected by a change in the global setting.

When you change a global setting, such as label alignment, only the current spreadsheet is affected. When you open another spreadsheet, the old defaults will be in effect. But since the global settings are saved with a spreadsheet, the next time you retrieve the spreadsheet whose defaults you changed, those new settings will be in effect.

The other global settings on the Options–Format menu include Numeric Format, Hide Zeros, and Global Width, all of which will be discussed later in this chapter.

System settings affect all Quattro Pro spreadsheets, not just the current one. The system settings, such as Hardware, Colors, and Display Mode, appear on the Options menu, above the default settings that were just discussed.

You can modify these settings for the current session only, or you can choose to save the new settings for all future sessions with Quattro Pro by invoking the Options–Update command. This command stores all the current system settings in the Quattro Pro resource files, RSC.RF and QUATTRO.MU (you may see your disk drive light blink for an instant as the information is

> The Options–Format–Align Labels command has no affect on the alignment of numeric or text values in the spreadsheet. The default is always left justified for values.

> In Lotus 1-2-3, the equivalent command is Worksheet–Global–Default–Update.

saved to disk). Every time you load Quattro Pro, it reads these files into memory and sets its defaults according to the information it finds there.

When you choose the Update command, all your system settings are saved, including the options on the Print–Layout menu. You should load Quattro Pro, immediately make any changes to the system settings, and then issue the Options–Update command. Otherwise, you may not know exactly what you have changed and which new settings will be saved.

APPLYING NUMERIC FORMATS

When you enter a number (or a numeric formula) into a cell, it is displayed in the default format, General (as determined by the Options–Format–Numeric Format command). In this style, no commas separate thousands, no dollar sign precedes the number, and only those decimal places that you enter will be displayed. As you saw in Chapter 3, when you enter a number that Quattro Pro cannot display within the current width of the column, it will display the number in Scientific format.

To change the display of a numeric entry, use the Style–Numeric Format command (Ctrl-F). There are ten basic formats from which to choose, plus five for dates and four for time. Table 6.1 shows examples of the formats.

Using this command requires the following steps:

1. Press Ctrl-F to display the Numeric Format menu.

2. Select the style of format from the menu.

3. When relevant, specify how many decimal places you want displayed (from 0 to 15).

4. Specify the block of cells you want to format.

When you choose the Fixed, Scientific, Currency, Comma, or Percent formats, you are prompted to specify the number of decimal places for the display. In these formats, the number that is displayed will be rounded, if necessary, to show the specified

Table 6.1: Quattro Pro Formats for Numeric Display

NUMERIC FORMAT	INPUT LINE	ACTUAL DISPLAY
Fixed	(F2)	1234.56
Scientific	(S2)	1.23E+03
Currency	(C2)	$1,234.56
Comma	(,2)	1,234.56
General	(G)	1234.56
Plus/Minus	(+)	+++++
Percent	(P2)	123456.00%
Date		
DD/MMM/YY	(D1)	18-May-03
DD/MMM	(D2)	18-May
MMM/YY	(D3)	May-03
Long Intl.	(D4)	05/18/03
Short Intl.	(D5)	05/18
Date–Time		
HH:MM:SS AM/PM	(D6)	01:26:24 PM
HH:MM AM/MP	(D7)	01:26 PM
Long Intl.	(D8)	13:26:24

Table 6.1: Quattro Pro Formats for Numeric Display

NUMERIC FORMAT	INPUT LINE	ACTUAL DISPLAY
Short Intl.	(D9)	13:26
Text	(T)	+C4+C5
Hidden	(H)	1234.56

Note: The table shows the numeric formats applied to a cell that contains the number 1234.56. The only exceptions are the Plus/Minus and Text formats,, which are for a cell that contains the number 5 and the formula +C4+C5,, respectively.

number of places. For example, if you enter the number 57.638, and then give it the format called Comma and specify two decimal places, the number will be displayed as 57.64. But remember that the cell still actually contains 57.638. Don't let the display fool you or the person who will ultimately be looking at the printout from this spreadsheet. See Chapter 4 for a discussion of how numeric formats can interfere with the actual results of your formulas.

As discussed in Chapter 3, when you have formatted a cell with a style that is too wide for the cell's column width, Quattro Pro will display asterisks in place of the number. The solution is simply to choose another style or widen the column.

ADJUSTING COLUMN WIDTHS AND ROW HEIGHTS

You may need to adjust the width of a column to accommodate its cell entries or just to make your display easier to read. You can also give a column no width, that is, hide it from view. Additionally, in Quattro Pro 3, you can adjust the height of rows.

SETTING THE WIDTH OF A SINGLE COLUMN

To widen or narrow a column, use the Style–Column Width command (Ctrl-W). You can set the width of a column from 1 to 254 characters. When you invoke this command, you are prompted to enter the new width of the column. You can either type the number at the prompt or use the ← or → key to shrink or widen the column, and then press ↵ to complete the change.

When the cell selector is on a cell that is in a column whose width has been adjusted, you will see the width indicated on the input line. If cell C35 contains the formula @PI*R^2, and column C is 15 characters wide, this is what you would see on the input line:

   C15: [W15] @PI*R^2

With a mouse, you do not need to use the Style–Column Width command. Simply point to the column letter in the spreadsheet and drag the column to the appropriate width—right to expand, left to contract. Release the mouse button to complete the task.

To return a column to its default width, use the Style–Reset Width command. This command resets the width of the current column, so be sure that the cell selector is in the column you want to change before you invoke the command.

You can also adjust the width of every column in the spreadsheet, globally, with the Options–Formats–Global Width command. This command behaves just like the Style–Column Width command, but it affects every column, except those that have been locally adjusted from the Style menu.

As with the other global settings, column widths will be saved with the spreadsheet but will not affect any other spreadsheets you create.

SETTING THE WIDTH OF MULTIPLE COLUMNS

You will frequently want to expand or contract more than one column at a time. To do so, use the Style–Block Size command.

As discussed in the last chapter, the width of a cell is one thing that is not copied with it to a destination cell when you use Edit–Copy.

A menu will appear with three choices for adjusting the widths of columns:

- Set Width: Prompts you for a block of columns to adjust. Either type in the address or point to the columns and press ↵. Then specify the width as you would for a single column. As with the Edit–Insert and Delete–Columns commands, you must use a valid block address. The rows you choose are not important; just be sure you have the column designations correct.

- Reset Width: Resets the width of a block of columns. Simply specify the block, press ↵, and the columns will be returned to the default width.

- Auto Width: Automatically sets each column's width to the longest entry found in that column, with a few adjustments, as described below.

The fourth choice on this menu, Height, is for adjusting the height of rows, as explained later in the chapter.

SETTING COLUMN WIDTHS AUTOMATICALLY

When you use the Style–Block Size–Auto Width command, you are prompted to enter the number of spaces you want to add to the longest entry in each column in order to determine the width of the cell. You can choose a number from 0 to 40, and that number represents the number of spaces that will separate an entry in one cell from that in the adjoining cell in the next column.

Then you specify the block of columns you want to adjust. If you specify the cells in one row, such as C5..H5, Quattro Pro will look at the entries in all cells in and below that row. The longest entry found in each column will determine the width of that column. If you specify more than one row, such as C5..H15, only the entries in the cells in that block will be used to determine the width of each column.

As an example, we'll use the Auto Width option to widen a sample column. Follow these steps:

1. In a blank spreadsheet, enter the following:

    A2: **A**

    B2: **BBBB**

    C2: **@DATE(91,12,13)**, formatted as (D1)

    D2: **'This label is 32 characters wide**

    E2: **12345678901234**, formatted as (G)

Your spreadsheet should look like Figure 6.1. The date in cell C2 is displayed as asterisks because the date format makes the display too wide for the column. The long label in cell D2 does not display because it is prevented from overhanging its column by the entry in cell E2. That cell has a very large number in it, which Quattro Pro has displayed in scientific notation because the column is not wide enough to display all 15 digits.

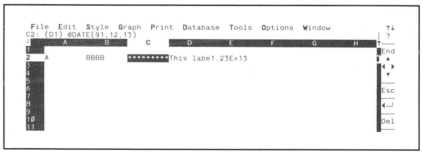

Figure 6.1: Sample spreadsheet for column adjustment

Now we will adjust the columns to the width of the entry in each of these cells. We will leave a single space between each one.

2. With the cell selector in cell A2, invoke the Style–Block Size–Auto Width command. You will be prompted to enter the number of extra spaces.

3. Type 1 (the default) and press ↵.

4. Specify the block of columns to adjust: Either point to or type the address A2..E2, and then press ↵.

Figure 6.2 shows the results. The width of each of the five columns will be adjusted according to either the length of the text entry or the size of the number and the type of numeric formatting it has.

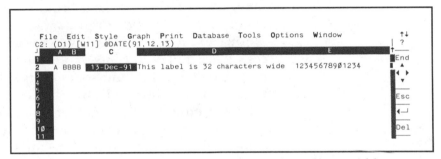

Figure 6.2: The Auto Width command adjusts the column widths

Column A was made two characters wide: one for the single letter in that cell and one for the space between cells. Column B is five characters wide, and column C was made 11 characters wide, which is one more than the minimum width required to display the number in the date format shown.

The long label in column D has caused that column to be widened to 33 characters. Finally, column E was made 16 characters wide, enough to display all 14 digits in the number, with the usual extra space that is required for a minus sign, plus the extra space we requested in the Auto Width command.

Note that the columns are now fixed at these widths; they will not automatically expand or contract to match the longest entry in them. But you can always invoke the command again and adjust the columns to the lengths of the current entries.

HIDING COLUMNS FROM VIEW

You can completely hide a column by using the Style–Hide Column–Hide command. When you hide a column, it literally disappears from the display, but it still exists in the spreadsheet. If you hide column B, for example, the spreadsheet will appear to skip directly from column A to column C.

Hiding columns can be very handy when you want to print a large block that contains columns that are unneeded and would only clutter the report. You can hide them before printing, and then use the Style–Hide Column–Expose command to display them again. The commands prompt you to specify the block of columns to either hide or display.

You can hide a column from view and still refer to any of its cells in formulas and most commands. For example, suppose you hide column B, and some of its cell entries are numbers. If you type the formula +B1, the result will be whatever is in cell B1, even though it is hidden from view.

If you are writing a formula and pointing to a cell, all hidden columns in the spreadsheet instantly appear when the Point mode indicator goes on. In this mode, hidden columns are indicated by an asterisk next to their column letter at the top of the spreadsheet, such as B*. The hidden columns will once again disappear when you leave Point mode.

Hidden columns will also be displayed for almost all other Quattro Pro commands that require you to input a block. However, they do not appear for the Print command because hidden columns are obviously not wanted in the printout. Pressing the F5 key (for the Goto command) does not display hidden cells because it is just not valid to go to a cell that is hidden.

Displaying and hiding columns can be very distracting as you build your spreadsheets. You usually don't need to hide columns until you're done with the construction process. You can save this enhancement for last.

ADJUSTING COLUMNS FOR A PLEASING DISPLAY

Sometimes, the proper column width for the data in a column may be too narrow to show the titles you have at the top of the column. You could widen the column so that the titles fit, but then the data will look crowded along one side of it. You could center the data in the widened column, but this almost never works for numbers, and even centered text entries can be difficult to read if they are of varying lengths. One way to solve this problem is simply to use an extra column.

Figure 6.3 shows a spreadsheet with three columns of the same data, each displayed in a slightly different style. The title at the top of each one is too long to fit in a narrow column.

Column A has been expanded to a width of 20 characters. The titles fit comfortably, but the numbers in the rest of the column are crowded along the right side.

Column C is also 20 characters wide. The numbers in it have been centered, but now they do not align along their decimal points, and are consequently difficult to read.

Column E provides the better solution. It makes use of two columns, not just one. It has been widened to 14 characters, and column F is set to 6 characters, to create a total width of 20. The column titles are allowed to overhang into column F. The numbers below the title are right justified (the default alignment) in column E. They align nicely along their decimals, while at the same time are also reasonably centered below the titles.

ADJUSTING THE HEIGHT OF ROWS

In Quattro Pro version 3, you can adjust the height of rows. However, there will most likely be few times when you will need

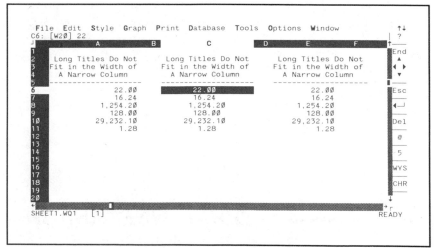

Figure 6.3: Arranging columns for the best display

to do so, because Quattro Pro adjusts row height automatically, according to the largest font that is used in the row. Row height is measured in the same units that are used to describe font sizes: points. By default, row heights are set to 15 points.

If you want to control the row height, perhaps to keep several rows the same height even though different sized fonts were used in each of them, you can set the height of one or more rows by using the Style–Block Size–Height–Set Row Height command. The procedure is the same as the one for adjusting column widths.

After you invoke the Style–Block Size–Height–Set Row Height command, select the rows you wish to adjust and press ↵. Specify the new row height by either typing in the number of points, from 1 to 240, or by using the arrow keys. The ← or ↑ key shrinks the row height; the → or ↓ key makes the row larger. When the row is the size you want, press ↵ to complete the task.

If you are using a mouse, you can quickly adjust the height of a row simply by pointing to the row number at the left of the row, and then dragging that number up or down to reduce or expand the row height, respectively.

Note that if the spreadsheet is not in graphics (WYSIWYG) mode, you will not see a visible change to the row heights in the spreadsheet. In graphics mode, the row heights will be clearly visible. You will also see the effects of varying row heights when you print your spreadsheet, whether to the printer or as a screen preview.

There is no indicator or cell reference to tell you the exact height of a row. To determine the current height of a row, invoke the Set Row Height command for that row, and the command will show you the current height when it prompts you for a new height.

You should be aware that when you manually adjust the height of a row, Quattro Pro will not adjust that row's height when you assign a font to a cell within it. If the row is too short for the font, a portion of the top of each character may be hidden.

To return a row to its default height, which Quattro Pro will then adjust as necessary, use the Style–Block Size–Height–Reset Row Height command.

ADDING LINES AND SHADING

Since practically all the work you will do in the spreadsheet will be based on rows and columns of data, it is frequently necessary to create horizontal or vertical dividing lines between different sets of data. A horizontal line can separate column titles and the data below them. You might want to place a vertical line between row titles and the data that stretches to the right across the rows, and between the data and a totals column on the right.

DRAWING LINES WITHIN AND AROUND A BLOCK

You have already seen how you can use the repeating label prefix, \, to fill a cell with hyphens or equal signs to create a dashed line that can be copied across a row. The vertical bar, |, can be used to create a vertical line. However, you can give your spreadsheets a more professional look by using the Style–Line Drawing menu options to add lines.

When you use the Style–Line Drawing command, you first must specify the block in or around which you want the lines. Next, you choose the line placement. The menu offers nine different locations for placing lines, including All, Outside, Top, Bottom, Left, Right, Inside, Horizontal, and Vertical. Finally, select the type of line: Single, Double, or Thick.

Back in Chapter 2, we used the repeating label prefix to draw horizontal lines in our Mileage spreadsheet. Let's remove those lines and use the Line Drawing command to enhance this spreadsheet.

⊙ In the Mileage spreadsheet, the @SUM formulas in row 12 summed only the data rows, 4 through 10, so we can delete rows 3 and 11 without causing these formulas to show ERR. Usually, however, your @SUM functions will include the rows above and below the data they sum, so use caution when deleting rows.

1. From any cell in the spreadsheet, issue the Edit–Delete–Rows command.

2. Specify A11 as the row to delete (remember, it is the row portion of the address that is important).

3. Invoke the Edit–Delete–Rows command again, and this time specify A3 as the row to be deleted.

Your spreadsheet should look like the one shown in Figure 6.4. Now we can add some line drawing.

4. Press Home to move the cell selector to cell A1 to begin the process.

5. Invoke the Style–Line Drawing command.

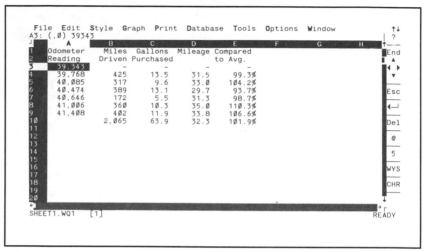

*Figure 6.4:*The Mileage spreadsheet after deleting the rows of dashed lines

6. To specify the block for the lines, press End-Home, which jumps the active corner of the highlighting to the lower-right corner of the spreadsheet, and then press ↵ .

7. When the Placement menu appears, select Outside to put a line around the outside of the entire block.

8. When the Type menu appears, specify Double as the line type.

A double-lined border will appear around the block. Once you select the type of line, the Type menu disappears, but the Placement menu remains. This allows you to continue to work with the block without having to start the command over again. Next, we will add vertical lines between columns.

9. Choose Vertical from the Placement menu.

10. Choose Single from the Type menu.

11. We are finished enhancing this block, so choose Quit from the Placement menu.

Now the block also has a vertical line between each column. The spreadsheet in Figure 6.5 shows the progress so far.

We will make two more enhancements to finish the job. A single horizontal line will be drawn between the column titles and the data, and between the data and the totals.

12. With the cell selector on cell A1, invoke the Style–Line Drawing command.

13. Press Escape to unanchor the block that is offered.

14. Point to cell A2 and press period to anchor the block at that cell.

15. Highlight the block A2..E2 and press ↵.

16. Choose Bottom from the Placement menu.

17. Select Single from the Type menu.

18. Choose Quit to leave the Line Draw command.

19. Repeat these steps to add a line *above* row 10. Specify the block A10..E10, select Top from the Placement

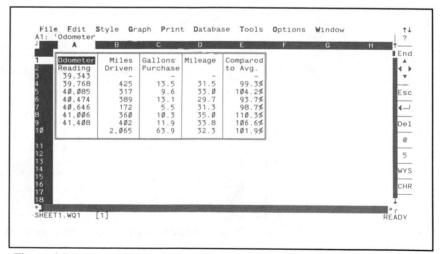

Figure 6.5: The spreadsheet after adding outside double lines and vertical single lines

menu, and choose Single from the Type menu. The finished spreadsheet is shown in Figure 6.6.

HANDLING LINES IN THE SPREADSHEET

As you may have noticed, Quattro Pro does not place the line drawings into the rows or columns of your spreadsheet. Instead, it adds space between the rows and columns and places the lines there. This makes it very easy to enhance your work without changing any cell addresses or formula references.

Note that vertical lines do diminish the usable width of a column by one space, so if you have fine-tuned your column widths, you may have to do it again after adding line drawing to your spreadsheet.

Line drawing is very much like a numeric format, in that it enhances a cell without changing its contents and will be copied with the cell when you use, for example, the Edit–Copy or Edit–Value commands. Unlike a format, however, line drawing is not indicated on the cell's input line. Of course, you will see the line drawing on the screen, but you really can't tell to which cell the lines are attached.

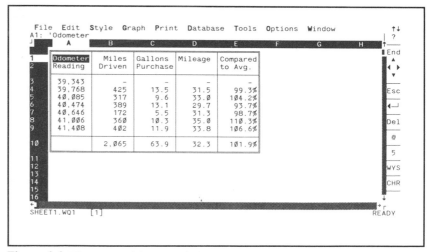

Figure 6.6: The spreadsheet with line drawing

For example, let's copy a few cells from our enhanced Mileage spreadsheet and see which lines get copied with them. Copy the block E1..E10 (the Compared to Avg. column) to cell G1. The result is shown in Figure 6.7. As you can see, the double line on the outside is attached to the left side of column F, and the double line at the bottom is attached to the top of row 11.

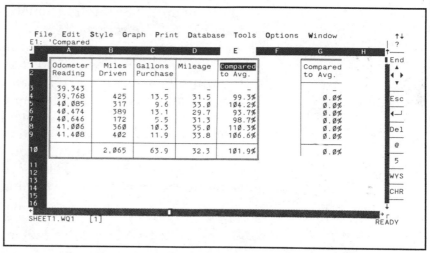

Figure 6.7: Copying a block that has line drawing may not produce the results you expected

REMOVING LINES

If you are dissatisfied with the results of your line drawing, it's easy to remove the lines. Just follow the same steps you used to add them, but choose None from the Type menu. Let's get rid of all the lines associated with the copied data in column G.

Just as with a cell's protection status or numeric format, you cannot remove line drawing effects by erasing the cell with the Edit–Erase Block command. You must use the None option from the Type menu to remove the lines.

1. Invoke the Style–Line Drawing command.

2. Specify the block G1..G10 and press ↵.

3. For line placement, choose All.

4. For Type, choose None, and all the lines associated with that block will be removed. Now let's remove the data, too.

5. Issue the Edit–Erase command and specify the block G1..G10.

PRINTING LINE DRAWINGS

You can print blocks that have line drawings associated with them in draft mode (using the Spreadsheet Print command on the Print menu), but the horizontal lines will be reproduced with dashes (–) the vertical lines with the vertical bar (|), and corners with a plus (+) sign. The advantage is that any type of printer can reproduce these characters.

To print the block in the best quality possible, with the lines treated as graphics characters and appearing as solid lines, use the Print–Destination–Graphics Printer command. Then use the Spreadsheet Print command to send the block to that printer.

Remember that the line drawing on one side of a cell may actually belong to the adjacent cell. In order to print that line, you must include the adjacent row or column.

ADDING SHADING TO A BLOCK

Another enhancement you can add to your spreadsheet is block shading. The Shading command is on the Style menu. It provides a second menu with the choices None, Grey, and Black. You then specify the block you wish to shade, and the shading will be applied.

Gray shading produces a gray background to the characters in the cells, and black creates a solid black cell—any characters in that cell will not be displayed. Choose None to remove shading from the cells in a block.

Let's add shading to the cells in the Mileage column of Figure 6.6.

1. Invoke the Style–Shading command and choose Grey.

2. Specify the block D4..D10 and press ↵.

Whenever you are printing a block for the first time, it is generally advisable (and a great paper-saver) to set the Print–Destination command to Screen Preview. The Spreadsheet Print command will then send the output to the screen, where you will see a crisp representation of how the spreadsheet will look on paper.

The cells in that block will now have a gray background, as shown in Figure 6.8. On the display, you do not see shading behind numbers or letters in the cell; you see it only in blank spaces on either side of the characters. When the spreadsheet is printed, however, the entire background of the cell will be shaded.

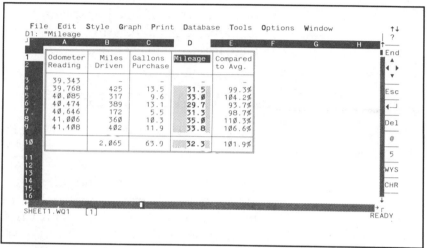

Figure 6.8: The spreadsheet with gray shading added to column D

INSERTING PAGE BREAKS

When you print your spreadsheet, Quattro Pro handles the pagination of the output, as you will learn in Chapter 7. It places the correct margins at the top and bottom of the page and divides the block among as many pages as necessary to complete the job.

In some cases, you may want to direct Quattro Pro to force a page break at a particular row in the spreadsheet. You can do this with the Style–Insert Break command, which inserts a new row into the spreadsheet and adds the special print command code |:: into the current cell. The broken vertical bar is a non-printing label prefix that precedes two colons, which direct Quattro Pro to skip to the next page when printing.

The only limitation to this command is that it must be entered in a cell within the very first column of your printout. If it appears in any of the inner columns, it will be ignored.

You could produce the same result as the Style–Insert Break command by using the Edit–Insert–Row command and then typing the special code.

The advantage to manually breaking pages becomes evident when you have many rows of data that contain several logical breaking points. For example, you might have data for the four quarters of the year and would like each quarter to begin on a separate page. You could use the Style–Insert Break command to insert a page break in the line above each quarter. When you print the spreadsheet, just specify the entire block of data as the block to be printed. Your inserted page breaks will force a new page for each quarter.

PRINTING BULLETS FOR YOUR LISTS

A very handy feature of Quattro Pro is its ability to include bullets in your printouts. You use a code to represent the bullet in your spreadsheet, so you won't see a bullet on the screen when the spreadsheet is in text mode. However, you will see the actual bullet character when the spreadsheet is in graphics mode, as well as when you print the spreadsheet with the destination set to the Graphics Printer or Screen Preview.

There are seven different styles of bullets from which to choose. You enter a bullet anywhere in your spreadsheet using the form

\bullet *n*\

Bullet is the keyword for the code, and *n* represents a number from 0 to 6. Since the code begins with a backslash, you must preface it with a label prefix when it is the first character in a cell.

Figure 6.9 shows a spreadsheet with seven labels in the block B2..B8. Each includes one of the bullet codes. As you can see on the input line at the top of the screen, cell B2 contains normal text that includes the special bullet command.

Figure 6.10 shows how this spreadsheet will look when it is printed. This is not a paper printout, however. The Print–Destination command was set to Screen Preview, and the spreadsheet was printed to the screen.

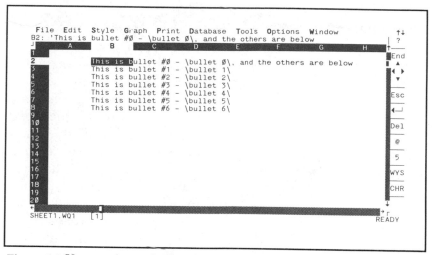

Figure 6.9: You can insert bullets in your printouts by using the special code

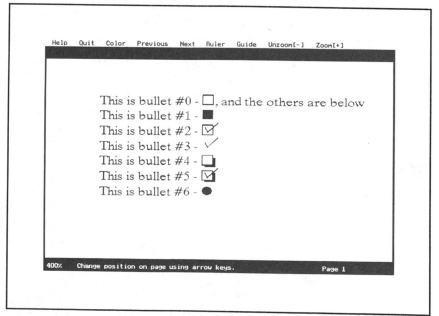

Figure 6.10: An example of bullets as shown on a screen preview

HIDING UNWANTED ZEROS

Some spreadsheets may have an excess of cells that display nothing but zeros. This may be due to your data, which simply might have a lot of zero entries, or it may be because your formulas produce zeros as their results. Either way, it can often be difficult to read a printout if there are many, irrelevant zeros.

The Options–Formats–Hide Zeros–Yes command lets you hide zeros from view. The command affects only the display; the contents of cells are left alone. It is a global setting, so you either turn off the display of every zero in the spreadsheet or none at all.

This command is most useful for printouts. Invoke it just before you print your spreadsheet. After printing, you can redisplay the zeros by selecting the No option for the Hide Zeros command.

USING FONTS
IN YOUR SPREADSHEETS

One of the most popular features of Quattro Pro is its capability to use a variety of fonts. This feature has absolutely nothing to do with managing, calculating, or organizing data, but it does affect the way that the data is perceived by others. Fonts not only appear in your printed spreadsheet, but in graphics mode, they are also displayed on the screen. There are three situations in which Quattro Pro will use screen fonts:

You need an EGA or a VGA monitor for WYSIWYG mode.

- Viewing a graph or working in the Graph Annotator
- Sending your printed output to the screen for a preview
- Working in graphics (WYSIWYG) mode (except in Quattro Pro versions 1 and 2)

Figure 6.11 shows the Mileage spreadsheet displayed in graphics mode. Fonts, which have been applied to the titles and totals, appear just as they will when the spreadsheet is printed.

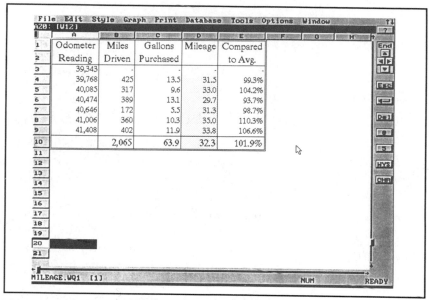

Figure 6.11: Fonts are displayed on the screen when Quattro Pro is in
graphics mode

TYPES OF FONTS

A *font* is a style of typeface. A Quattro Pro spreadsheet can
have up to eight different fonts in it. Fonts are referred to by
typeface names, such as Roman, Dutch, Swiss, and Sans Serif,
and may have a style such as bold, italics, or underlined. Each
font comes in a size that is measured in points. A 12-point font
is bigger than a 10-point font. Quattro Pro can work with three
different types of fonts:

- Built-in fonts: Quattro Pro can access the fonts built into
  your printer, as long as your printer was correctly installed using the Options–Hardware–Printers command.

- Bit-mapped fonts: These are printed in graphics mode
  on your printer, which implies that you need a printer
  that is capable of graphics printing. Bit-mapped fonts
  take longer to print than built-in fonts, but their output is generally more pleasing (or more interesting).

- Downloadable fonts: These are the highest quality fonts and are supplied by the font-making company, Bitstream. Downloadable fonts reside on disk and are downloaded to the printer at print time.

USING DOWNLOADABLE FONTS

There are a few drawbacks to downloadable fonts that will restrain you from using them for every printout. Each font, style, and size is a separate file on disk, so that Bitstream Dutch Italic 12-point is one file. If you want that font in bold, you will need another file of equal size. Font files grow in size with the point size; a 12-point font's file may be about 20K in size, but a 72-point font's file may be 150K. The number of different fonts you can access is therefore limited by the disk space you have available for storing them.

Quattro Pro doesn't come with downloadable fonts already made. Instead, it makes them when they are needed, either for printing or screen display. New fonts will be made only when you have chosen Final for the Options–Graphics Quality command, as discussed shortly. When Final is selected, a font will be built when you are printing to the Graphics Printer or Screen Preview, if the spreadsheet is in graphics mode, or if you are viewing a graph or working in the Graph Annotator. You will see the message

> Now building font

Fonts will also be built if you select Screen Preview as the destination, and then use the Zoom command to enlarge the preview text.

as Quattro Pro builds the font it needs to print or display your spreadsheet. The faster your computer, the less time it will take to build a font.

When you installed Quattro Pro, you were given the opportunity to build a group of fonts all at one time. This was to give you an initial set of commonly used fonts and reduce the number of fonts to be built while you are working in Quattro Pro.

After a font has been built, it will be available on disk for any spreadsheet that require that font. This means that the building process will happen less and less frequently when you work in final-quality mode. However, when printing, the font still must be downloaded to the printer at print time. This takes some time, but very little compared to the font-building process.

CHOOSING DRAFT OR FINAL-QUALITY MODE

Two modes of operation in Quattro Pro affect its use of fonts for printing and displaying text on the screen: Draft and Final. You set the mode with the Options–Graphics Quality command.

When Quattro Pro is in its text mode (called 80x25 on the Options–Display Mode menu), fonts are not shown in the spreadsheet. When you switch to WYSIWYG (graphics) mode, however, the fonts you used appear, so the spreadsheet looks very much as it will when it is printed. Hence, the acronym WYSIWYG, for *what you see is what you get.*

Use the draft mode for most of your printouts. Use the Final option only when you actually want to get a final printout (either as a test copy or for distribution).

Regardless of whether the spreadsheet is in text or graphics mode, fonts are displayed when you print with the destination set to Screen Preview. When you display a graph or work in the Graph Annotator, you will also see Quattro Pro fonts.

It is when Quattro Pro is in one of these font-displaying modes that the Draft or Final option comes into play. When you select Final mode from the Options–Graphics Quality menu, Quattro Pro will show every font you have used. If the font file does not yet exist on disk, Quattro Pro will build it.

In Draft mode, however, if a font you selected does not yet exist on disk, Quattro Pro will not take the time to build it. Instead, it will approximate the font by substituting one of its Hershey fonts, which can be displayed in any size. However, any specified font that is already on disk will appear on the screen. In other words, Quattro Pro will do the best job it can while avoiding the somewhat time-consuming job of font building.

PRINTING TO THE DEFAULT OR GRAPHICS PRINTER

You select the printer to use for the current print job by using the Printer–Destination command. The options offered are

Printer (the default, draft-quality printer) and Graphics Printer (for high-quality output). If you choose Printer, Quattro Pro will produce a draft-quality printout using your printer's internal fonts, even if you set the Options–Graphics Quality command to Final.

You will get the best results when you choose the Graphics Printer option. However, the quality of the printout will now depend on whether you selected Draft or Final on the Options–Graphics Quality menu.

Just as with screen fonts, if you have selected Draft quality, Quattro Pro will not build any fonts that do not already exist on disk. Printouts are produced quickly, but the quality may be less than what is possible if the necessary fonts do not already reside on disk.

If you have chosen Final quality, each font in the spreadsheet will be printed, even if Quattro Pro has to first build a new font file for it. The printouts may take longer to produce, but they will be the highest quality possible.

Therefore, the highest quality printouts are obtained when you have chosen Final mode and directed the printing to the Graphics Printer. Quattro Pro will use any Bitstream fonts you have specified, and your spreadsheet will take a little longer to print. Chapter 7 discusses the options associated with print quality in greater detail.

SELECTING FONTS

You apply a font to a cell in the same manner that you apply a numeric format. Invoke the Style–Font command and select from the eight fonts that are offered. The menu shows a fixed list of font *numbers*, and it is the number that you are applying to a cell. You can change the font associated with any of the numbers by using the Edit Fonts command on the Fonts menu.

Any cells that have not had a font applied to them are assigned font number 1 by default. If you look on the Fonts menu, you will see that this font is Bitstream Dutch 12-point Black. This font will be printed if you selected the Options–Graphics Quality–Final command and are printing to the Graphics Printer.

When you select a font number for a cell, that number will appear on the input line for that cell. For example, if you choose font number 3 for cell A1, the input line would look like this:

A1: [F3]

By default, font number 3 is Bitstream Dutch 8-point Black, and that font would be used for cell A1 in this example. But if you change the font associated with font number 3, that new font will be used to print cell A1.

CHANGING DEFAULT FONTS

To change one of the fonts on the list, use the Style–Fonts–Edit Fonts command and then choose one of the eight fonts on the list. The font-editing menu provides four options:

- Typeface: Offers a number of different typefaces in the built-in, bit-mapped, and downloadable categories. These include Bitstream Dutch, Bitstream Courier, Roman, Sans Serif, and many more, depending on the number of fonts built into your printer.

- Point Size: Offers a long list of sizes, ranging from 6 to 72 points, although the range will vary depending on the typeface you have selected.

- Style: Lets you choose from Bold, Italic, or Underlined.

- Color: Allows you to choose a different color for each of the eight fonts (if you have a color printer).

If you change font number 1, all cells in the spreadsheet, except those you have specifically assigned another font, will now be printed in the new font. If you change font number 3, any cell to which you had applied that font will now be printed in the new style.

The list of eight fonts is saved with the current spreadsheet. The next time you retrieve the spreadsheet, the same list will be available, and your printouts will use the same fonts as they did in the previous session. You can use the Style–Font–Update command to save the current set of fonts as the default for future sessions.

Now that you are able to control the look of your spreadsheets, the next chapter will tell you all you need to know about printing them.

7

Printing Your Spreadsheets

Fast
Track

NO MATTER WHAT THE PURPOSE OF ONE OF YOUR spreadsheets, you will undoubtedly print it at least once in its life. For most of your work, you will find that you print spreadsheets many, many times. Because printing is such a frequent and repetitious task, you will find this chapter to be of great value. The process of printing is discussed as follows:

- What to print: The commands and procedures for defining what will be printed.

- Page layout: How the material will be arranged on the page.

- How to print: The use of setup codes and other formatting techniques for changing the appearance of what is printed.

- Where to print: The various destinations for your printout, including the printer, a file, the screen, or a binary file.

CHOOSING WHAT TO PRINT

Unlike a word processor, Quattro Pro does not generate just one long continuous string of text. You may have data scattered throughout the 256 columns and 8192 rows of your spreadsheet. Printing, therefore, is a selective process in which you specify the exact block you wish to print.

If you discover after the printing begins that you have chosen the wrong block, you can cancel the print job by pressing Ctrl-Break. Quattro Pro will interrupt the printing and return you to the Print menu. Your printer may or may not stop immediately, depending on whether it is buffered.

SPECIFYING THE BLOCK TO PRINT

You cannot print a spreadsheet until you have defined the block you want printed. Therefore, the Print–Block command will usually be the first Print command that you invoke.

That command prompts you for a block, which you can specify in the usual manner: type the cell address, point to the block, use a block name, or use the Select key (Shift-F7).

When defining the block, include only the rows and columns that you want to print. Avoid the temptation to include extra blank rows or columns to serve as margins; instead, let Quattro Pro's print options define the page layout for you. ·

If there are any long text entries in cells within the print block, check to see if their text overhangs the last column of the block. If so, be sure to expand the block to include enough extra columns so that all the text is included in your printout. This is an important point to remember, because Quattro Pro prints what is on the display, not what is within the cells.

Now we will print our Mileage spreadsheet, which we created and enhanced in earlier chapters.

Make sure that your printer is on and, if you are using a dot-matrix or other continuous-feed printer, that the top edge of the paper is aligned with the print head. Then follow these steps:

When your print block includes line drawings, you may have to extend the print block an extra column or row in order to include all the outlines around the block.

1. Invoke the Print–Block command and specify the block A1..E12. You will see the block's address to the right of the Block command on the Print menu. If you don't see it there, expand the Print menu by pressing the + key.

2. To begin printing, select the Spreadsheet Print command from the Print menu.

The block will be printed, but the paper will not be ejected from the printer. Quattro Pro prints only what you tell it to print.

3. From the Print menu, use the Adjust Printer–Form Feed command to eject the rest of the page from the printer (this command will be discussed later).

If you had not issued the Form Feed command, you could have printed other blocks on the rest of the page, as discussed in the next section.

PRINTING MULTIPLE BLOCKS

Quite often, you will want to print several blocks in one print-out. There are two ways to include multiple blocks within the same printout:

- Simply arrange your blocks so that they all fall directly below one another in the spreadsheet, separated by a few blank rows. You can then print them as one block, which works if you will always print the data in that arrangement.

- Specify each block, print it, specify the next one, print it, and so on. This will work no matter where the blocks fall in the spreadsheet, and it allows you to print the blocks in any order you wish. You are not locked in to the same arrangement each time you print.

If you will print several areas in your spreadsheet on a regular basis, give each block a name. Then specifying the blocks to print turns into a simple process of picking their names from the Choices list (press F3). The names might be descriptive, such as NEW_YEAR, LAST_YEAR, or TOTALS, or more generic, such as PRINT1, PRINT2, and PRINT3.

PRINTING MULTIPLE COPIES

You can use the Print–Copies command to specify the number of copies Quattro Pro should print. The default is 1, but you can request as many as 1000. If your block takes up several pages, one copy of the complete set will be printed first, then another complete set, and so on until all the copies you specified are printed. Page numbering in headers and footers will be reset after each complete printout of the block.

The Copies command is reset to 1 after each printing (so you do not accidentally print too many copies the next time), and Quattro Pro does not save this setting with your file. Therefore, you must issue the command each time you want to print multiple copies.

Many other Quattro Pro commands retain their settings when you save the spreadsheet. These include the Edit–Search & Replace, Database–Sort and Query, Graph, and Tools–Advanced Math commands.

REUSING BLOCK SPECIFICATIONS

When you save your spreadsheet, Quattro Pro saves all the information associated with your last printout, including the address of the block that was printed. This means that the next time you want to print, you need only issue the Print–Spreadsheet Print command. But this only works if you want to print exactly the same block as before, so it will not work for multiblock printouts.

The easiest and most reliable ways to specify blocks are by using block names and by putting all the print settings into a print macro. Macros are discussed in Chapters 16 and 17.

INCLUDING PAGE HEADINGS

Almost all spreadsheets are organized around columns of similar data, such as the months of the year, and rows of related information, such as for each employee. Columns are labeled with titles at the top, and rows are labeled down a column on the left side.

When you print a block (or series of blocks) that is too long to fit on one page, Quattro Pro lets it spill over to as many pages as needed, until all the rows are printed (how the block is formatted is discussed in the next section).

When that block includes titles at the top of each column, those titles would appear only on the first page of the printout. The pages to follow would show only the data. The same would be true for a very wide printout: the titles in the columns on the left would not appear on later pages.

To print these titles on subsequent pages, use the Print–Headings command. The command offers choices for left headings (titles down one or more columns) and top headings (titles across one or more rows).

For example, suppose that we added several new columns and many more rows of data to our Mileage spreadsheet, as shown in Figure 7.1. Only part of the spreadsheet can be seen on the screen, and you would have to move the cell selector to find the new dimensions of the block, A1..I140.

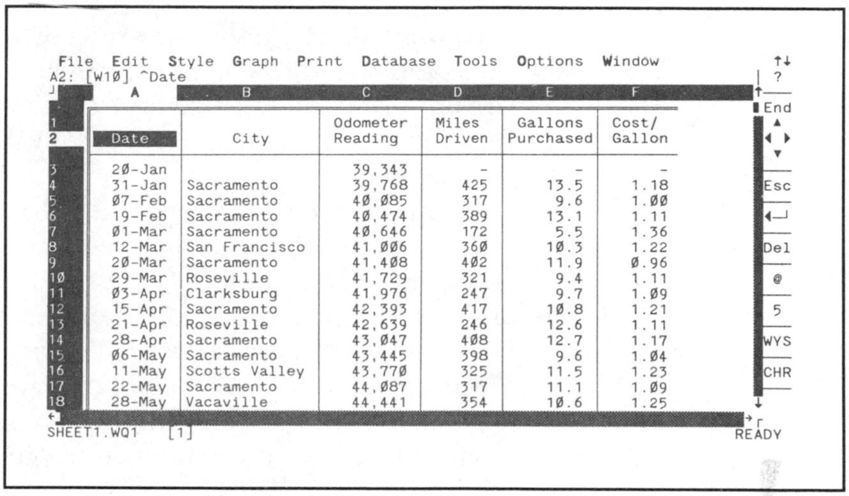

Date	City	Odometer Reading	Miles Driven	Gallons Purchased	Cost/ Gallon
20-Jan		39,343	-	-	-
31-Jan	Sacramento	39,768	425	13.5	1.18
07-Feb	Sacramento	40,085	317	9.6	1.00
19-Feb	Sacramento	40,474	389	13.1	1.11
01-Mar	Sacramento	40,646	172	5.5	1.36
12-Mar	San Francisco	41,006	360	10.3	1.22
20-Mar	Sacramento	41,408	402	11.9	0.96
29-Mar	Roseville	41,729	321	9.4	1.11
03-Apr	Clarksburg	41,976	247	9.7	1.09
15-Apr	Sacramento	42,393	417	10.8	1.21
21-Apr	Roseville	42,639	246	12.6	1.11
28-Apr	Sacramento	43,047	408	12.7	1.17
06-May	Sacramento	43,445	398	9.6	1.04
11-May	Scotts Valley	43,770	325	11.5	1.23
22-May	Sacramento	44,087	317	11.1	1.09
28-May	Vacaville	44,441	354	10.6	1.25

Figure 7.1: A large spreadsheet that could use left and top headings on each page of the printout

When you define the print block, do not include the heading rows or columns within the block. If you do, those headings will appear twice on the first page of the printout—once as the headings and again as a part of the print block. Therefore, in Figure 7.1, the print block will be the rows below rows 1 and 2, and the columns to the right of columns A and B.

Since the block appears to be too long to fit on one page, we will specify the column titles, rows 1 and 2, as the top headings. And, because it is probably too wide, we will specify columns A and B as the left headings. You can include as many columns or rows as you want to see on every page.

Here are the steps to follow to specify these settings:

1. Invoke the Print command and choose Block.
2. Specify the block C3..I40 as the block to print.
3. Choose Headings–Top Headings from the Print menu.
4. Specify the block A1..A2 as the rows that will print across the top of each page. You need to specify only one column with the correct number of rows, not all the columns above the print block (B through I).
5. Choose Headings–Left Headings from the Print menu.
6. Specify the block A1..B1 as the columns to be printed at the left edge of each page.

Now, no matter how many rows or columns are in the block, the column and row titles will appear on every page. However, you must remember to exclude the title rows and columns from the block itself; otherwise, the titles will be printed twice on the first page.

If you do not want any headings for your next print job, you must reset them by using the Print–Layout–Reset–Headings command. Do not simply use the Print–Headings command and press Escape when you are offered the previously defined block—when you press ↵, you will actually be defining a new block as the heading. Use the Reset command.

After you have defined the block and headings you want to print, you can set the options that will determine the layout of the blocks on the printout.

DESIGNING THE PAGE LAYOUT

Even though the block you print is of a fixed width and depth, you can control precisely where on the page that block will appear. Quattro Pro provides the following settings and features that allow you to design the layout of the printed page:

- Page length
- Margins at the left, right, top, and bottom, specified in inches, centimeters, or characters
- Portrait, landscape, or banner orientation
- Include page breaks or print from the top to bottom edge of the page
- Header and footer on each page
- The ability to control the printer from the keyboard
- The ability to set a scaling factor to size all the fonts in the spreadsheet

If you don't specify otherwise, Quattro Pro will print your work with its built-in, default print settings. These are designed for 8½- by-11-inch paper.

CHOOSING LAYOUT DIMENSIONS

By default, Quattro Pro measures your work in characters. When used in terms of horizontal measurements, these are standard print characters that are counted ten characters per inch (10 cpi). A left margin of four characters, for example, leaves a margin of a little less than ½ inch (⁴⁄10 to be exact) between the left edge of the page and the beginning of the printed block.

Vertical measurements are made in standard printer lines, which are counted six lines per inch (6 lpi). Setting the top margin to three lines would produce a ½-inch margin at the top of the page.

Measuring in inches or centimeters may prove to be more convenient than using characters or lines. You will avoid having to convert characters into tenths of an inch or lines into sixths of an inch to see where your block will fall on the page. To change the measurement system, use the Print–Layout–Dimensions command, and choose either Inches or Centimeters.

In Quattro Pro, whenever you measure dimensions in characters, you are using the standard, 10 cpi horizontal and 6 lpi vertical measurements. You can print in any size font, and the left margin will always remain the same.

SPECIFYING MARGINS

The Print–Layout–Margins command allows you to specify the length of the paper you are using and the left, right, top, and bottom margins. The settings Quattro Pro uses by default, along with the acceptable range of values, are listed below.

- Page length: 66 lines (1 to 100)
- Left margin: 4 characters (0 to 254)
- Top margin: 2 lines (0 to 32)
- Right margin: 76 characters (0 to 511)
- Bottom margin: 2 lines (0 to 32)

In Lotus 1-2-3, all margins are measured in characters, but the actual size of the character depends on which size your printer is using. A left margin of 10, for example, produces a 1-inch margin in standard character size. But when you switch to a smaller font, such as 17 cpi, the left margin will be a little more than ½-inch. You may have to adjust the settings if you are printing the same spreadsheet in both programs.

If your printer uses 10 cpi, you can print a block of exactly 72 characters within the default left and right margins. Note that 72 is also the maximum number of characters that can be displayed on the Quattro Pro screen.

SETTING LEFT AND RIGHT MARGINS

The left and right margins are measured from the left edge of the paper. You can calculate the length of the line that will print between these margins by subtracting the left margin, 4, from the right margin, 76, leaving a line length of 72 characters, or 7.2 inches.

If you are printing on standard, 8½-by-11-inch paper, you can determine the amount of blank space to the right of your printout by subtracting 7.6 inches (the right margin) from 8.5 inches (the width of the page), for a blank margin of about 9/10 inch.

SETTING TOP AND BOTTOM MARGINS

The top and bottom margins are measured from the top edge and bottom edge of the paper, respectively. The default of two lines equals a ⅓-inch margin, but this margin does not define where your block will begin printing. Instead, it is the margin between the edge of the paper and either the header, at the top of the page, or the footer, at the bottom (headers and footers will be discussed shortly).

In summary, with the default settings, your printouts will have about a ½-inch margin on the left, top, and bottom, and about a 1-inch margin on the right.

ADJUSTING PAGE LENGTH

The standard printer line height is ⅙ inch. For 11-inch tall paper, that equals a total of 66 lines per page, the default setting in Quattro Pro. From that 66 lines, subtract the top and bottom default margins, which leaves 62 lines for the body of your printout including the header and footer.

You may want to adjust the Page Length setting to change to a new printer or paper size or when you reset the line spacing.

CHANGING TO A NEW PRINTER OR PAPER SIZE

If you change to a new paper size in your printer, you must change the Page Length setting in Quattro Pro. For example, if you change to 11-by-8½-inch paper, the Page Length should be 8½ times 6, or 51 lines.

Even with standard sized paper, some printers cannot print to the very edge of the page. These include laser printers and ink-jet printers, which generally leave about ¼ to ½ inch of blank space along each edge. You must adjust the page length for these printers; Quattro Pro will not do it automatically.

You should check the manual for your specific printer, but in general, use a page length of 60 for 11-inch paper on most laser printers. Whatever size paper you are using, you can usually just subtract 1 inch from its height and consider that the page length.

If the paper size and printer settings don't match the Page Length setting, your printouts will be a mess, with the text running right across the page breaks in the printer, and groups of blank lines being printed in the middle of a page. Remember, if you change paper in the printer, you should verify that the Page Length setting is adjusted accordingly.

CHANGING LINE SPACING

Practically all printers have the ability to vary their line spacing in fractions of an inch. They also have built-in line spacing in the even increments of both 6 (the Quattro Pro default) and 8 lpi. On some printers, you can select the line spacing by pressing a button or two on the printer's control panel. Quattro Pro can send a setup code to the printer and achieve the same result.

A *setup code* is a special command that a program sends to the printer. The printer interprets the code and adjusts its settings accordingly.

For example, you can enter the proper setup code for your printer to print 8 lpi. You would then have 88 lines available on 11-inch paper. You must tell Quattro Pro about this, too, by changing the Page Length setting to 88. For 11-by-8½-inch paper, at 8 lpi you would have 68 lines for printing (8½ times 8).

Setup codes will be discussed in more detail later in this chapter.

SETTING PAGE ORIENTATION

The Print–Layout–Orientation command allows you to shift the orientation of the printout by 90 degrees. There are three options on this menu:

- Portrait: Refers to a page that is taller than it is wide, such as standard 8½-by-11-inch paper. This is the default orientation.

- Landscape: Refers to a page that is wider than it is tall, such as 11-by-8½-inch paper.

- Banner: Similar to landscape orientation, except the width of the printout spans as many pages as needed, as though there were one infinitely wide piece of paper.

In order to use this command to print in landscape or banner mode, however, you must select Graphics Printer as the destination for the printout.

When you print to the Graphics Printer, Quattro Pro can send special fonts and print in landscape or banner mode without your physically turning the paper. This is done with either Quattro Pro's bit-mapped or downloadable fonts (as discussed in Chapter 6), which are graphic images of letters that are sent to the printer as "sideways" characters.

Be aware that when you print in landscape or banner mode, you must also change the appropriate page layout settings. For example, you must adjust the Page Length and Right Margin settings to account for the wider paper.

When you print in banner mode, Quattro Pro formats the printout without paper width boundaries. This allows you to print all the columns of a very wide spreadsheet in one contiguous block, rather than dividing it among several pages. For example, suppose that you would like to present a 60-column spreadsheet showing a 5-year business forecast. Rather than printing several pages, you could print the spreadsheet in banner mode so that the entire forecast appears on extra-wide paper.

Remember that when you are printing to the Graphics Printer, the speed and quality of the printout depend on the resolution you have chosen for your printer from the Printer Type menu under the Options–Hardware–Printers command.

In order to use banner printing, you must choose the Graphics Printer as the destination, just as you do for landscape printing. You must also have a printer that uses continuous-feed paper, as most dot-matrix printers do. Printers that feed single sheets, such as laser and daisy-wheel printers, cannot be used for banner printing.

Banner printing is rotated 90 degrees, just as with landscape printing. But the right margin is ignored, and the entire width of each line in the print block is printed in a continuous row, spanning across as many pages as necessary.

Because the printout is considered to be infinitely wide, headers and footers print only once, just as on a one-page printout.

ADDING HEADERS AND FOOTERS

A *header* is text that is printed at the top of every page. In Quattro Pro, the header is the first line that is printed below the top margin. A *footer* is text that appears at the bottom of every page, and it is the last line to print before the bottom margin.

Typical text for headers and footers includes a report title, file name, author, company name, and version number of the spreadsheet.

You specify the text for the header or footer on the Print–Layout menu. The text is not a part of your print block or headings. You can type in as many as 240 characters, which is generally about as long a line as any printer can print.

Quattro Pro provides three characters that have special meaning when included in a header or footer:

- ¦ (vertical bar): Text justification

- # (pound sign): Page number

- @ (at sign): Current date

You include the broken vertical bar to either center or right justify the text in the header or footer. If you do not include it, all text is left justified. A single vertical bar centers all the text that follows it. The following text would print as a centered header or footer:

ǀThis is centered

A second vertical bar right justifies all text that follows it. The @ symbol is used to signify the current date, which Quattro Pro substitutes in the printout. The following would print a right-justified date:

ǀǀToday's Date: @

On December 12, 1991, the header or footer would appear right justified on the printout, like this:

Today's Date: 12-Dec-91

The # symbol is similar to the @ symbol, except that it is replaced with the current page number when printed. If you enter this into your footer:

ǀPage [#]

you would get a centered footer that looks like this on page 11 of your printout:

Page [11]

A header or footer is a single line only, which prints whether or not you specify any text. This means that a line is reserved at the top and bottom of the printout; you can add text to these lines or leave them blank, but they are part of your line count.

If your top margin is set to the default of two lines, there will be two blank lines above your header. The body of your print block always begins two lines below the header, and ends two lines above the footer. This means that the header and footer each take up three lines of the page, for a total of six lines.

FIGURING LINES PER PAGE

Now that we have discussed the page length, top and bottom margins, and header and footer lines, we can finally calculate just how many lines are available for your print block on each page. The default page length is 66 lines, and here is how each of those lines is used:

Top margin	1–2
Header	3
Two blank lines	4–5
Print block	6–61
Two blank lines	62–63
Footer	64
Bottom margin	65–66

Counting the rows from 6 to 61, there are 56 lines available on the default page in Quattro Pro. Figure 7.2 provides a graphic representation of the page layout, including the left and right margins.

Knowing how Quattro Pro uses a page allows you to print in a variety of formats. For example, suppose you want to print a block of 10 columns (each of which is nine characters wide) and 58 rows, and you would like it to fit on one piece of paper. You can easily determine what settings you will need from what we know about the page layout in Quattro Pro.

The block is 90 characters wide, so it will not fit within the width of a standard page at 10 cpi. You can either shrink the character size to fit more characters on a line or use wider paper. Let's explore both options.

First, you can use 11-by-8½-inch paper, which has room for about 100 standard characters on a line, plus the margins. You would change the Right Margin setting to 105 and the Left Margin to 5 to handle the long line length. But the page has room for only 51 lines, which is not enough for your block of 58 rows. You could try an even larger paper size, such as 14-by 11-inch,

Whenever you have to start adjusting your margins to fit a block onto the page, you should change the Print–Destination option to Screen Preview. Then, you can test your print settings via the screen preview, which will save both time and paper.

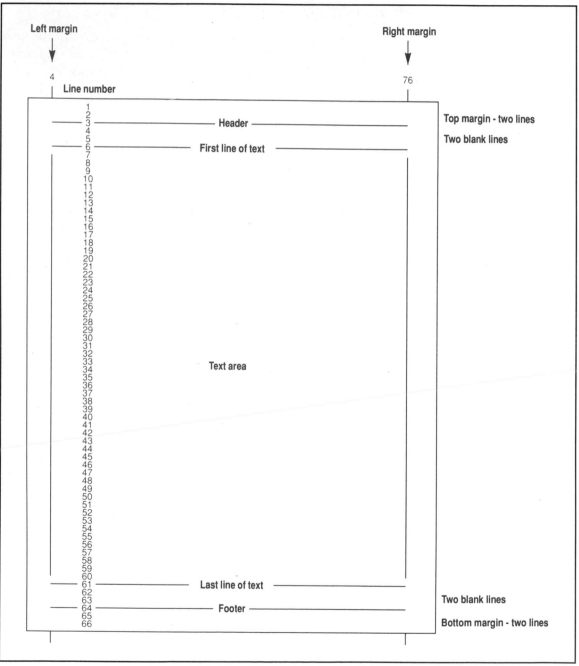

Figure 7.2: Quattro Pro page layout

or use a setup code to change the line spacing to 8 lpi, giving a total of 68 lines. You would then have to change Quattro Pro's Page Length setting to 68.

You could also fit this printout on 8½-by-11-inch paper. Its 66 rows are more than enough for the block to fit vertically. You could then try a smaller font size, such as 8 points. Or use a font that fits 17 cpi, which would allow about 125 characters per line. Change the Right Margin setting to about 120, which would be more than enough to handle the 100-character line.

HANDLING WIDE BLOCKS

You may want to try banner-mode printing when you have a very wide printout that will look best on one wide page. Use the Print–Layout–Orientation–Banner command.

When faced with an overly wide block, Quattro Pro simply prints as many columns as it can fit on one page. After all the rows of the block have been printed, it then prints the excess columns on another set of pages. When all the printing is done, you can place the pages with the excess columns alongside of the first set of pages to complete the picture of the block.

You may remember to increase the margin settings for a wide block but forget that these margins are too wide for your printer to handle. Printers with an 8½-inch carriage width generally cannot print more than 85 characters on a line. If you try to send more, the printer may accept them and simply dump the excess characters on a second line of print.

This is very unsatisfactory, and you might not realize what is happening at first. Sometimes the excess characters are just blank columns, so your printout will look like it's double spaced. So keep your printer's maximum line length in mind, and be sure not to exceed it when specifying the Right Margin setting.

SCALING YOUR PRINTOUTS

It can be frustrating when just a few lines of your printout spill onto a second page. You could try adjusting font sizes and page margins yourself until the entire printout fits on a single page, but there's an easier way to get the job done.

Instead of issuing the Print–Spreadsheet Print command to begin printing, set the Destination to Graphics Printer and invoke the Print–Print to Fit command. Quattro Pro will adjust the printout's font size and line spacing in order to print the spreadsheet block on a single page, or at least as few pages as possible.

Quattro Pro will avoid font sizes that are unreasonably microscopic, but the resulting font might still be too small for your purposes. You will have to decide whether to use fewer pages or a more readable font.

Note that the Print to Fit command will not change your margin settings. This means that all the pages of a spreadsheet can have the same margins, even if some of them have been reduced to fit on fewer pages.

You can also scale your printouts manually with the Print–Layout–Percent Scaling command. Again, you must select the Graphics Printer for the Destination command. By default, Percent Scaling is set to 100, so that your fonts are printed in the sizes you have specified. Set this command to a lower or higher number, from 1 to 1000, and Quattro Pro will shrink or expand your printout to the specified scale. In this way, all the fonts in the spreadsheet will be adjusted the same amount, and you avoid changing each font size yourself.

Note that this command does not work in conjunction with the Print to Fit command. You must use the Spreadsheet Print command in order for the Percent Scaling command to take effect. If you choose Print to Fit to start your printing, the Percent Scaling command setting will be ignored.

PRINTING WITHOUT PAGE BREAKS

To maximize the number of lines that you can print on a page, you can shrink the top and bottom margins to zero. This saves four lines, leaving sixty for the print block. And that's the most you can get without resorting to an 8-lpi line height.

If you want to print to the very edge of the page (assuming your printer can do that), you can choose the Print–Layout–Break Pages–No command. Quattro Pro will now print on the lines

If you are using a laser or ink-jet printer that cannot print to the edge of the page, you really don't need to add a top and bottom margin to that blank space. Consider setting the top and bottom margins to zero.

reserved for the top and bottom margins, as well as the header, footer, and the blank lines between them and the print block. This gives you a full 66 lines on the page.

Even when you are printing without page breaks, Quattro Pro still counts lines, and it knows how far it has printed on the current page. When you want to eject the page from the printer, you can still use the Print–Adjust Printer–Form Feed command. Quattro Pro will advance the paper so that the top of the next page is aligned and ready to go. Also, hard page breaks within the print block are recognized and the printout will be divided accordingly.

VIEWING, CLEARING, AND RESETTING THE LAYOUT

The last three commands on the Print–Layout menu are Reset, Update, and Values. When you want to change some or all print settings back to their default, choose the Reset command. It has the choices All, Print Block, Headings, and Layouts. Choose the option you want to clear, and just those settings will be reset to those that are in effect each time you load Quattro Pro.

You would generally use the All option when you move on to print a different block with many different settings. By resetting all the print options, you ensure that you don't forget to change any of them. Note that when you use the Reset All command, all the options under the Graph Print menu are also reset.

The Update command allows you to save the current print settings as the default for all future sessions of Quattro Pro. Just as with the Options–Update command, the best time to save default settings is just after you load the program. That way, you will know exactly what changes you have made and what will be saved as the new print settings.

The Values command pops up a window that shows all the current settings for the page layout, including margins, page length, setup string, orientation, and so on. You can see all the relevant page layout settings at one glance. These settings are also the ones that are saved when you invoke the Update command, so you can use the Values command to verify which settings will be saved. Press any key to clear the window and return to the Print–Layout menu.

USING SETUP CODES
TO CONTROL THE PRINTER

Quattro Pro offers quite a few menu options for controlling the appearance of your printouts, but sometimes you will have to take control yourself and tell the printer what you want. You do this by using setup codes. As mentioned earlier, a setup code is a special command that a program sends to the printer. If the code is a valid one, the printer will interpret it and adjust its settings accordingly. Setup codes are also called Escape codes because they always begin with the Escape character.

There are dozens and dozens of codes you can send to the printer to adjust almost any aspect of printing. Each printer has its own set of commands, so you will have to refer to your printer manual for specific ones. But printers typically share one of several, industry-wide standards. Many dot-matrix printers use the Epson printer's set of control codes. Many laser printers share the language used in Hewlett-Packard's line of LaserJet printers.

SPECIFYING A CODE WITH THE PRINT COMMAND

You can send a setup code to the printer by using the Print–Layout–Setup String command and entering the appropriate Escape code. But you don't actually press Escape to begin the sequence. Instead, you enter the ASCII code for it, which is 027. You must also always begin the code and separate each portion of it from the others with a backslash (\).

For example, the code Escape 0 instructs an Epson printer to use 8-lpi spacing. You would enter that code this way: \027\048. To use compressed print (17 cpi) with an Epson printer, the code is \027\015. If you wanted to print in compressed mode with 8 lpi, you could combine these codes like this:

\027\048\015

The setup codes for a laser printer can be quite complex. For example, the code to send to a Hewlett-Packard LaserJet for compressed, 8-lpi printing is

\027&l8d\027(s16.66H

Quattro Pro's built-in fonts and orientation and margin settings take care of the most common uses for setup codes.

Quattro Pro sends the printer the setup code, but it is not aware of what that code is actually doing. You must change its settings to match the printer's. For example, if you change line spacing using a setup code, you must tell Quattro Pro by adjusting the Page Length setting; otherwise, it would use the existing page length. If you change the printer's font size with a setup code, you must in turn adjust Quattro Pro's margin settings to tailor the line length to the print size.

If you use a setup code that your printer does not recognize (enter the wrong one or make a typing mistake), the printer will simply try to print the code, as though it were text. If your printouts are ever plagued by a few strange characters in the very first row of the page, this may be your problem.

When you enter a setup code with the Setup String command, that code is the first thing sent to the printer when printing begins. If you need to have a printing command take effect in the middle of a printout, you can place the codes within the spreadsheet itself, as explained in the next section.

EMBEDDING SETUP CODES IN SPREADSHEETS

The broken vertical bar character is used for the nonprinting label prefix. It is typed from the keyboard by pressing Shift-\.

In Chapter 6, you learned how to embed a page-break command within the spreadsheet by using the special nonprinting label prefix, |, to preface a pair of colons. The broken vertical bar can also be used to send Escape codes.

For example, to shift to 17 cpi within your printout, you could include the appropriate setup string in the spreadsheet. Begin with the nonprinting label prefix and add a second one before typing the code:

||\027\015

The setup codes must be placed in a cell within the first column of the print block. The rest of that row will be ignored when printed, so be sure to place the code in an empty or otherwise unnecessary row.

Embedded codes are handy, but you can't use them to switch too many settings within a print block. Although you could include five or ten codes in the print block, Quattro Pro print settings cannot be changed while that block is printing. If you were to change the number of lines per inch with an embedded code, Quattro Pro would continue to count lines at whatever page length it started with because it would not be aware of the change, and it and the printer would be out of sync.

PRINTING ACTUAL CELL CONTENTS

By default, your printout is an image of your spreadsheet as it appears on the display. The results of formulas are shown, not the formulas themselves. In fact, you really can't tell from a printout if a value is a number, text that looks like a number, or a formula that produces the number.

In some cases, you will want a printout that shows cells with their actual contents. You can do this by invoking the Print–Format command. This command is preset to As Displayed, and your spreadsheet is printed just as it appears on the screen. Change the setting to Cell-Formulas, then print the spreadsheet. The block you print will be printed in one long column. Each row is a cell, and what is printed is basically what you see on the input line when highlighting that cell.

Figure 7.3 shows the result of printing the last two columns of the Mileage spreadsheet (D1..E12) with the Print–Format command set to Cell-Formulas. As you can see, each line of the printout shows the cell addresses, the cell attributes that you would see on the input line, and the cell contents.

A printout such as this one can be useful for documentation or debugging purposes, although you will rarely want to print the entire spreadsheet. Instead, you might print just those

```
D1:  "Mileage
E1:  'Compared
E2:  'to Avg.
D3:  \-
E3:  \-
D4:  "-
E4:  "-
D5:  (F1)  +B5/C5
E5:  (P1)  +D5/[FIG02-05]$C$3
D6:  (F1)  +B6/C6
E6:  (P1)  +D6/[FIG02-05]$C$3
D7:  (F1)  +B7/C7
E7:  (P1)  +D7/[FIG02-05]$C$3
D8:  (F1)  +B8/C8
E8:  (P1)  +D8/[FIG02-05]$C$3
D9:  (F1)  +B9/C9
E9:  (P1)  +D9/[FIG02-05]$C$3
D10: (F1)  +B10/C10
E10: (P1)  +D10/[FIG02-05]$C$3
D11: \-
E11: \-
D12: (F1)  +B12/C12
E12: (P1)  +D12/[FIG02-05]$C$3
```

Figure 7.3: Last two columns of the Mileage spreadsheet printed in the Cell-Formulas format

areas that are particularly important or worthy of further written explanation.

Perhaps the best way to take advantage of a Cell-Formulas printout is by sending the output to a file, not the printer, so it can be stored for future reference. You can then edit and save it as documentation or print it. Printing to a file will be covered a little later in this chapter.

ADJUSTING THE PAPER

If you print a small block, Quattro Pro does not eject the rest of the page; it waits for you to issue another print command. You can print another block if you wish or eject the paper from the printer and be done with it. But don't use the controls on your printer to eject the completed page.

If you manually eject the paper at this point, the paper will be aligned as you wanted, but Quattro Pro will not be aware of this; it will still think that there are a certain number of lines left on the current page.

To eject the paper from the printer, use the Printer–Adjust Printer–Form Feed command. Quattro Pro knows how much of the page is left in the printer and will advance it just enough to

Avoid the habit of pressing the Form Feed button on the printer or turning the platen to eject the page. Quattro Pro will not know that the next page is in place.

eject it from the printer and ready the next page for printing. Now Quattro Pro knows that the next time it prints, it will be at the beginning of a new page; its line count will be set to line 1.

The Adjust Printer command has two other choices, Skip Line and Align. Use the Skip Line command to advance the paper by a single line. This command is useful when you are printing multiple blocks. Print the first block, issue one or more Skip Line commands, print the next block, and so on. If you want 1 inch of blank space between blocks on the printout, issue the command six times. Quattro Pro includes these blank lines in the line count, and if you press Skip Line enough times in a row, eventually you will get to the end of the page, and Quattro Pro will insert the bottom margin and begin printing on the next page.

You use the Adjust Printer–Align command when you have manually adjusted the paper in the printer. This command tells Quattro Pro to reset its line count to line 1, because the paper is now at top of form. For example, if your printer runs out of paper during a printout, you would press Ctrl-Break to cancel the print job. After you have loaded the new paper and aligned the first page at the top-of-form position, you will want to start the print job over again. Before you print, use the Align command to tell Quattro Pro to reset its line count to line 1.

Note that the Align command also resets the page count to page 1. The pages of all print jobs are numbered consecutively, and the page number appears in either the header or footer if you have used the # code.

When starting a new printout, you should invoke the Align command so that the page count returns to 1. Your header or footer will then display the correct page numbers for the new print job.

Both the Form Feed and Skip Line commands have the same effect as pressing the corresponding buttons on your printer, which are usually called Form Feed and Line Feed.

Lotus 1-2-3 users should note that, unlike 1-2-3, Quattro Pro does not automatically reset the page count to 1 when you return to Ready mode after printing. Page numbers are retained for all print blocks in the current session.

CHOOSING PRINT DESTINATIONS

In Chapter 6, you learned that the Print–Destination command directs your printout to either the Printer or the Graphics Printer. In fact, these two printers are actually one and the same, but the output is treated differently for each.

When you set the print destination, the currently selected printer is displayed to the right of the Destination command on the Print menu.

Don't confuse the Graphics Printer destination with the Graph Print command. Use the latter command when you are printing a graph, not when you are printing data in the spreadsheet.

Remember, no matter how many fonts you may have used in your spreadsheet, they will not be printed if the Print–Destination command is set to Printer, the default. When you then invoke the Print–Spreadsheet Print command, output is sent to the printer strictly as text. Your printouts are produced in the least amount of time but with the fewest embellishments.

If you set the Print–Destination command to Graphics Printer, however, Quattro Pro will take its time and do the best job possible in applying fonts, line drawing, and shading, as well as print any graphs you have inserted into the spreadsheet.

SETTING THE GRAPHICS QUALITY

You also learned in Chapter 6 that for the best possible output, you first need to set the Options–Graphics Quality command to Final. If you print to the Graphics Printer while the Options–Graphics Quality command is set to Draft, Quattro Pro will not build any Bitstream fonts. If a Bitstream font you have applied to a cell is not already on disk, Quattro Pro will substitute one of the Hershey fonts. This avoids the delay of font building, although the Hershey fonts are not as attractive as the Bitstream ones (but they are very similar to the fonts in Quattro 1).

When you set the Options–Graphics Quality command to Final and then print to the Graphics Printer, Quattro Pro will build any fonts that are not on disk to produce the printout or, if the Print–Destination command is set to Screen Preview, to generate screen fonts. On a slow computer, final-quality printouts might take a little longer to produce if several fonts must be built.

There are three other choices on the Print–Destination menu:

- File: Directs the printout to a plain text file that can later be imported into a word processor or other program.

- Binary File: Sends the printout to a complete, final mode binary file that can later be sent directly to a printer.

• Screen Preview: Eliminates the printer altogether and directs the output to the screen, where you can view it before you send it to the printer.

You have two printers from which to choose in Quattro Pro, although only one can be active at a time. You select the printer from the Options–Hardware–Printers menu. On that menu, you specify each printer's type (make, model, and so on) and which printer should be the active, or default, printer. See Chapter 18 for more information about configuring Quattro Pro.

USING SCREEN PREVIEWS TO SAVE A TREE AND YOUR TIME

To see the print block in its printed format, your computer's video card and monitor must be capable of displaying graphics; otherwise, Quattro Pro will issue an error message and cancel the command. Quattro Pro supports many different video standards, including CGA, EGA, VGA, and Hercules.

The Screen Preview option is perhaps the most useful of the three nonprinter destinations. When you choose Screen Preview as the Destination, the Spreadsheet Print command sends your spreadsheet to the screen, in the exact same format as would have been printed if you used the Graphics Printer option.

Figure 7.4 shows the Mileage spreadsheet with a title added above the main body of the spreadsheet and fonts applied to some of the cells. If you look on the input line, you can see that font number 2 (18-point Bitstream Dutch) has been applied to the current cell, A5. The titles in rows 5 and 6 and the totals in row 14 all have this font. The title in row 2 has been enhanced with font 6 (18-point bold italic Bitstream Swiss). As you may remember, column D had shading applied to it.

If you used the Print–Destination–Screen Preview command, specified the block (in this case A2..F15) and any necessary print settings, and issued the Print–Spreadsheet Print command, a graphics screen display would show the printed page as it appears in Figure 7.5.

This is how the printed page will look in its entirety. You can see all the larger text that was in 18-point type, but the numbers are too small to be displayed, as is a line of text at the top of the screen. Quattro Pro simply represents them with a pattern.

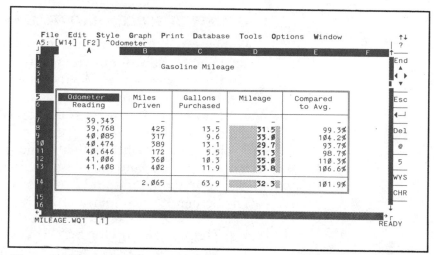

Figure 7.4: The spreadsheet as it appears before printing to the screen

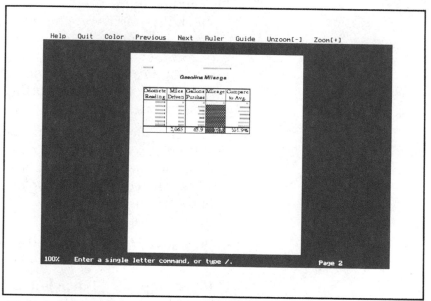

Figure 7.5: The spreadsheet in preview mode

THE PREVIEW SCREEN AND ITS MENU

At the bottom of the screen is a prompt that tells you how to select a command from the menu. To its right is the page number of the displayed page. To its left, the number *100%* means that the screen has not been expanded with the Zoom command (more on this later). At the top is the menu bar.

There is no cell selector to move around the screen, so you can select a command from the menu just by typing its first letter. Or, press / and pick the command from the menu by moving the highlighter and pressing ↲.

The Screen Preview menu provides the following commands:

- Help: Brings up the Screen Preview Help system, which you can also get by pressing F1. You choose Help topics in the usual way.

- Quit: Leaves the preview and returns to the spreadsheet. Pressing Escape has the same effect. Remember that this is merely a temporary picture of the printed page, and there is nothing to save for future use. You can pop in and out of preview mode as often as you need to test your current print settings and spreadsheet layout.

- Colors: Switches the screen colors to one of the available color sets. For example, on a monochrome system, you have a choice of black on white or white on black. This command has no effect on the final, printed output; it just provides you with another way to fine tune the display.

- Previous or Next: Displays the previous or next page, respectively. You can also use the PgUp and PgDn keys.

- Ruler: Imposes a 1-inch grid over the page. This gives you a reasonably accurate means to gauge the layout of the page. Invoking the command a second time removes the grid from the screen.

- Zoom (+): Expands, or magnifies, the page. Each time you invoke the command, the screen magnification doubles. You can only zoom twice, which expands the display to 400 percent, as the indicator in the lower-left corner of the screen will tell you. To reduce the magnification, choose Unzoom (−). Figure 7.6 shows the sample preview screen magnified by 200 percent. Now you can see the smaller text in the header, as well as the numbers in the block.

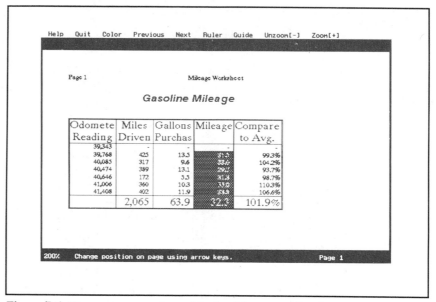

Figure 7.6: The screen preview with double magnification

- Guide (Ins): Displays a small image of the page in the upper-right corner of the screen. On that page is superimposed a small box, called the *zoom box*, which represents the portion of the page that you are currently viewing. Use the arrow keys or your mouse to move the box to a different portion of the page, press ↵, and that portion will be displayed. To remove the small page and zoom box from the screen, invoke Guide again or press Del.

DISPLAYING SCREEN FONTS

Whether you are printing to a printer or to the screen, Quattro Pro will use the fonts you specified. When the Options–Graphics Display command is set to Draft, no fonts will be built for the preview. When it is set to Final, all fonts will be displayed, and those that aren't already on disk will be built as needed. As the screen is being prepared, you may see the familiar message

Now building fonts

These are the same fonts that are used when printing on a printer, but they are used as display fonts here.

If you have used several fonts in the spreadsheet, none of which are on disk, be prepared for some delay if you use the Zoom command to magnify the preview screen. Each level of magnification requires a larger font size for the fonts, and the new fonts will need to be built.

PREPARING FOR PRINTING ELSEWHERE

Besides saving time and paper, the Screen Preview option also allows you to preview printouts that you could never print on your printer. Suppose you have a daisy-wheel printer that cannot print graphics or fonts, but a coworker is going to let you use his first-rate laser printer for a special spreadsheet. You could prepare the spreadsheet for laser printing following these steps:

1. Use the Options–Hardware–Printer command to select the laser printer that you will be using.

2. Lay out your spreadsheet with the fonts, graphs, or other enhancements.

3. Select Print–Destination–Screen Preview for the output.

4. Select Spreadsheet Print to view the printout on the screen and verify that it looks the way you want.

5. Change the Print–Destination option to Binary File (read the next section to learn why).

PRINTING TO A BINARY FILE

■ If you don't specify a file extension, Quattro Pro will automatically append the extension PRN to it.

When you choose the Binary File option for the Destination of your printout, you are prompted to enter the name of a file. Type in the name you want and press ↵. When you later invoke the Spreadsheet Print command, the output will be sent to that file on disk. The file will contain every bit and byte that would have been sent to the printer, including all the control codes, fonts, and spreadsheet data.

You now have a transportable printout—one that you can copy to a floppy disk and take to your fellow worker's computer, where it can be printed on the laser printer.

To print the file, you simply use the COPY command from the DOS prompt to copy the file to the printer. Be sure to append the parameter /B to the command, which tells DOS that the file is a binary file. If you don't, the spreadsheet will not print properly.

For example, if you named the output file MYPRINT.PRN, and the printer was connected to the parallel port, you would use this command to print the file:

COPY MYPRINT.PRN PRN: /B

The printer will accept the data as though it were coming directly from Quattro Pro, and you will have your printout.

PRINTING TO A TEXT FILE

Unlike printing to a binary file, which creates a file that can produce a complete, fully enhanced printout, setting the Print–Destination to File creates a file of very plain, unadorned text. The resulting file is often called a text or ASCII file, and it consists only of standard PC characters. These include the letters of the alphabet, numerals, and punctuation, as well as the extended characters available on the PC, such as pi, square root, or the degree sign.

The data that is printed will be formatted just as it would be when printed on a plain text printer. There will be blank lines for the top and bottom margins, blank spaces on the left for the left margin, and the headers and footers will appear as they should.

This file can be copied to a printer, just as you can copy the binary file, only you do not need the /B parameter after the COPY command. But printing a text file is usually not the primary reason for creating one. Instead, text files are typically used for transferring data from one program to another.

For example, suppose you are writing a report in your word processor and would like to include the Mileage spreadsheet. Here are the steps to follow to transfer the data:

> Notice that the File option on the Destination menu is in the section of that menu labeled Draft Mode Printing. The Binary File option, on the other hand, is in the section labeled Final Quality Printing.

1. Select Print–Destination–File.

2. Enter a file name at the prompt, such as Mileage (Quattro Pro will append a PRN extension to the name).

3. Use the commands on the Layout–Margin menu to set the left margin to 0 and the right margin to 511S.

4. Set Break Pages to No.

5. Choose Quit to leave the Layout command.

6. Choose Spreadsheet Print.

7. Choose Quit to complete the job. You will return to Ready mode.

You will see the light on your disk drive blink on briefly as the data is sent to disk. Let's look at this file from DOS.

8. Use the Quattro Pro File–Utilities–DOS Shell command to temporarily exit to DOS.

9. Use the DOS TYPE command to display the print file on the screen. If the file is on the D drive, use the command **TYPE D:MILEAGE.PRN**.

10. Type **EXIT** to return to Quattro Pro.

The text file is displayed as shown in Figure 7.7. It consists of nothing more than text characters, with the draft-mode formatting of margins. This is exactly how it will look when you import it into your word processor.

When creating a text file, you will generally use the same layout settings that were used in the example above:

- Left margin: 0

- Right margin: 254

- Break pages: No

You can import a text file into Quattro Pro by using the Tools–Import command, which will be covered in the next chapter.

You do not need page breaks and left margins when you use the file in some other program. You would usually want that other program to handle the formatting. By setting the right

```
D>TYPE D:MILEAGE.PRN
                        Gasoline Mileage


+------------+-----------+-----------+-----------+-----------+
¦ Odometer   ¦ Miles     ¦ Gallons   ¦ Mileage   ¦ Compared  ¦
¦ Reading    ¦ Driven    ¦ Purchased ¦           ¦ to Avg.   ¦
+------------+-----------+-----------+-----------+-----------+
¦   39,343 ¦         - ¦         - ¦         - ¦         - ¦
¦   39,768 ¦     425 ¦     13.5 ¦    31.5 ¦    99.3%¦
¦   40,085 ¦     317 ¦      9.6 ¦    33.0 ¦   104.2%¦
¦   40,474 ¦     389 ¦     13.1 ¦    29.7 ¦    93.7%¦
¦   40,646 ¦     172 ¦      5.5 ¦    31.3 ¦    98.7%¦
¦   41,006 ¦     360 ¦     10.3 ¦    35.0 ¦   110.3%¦
¦   41,408 ¦     402 ¦     11.9 ¦    33.8 ¦   106.6%¦
+------------+-----------+-----------+-----------+-----------+
¦          ¦   2,065 ¦     63.9 ¦    32.3 ¦   101.9%¦
+------------+-----------+-----------+-----------+-----------+

D>
```

Figure 7.7: The text file output of the Print–Destination–File command, as displayed from DOS

margin as large as possible, you ensure that you export the longest line that Quattro Pro can handle during printing.

Much of your work in Quattro Pro will involve files, whether they are spreadsheets, text printouts from your spreadsheet, data from a database program, or a text file exported from a word processor. The next chapter provides information that can help you deal with all these files.

8

Managing Your Files

Fast
Track

JUST ABOUT ALL YOUR WORK IN QUATTRO PRO WILL AT some point end up in a file on disk. This chapter covers the various file operations that allow you to handle those files. Using the very practical File Manager is discussed in the next chapter.

SAVING YOUR FILES

The default file name extension can be changed with the Options–Startup–File Extension command. See Chapter 18 for more information about configuring Quattro Pro.

When you save your work to disk in Quattro Pro, it is by default given the file name extension WQ1. For example, if you specify the name MYFILE, the file will be named MYFILE.WQ1. There are many other operations that create files with specific file name extensions. Some of them are related specifically to the Quattro Pro program, and others are related to your data files. Table 8.1 lists the extensions that are automatically appended by Quattro Pro.

Table 8.1: Quattro Pro File Extensions

EXTENSION	FILE TYPE
BAK	Backup file for your spreadsheet
CHR	Hershey font
CLP	Graph annotator Clipboard picture
EPS	Exported graph, encapsulated PostScript
FON	Bitstream font
MU	Quattro Pro menu and system defaults
PCX	Exported graph, PC Paintbrush
PIC	Exported graph, Lotus 1-2-3 compatible

Table 8.1: Quattro Pro File Extensions (continued)

EXTENSION	FILE TYPE
PRN	Plain text file or binary output file
SFO	Bitstream font outline or description
WQ1	Quattro Pro spreadsheet
WQ!	Compressed Quattro Pro spreadsheet
WSP	Workspace settings

Generally, whenever you are prompted for a file name, you can specify your own file name extension as well. Bear in mind, however, that the extension serves as a means of grouping similar files. If you specify a different extension, such as DOC for a spreadsheet file, it will no longer be clear that the file is similar to all the other files that have WQ1 extensions.

When you first load Quattro Pro, the spreadsheet displayed is by default referred to as SHEET1.WQ1. This is not a file name, but simply a name by which to refer to this particular window. When you are ready to save your work to disk, invoke the File–Save command (Ctrl-S). That command will prompt you for a file name.

Shown below the prompt are the current default drive and directory, such as C:\ or C:\DATA, followed by the current file name filter, such as *.WQ1. The complete drive, path, and filter might look like this:

```
C:\DATA\*.WQ1
```

Below this is a list of the files in the current drive and subdirectory that have extensions that match the filter. In the example above, the list would include all files with a WQ1 extension in the subdirectory DATA on drive C.

MODIFYING THE LIST OF FILES

The same file prompt and list appear when you use any of the commands that work with files.

You can manipulate the display of files to show you more or different information. When the list is displayed, press the + key to expand the list and show each file's date and time of creation, as well as its size. Press the − key to return the display to file names only.

Press F3 to expand the list to full-screen size. Press it again to shrink the list back to its original size.

To display a list of files in the parent directory, press Backspace. To display files in a subdirectory of the current directory, just highlight that directory name in the list and press ↵ (or click on it with your mouse).

Press Escape once to type in a new file list filter, or press it twice and then type in a completely different drive or subdirectory.

NAMING FILES

When you are saving a new spreadsheet (one that has not yet been saved), you can either choose a file from the list (which will be replaced by the data in the current spreadsheet) or type in a new name.

If you want to replace an existing file with the current spreadsheet, just highlight that file name and press ↵ (or double-click on it with your mouse). Quattro Pro then offers a menu with the options Cancel, Replace, and Backup. Choose Cancel to cancel the save routine (this is the same as pressing Escape several times to return to Ready mode). Choose Replace to overwrite the existing file with the data from your current spreadsheet. Select Backup to rename the file on disk with a BAK extension, and then save the current spreadsheet. This creates two files on disk with the same name but different extensions; the original file now has the extension BAK, and the new one has WQ1.

To give your spreadsheet a new name, type the name at the prompt. As soon as you type the first character, the list of files disappears and is replaced by what is called a *prompt box*.

Now you are typing a name after the drive and path. Below the name are two mouse buttons, Enter and Esc. When you have typed a name, press ↵ or click on the button labeled Enter with your mouse. If the name you typed is not already in use by a file in the current directory, your spreadsheet will be saved under that name. However, if the file name already exists on disk, you will see the same menu that appears when you highlight a file name on the list. Choose to cancel, replace, or back up the file.

After you have named a spreadsheet, you no longer have to enter the name after you issue the File–Save command. Since the file already resides on disk, you will simply be offered the menu with the choices Cancel, Replace, and Backup.

SAVING UNDER A NEW NAME

The file will retain its name until you specifically change it. If you want to save the current spreadsheet under a different name, use the File–Save As command. The prompt box will appear with the drive, path, and file name of the current spreadsheet. You can type a new name, press F2 and edit the existing one, or specify a new drive and path and save the file in a new location.

As always, if you specify a name that is already in use, you will have to decide whether to cancel, replace, or back up the file.

SAVING ALL OPEN FILES

You can open as many as 32 files at the same time in Quattro Pro. Although you may never need that many open files, it is likely that you will work with several files at once. When you have more than one spreadsheet open, it's particularly important to save your work frequently because there is more of your work at risk.

You could issue the File–Save command to save each active spreadsheet, but this would be tedious with many spreadsheets, and you could easily skip one by mistake. The better method is to use the File–Save All command. Each open worksheet will be saved, just as though you had issued the File–Save command. If a file already exists on disk, you will be prompted to cancel, replace, or back up the file, as with other save operations.

PASSWORD PROTECTING A SPREADSHEET

When you save a spreadsheet, you can specify a password that must later be supplied whenever the spreadsheet is retrieved into Quattro Pro. Only those who know the password will be able to access the file.

A password can be as long as 15 characters and include any characters you can type from the keyboard. Note that this is one instance where the case of letters does matter; uppercase and lowercase letters are considered different.

A password-protected spreadsheet is not saved in its usual format. Quattro Pro encrypts the file so that it cannot be read by anyone without the correct password.

Password-protected files are very well protected. If you forget the password for a spreadsheet, you will never be able to access it again.

You enter a password when you specify the file name, following this procedure:

1. Type the name under which you want to save your work.

2. Type a space and then the letter **P** (for password), and then press ↵.

3. Type the password at the prompt. You won't see the characters you type. Instead, Quattro Pro displays a square for each one to prevent anyone from seeing your keystrokes.

4. Press ↵, and you will be prompted to verify the password by typing it again. This ensures that you typed it exactly as you had intended.

5. Press ↵, and if you typed the password the same both times, your spreadsheet will be saved.

You can apply a password whenever a file command prompts you for a file name. This includes the File–Save and File–Save As commands, as well as some of the other file commands that will be covered in this chapter.

SAVING THE WORKSPACE

Restoring a work-space is simply a shortcut. The process is equivalent to using the File–Open command for the files you want to load, and then sizing and positioning their windows. Any other files that are open are unaffected by the addition of the files that are loaded by the workspace.

When you are working with several open files, it is often the case that those files are related and will always be used as a group. The current configuration of open files and their windows is known as a *workspace.*

You can save the workspace for future use by invoking the File–Workspace–Save command. Specify a name as you would for a file (Quattro Pro appends the extension WSP), and a new file will be created that contains a simple list of the spreadsheets that are open and their window sizes and positions. The spreadsheets themselves are not saved.

When you again want to work with the same group of files, just use the File–Workspace–Restore command and specify the name of the workspace file. Quattro Pro will load all the spreadsheets that are part of that workspace and position them just as they were when you saved the workspace.

CLOSING A SPREADSHEET

When you are finished working with a file, you can use the File–Close command to remove the active spreadsheet and its window from Quattro Pro. If you have changed any data in that spreadsheet since last saving it, Quattro Pro will prompt you with the message

Lose your changes?

and offer a menu with the choices No and Yes. Choose No to cancel the Close command and return to the spreadsheet in Ready mode (so you can save your work if you want to). Choose Yes to close the window and lose any changes you have made to it since the last time you saved it.

You can close all open windows with the single command File–Close All, which is equivalent to issuing the File–Close command for each open file. Any files that have been changed since last saved will cause the prompt shown above to appear, giving you the opportunity to cancel the operation.

Lotus 1-2-3 users take note: The File–Erase command in 1-2-3 is used to erase a spreadsheet file on disk. It is the Worksheet–Erase command in 1-2-3 that is equivalent to Quattro Pro's File–Erase command.

Another way to remove a file from memory is with the File–Erase command. This leaves the window open for the active spreadsheet but erases all data and settings for it, leaving a blank, unnamed spreadsheet.

Yet one more way to close all open spreadsheets is by exiting Quattro Pro with the File–Exit command (Ctrl-X). You will be asked if you want to save the spreadsheets in any windows that have changed since the last time they were saved. When all the windows have been closed, you will be back at the DOS prompt.

RETRIEVING A SPREADSHEET

When you first load Quattro Pro, you are presented with a single, blank, unnamed spreadsheet. From here, you have several means for accessing other files.

REPLACING THE CURRENT SPREADSHEET

This command is equivalent to the Lotus 1-2-3 command File–Retrieve. But Quattro Pro can handle 32 windows at once, so there are other commands that allow you to open other spreadsheets in other windows.

The File–Retrieve command replaces the spreadsheet in the current window with the one you specify from disk (use the File–Open command to open a spreadsheet in another window). Because you will lose your current work, Quattro Pro asks you if you want to lose your changes (if any were made since you last saved the spreadsheet) before bringing in the new spreadsheet.

The same prompt and list of files that you see when you issue the File–Save command appear. Either type the name of the file you want to retrieve or select it from one of the listed files, and the file will be loaded into the current window.

OPENING ANOTHER SPREADSHEET

The File–New command opens another window that contains a blank spreadsheet, with the name SHEET#, where # is the number of windows that you have opened during the current session with Quattro Pro. Once created, the new spreadsheet will be the active one.

To load an existing spreadsheet file into its own window, use the File–Open command. That window will then be the active one. This command is equivalent to using the File–New command to create a blank spreadsheet, and then using the File–Retrieve command to load a spreadsheet into that new window.

As described earlier, you can use the File–Workspace–Restore command to open all files that belong to a saved workspace.

LOADING A SPREADSHEET AT STARTUP

You may find it convenient to load Quattro Pro and a spreadsheet at the same time. In other words, when Quattro Pro appears on the screen, there will be a spreadsheet ready and waiting for you. This spreadsheet may be one that you work with each day, or it may be one that contains an autoload macro that calls other spreadsheets or performs some other daily routine.

LOADING THE SAME SPREADSHEET EVERY TIME

In Lotus 1-2-3, a file to be loaded with the program must be named AUTO123.

One way to automatically load a file is by using the Options–Startup–Autoload File command and entering the name of the file. By default, the file name is QUATTRO.WQ1. Each time Quattro Pro is loaded, it will look for that specific file in the default subdirectory. If it finds the spreadsheet, it loads that file into memory.

You can also use an autoload macro name. If a macro with that name exists in a spreadsheet, Quattro Pro will run the macro whenever it loads that spreadsheet. Chapter 17 provides more information about autoload macros. See Chapter 18 for more information about configuring Quattro Pro for your computer system and work habits.

SPECIFYING A FILE NAME FROM DOS

When you load Quattro Pro from the DOS prompt, you can specify the name of the spreadsheet that you want it to retrieve as soon as the program is loaded into memory. For example, to have it retrieve the file named MYFILE from a subdirectory named DATA on drive C, you would type this command:

    Q C:\DATA\MYFILE

You do not need to specify a file extension unless it is not the default extension.

You can include a macro name after the file name, so that Quattro Pro will not only load the named file, but will also invoke the named macro. To run the macro START, for example, you would enter this command:

    Q C:\DATA\MYFILE START

You can also specify the name of a workspace in this same manner. To open the workspace named BUDGET that is located in the default, startup directory, you would type the command:

    Q BUDGET

Quattro Pro will open all the windows and files associated with that workspace.

CHANGING THE DRIVE OR DIRECTORY

There is always one drive and subdirectory (a *path*) in Quattro Pro that is considered the default. Just as when you are working from the DOS prompt, if you do not specify another location for a file, the default location will be used.

When saving or retrieving files in Quattro Pro, you have two ways to specify another path: change the default one or specify the location for a particular file.

CHANGING THE DEFAULT PATH

From the DOS prompt, you can make another drive the default simply by typing the drive letter followed by a colon. For example, entering the command D: and pressing ↵ makes the D drive the default. You can change to a new subdirectory by using the CD command.

In Quattro Pro, you can perform the same function by invoking the File–Directory command. Type in a new drive, subdirectory, or both, and that will become the default path for the current session of Quattro Pro. Whenever you access a file on disk, Quattro Pro will look in this new location. The File–Retrieve command, for example, will offer a list of all the spreadsheet files in that new default directory.

You can also change the default directory at startup for all future sessions of Quattro Pro by using the Options–Startup–Directory command, as explained in Chapter 18.

SPECIFYING A PATH FOR A SINGLE OPERATION

When you are accessing a file at the DOS prompt, you can override the default path by naming the location where the file can be found. You can do the same thing in Quattro Pro.

If you need to access just a single file from another location, there is no need to change the default directory. Instead, just specify exactly where that file can be found, using the following procedure.

1. Invoke the File–Retrieve command.
2. Press Escape once to erase the file filter (*.WQ1) that is offered.
3. Press Escape a second time to erase the drive and path.
4. Type in the new drive, subdirectory, and file filter.
5. Press ↵, and Quattro Pro will now list the files in that location.

You do not need to specify all three components of the path: drive, subdirectory, and file filter. If you specify just the drive, Quattro Pro will log onto that drive and to whatever subdirectory is currently its default.

Remember that pressing Backspace in the file list moves you up to the parent directory.

You can also choose a different subdirectory by picking it from the list of files that is offered by the various file commands. Just highlight the subdirectory name and press ↵, or double-click on it with your mouse.

WORKING WITH PORTIONS OF A SPREADSHEET

The file commands that we have discussed so far deal with complete files. But you can also save and retrieve smaller parts of a file.

SAVING PART OF A SPREADSHEET

The Tools–Xtract command saves a single block of the current spreadsheet to a file. The resulting file retains all the settings of its parent spreadsheet, including the widths of columns, block names, default settings, and cell formats.

This command has two options for saving the block: Formulas and Values. If you choose Formulas, any formulas in the block you specify will be saved as formulas. Use this if you want a clone of all or part of the source spreadsheet.

A problem can arise if the formula cells you extract refer to cells that are not included in the extracted block. In the new spreadsheet, those formulas will refer to blank cells, and they will not produce the same results as they did in the source spreadsheet.

If you choose Values, only the values in the cells will be saved. Use this to retain a "snapshot" of the data found in the source spreadsheet. These options are equivalent to the Edit–Copy and Edit–Values commands, respectively.

After you have chosen Formulas or Values, the Tools–Xtract command prompts you for the name of the file to which you want this block saved. Again, this is the same process you use when saving a file with the File–Save command. Then specify the block you wish to extract to its own file. Designate the block in the usual way: by typing the cell address, pointing, or using a block name.

The resulting file will contain only the block you specified. That data will begin in the upper-left corner of the new spreadsheet, in cell A1.

Figure 8.1 shows a spreadsheet named Yearend, which contains a small table of data that occupies the block B4..G18. It has column titles in rows 4 through 6, and totals in row 18 and column F. The block with the data and year-end totals, B7..G16, has been given the name ALL_DATA. To extract this block, you would issue the Tools–Xtract command, select Values (because you do not need active formulas in the extracted file), specify a new name for the file, and specify the block name ALL_DATA. You must be sure to use a file name that is different from the name of the active spreadsheet, or you will overwrite the original spreadsheet. The results of extracting this block are shown in Figure 8.2.

RETRIEVING PART OF A SPREADSHEET

The Tools–Combine command lets you specify all or just a portion of another spreadsheet to combine into the current spreadsheet. The original spreadsheet remains active, but it now contains data from the second spreadsheet.

The cells from the other spreadsheet will be brought into the active spreadsheet at the cell selector's location. In other words, if the cell selector is on cell M201, and you specify the block F21..G30 as the block to bring in from the other file, the 20 incoming cells will overlay the cells in the block M201..N210.

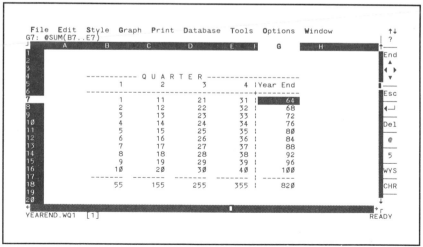

Figure 8.1: A spreadsheet with a block to be extracted

The Tools–Combine command provides three options to determine the manner in which the data will be combined into the current spreadsheet: Copy, Add, and Subtract.

COMBINING WITH COPY

When you choose Tools–Combine–Copy, all incoming cells will replace (overwrite) cells in the current spreadsheet. This is similar to the Edit–Copy command, which replaces cells in the destination block with the copies of the cells in the source block, but blank cells are treated differently.

An incoming cell that happens to be blank will not affect an occupied cell in the current spreadsheet. But the cell must be entirely blank. If it has been given a numeric format, that empty but formatted cell will replace a cell in the active spreadsheet.

COMBINING WITH ADD OR SUBTRACT

The Add and Subtract options perform arithmetic with the incoming cells and the corresponding cells in the active spreadsheet. With the Add option, an incoming cell is added to the cell

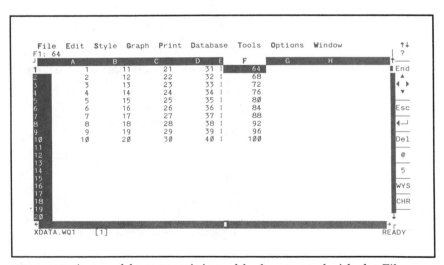

Figure 8.2: A spreadsheet containing a block extracted with the File–Xtract command

it overlays, leaving a total in that cell. With the Subtract option, the incoming number is subtracted from the cell it overlays.

The cell in the active spreadsheet must contain a number in order for the addition or subtraction to occur. If the cell contains a formula, text, or a text value, nothing will happen—the incoming cell will be ignored. An incoming cell must be either a number or a formula that equates to a number; otherwise it, too, will be ignored.

For example, suppose that you have several income spreadsheets for rental property. The spreadsheets all have different data, but they are all structured in exactly the same fashion. With the Tools–Combine–Add command, you can quickly and easily consolidate all the reports into one grand total in the current spreadsheet.

Figure 8.3 shows the result of using this command to bring the spreadsheet shown in Figure 8.2 into the one shown in Figure 8.1 (the active spreadsheet). The cell selector was on cell B7 when the Tools–Combine–Add command was issued. You can't see it in this figure, but the formulas in column G were not affected by the incoming data; they are still formulas that sum the same cells they summed before the file operation.

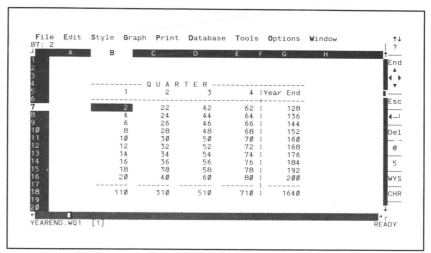

Figure 8.3: The Tools–Combine–Add command adds the value of incoming cells with those in the current spreadsheet

If you were to continue this process and bring in data from other spreadsheets, each succeeding block would be added to the current block. You could simply repeat the command for as many files as you wanted to combine.

COMBINING VERSUS LINKING SPREADSHEETS

The ability to combine one or more spreadsheets into another can be a very powerful feature. But note that you can perform the same task by writing linking formulas that refer to those other spreadsheets. In some instances, you will find one method is preferred over the other.

For example, if you need to access a dozen cells that are scattered in various locations in another spreadsheet, linking formulas will definitely be the best way to proceed. It is much easier to write a dozen formulas that, once written, can be left alone, than to perform 12 file operations each time you want to update the information in the master spreadsheet.

On the other hand, if you need to access a single, named block in a dozen spreadsheets, you will very likely find that using the Tools–Combine command is the way to go. If you write a short macro to automate the 12 file operations, the task will take but a few seconds to complete, and your spreadsheet will not be burdened with many linking formulas.

Of course, if you don't write a macro to do the job for you, you may find formulas more convenient. But be sure to read Chapters 16 and 17 to find out how powerful an ally macros can be.

TRANSLATING OTHER FILE FORMATS

Quattro Pro can save to and retrieve from other types of files besides its own. You can save your spreadsheet to another file format simply by specifying the appropriate file name extension when prompted for a name by the File–Save or Tools–Xtract command. For example, if you specifically include the extension WK1 when saving your spreadsheet, it will be saved as a Lotus 1-2-3 release 2.2 file.

Retrieving a file that is in another format is even easier. Just treat it as though it were a Quattro Pro file, and Quattro Pro will do the rest. For example, to retrieve a dBASE III file into a spreadsheet, just specify the name of the file and its extension when you use the File–Retrieve or File–Open command.

Whether you are saving or retrieving a non- Quattro Pro file, the file extension is of critical importance. The extension not only determines the format in which the file will be saved, but it is also what Quattro Pro looks for when you retrieve it. If a dBASE file does not have a DBF or DB2 extension, it cannot be retrieved. Quattro Pro can handle any of the file formats listed in Table 8.2.

Table 8.2: File Formats Saved and Retrieved by Quattro Pro

EXTENSION	FILE TYPE
DB	Paradox
DB2	dBASE II
DBF	dBASE III, III Plus, and IV
DIF	VisiCalc
RXD	Reflex, release 1
R2D	Reflex, release 2
SLK	Multiplan
WKS	Lotus 1-2-3, release 1A
WK1	Lotus 1-2-3 release 2.01 and 2.2
WK3	Lotus 1-2-3 release 3.0 and 3.1—must save in WK1 format
WKE	Lotus 1-2-3, academic

Table 8.2: File Formats Saved and Retrieved by Quattro Pro (continued)

EXTENSION	FILE TYPE
WRK	Symphony, release 1.2
WR1	Symphony, release 2.0
WKQ	Quattro 1
WQ1	Quattro Pro
WKP	Surpass
WK$	Lotus 1-2-3, release 1A, compressed with SQZ!
WK!	Lotus 1-2-3, release 2.01 and 2.2, compressed with SQZ!
WR$	Symphony, release 1.2, compressed with SQZ!
WR!	Symphony, release 2.0, compressed with SQZ!
WKZ	Quattro 1, compressed with SQZ!
WQ!	Quattro Pro, compressed with SQZ!

To bring a 1-2-3 release 3 worksheet into Quattro Pro, you must first save the worksheet as a WK1 file (release 2.2 format). Then retrieve the WK1 worksheet into Quattro Pro.

DEALING WITH LINKING FORMULAS IN LOTUS 1-2-3 2.2 SPREADSHEETS

If you retrieve a Lotus 1-2-3 release 2.2 worksheet into Quattro Pro version 1, any linking formulas will not be converted to the Quattro Pro linking syntax. For example, a linking formula that refers to cell A1 in a file named MYFILE would look like this in 1-2-3 release 2.2:

    +<<MYFILE>>A2

Quattro Pro version 1 would simply bring in the formula without converting it to valid linking syntax, so that it would appear like this:

    @@("<<MYFILE.WK1>>A1")

With Quattro Pro version 2, however, Lotus 2.2 links are converted to Quattro Pro links, so that the formula shown above appears like this:

    +[MYFILE]A1

Because Lotus 1-2-3 release 2.2 had to remain file compatible with release 2.01, it stores linking formulas in the same manner. You would see the same @@ function if you were to retrieve this 1-2-3 release 2.2 spreadsheet into 1-2-3 release 2.01.

When you retrieve a 1-2-3 release 2.2 worksheet that has one or more linking formulas, Quattro Pro offers the same menu of link options that is provided when you retrieve a linked Quattro Pro spreadsheet:

Refer to Chapter 11 for a discussion of linking formulas and your options when retrieving or saving a Quattro Pro spreadsheet that contains them.

- Load Supporting: Load all the spreadsheets that are referenced in the linking formulas and recalculate the linking formulas.

- Update Refs: Calculate the results of the linking formulas without loading the other spreadsheets.

- None: Ignore the linking formulas for now and do not update their values.

Quattro Pro version 2 will also retain linking formulas when you save your spreadsheet in a 1-2-3 release 2.2 format. Of course, those formulas must be valid for release 2.2 and contain just one external reference with no other formula components.

If you give a WK1 extension to such a spreadsheet, you will see the message

Formula with Hotlink translated to value. Save the file?

Your choices are Yes, No, or Use 2.2 Syntax (Quattro Pro version 1 options are just Yes and No).

If you choose Yes, Quattro Pro saves the spreadsheet but converts all linking formulas to the values of their results. This allows you to save a spreadsheet that can then be loaded into 1-2-3 release 2.01, which does not provide a linking syntax.

If you choose No, your spreadsheet will not be saved, but Quattro Pro will immediately prompt you with the message:

Warning, file has been erased. Please save again.

If you do not save the current spreadsheet, your previous work in the file on disk will be gone forever.

Choosing Use 2.2 Syntax converts any linking formulas to the 1-2-3 release 2.2 syntax. Just remember that linking formulas in Lotus 1-2-3 version 2.2 must contain only one external reference. A more complex linking formula in Quattro Pro will be converted to its value when saved as a Lotus 1-2-3 worksheet.

EXPORTING DATABASE FILES

When you see the database structure menu, the file has already been partially created on disk, and any existing file has been erased. If you choose Quit at this point, the previous version of the file will be gone, and no new version has been saved. When in doubt, it's best to save the file under a completely new name so you do not overwrite an existing database file.

When you are saving all or part of a spreadsheet to either a dBASE, Reflex, or Paradox file, Quattro Pro prompts you with a translator menu that contains the choices View Structure, Write, and Quit.

The Write choice proceeds with the save process, and the file is created. The Quit choice cancels the command and returns you to the spreadsheet in Ready mode.

The View Structure option displays a list of the database fields and data types that will be created. Each field is based on a column in the spreadsheet. The field name is taken from the column title, the width is taken from the column width or the longest entry in the column, and the data type is based on the first entry below the column title. An example is shown in Figure 8.4, in which a spreadsheet is being saved to a Paradox file.

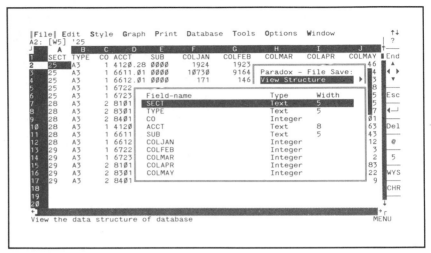

Figure 8.4: The database structure displayed by the View Structure option when creating a database file

From the View Structure display, you can change both the name and type of any field before the file is saved. Move the cursor through the list of field names, highlight the one you want to change, and press ↵. Another menu will appear with the choices Name and Type. If you want to change the name of the field, choose Name and enter the new name. Choose Type to change the field type, and yet another menu will appear, from which you can select the field type you want for this field. This menu is shown in Figure 8.5.

When you are exporting to a dBASE II file, you must use the extension DB2. Although both dBASE II and III use the same extension, DBF, Quattro Pro needs to use a unique extension for dBASE II in order to know you mean that version of the program. Therefore, once you have created a dBASE II file from your spreadsheet, you must rename the file with a DBF extension in order to use it with the dBASE II program. Use either the RENAME command at the DOS prompt or the File Manager's Edit–Rename command (discussed in the next chapter).

When you are retrieving a dBASE file from either dBASE II or III, you can leave the file extension as DBF.

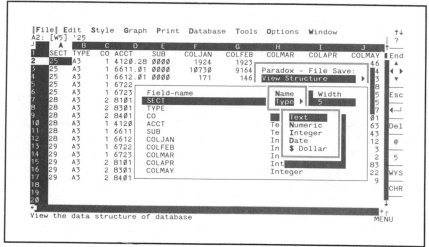

Figure 8.5: Choosing another field type for a field while saving a database file

IMPORTING TEXT FILES

In the last chapter, you learned that you can print your spreadsheet to a file and use that file in any program that imports plain text files. You can import text files into Quattro Pro by using the Tools–Import command.

The Tools–Import command is somewhat like the Tools–Combine command in that data from a file is combined into the cells of the current spreadsheet. However, the Tools–Import command deals only with text files. Most word processors can export a document to a text file. The resulting file will be almost completely unformatted, in that only text characters will remain.

If the data in the text file is formatted properly for a spreadsheet, Quattro Pro can break each item into a separate cell. This creates columns of text or numbers that can then be manipulated in the spreadsheet.

If the data is not correctly formatted, you can still bring it in so that each row is one long string of text. You can then use

A text file is the simplest file that you will find on a PC. It consists of nothing but rows of text characters. For example, your bootup files CONFIG.SYS and AUTOEXEC.BAT are text files, as are any batch files you might have on your system.

Quattro Pro's powerful Tools–Parse command to break each item into a separate cell, creating columns of data that can then be used in the normal fashion.

IMPORTING UNFORMATTED TEXT

The equivalent command in Lotus 1-2-3 is File–Import–Text.

It is easy to import text when formatting is not important, and each line of text will become a single entry in the spreadsheet. For example, if you export a document from your word processor, you could then import that text into Quattro Pro with the command Tools–Import–ASCII Text File.

You can experiment with this command by bringing in a text file from your disk. Use the following procedure to import the CONFIG.SYS file, which is in your root directory (if you don't have this file, you can substitute a batch or another text file).

1. On a blank spreadsheet, move the cell selector to cell B4 (an arbitrary location for this example).

2. Invoke the Tools–Import–ASCII Text File command.

3. Press Escape once or twice to clear the drive, path, and file filter from the prompt.

4. Type in the path and file name **C:\CONFIG.SYS**, and then press ↵.

If you spelled the name of the file correctly, the text from that file will be brought into the spreadsheet at cell B4. Figure 8.6 shows how this looks (although the text in your CONFIG.SYS file will be different). As you can see on the input line, the entry in cell B4 is one long string of text.

The Tools–Import–ASCII Text File command can handle lines as long as 254 characters. The lines in the text file end up as rows of long labels down a column in the spreadsheet, as you can see in the example. This is perfect for bringing in unformatted text, but it is impossible to perform any arithmetic with this data. Later in this chapter, you will learn how to split up lines of text into individual cells by using the Tools–Parse command.

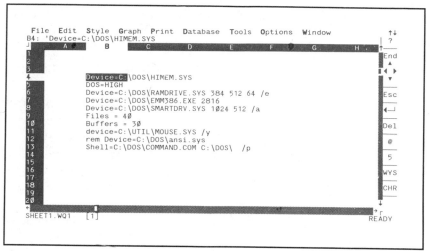

Figure 8.6: Importing a text file with the Tools–Import–ASCII Text File
command

IMPORTING FORMATTED TEXT

In Lotus 1-2-3, the
command is File–
Import–Numbers.

If you want to import text data into separate cells, the data
must be formatted in such a way that Quattro Pro knows how to
split the components. If the file is formatted properly, you can
use either the Tools–Import–Comma & " " Delimited File or
Tools–Import–Only Commas command.

Many programs can export data as a *comma and quote delimited
file*, sometimes called a *comma separated file*. This is a text file that
has unique data items within each line of text. Each item is
separated from the next with a comma, and text items are
enclosed in quotation marks.

Because commas
are used as delimit-
ers, do not use any com-
mas in numbers in the
text file to be imported.

For example, suppose that you wanted to import data col-
lected from a weather station. In the file, each row contains
weather information, including the weather station name, date,
time, temperature, pressure, humidity, and wind speed. This is
the type of data that you would want to break into individual
cells, so that the weather station name was in the first column,
the date in the second, the time in the third, and so on. In the

proper format, the text file might contain these lines of data:

"IW-099","11-Oct","03:25",52.4,29.45,48.7,12.4

"IW-103","12-Oct","14:07",68.9,29.6,36.3,8.5

If you used the Tools–Import–Comma & "" Delimited File command to import this file into Quattro Pro, the result would be as shown in Figure 8.7. The cell selector was on cell A6 when the command was invoked. As you can see on the input line for cell A6, each item from a line was split into a separate cell in a row.

PARSING UNFORMATTED DATA

If you have imported unformatted text (not comma and quote delimited) into Quattro Pro, it will just be a long string of characters. You can't manipulate the individual items because they are part of a single cell entry. To split each component of a long label into a separate cell, or *parse* the data, use the Tools–Parse command. You must specify the input block, which is the column of labels that make up the text data plus one row above it (you'll see why shortly), and the output block, which is the

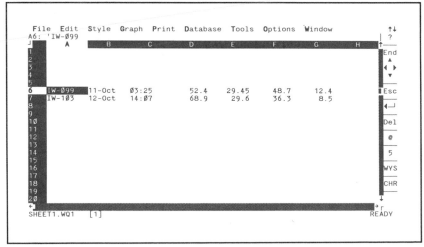

Figure 8.7: Importing formatted data that is split into individual cells

upper-left corner of the block where you want the parsed data to be copied. The output block will contain as many columns as there are data elements in each row of the input block.

The Create and Edit options on the Parse menu produce a format line, which is a special line of text that tells Quattro Pro how to parse each succeeding line in the data. You must have at least one format line in the first row of the input block, but you can include more lines in other rows within the data. Quattro Pro parses each row of data according to the format line above it. The Reset command simply resets all the options to their default values.

To demonstrate how the Tools–Parse command works, we will use a directory listing of files on your disk, which is not comma and quote delimited. After you import and parse the data, you could sort this list by date or time, or sum the total number of bytes used by these files. Follow these steps to create, import, and parse the file:

1. Invoke the File–Utilities–DOS Shell command to temporarily exit to the DOS prompt.

2. Type the DOS command **DIR > FILELIST.PRN** to create a text file named FILELIST.PRN that contains a directory listing of your Quattro Pro subdirectory.

3. Type **EXIT** to return to your spreadsheet in Quattro Pro.

You have just created a file on disk that has all the text that would normally be sent to the screen by the DIR command. Now you can import this file into the spreadsheet.

4. With the cell selector in cell A1, invoke the command Tools–Import–ASCII Text File.

5. Specify the name **FILELIST.PRN**, which should be in your Quattro Pro subdirectory. The file will be imported into the cells down column A.

6. Move the cell selector to the first file entry, which should be in cell A7.

Figure 8.8 shows a sample list of files (your list of files will be somewhat different). The input line reveals that each row is a long label.

7. With the cell selector still on the first file entry, in cell A7, invoke the Tools–Parse–Create command.

8. Select Quit from that menu.

The command inserts a new row and creates a format line that is based on the first row of data, as shown in Figure 8.9. This format line specifies how each row of data should be parsed into separate columns. A format line must begin with the nonprinting label prefix, the broken vertical bar.

The special characters on the format line indicate Quattro Pro's best guesses of the type of data that will be parsed. The following symbols are used on format lines:

- D: Recognizable date value

- L: Label

- T: Recognizable time value

- V: Numeric value

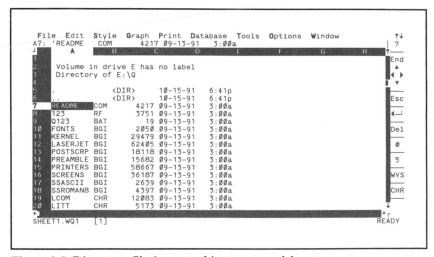

Figure 8.8: Directory file imported into a spreadsheet

- >: Item continues
- *: Ignores blank spaces
- S: Skips characters below

As you can see in the format line of Figure 8.9, Quattro Pro did not recognize the DOS date and time entries. This is because they do not appear in one of the styles used by Quattro Pro, such as 23-Jul-91. Instead, they have been designated as labels. The file size entries are marked as values. This is fine, but only four characters have been assigned to this column (>>>>) because the first file size is only four characters, 4217. However, there are larger file sizes in the list, which require a wider column in the format line.

EDITING A FORMAT LINE

Instead of editing a format line, you can insert a second one farther down in the data, which would define the parse for the rows below it.

You can create or edit a format line without using commands on the Parse menu, but it is generally more convenient to take advantage of this command's built-in capabilities. Follow these steps to modify the format line:

1. With the cell selector still on the format line, cell A7, invoke the Tools–Parse–Edit command.

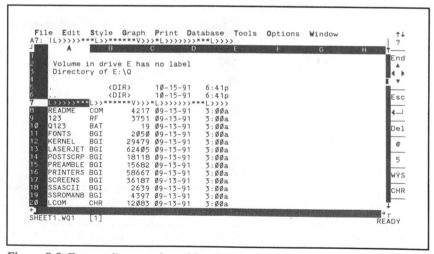

Figure 8.9: Format line produced by the Tools–Parse–Create command

2. Press ↓ several times to scroll the rows of data up to the format line. Look for the entry that has the largest file size.

3. Move the cursor to the file size column and type a **V** over the first digit of the largest file size.

4. Type a **>** over the * and old V to the right. Your screen should look like Figure 8.10 at this point.

5. Press ↵ to finish editing the line and accept the change.

6. Select the Tools–Parse–Input command, and specify the block that begins with the format line in cell A7 and ends with the last data-file entry in column A. There is no need to specify any other columns.

7. Specify the output block by indicating the upper-left cell of the block in which you want the data parsed and copied. You could choose a cell below the bottom of the file list.

8. Choose the Go command, and the job is finished.

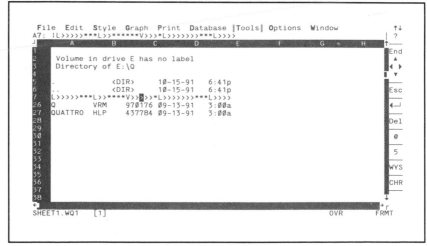

Figure 8.10: Editing the format line

9. Move the cell selector to the cell you chose as the output block. You will see that each item in each line of text has been parsed into a separate cell, as evidenced by the input line shown in Figure 8.11.

This process may seem like a lot of work, but it really isn't when you consider the tremendous amount of flexibility it can provide when your data is not in a comma and quote delimited format.

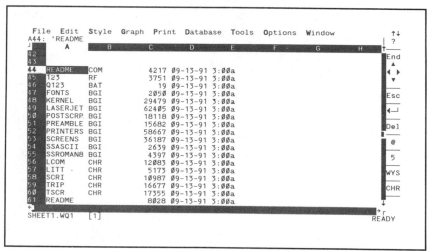

Figure 8.11: After parsing, each item is in a separate cell

EXITING TO DOS TEMPORARILY

You have already seen how convenient it is to temporarily return to DOS via the File–Utilities–DOS Shell command. A quick exit to the DOS prompt allows you to format a floppy disk, view a text file before importing it into Quattro Pro, or run another program. To return to Quattro Pro, you simply type the DOS command EXIT.

In the first two releases of Quattro Pro, the DOS Shell command takes you directly to the DOS prompt. In version 3, the DOS Shell command first prompts you for the name of a file to be run from DOS. You can enter the name of a DOS command, a program, or a batch file.

If you just press ↲ at the prompt without entering a name, the DOS prompt will appear. However, if you specify a program or DOS command, such as FORMAT, Quattro Pro will run it. After the program or command is executed, such as when the disk formatting is complete, you will be returned directly to Quattro Pro, without ever seeing the DOS prompt.

This additional step of specifying a program has tremendous potential. It allows you to create Quattro Pro macros that run programs outside Quattro Pro and then have control returned to them. For example, suppose that you write a macro in Quattro Pro that uses the DOS Shell command to run your telecommunications program. That program calls a telephone number and downloads information to your disk. When the program has finished, control returns to the macro in Quattro Pro. Finally, the macro imports the data from the disk into your spreadsheet. By taking advantage of this small feature, you can automate quite a bit of work.

When you use the DOS Shell command, there are a few caveats of which you should be aware:

- Remember that Quattro Pro and your spreadsheets are still in memory while you are at the DOS prompt. If any problems should occur, your work is in jeopardy of being lost.

- Although you do not have to save your work before invoking the DOS Shell command, you should do so if you are performing any long or involved operations outside Quattro Pro, such as running another program that could have problems of its own.

- You may have as much as 300K of RAM available at the DOS prompt, but that may not be enough to run a large program. If you do not have enough memory, you will have to return to Quattro Pro and exit from the program.

- Never run a memory-resident program while Quattro Pro is still in memory. This includes those that you

Your use of this small but powerful feature in the DOS Shell command will depend on your needs and your macro programming skills. Even if you don't use it today, keep this feature in your Quattro Pro tool box, where it could play an important role.

may not have considered as being memory-resident. For example, a mouse driver, the DOS PRINT command, and a screen-capture utility are all programs that remain in memory after they are run.

• If you loaded a memory-resident program after Quattro Pro, you may not be able to return to your spreadsheet—typing EXIT may not work. Even if you can access Quattro Pro, you may run into problems when you try to print, save your spreadsheet, or exit from the program.

You can use the File–Utilities–DOS Shell command frequently while working in Quattro Pro, but exercise a little caution while you are at the DOS prompt.

SAVING DISK SPACE WITH SQZ!

Quattro 1 came with an add-in called SQZ!, which is a file-compression utility designed specifically for spreadsheet files. SQZ! has been further integrated into Quattro Pro.

This very practical utility simply compresses your spreadsheet when you save it so that it takes up less space on disk. The amount of compression depends on the type of data that is saved. A compressed file is generally at least 40 percent smaller than the uncompressed file would be, so that a 100K spreadsheet would end up being about 60K.

By compressing a file, you can put a 500K spreadsheet on a 360K floppy disk, fit twice as many spreadsheets within a given space on your hard disk, and transmit a spreadsheet through a modem in half the time that would be required for an uncompressed file.

SQZ! compresses spreadsheets as they are saved to disk, and it does not affect the amount of RAM that a spreadsheet uses while it is in Quattro Pro. When a compressed file is retrieved, it is expanded back into a normal spreadsheet.

To have SQZ! compress your spreadsheet, just specify the file extension WQ!, and SQZ! will do the rest. You can also compress files for other spreadsheet formats by using one of the following valid file extensions:

- WQ!: Quattro Pro
- WKZ: Quattro 1
- WK$: Lotus 1-2-3 release 1A (WKS file)
- WK!: Lotus 1-2-3 release 2.01 and 2.2 (WK1 file)

Remember that a file that has been compressed with SQZ! is no longer a normal spreadsheet file. If you plan to use that file with another program, such as a database that can read spreadsheet data, you should not compress it. If you did, the other program would most likely not be able to interpret the file.

The File–Utilities–SQZ! command offers several options that affect the way SQZ! compresses your spreadsheets. The first two options give you the choice of losing some of the spreadsheet's components in order to compress the file even further.

The Remove Blanks option is by default set to No. If you change this to Yes, any cells that are empty but have been given a numeric format or are unprotected will be left out of the spreadsheet when it is saved. This not only saves space on disk, but it is also a good way to strip out any formatted but otherwise unused cells.

The Storage of Values option is by default set to Exact. The values referred to are those that are the results of formulas. Quattro Pro stores both the formula and its result when the spreadsheet is saved to disk. You can set this option to Remove to save formulas without their results. This conserves disk space, and the results will be recalculated when the spreadsheet is next retrieved. Your other choice is Approximate, which saves only 7 significant digits of formula results, instead of the usual 15. This does not compress the file as much, but it leaves the formula results within the file.

If your spreadsheet is set to Manual recalculation, all formulas will display zeros when you first retrieve the spreadsheet. Press F9 to recalculate them.

Finally, the Version option on the SQZ! menu lets you choose between SQZ! and SQZ! Plus. Use the second option, SQZ! Plus, unless you need to save a spreadsheet in a format that is compatible with the original version of SQZ!.

In this chapter, you learned how to manipulate files in Quattro Pro. A final reminder is that you should save your work on a regular basis. How often? Save your work whenever you feel that you would regret losing the work you have done since the last time you saved the spreadsheet. That may be every minute, or it might be every six hours. Most likely, it will be about every ten minutes.

In the next chapter, you will learn how the File Manager can be a ready assistant in handling your files.

Navigating Your Disks with the File Manager

Fast
Track

THE FILE MANAGER IS A BUILT-IN APPLICATION FOR helping you manage files on your hard disk and floppy disks. It is not specifically a spreadsheet tool, but Quattro Pro's ability to work with 32 files at a time makes it a most welcome feature.

OVERVIEW OF THE FILE MANAGER

Figure 9.1 shows a File Manager window that is currently logged onto the Quattro Pro subdirectory, named Q, on the E drive. This example shows all the major components of the window:

- The File Manager menu bar at the top of the screen is similar to the menu bar of a spreadsheet window. The mouse palette is on the right side of the screen.

- The Control pane is in the upper-left quadrant of the screen. The options in this pane control where the File Manager looks for files.

- The File List pane, below the Control pane, is where the files in the current location are displayed.

- The Tree pane, to the right of both of the other panes, displays a line-drawing representation of the subdirectory structure of the current drive.

In the same way that you can open multiple spreadsheet files, you can also open multiple File Manager windows. Each one can be showing the files on a different drive and subdirectory, or looking at the same location but filtering the file list in a different way.

OPENING A FILE MANAGER WINDOW

You open a File Manager window by invoking the File–Utilities–File Manager command. A new File Manager window will open, even if another File Manager window was already open. This command is similar to File–Open, which can open more than one spreadsheet window at a time.

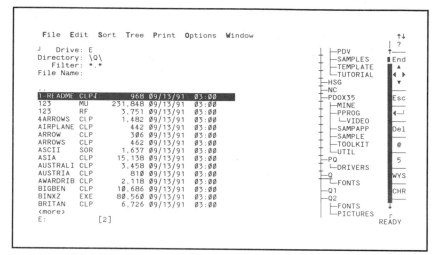

Figure 9.1: The File Manager window and its three panes: Control, File List, and Tree

You access a File Manager window in the same way that you access a spreadsheet window, which will be covered in detail in the next chapter. For example, you can press Alt and the number of the window, such as Alt-2, or invoke the Window–Pick command (Alt-0) and select the window from the list of all open windows. A File Manager window is named after the drive onto which it is logged, such as C: or E:, and will also be identified by its window number, such as [2] or [9].

With a mouse, if there are several windows displayed on the screen, you can simply click on the File Manager window to make it the active one.

Each File Manager window is separate and unique from the others. Each one can be logged onto a different drive and display a different list of files. Having more than one open at a time makes it very easy to perform file operations such as copying and backing up files. You can simply point to the source file in one window and the destination location in the other.

MOVING AMONG THE PANES

You can move between the File Manager window panes by pressing either the Tab or F6 key (or by clicking the mouse in the desired window). You will know which pane is active because the cursor appears in that window.

When you are finished working with the File Manager, you can go to another window, such as a spreadsheet, by using one of the methods described earlier.

USING MENU COMMANDS

The File Manager menu commands are oriented toward manipulating the components of the window and the files that are listed in it:

- File: Provides several choices that are found on the spreadsheet menu. It lets you open a spreadsheet or create a new one and close the current File Manager window or close all open windows. The commands Workspace, Utilities, and Exit are on this menu, too. There are also commands to make a subdirectory and read the disk again to refresh the display of files and subdirectories.

- Edit: Provides commands with which you can select one or more files, and then copy, move, rename, or erase them.

- Sort: Rearranges the list of files in the order you select.

- Tree: Lets you open, close, or resize the Tree pane. You may not want the Tree pane displayed all of the time because the process of reading your entire disk to determine the directory structure causes a delay.

- Print: Prints either the list of files or the subdirectory structure of the Tree pane.

⊙ The Options–Update command on the File Manager menu performs the same task as that command on the spreadsheet menu. All system settings in both the spreadsheet and File Manager menus are saved as the new defaults, so don't issue this command unless you are sure that all these settings are as you desire.

- Options: Provides some choices that are found on the spreadsheet menu and some that are not. All the options affect the overall use of the File Manager and can be used to set the system defaults for future sessions.

- Window: Offers the choices of switching windows and changing the size of or moving the current window (you cannot split the current window as you can for a spreadsheet).

Just as the menus are different, so are the function keys. The Help key is still F1, and F6 jumps the cursor between window panes, but all the other keys perform a different function (if they are used at all). You will see how the keys are used as each pane of the File Manager window is discussed.

SPECIFYING FILES IN THE CONTROL PANE

The Control pane is where you specify the drive and subdirectory to be viewed, as well as the file list filter. As shown in Figure 9.1, the Control pane contains four settings: Drive, Directory, Filter, and File Name.

SETTING THE DRIVE AND DIRECTORY

Each time you open a File Manager window, it reads the file list from the drive and directory specified by the Options–Startup–Directory command on the File Manager menu. This command has two choices, Previous and Current. By default, it is set to Previous, so that the File Manager always looks in the drive and subdirectory that was active during the previous session in the File Manager. If you change the setting to Current, the File Manager will always log onto the drive and directory that are current (the default) when the File Manager is loaded.

You can change the drive letter in the Drive option to any available disk drive on your system. Nothing happens until you either press ↵ or move the cursor to another item. Then the File Manager reads that disk and displays the files that it finds there, in whatever directory is currently active for that drive.

The Directory option in the Control pane shows the current subdirectory. You can change to a new one by editing it. You can also change to either the parent or a child directory of the current directory simply by picking the appropriate directory name from the list of files and subdirectories in the File List pane, as discussed shortly.

LIMITING THE FILE LIST WITH A FILTER

The Filter option determines what file names will be displayed in the File List pane. In Figure 9.1, the filter *.* uses the DOS wildcards that represent any and all characters in the file name and extension, so that all files will be displayed.

If you cannot find a file in the File List window that you are sure must be there, check the Filter setting in the Control pane—it may contain a filter that excludes the file for which you are searching.

You can edit the filter to display a revised list of files using any of the usual DOS characters, including wildcards. Here are some examples of filters and the file names they display:

- *.*: Any and all files.

- *.WK?: File names with an extension that begins with WK.

- *.?Q?: File names with a three-letter extension where the middle letter is Q.

- QTR?.WKQ: File names that begin with QTR plus any one character, with an extension of WKQ.

- QTR*.WKQ: File names that begin with QTR plus one to five characters, with an extension of WKQ.

- MYFILE.PRN: The single file named MYFILE.PRN.

Unlike file filters in DOS, you can specify more than one filter by separating them with a comma. For example, to display all files that have a WQ1 extension as well as all files that have a PRN extension, you would use the filter *.WQ1,*.PRN.

You can also specify those files that you do not want to see by enclosing the filter within square brackets. For example, specifying [*.WK1] means that all files except those with a WK1 extension will be shown. You can combine filters to create a very specific list of files:

    .WQ1,.WKQ,[MY*.*]

This filter will list all Quattro Pro (WQ1) and Quattro 1 (WKQ) files, but no files that begin with MY.

FINDING FILES

No matter what pane the cursor is in, you can press Shift-Tab to send it directly to the File Name option.

The final setting in the Control pane is File Name. By default it has no entry. When you type a character here, the cursor will jump to the first file name in the File List pane that begins with that character. Type a second character, and the cursor will again move to the first file that begins with both of those characters. In this way, you can search for the file you want in the current subdirectory. You can also include wildcards in the name you type to make the search more general.

If you don't find the file you want in the current directory, you can have the File Manager search for it in all the directories on the current drive. Simply type the name, or as much of it as you can remember, and then press F5. The File Manager will search through all directories on the disk. When it finds the file, it will display the files for that subdirectory, with the cursor highlighting the specified file.

When you type the name of a spreadsheet file into the File Name option and press ↵, Quattro Pro will open that spreadsheet. This is the same as using the File–Open command. Unlike that command, however, if you specify a name that does not exist, the File Manager will create a new, blank spreadsheet under that name.

MANIPULATING FILES IN THE FILE LIST PANE

The File List pane displays the files and subdirectories that were found on the current drive and directory. The contents of the list are also determined by the Filter setting, which may be filtering out certain names.

ELEMENTS OF THE FILE LIST PANE

The list of files in this pane is made up of five columns. From left to right, these columns contain the file names, extensions, size, and the date and time they were created.

By default, any subdirectories are shown after any files, and all the items in either of these sections are arranged in alphabetical order. The first entry is always the twin periods, .., which represent the parent directory of the current subdirectory. When you are looking at the root-level directory, the word *<ROOT>* appears in place of the two dots.

At the bottom of the list of files in Figure 9.1, you can see the word *<more>*. This indicates that there are more items on the list. You can view all the entries on the list by moving the cursor up or down, as follows:

↓ or →	Down one item
↑ or ←	Up one item
PgDn	Down a screen
PgUp	Up a screen
End	End of list
Home	Beginning of list

You can open any spreadsheet file on the list simply by highlighting it and pressing ↵. Later in this chapter, you will learn how to mark several spreadsheet files and open them all with one command. You will also learn how to perform DOS-type operations with the files on the list.

Figure 9.2 shows the file list from Figure 9.1, but this time the list has been filtered so that only files with an extension of COM are displayed. This makes a very short list of files, so that you can now see some disk-related information below the list:

4 of 128 Files 33,090 Bytes Used 6,520,832 Bytes Free

This indicates that there are 4 entries displayed in the list, out of a total of 128 entries in the current subdirectory; the total number of bytes used by the four files is 33,090; and 6,520,832 bytes are still available on the current drive. Knowing how many bytes are used is quite helpful if you are going to copy all these files to a floppy disk. The total size will tell you whether or not they are going to fit on one disk. Remember that this number will change depending on what you have specified for a file filter.

REARRANGING THE LIST OF FILES

The list of files and subdirectories gives you a dynamic view of the contents of your hard disk or floppy disk. The File Manager provides several means of arranging that list to make it even more useful.

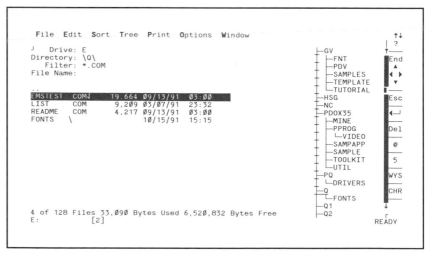

Figure 9.2: Disk information displayed in the File List pane

CHOOSING A VIEW

When you issue the DIR command at the DOS prompt, the list of files looks very similar to the list in the File List pane. When you include the parameter /W, the DIR command shows you a wide listing of files; only their names and extensions are shown, and many more file names can fit on the screen.

You can change the display of the files in the File List pane in the same way. The Options–File List command has the choices Wide View and Full View. Figures 9.1 and 9.2 show the list in full view. Choose Wide View to display more files, listed without their size and date and time of creation.

SORTING THE LIST

You can also sort the list of files. Note that you are sorting just the list as it appears in the File List pane, not the actual directory listing on disk.

The Sort command offers five choices: Name, Timestamp, Extension, Size, and DOS Order. Choosing one of the first four choices will arrange the list by the corresponding element in each file. For example, choosing Size will arrange the list in order of file size, with the smallest files at the top and the largest files at the bottom.

The DOS Order choice simply displays the files in the order in which they appear on disk—in the order you would see them with the DOS DIR command.

REFRESHING THE LIST

When you are working in a spreadsheet, F9 serves as the Calc key. In the File Manager, this function key invokes the File–Read Dir command, which performs a similar task. It refreshes the list of files by reading the current disk and updating the list.

This is especially useful when you are logged onto a floppy disk drive. The File Manager won't know when you put in a new disk, so that is the time to press F9 and have the File Manager read the disk and display the list of files that it finds there.

If you temporarily exit to DOS and perform some file operations there, when you return to Quattro Pro and the File Manager, you will need to press F9 so that the changes you made to the disk will be included in the file list.

DEALING WITH DIRECTORIES IN THE TREE PANE

The Tree pane occupies the right half of the screen in Figure 9.1. It displays the entire subdirectory structure for the current drive. The root level is at the top, and subdirectories appear down the tree, with each one's child subdirectories branching to the right below it. The current directory, as specified in the Control pane, will be highlighted in the Tree pane. The order of the subdirectories in the list is determined by the Sort command.

The Tree pane's visual statement is its strongest point. In one simple diagram is contained the otherwise hidden structure of your hard disk, a structure that you never really see but must contend with daily.

Note that you can create a new subdirectory on the active disk with the File–Make Dir command. The directory will be made within the current subdirectory, the one that is shown in the Directory option in the Control pane.

To delete a directory, the directory must first be empty of any files or subdirectories. Then use the Edit–Erase command to remove it.

ACCESSING THE TREE PANE

The commands Tree–Open and Tree–Close let you choose whether or not the Tree pane should be displayed. Whenever you open a new File Manager window, log onto another disk, or invoke the File–Read Dir command (F9), the File Manager must read the subdirectory structure of the entire disk in order to draw the tree. This can take some time on a heavily populated disk (perhaps up to 10 or 15 seconds).

If the Tree pane appears below the File List pane, it is because the File Manager is not zoomed to its full size. Use the Window–Zoom command (Alt-F6) or click on the zoom box with your mouse, and the Tree pane will be moved to the right side of the screen.

Besides the delay when first drawing the tree, the tree also takes up room on the screen and may detract from your use of the file list. Therefore, you may want to use the Tree pane selectively. Remove it from the screen with the Tree–Close command, and open it only when you need it.

You can also adjust the size of the Tree pane to suit your needs. The Tree–Resize command prompts you to enter a percent, and then sizes the Tree pane as that percent of the File Manager window. Fifty percent is a reasonable size that usually leaves plenty of room for the File List pane, although you might want to make the Tree pane larger if you have many levels of subdirectories.

MOVING THROUGH THE TREE PANE

Besides offering a visual representation of the subdirectory structure of your disk, the Tree pane also lets you access them. Instead of typing the path into the Directory option of the Control pane, you can simply pick the one you want from the tree.

Without a mouse, the process of moving past subdirectories can be somewhat slow. This is because the files in each subdirectory you pass are displayed in the File List pane, and this takes a second to process.

With the Tree pane active (press F6, Tab, or click with your mouse), you can simply use ↓ or ↑ to move the cursor through the list until you have highlighted the subdirectory you want. To go into a subdirectory to access its own subdirectories, press →. To move back out of a subdirectory to its parent, press ←. As you move to a new subdirectory in the tree, the Directory option in the Control pane will reflect the change.

If you have a mouse, you will find it even easier to navigate through your tree. If the subdirectory you want is visible on the tree, simply point at it and click the mouse, and that subdirectory becomes the current one.

If the subdirectory you want is not on the visible part of the tree, you will have to scroll through the tree until the one you want appears. Use ↑ or ↓, or hold down the mouse button and drag either to the top of the pane to scroll upwards, or to the bottom to scroll downwards. Note that the mouse scroll bar on the right side of the screen is used only for the File List pane. You cannot use it to move through the Tree pane.

ACTING ON FILES

If you have marked several files, you can open them all by invoking the File–Open command once. This is a quick way to open multiple files when you have not already saved a workspace that includes them. You can also perform DOS-style operations on one or more marked files, including copying, erasing, renaming, and even moving—something you can't do from the DOS prompt.

Before you can perform these file operations, however, you must indicate the files on which you want to act.

SELECTING FILES

The simplest way to select a file is to highlight it in the list of files. You will notice that a small check mark appears next to the extension of the highlighted file.

You can select more than one file at a time by marking each file. Highlight a file and invoke the Edit–Select File command, or press either the + key or Shift-F7. With a mouse, just click on the file. Note that when you have multiple File Manager windows open, you can mark files in only one window at a time.

When you move the cursor off the selected file name, you will see that the name is now in a different color than the other names on the list (or in boldfaced type on a monochrome system). The file has been marked, but note that the file that is currently highlighted by the cursor is also a marked file. Even though you haven't specifically marked it, the fact that it is highlighted means it has been selected.

The Edit–Select File command is a toggle, so that you can unmark a file by highlighting it and again invoking the command or one of its shortcuts.

You can use the Edit–All Select command (Alt-F7) to mark every file shown in the list (or unmark them all if some are already marked). This is a very handy command when you have filtered the file list so that only those files that you want to use are shown. You can mark them all in one step.

Because a command will work on all marked files, use caution when invoking a destructive command such as Erase. You may have accidentally marked files that you do not want included in the operation. Verify which files will be affected before you invoke the command.

It is also useful when you have filtered the list as much as you can, and although you want most of the files, there are still a few that you don't want included in the group. In that case, just issue the Edit–All Select command to mark them all as a group. Then unmark each of the files that you don't want.

ERASING FILES

The simplest file command is Edit–Erase (Del). If no other files are marked, it will erase the file that is currently highlighted. Before it does, however, it will offer a Yes/No menu so that you can confirm the erasure. Once erased, a file is gone forever, so use caution.

Remember that you can also erase subdirectories with this command. The subdirectories must be empty, without any files or other subdirectories.

If you have marked several files, all of them will be erased as soon as you respond with Yes to the confirmation menu. You will not be asked to confirm each one. *Do not* accidentally use the Edit–All Select command and then choose Edit–Erase!

COPYING FILES

When you invoke the Edit–Copy command (Shift-F9), the File Manager issues a short beep (or click), and the file names of all marked files are immediately copied to a behind-the-scenes area called the *paste buffer*. The source file names will remain highlighted in the list, and you won't see them anywhere else. With the names waiting in the paste buffer, you then change to the destination drive or directory.

Once you are logged onto the destination location, invoke the Edit–Paste command (Shift-F10). The File Manager will copy each of the files named in the paste buffer to this location. Unlike the DOS COPY command, you cannot rename the files in the process of copying them (but you can with the Edit–Duplicate command, discussed shortly).

It's very convenient to have two File Manager windows open before you copy any files. Set one window to the source location and the other to the destination. Figure 9.3 demonstrates this. The File Manager window number 2, on the left side of the screen, is the active window, and it is logged onto the E drive in the Q subdirectory. The file list has been filtered so that only files with a name that begins with an S and ends with a WQ1 extension are shown, except for those named SLIDES. By filtering the list so tightly (only 4 files, plus 1 subdirectory, out of 128 are displayed), it is a quick job to mark all the files in the list (they are all highlighted in the figure). That's much easier than looking through 128 files for the 4 that you want.

Figure 9.4 shows the result of copying the marked files to the other File Manager window, number 3, on the right side of the screen, which is logged onto the G drive. Their names now appear in the File List pane of this window.

MOVING FILES

When you want to move a file to a new location, you normally have to copy it there first, and then delete it from the source location. In Quattro Pro, you can perform this operation in one step with the File Manager's Edit–Move command (Shift-F8).

Just as with the Edit–Copy command, first mark those files that you want moved. Change to the destination location and

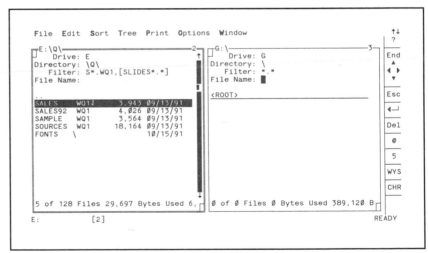

Figure 9.3: Copying files between two File Manager windows

invoke the Edit–Paste command (Shift-F10). The marked files will be moved to the new location, and they will be gone from the source location.

DUPLICATING FILES

The Edit–Duplicate command works very much like the DOS COPY command, except it works with only one file at a time. It does not use the paste buffer during the duplication process.

Highlight the file you want to duplicate and invoke the Edit–Duplicate command. You will be prompted to type in the new name. You can include a new drive, path, and file extension as well, just as you can with the DOS COPY command.

The file will be duplicated under the name you specify. If you are duplicating spreadsheet or database files that will be used by Quattro Pro, you should not change their file extensions; otherwise, Quattro Pro might not be able to identify the type of file when you later try to open it.

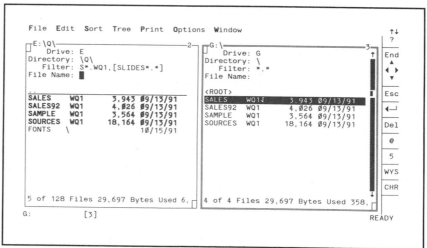

Figure 9.4: The copied files in the second File Manager window

RENAMING FILES

The Edit–Rename command (F2) is somewhat like the DOS RENAME command. This command operates on only one file at a time, but you can include a new drive and subdirectory in the name, which is equivalent to moving the file to that new location.

Highlight the file you want to rename, invoke the Edit–Rename command, and you will be prompted to enter the new name. Type the name, press ↵, and the job is done.

As with the Duplicate command, you should avoid changing the file extension of a spreadsheet or database file that will be used by Quattro Pro.

PRINTING A FILE LIST OR TREE

The Print menu in the File Manager is similar to the one in the spreadsheet window, but the block you select with the Print–Block command is not a spreadsheet. Instead, you can print the list of files in the File List pane, the subdirectory tree in the Tree pane, or both.

With the Print–Destination command, you can choose to send the output to either the printer or to a text file (not to a binary file). The options on the Print–Page Layout menu let you adjust the layout of the printed page.

Note that you cannot choose to send the output to the graphics printer. If you really need a fancy printout, print the file list or tree to a text file, and then use the Tools–Import–ASCII Text File command to import the file into a spreadsheet. Then you can print the file list or tree from your spreadsheet in any style you want.

This chapter has shown you how to take advantage of the File Manager so that you can integrate it with your day-to-day use of Quattro Pro. The next chapter will delve into the many ways that you can use multiple windows in Quattro Pro.

10

Arranging Your Work in Windows

Fast
Track

PERHAPS THE MOST POWERFUL FEATURE OF QUATTRO Pro, and the one that separates it from much of the competition, is its ability to work with multiple windows. In the example in Chapter 2, you saw how easy it is to open more than one spreadsheet window at a time and link one to data in another. In the last chapter, you saw how you can open multiple File Manager windows and perform file operations between them.

Now we will examine the ways you can manipulate windows while working with spreadsheets or the File Manager. The discussion includes the methods to size and move a window, select a window, split a window into two panes, lock row or column titles on the screen, and use the Map View command to inspect your spreadsheet.

ADJUSTING A WINDOW'S SIZE AND POSITION

In Quattro Pro, you view a small portion of the spreadsheet through a window. The window delimits the size and shape of the visible portion of the spreadsheet.

When you first enter Quattro Pro in text mode, the spreadsheet is in a full-sized window. This allows you to see twenty rows and eight columns, each of which is nine characters wide. If you open a second spreadsheet with either the File–New or File–Open command, that spreadsheet will also be full size, and it will overlay and hide the first spreadsheet.

You can easily move back and forth between the two windows, which will be discussed later in this chapter, but you may want to see both windows at the same time. In order to do so, you must make one or both of the windows less than full size. You can use the cursor-control keys on the keyboard or your mouse to make the change.

SIZING AND
MOVING A WINDOW WITH THE KEYBOARD

You use the Window–Move/Size command (Ctrl-R) to change the size or position of both spreadsheet and File Manager windows on the Quattro Pro screen.

Let's adjust the size of one window by using the keyboard. Start with a single, blank worksheet and follow these steps:

1. Use the Window–Move/Size command or press Ctrl-R. You will see the Move indicator appear in the upper-left corner of the spreadsheet. Since the window is already full size, you cannot move it until you first resize it.

2. Press the Scroll Lock key, and the indicator will change to Size. Now you can use the cursor-control keys to change the size of the window.

3. Press ← about 35 times, which will move the right edge of the window in toward the center of the screen.

4. Press ↑ about 10 times, which moves the bottom edge of the window up toward the center of the screen. Now the window fills up about a quarter of the screen, and we can move it to a new location. Let's put it in the lower-right quadrant of the screen.

5. Press Scroll Lock again so that the indicator changes back to Move.

6. Press → to move the window all the way to the right side of the screen.

7. Press ↓ to move it all the way to the bottom of the screen.

8. Press ↵ to complete the job.

Your screen should look like Figure 10.1, with the active spreadsheet's window filling the lower-right portion of the screen. The spreadsheet within this window is the same as it was before, only the viewing window has changed.

When the spreadsheet is in graphics (WYSIWYG) mode in Quattro Pro 3, you cannot move or adjust the size of a window. You can, however, use the Window–Tile command to view all open windows at the same time, as well as switch between them quickly.

You can resize and move a window in one step. Instead of using the arrow keys or a mouse, just press L for left, R for right, T for top, or B for bottom, and the window will immediately fill that portion of the screen.

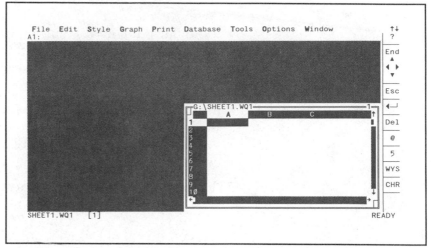

Figure 10.1: Adjusting the size and position of a window with the
Window–Move/Size command

Notice that once a window is no longer full size, it is enclosed in a double-lined box. On the left side of the top border is the file name associated with that window, and on the right side is the window's number. You can have as many as 32 windows open at the same time, so the window number and file name are important pieces of information.

SIZING AND MOVING A WINDOW WITH A MOUSE

If you have a mouse, you can quickly resize and move windows by dragging the resize box. Now let's see how easy it is to use a mouse to size a second window:

1. Use the File–New command to open a second worksheet. The new spreadsheet will fill the screen, completely hiding the first window.

2. Move the mouse pointer to the resize box, located in the lower-right corner of the spreadsheet, above the mode indicator. It is just to the right of the horizontal scroll bar's → and below the vertical scroll bar's ↓.

3. With the mouse pointer on the resize box, press and hold down the mouse button. Immediately, the window will be enclosed in a double-lined outline, and the Size indicator will appear. You can now resize the window.

4. While holding down the mouse button, drag the resize box to the left and up (toward the center of the screen) to shrink the width and height of the window. Move the lower-right corner of the window until the window fills the upper-left quadrant of the screen.

5. Release the mouse button, and the window is resized and relocated.

Your screen now looks like Figure 10.2. Notice that because the first window, in the lower-right corner of the screen, is an inactive window, it has a single-line border and no scroll bars. The second window is the active one, and therefore has a double-line border and two scroll bars. This is the window that will receive your keystrokes and be the target of any commands you issue.

It is easy to move the resized window with a mouse. You simply drag the window from any spot on it's outline (border). Let's

No matter which portion of the window border you drag, the entire window will be moved.

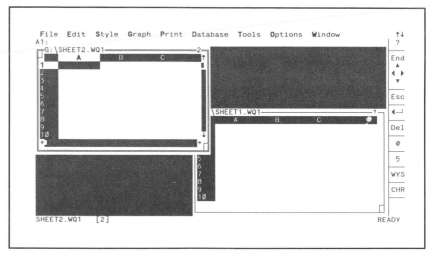

Figure 10.2: Two spreadsheet windows displayed on the screen

demonstrate by moving the second window.

6. Using your mouse, point to any part of the active window's double-line outline.

7. Press and hold down the mouse button. The Move indicator appears in the window.

8. Drag the window to a new position on the screen.

9. When the window is where you want it, release the mouse button.

It's that easy; the mouse is a great tool for this kind of task.

EXPANDING OR SHRINKING A WINDOW WITH THE ZOOM COMMAND

Remember, in order to change the size of a window, the spreadsheet display must be in a text mode, not graphics (WYSIWYG) mode.

You can use a shortcut to expand a window to full size. Instead of issuing the Window–Move/Size command or dragging the resize box with your mouse, you can invoke the Window–Zoom command (Alt-F6).

The Zoom command is a toggle command that expands a window or contracts it again. The first time you use the command, the active window expands so it occupies the entire screen, giving you a full view of the active spreadsheet. The next time you invoke the Zoom command for the same window, the window will shrink to the size it had been before you expanded it. If you use the Zoom command on a new full-size window that you have not yet resized, it will shrink the window to about a half of the screen.

You can also use your mouse to expand or contract a window. Just click on either the ↓ or ↑ in the zoom box in the upper-right corner of the screen.

ARRANGING WINDOWS WITH THE TILE AND STACK COMMANDS

When you are working with several windows on the screen, you may find it convenient to rearrange them by using either the Window–Tile (Ctrl-T) or Window–Stack command. These commands simply arrange all the windows in an orderly fashion so that you can see a portion of all of them at the same time.

The Window–Tile command sizes each window so that all share the screen equally. If you have just two windows open, this command will place one window on the left side of the screen and the second window on the right. With three windows open, two will share the right side of the screen, and one will occupy the left. With four windows, each will occupy one quadrant of the screen. With eleven windows open, the screen is arranged as shown in Figure 10.3.

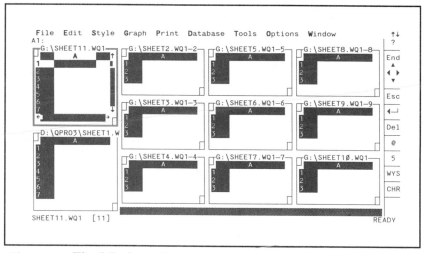

*Figure 10.3:*The Window–Tile command arranges all open windows

As you can see, the windows are laid out in an orderly fashion so that you can see the name of each one. On the other hand, there are only three cells shown in most of the windows, so you would probably not want to work in this layout for very long. With 32 windows tiled, there is even less to view of each window.

Use the Window–Tile command as a convenient way to get a quick view of all the windows that are currently open. You can choose the one you want (as explained in the next section), and then expand it to full size with the Window–Zoom command.

The Window–Stack command also arranges all the open windows in an orderly fashion, but it takes a different approach. Windows are overlaid, one on top of the other, like a deck of cards. The window on top is completely in view, although less than full size. The other windows are behind it, and they are hidden except for each one's top border, showing its name and window number.

Figure 10.4 shows the 11 windows from Figure 10.3 after they have been arranged with the Window–Stack command.

Just as with sizing and moving a window, the Window–Stack command only works when the spreadsheet display is in a text mode, not graphics (WYSIWYG) mode.

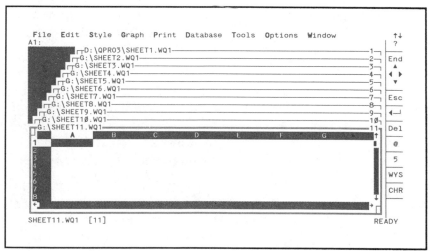

Figure 10.4: The Window–Stack command arranges all open windows in a stack

SELECTING A WINDOW

When you have more than one window open, only one of them is the active, or current, window. The others are inactive but accessible. It is the active one that has complete control of the program. All keystrokes that you type are sent to it, and menu commands you issue affect it only. When you want to access another spreadsheet, whether to view, change, or print it, you must make that window the active one. There are several ways to do this:

- Use the Window–Pick command (Alt-0), which offers a menu listing the names and window numbers of all open windows. Just highlight the window you want, press ↵, and that window will become the active one. If you had arranged the windows with the Window–Stack command, the window you pick will be displayed on top of the stack.

- Use the shortcut to reach any of the first nine windows that are open (those that are numbered 1 through 9). Simply press Alt and the window number, such as Alt-4 to activate window number 4. For windows numbered greater than 9, you must use the Window–Pick command's menu.

- Press Shift-F6, the Next Window key. It activates the next window in line. For example, when window 5 is active, pressing Shift-F6 activates window 6. When your windows are stacked, this is a convenient way to step through the stack, looking at each window in turn.

- Press F5, the Goto key. In response to the command's prompt, type the window's file name, enclosed in square brackets, and then specify a cell address or block name. For example, to go to cell M29 in an open spreadsheet named Mysheet, you would press F5, type: [Mysheet]M29, and then press ↵.

- With a mouse, you can activate any window that is visible on the screen simply by clicking on or within its borders.

You will learn more about referencing cells in other windows in the next chapter, which explains how to write linking formulas.

If the file you want to activate did not originate in the same drive and directory as that of the active window, you must include its path along with its name. For example, if the active window came from a subdirectory on your C drive and you want to activate the MYFILE file that came from the subdirectory DATA on your D drive, you would specify [D:\DATA\MYFILE]M29.

DEALING WITH PANES IN YOUR WINDOW

In Quattro Pro, you can split one window into two panes. Each pane can be positioned on a different portion of the spreadsheet, and you can choose to have them scroll together or independently.

SPLITTING A WINDOW INTO PANES

The Window–Options command provides the options Horizontal, to split the window horizontally (at a row), and Vertical, to split it vertically (at a column). When you choose either of these options, the window will be split in two, with the split occurring at the cell selector's location.

Figure 10.5 shows an example of splitting a screen into two horizontal panes of approximately the same size. The spreadsheet in the figure is the expanded Mileage spreadsheet (Figure 7.1), which demonstrated adding row and column headings when printing. The screen is split horizontally by a duplicate set

When splitting the screen horizontally, the cell selector must not be in the very first or last row on the screen. In order to create two panes, there must be at least one row between it and the edge. The same is true when splitting the screen vertically; there must be at least one column between the cell selector and the edge of the screen.

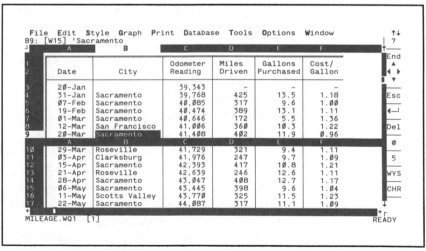

Figure 10.5: Splitting the screen horizontally with the Window–Options–Horizontal command

of column labels. Row 10 (where the cell selector was before the Window–Options–Horizontal command was issued) appears in the lower pane, and the cell selector is in the upper one, on row 9.

To move the cell selector to the lower window, just press function key F6, the Window key. To move back, press F6 again.

KEEPING PANES SYNCHRONIZED

The Sync option on the Window–Options menu sets each pane to scroll when the other is scrolled. By default, both panes are synchronized when you scroll through the spreadsheet, just as though you had previously used the Window–Options–Sync command. With the screen split horizontally, if you move the cell selector past a vertical edge of one pane so that its screen scrolls, the screen will also scroll in the other pane.

Synchronized windows are handy when your work area is larger than the dimensions of the screen, as is the one in Figure 10.5. In that spreadsheet, if you were to move the cell selector to column M in the upper pane, the lower pane would also scroll to column M.

When the window is not split into panes, the titles at the top of each column will disappear off the top of the screen when you scroll down past row 20, as will the rows of data in the upper portion of the spreadsheet. But with the window split into panes, you can keep two distant areas of the spreadsheet on the screen at the same time.

In Figure 10.6, the window is still split horizontally, but now the cell selector has been moved to the lower pane, and down to row 140 in column H. The upper window has scrolled to the right also, so that all columns are still aligned in both panes. You can see the top rows of data and the column titles in the upper pane, and the bottom rows of data and the totals in the lower pane.

When you move the cell selector from pane to pane while the panes are synchronized, it will always jump to the same column in the other pane. For example, in Figure 10.6, pressing F6 would send the cell selector from column H in the lower pane to column H in the upper one. If you then moved it to column C

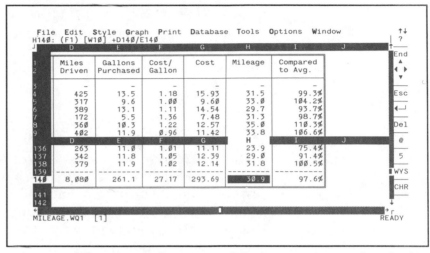

*Figure 10.6:*When you scroll one pane while the panes are synchronized, the other pane scrolls as well

in the upper pane, pressing F6 would send it back to column C in the lower pane.

The row to which the cell selector goes depends on the row it was in the last time it was in that pane. In Figure 10.6, the cell selector is in cell H140. If you jump the cell selector to the upper pane and move to column C, when you then press F6, the cell selector would jump to cell C140 in the lower pane.

WORKING WITH UNSYNCHRONIZED PANES

Invoking the Window–Options–Unsync command releases the tie between the panes. When you scroll one pane, the other will not be affected. Use this option to view two portions of the spreadsheet that do not share the same columns or rows.

For example, in Figure 10.6, you could leave the lower pane displaying the cells around cell H140, and then move to the upper pane and display the cells around cell A1. You would then see both portions on the screen at the same time.

When you move the cell selector between unsynchronized panes, it will always jump to the cell it occupied the previous time it was in that pane.

With the cell selector in cell H140 in the lower pane, you could press F6 and then move to cell IV1 in the upper pane. The lower pane would still be displaying the same cells, and if you press F6 again, the cell selector would return to cell H140 in the lower pane.

TAKING ADVANTAGE OF THE PANES

Besides allowing you to view or work in two distant areas of the same spreadsheet, a split screen can also assist you when you are carrying out Quattro Pro commands. Anytime you are specifying a block for a command, you can use the F6 key to jump to the other pane and point to a cell there. If you split the screen before you begin the command, you can arrange the panes so that the cells you need will be in easy reach.

Generally, you will want the panes synchronized when you are performing an operation along many cells in the same group of rows or columns. For example, suppose you wanted to copy several rows from the upper rows of Figure 10.6, such as the block A4..I6, to the bottom of the data, such as cell A136. With synchronized panes, it is easy to point to the source cells in the upper pane that start in column A, and then to the destination cell in the lower pane in column A.

On the other hand, you will want the panes unsynchronized when you are copying cells from two unrelated locations. You might, for example, have the upper pane displaying cell V1059 and the lower pane displaying cell C128, and then copy cells from one of those areas to the other.

CHANGING THE LOOK OF EACH PANE

When the window is split into panes, you can adjust the look of certain features in each one independently of the other.

SETTING GLOBAL EFFECTS IN ONE PANE

You can change the width of one or more columns in one pane, and the widths of those columns will remain unchanged in the other. You can also change global settings without affecting those settings in the other pane. These include the settings on the Options–Formats menu for global column width and cell format and alignment.

However, if you specifically apply a format or alignment to a cell or block of cells (using the Style–Numeric Format command, for example), that change affects the cell or block itself. The change will be visible no matter which pane happens to be displaying it.

HIDING THE BORDERS

The spreadsheet row identifiers to the left of each row and the column identifiers at the top of each column can be turned off by using the Window–Options–Row & Col Borders–Hide command. This command not only removes what may be unnecessary information from the screen, but it also allows a little more room for data to be displayed.

Normally, the largest window displays 72 characters across by 20 rows deep. With the row and column borders hidden, you can see 76 characters by 21 rows.

You certainly won't want to turn off the borders while you are building a spreadsheet, but you may later want to hide them in order to enhance the appearance of your work. This is especially so if you have written an application that will be used by others, including macros to handle most of the routines. Turning off the borders allows you to customize the look of your work. For example, you could turn the borders off in the lower window and display a message there while the user works in the upper window.

To redisplay the borders, use the Window–Options–Row & Col Borders–Display command.

Note that when the window is split, the Hide command, like most of the other global formatting commands, affects only the pane in which the cell selector was positioned when the command was issued.

HIDING THE GRID LINES

When you are working in graphics (WYSIWYG) mode, you can use the Window–Options–Grid Lines–Hide command to remove the spreadsheet grid lines from the screen display. Unlike the other commands on the Window–Options menu, this command affects both panes of the active window. Use the Display command on the Grid Lines menu to once again bring the spreadsheet grid lines into view.

CLEARING THE PANES

You can remove the panes and return to a single window by using the Window–Options–Clear command. The screen will revert to displaying the section of the spreadsheet that had been displayed in either the upper pane when split horizontally, or the left pane when split vertically.

Any column width settings, as well as all global settings for column widths and cell formats and alignment, will revert to those that were in effect in the upper or left pane. In that sense, the upper or left panes are dominant over the lower or right panes.

LOCKING TITLES IN THE WINDOW

You don't have to split the window into panes in order to display a work area's column titles while you are working many rows below them. Instead, you can use the Window–Options–Locked Titles command to lock rows (or columns) at the top (or left side) of the screen. Choose Horizontal, Vertical, or Both.

For example, the spreadsheet in Figure 10.5 has column titles in rows 1 and 2 and is 140 rows deep. Without splitting the window, you could freeze the column titles at the top of the screen, and they would not scroll out of sight as you move the cell selector down to rows below row 20. You would move the cell selector to row 3 and issue the Window–Options–Locked Titles–Horizontal command.

The line drawing below row 2 does not stay locked in place with row 2 itself. Quattro Pro considers the line to be a top line for row 3.

If you have a color monitor, you will see that a different color is used for the entries in the cells within locked titles (rows 1 and 2). Otherwise, you wouldn't notice any difference in the display until you tried to move the cell selector up to cell A2. Then Quattro Pro would beep to tell you that you reached the upper limits of the spreadsheet. Row 3 is now the top row of the spreadsheet—rows 1 and 2 are locked in as titles.

When you moved the cell selector down past row 20, you would see that rows 1 and 2 remain at the top of the screen, locked in place. Figure 10.7 shows the spreadsheet scrolled all the way to the bottom of this data, row 140, and out to column H. The column titles remain locked in place so you can navigate the depths of your data.

To clear the locked titles, invoke the Window–Options–Locked Titles–Clear command. The spreadsheet display will return to normal.

You can also lock in one or more columns on the left side of the screen by using the Window–Options–Locked Titles–Vertical command. This allows you to scroll far to the right while having the column labels on the left remain on the screen.

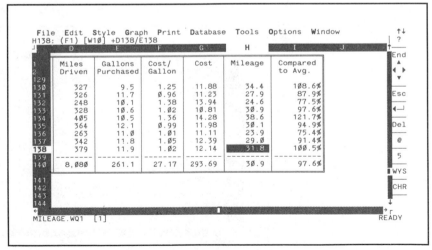

Figure 10.7: Locking in column titles with the Window–Options–Locked Titles–Horizontal command

Finally, you can choose the Both option, which locks in the rows above and the columns to the left of the cell selector. For example, for the spreadsheet in Figure 10.5, you might set both titles while the cell selector is on cell C3. This would lock rows 1 and 2 at the top of the screen, and columns A and B on the left side. Now when you scrolled down to cell H140, you would have both column and row titles to indicate your position in the data. Figure 10.8 shows how this would look.

When you have locked titles on the screen, the rows above, if horizontal, or to the left, if vertical, cannot be accessed simply by moving the cell selector to them. When you press the Home key, the cell selector does not jump to cell A1. Instead, it jumps to the first cell below any row titles (horizontal) and the first column to the right of any column titles (vertical).

This adds another advantage to locking titles. When you lock both row and column titles at the top-left corner of a data section in which you want to work, pressing Home will always return you to the top of your data.

However, whenever you are writing a formula, you can point to cells anywhere in the worksheet, including within the titles. This allows you to include any of those cells in your formula.

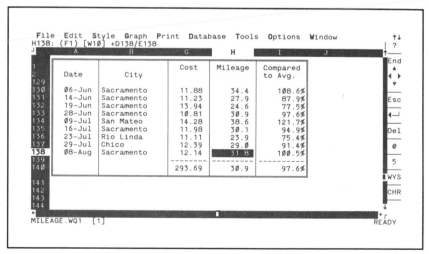

Figure 10.8: Locking both column and row titles

You can also use the Goto key (F5) to access cells in locked title areas. The cell selector will jump to the cell you choose, but the titles will still be locked in the same position. Therefore, you will see two images of those cells: one for the titles at the top (or left side) of the screen and another for the cells surrounding the cell selector.

You are free to move the cell selector anywhere you want once you have entered the titles area. But once you move the cell selector out of that area, you will again be locked out until you use the F5 key or point while writing a formula.

USING THE MAP VIEW TO SEE THE WHOLE PICTURE

The Window–Options–Map View–Yes command provides a fast and convenient way to survey a large area of your spreadsheet on one screen. The command has two effects: it shrinks all column widths to one character, and it changes the display to reflect the contents of each cell. There are six characters that are used to denote the cell contents of each occupied cell.

l   Label (or text)

n   Number

+   Formula

–   Linked formula

c   Circular formula

g   Graph inserted into spreadsheet

In Chapter 4, you saw how the map view can serve as an aid for tracking down formula cells that have been overwritten by numbers. In a block of cells that should be all formulas, and therefore displaying nothing but a + in each cell, a cell that contains a number will display an n and stand out from the rest.

You can extend the utility of the map view by viewing the same area of the spreadsheet in both normal and map view. Split the window either horizontally or vertically, and invoke the Window–Options–Map View–Yes command in one of the panes. The other pane will remain in its normal state.

If you leave the panes synchronized, as you scroll through the map, the other pane will scroll the corresponding cells into view. In this way, you can inspect any portion of the spreadsheet in both views.

Figure 10.9 shows the same spreadsheet as Figure 10.6, but this time the lower pane is in map view. The cell selector is still on cell H140, although it's difficult to see when the columns are so narrow.

To return to the normal view, just issue the command Window–Options–Map View–No.

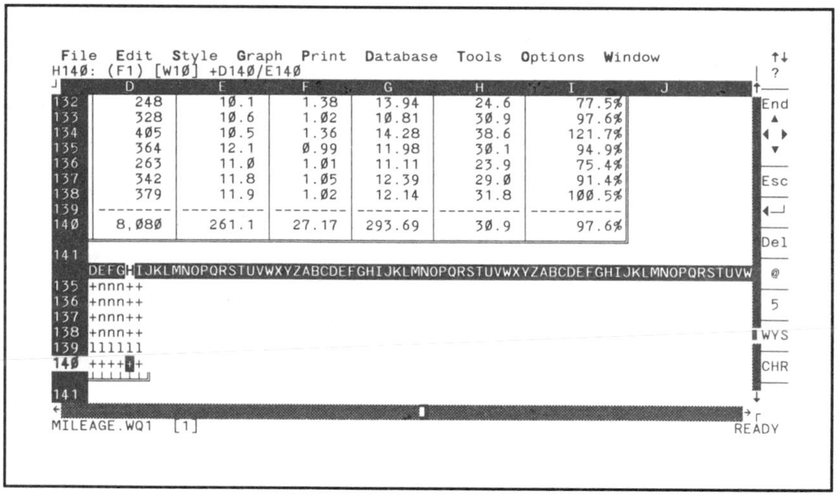

Figure 10.9: Inspecting the spreadsheet while one pane is in map view

You have seen how to open multiple spreadsheet files with the File–Open command; how to open one or more File Manager windows with the File–Utilities–File Manager command; and how to move among those windows, size and move them, split them into panes, lock titles, and inspect them in the map view.

In the next chapter, you will see how to write linking formulas that tie multiple spreadsheets together.

11

Using Formulas to Link Spreadsheets

Fast
Track

To create very long linked formulas,   **327**
    break the formula into several cells in order to stay within the
    254-character cell limit.

To bring in a large block of data,   **328**
    consider using the Tools–Combine command instead of link-
    ing formulas.

THE ABILITY TO WORK WITH MULTIPLE SPREADSHEETS brings with it the need to reference data in more than one spreadsheet. You do this in Quattro Pro through the use of linking formulas, which are formulas that refer to cells in other files.

Linking formulas have been mentioned in Chapter 2 (a linking formula was used in the Mileage spreadsheet) and Chapter 4. This chapter describes the components of linking formulas and how to write, update, and maintain them.

TAKING ADVANTAGE OF LINKING FORMULAS

The simplest of all formulas is one that refers to another cell in the current spreadsheet, such as +A1. A linking formula can be just as simple, except that it refers to a cell in another spreadsheet. In Quattro Pro, you enclose that spreadsheet's file name in square brackets, and then reference the cell in that file. Here's how you would refer to cell A1 in the file named Mywork:

+[MYWORK]A1

You can write a formula that refers to cells in an active spreadsheet (in memory) or one that resides on disk, so the formula shown above would be valid whether or not the file Mywork was in memory.

The power of linking formulas can be quite extensive. By using a linking formula, you avoid having to include data in one spreadsheet that exists in another. You save time by not having to reproduce the data, and you also save memory and disk space by avoiding duplication. With linking formulas, you can refer to megabytes of data, spread over many files, that you could never fit into a single spreadsheet.

Linking formulas allow you to refer to spreadsheets that have been updated by others but that you may never see. You can let the others perform their work in their spreadsheets, and let Quattro Pro handle the updating of your spreadsheet.

When many people must access the same table of information, they can do so with linking formulas to avoid having to bring the table into their spreadsheets. This means that one table can be updated on a regular basis to keep its data current, and all those with spreadsheets that refer to it get the most current information automatically.

CREATING A LINK

A linking formula behaves in essentially the same manner as a regular formula, and it follows all the rules that govern formulas (see Chapter 4). It has the same components as a regular formula, with the addition of one or more file references.

SPECIFYING THE FILE NAME

There are two ways to include a file name within a formula: type the name or point to the spreadsheet itself. You can type the name of the file whether or not that spreadsheet is currently open. Just be sure to enclose the file name within square brackets.

To point to the spreadsheet you want, the spreadsheet must be open. If you have a mouse, just click in the window that you want. With the keyboard, use the Window–Pick command (Shift-F5), press Alt and the window's number, or press Shift-F6 to rotate through the open windows until the one you want is active.

For example, if you are writing an @SUM formula in spreadsheet 1, and want to refer to the block G5..G20 in spreadsheet 5, named Yourfile, you could type the formula:

@SUM([YOURFILE]G5..G20)

Or you could point to the block in this manner:

1. Type **@SUM(** to begin the formula.

2. Point to the other spreadsheet, for example by pressing Alt-5.

3. Move the cell selector to cell G5 in that spreadsheet.

4. Press the period key to anchor the block.

5. Highlight the rest of the block, G5..G20.

6. Type the closing parenthesis, and the formula is finished.

Pointing is certainly the easiest method when the other spreadsheet is open. You avoid having to type the file reference.

SPECIFYING THE FILE NAME EXTENSION

When you refer to a file in a linking formula, you do not need to specify the file name extension unless it is different from that of the active spreadsheet. If all your spreadsheets use the WQ1 extension, you will never have to think about this. On the other hand, if you are linking to Lotus 1-2-3 or Quattro 1 spreadsheets, you will need to specify the WK1 or WKQ extensions.

This is especially important if the file to which you are linking resides on disk but is not open. If you forget to include the extension, you might end up referring to a Quattro Pro file of the same name, which could produce disastrous results without your even being aware of the mistake.

If Quattro Pro fails to find a spreadsheet with the name you specified and a WQ1 extension, it will issue an error message and prompt you to change the name.

SPECIFYING THE FILE'S PATH OF ORIGIN

If the spreadsheet to which you are linking originated in a drive or subdirectory that is different from the current spreadsheet, you must specify its complete path of origin.

For example, if the spreadsheet in the example above came from your D drive and the subdirectory named Qtr1, the formula would look like this:

@SUM([D:\QTR1\YOURFILE]G5..G20)

That is what you would have to enter if you were typing the formula. But when you point, Quattro Pro automatically includes the file's path if it is different from that of the current spreadsheet.

Therefore, when you are linking to other files, you might consider keeping them all in the same drive and subdirectory so you don't have to include a path in a linking formula. If you don't, you must not move any of the spreadsheets to a new location or rename them. Otherwise, when you later use your spreadsheet, the formula links will not be found.

CREATING LINKS WITH WILDCARDS

Suppose you have four spreadsheets open that are named Qtr1, Qtr2, Qtr3, and Qtr4. You now want to write a linking formula in a fifth spreadsheet, named Yearly, to total the cell B20 in each of them. You could write a formula that refers to each spreadsheet and cell, as in +[Qtr1]B20+[Qtr2]B20, or you could point to cell B20 in each of the spreadsheets.

An easier method would be to refer to all the files with one reference. You can do this by using a wildcard character in the file name reference.

As you may already know, when you are referring to file names in a DOS command or Quattro Pro file command, you can use the * to represent any and all characters and the ? to refer to any single character. This allows you to refer to a group of files with one command, and you can do the same thing with your link references.

To write the formula that refers to cell B20 in the four spreadsheets, you could type the formula +[Qtr?]B20, and the job would be done. Quattro Pro would check the name of each open file, and if it matched the filter you applied, it would include that spreadsheet in the formula. The result is the same, whether you had typed, pointed, or used the wildcard:

+[Qtr1]B20+[Qtr2]B20+[Qtr3]B20+[Qtr4]B20

In the Quattro Pro *User's Guide*, this technique is known as *3-D linking*, because with it you can refer to a "block" of spreadsheets with one reference.

All the spreadsheets should be laid out in precisely the same style, or your one reference will be picking different data from each spreadsheet. As with any formula, block names can come to the rescue.

If there are specific areas of each spreadsheet that you will later be referencing, you should consider giving those areas a block name in each file. Then each spreadsheet will contain the same name, and no matter where the named block might end up in each one, the linking formula will still be able to find it. In the formula above, if cell B20 were an important cell, you could have named it THISCELL. You would then write the formula as +[Qtr?]THISCELL.

A word of caution is now due. As shown in the above example, when you include wildcards in a link, Quattro Pro creates a formula that actually contains the file names of each file that matched the filter. The formula works fine, but it will no longer include any other files; it is now fixed.

For example, if you later created a new spreadsheet named Qtr5 and wanted to include it into the formula shown above, you would either have to write the formula again using the same wildcard or edit the existing formula and add the new reference.

CREATING LINKS PASSIVELY

Normally, you will create a linking formula by typing, pointing, or a combination of the two. You can also create one without necessarily intending to; Quattro Pro will work behind the scenes to set up formula links, even if you didn't know that they were necessary.

The situation arises when you have two or more open files and you move a formula or the cells it references (but not both) to the other file. If the cells to which the formula referred are not also moved to the second spreadsheet, you will have created a linking formula in the second spreadsheet.

For example, in Figure 11.1, the spreadsheet on the left contains a formula that sums the numbers above it. You can see the formula, @SUM(B2..B7), on the input line. If you moved the formula to the spreadsheet on the right, but not the data to which it refers, the result would be as shown in Figure 11.2. The input line shows that the formula still refers to the same cells: @SUM([SHEET1]B2..B7). The formula became a linking one because the cells are in the other file.

You can take advantage of this feature when you have many linking formulas to write. Create them in the spreadsheet to which they will refer, and then move them to the spreadsheet where the formulas belong. They will maintain their reference to the same cells and thereby become linking formulas.

> Remember that when you move a formula, it always maintains its references to precisely the same cells. It is only when you copy a formula that cell references will adjust.

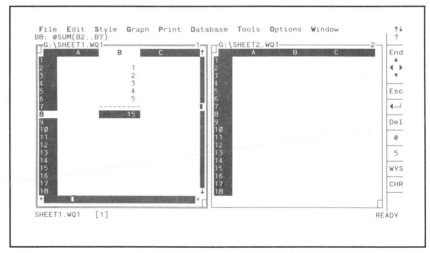

Figure 11.1: The formula references cells in its spreadsheet

USING RELATIVE AND ABSOLUTE REFERENCES

Like any other formulas, when a linking formula has a relative reference, such as +[Filename]A1, that reference will adjust when the formula is copied. For example, if you copied the preceding formula to the cell below, it would appear as +[Filename]A2.

You do not have to worry about whether the file name is absolute or relative—no matter how or where you copy the formula, it will always refer to the same file. Only its cell references can adjust.

You create an absolute reference in a linking formula cell address in the same way that you do for any other formula: put a dollar sign before the column or row (or both) of the address. To make the formula shown above an absolute reference, you would write it this way: +[Filename]$A$2.

When the file you want to reference in your linking formula is open, you may not know which cell or block address you want to reference. You may have forgotten, or that other spreadsheet may have been worked on by someone else since you last saw it.

You can avoid this problem by naming one cell, a *beacon cell,* in that spreadsheet. Write one formula that refers to the named cell, and you will now have a link to that location. You can then copy that formula to any other cells in the active spreadsheet, and it will adjust its references relative to its starting address with the named block.

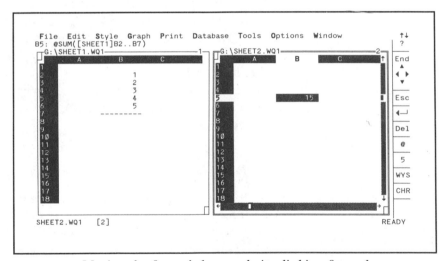

Figure 11.2: Moving the formula has made it a linking formula

KEEPING LINKS CURRENT

A formula that links to another spreadsheet is very much like a regular formula and, in fact, may contain many other formula components besides the link. But linking formulas go outside the spreadsheet for their source data, and therefore follow a different set of rules for calculations and updates.

RETRIEVING FILES THAT CONTAIN LINKS

Whenever you open a spreadsheet file that contains one or more linking formulas, Quattro Pro offers you a menu with the choices Load Supporting, Update Refs, and None. Selecting one of these tells Quattro Pro how to treat the links.

If you choose Load Supporting, all the spreadsheets to which the current spreadsheet is linked will be opened, too. The linking formulas will then be referring to spreadsheets that are in memory, and will be updated during normal spreadsheet recalculation.

If you want to update the linking formulas but do not want to open the supporting spreadsheets, you can choose Update Refs. The other spreadsheets will remain on disk, but Quattro Pro will read each file in order to evaluate the linking formulas.

If you have many linking formulas, updating their values may take time, so there may be occasions when you choose None. The linking formulas will now result in NA, indicating that their sources are not available. You can work on the spreadsheet, but remember that the results those formulas are displaying are not the correct ones.

UPDATING LINKS

Formulas that link to an active spreadsheet are evaluated during normal spreadsheet recalculation.

Once a spreadsheet is loaded into memory, you can evaluate its links at any time by using the Tools–Update Links command. This command provides the choices Open, Refresh, Change, and Delete. The first two options are equivalent to the Load Supporting and Update Ref options that are offered when you first open a spreadsheet that contains linking formulas. Either command will update all linking formulas in the spreadsheet.

If you are working on a stand-alone computer, there will probably be few times, if any, when this will be necessary. After all, who will be changing the source files while you are working in Quattro Pro?

If you are connected to a network, however, you may need to update all the linking formulas on a regular basis. Your spreadsheet may be linked to others that are also in use, so that the data in them can change at any time. In order to maintain the accuracy of your spreadsheet formulas, issue the Tools–Update Links–Refresh command. Do this whenever necessary, such as before printing or before performing any data analysis that uses those formulas.

If you have other spreadsheets that link to your current spreadsheet, you should also update all links before saving your work, so that their results are current.

CHANGING OR DELETING LINKS

File names are not necessarily static. You may need to rename a file or save a file under a new name. If the file is used in linking formulas, you would need to change the formulas so that they continue to reference the correct spreadsheet. You do this with the Tools–Update Links–Change command.

This command offers you a list of all spreadsheets to which the current one is linked. Pick the spreadsheet you no longer want referenced (highlight it on the list and press ↵ or click on it with your mouse).

You are then offered the usual file-selection prompt box, where you can either type in the name of a new spreadsheet or press Escape and then pick one from the menu of all files on disk. That file name will then appear in all the linking formulas which had previously linked the other file.

There may be other times when you will want to dissolve a link to another spreadsheet. Perhaps that file was lost (what, no backups?) or is no longer relevant. Use the Tools–Update Links– Delete command, which also displays a list of all the files to which the current one is linked.

To delete a single name, just highlight it and press ↵. You are offered a final No/Yes menu before the links are dissolved. You can delete more than one name with this command by marking each one. Just highlight it on the list and press Shift-F7, the

Select key. You can choose all the names on the list by pressing Alt-F7, the Select All key. Selected files will have a check mark next to their name.

After a file reference is deleted from the list, any formulas that had referred to that file will refer to ERR. You will have to edit them and either delete the reference or rewrite it so that it refers to another block or file.

You can use the Edit–Search & Replace command to find all files that refer to ERR.

AVOIDING PROBLEMS WITH LINKS

In Chapter 4, a few of the common recalculation problems that can be encountered with regular formulas were covered. Formulas that contain links have a few pitfalls of their own, as discussed in the following sections.

WATCHING THE CHAIN OF LINKS

One common problem with linking formulas occurs when you neglect to update one spreadsheet that is part of a chain of linked spreadsheets. Although the chain of links can be quite complex, a simple example will demonstrate the problem that can arise.

Three spreadsheets are linked in a chain: spreadsheet 1 has linking formulas that reference spreadsheet 2, and spreadsheet 2 has links to spreadsheet 3. If you update the information in spreadsheet 3, save the file, and then retrieve spreadsheet 1 (not 2), the results of spreadsheet 1 will not be accurate.

This is because it has links to spreadsheet 2, but that spreadsheet has not been opened since the changes were made to spreadsheet 3. Therefore, spreadsheet 1 is not getting the most current data.

The routine should have been:

1. Revise the data in spreadsheet 3 and save it to disk.

2. Open spreadsheet 2 and refresh its links, then save it to disk.

3. Open spreadsheet 1 and refresh its links.

It is very important that you keep this in mind because the problem will not make itself known. The linking formulas will be updated as always, but they will not be getting the most current information. If you use a standard set of linked spreadsheets, you might want to draw a simple map showing the spreadsheets upon which each one relies, or is dependent.

CREATING A LINK LIBRARY

Using a *link library,* which is simply a spreadsheet that contains links to other spreadsheets, not only saves you time writing your linking formulas, but also ensures that the links are all current.

When you created the Mileage spreadsheet in Chapter 2, you opened a second spreadsheet that contained a value representing a national mileage average. Suppose that other numbers for other comparison figures—nation-wide figures for the cost of gasoline per gallon, the average number of miles driven between fill-ups, average number of gallons purchased, and so on—were stored in several other spreadsheets.

Instead of writing a linking formula to find each of these figures in its own spreadsheet, you could create a link library containing formulas that link to each of the other spreadsheets. The Mileage spreadsheet (and any other spreadsheet that needed to reference those figures) could then refer strictly to the link library. Figure 11.3 shows how this link library might appear.

Each row of a small table contains the linking formula in column B. As you can see on the input line, the formula in cell B3 refers to the spreadsheet used in Chapter 2 and displays the number that represented the national mileage average.

To the left of each formula, in column A, is a short description of the formula. Each formula has been given a block name, which is shown to its right in column C. Columns A and C are just for reference while maintaining or adding to the list; they are not used by any linking formulas.

You could refer to the link library from any spreadsheet to reference these values. This saves you from having to remember the name and location of each of the source spreadsheets and

For Figure 11.3, instead of typing in the block name for each cell in column C, a formula was written that referred to the named cell in column B. Cell C3 has the formula +B3. The formula (in column C) was given a text numeric format so the block name appears exactly as it is spelled, which is why there is a + in front of each name in column C.

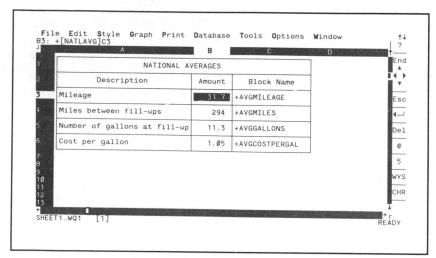

Figure 11.3: A table of linking formulas that are used as a link library

can simplify the formulas as well. But first you should ensure that the library had been opened and updated, so that all its links are current.

For example, suppose the national mileage average had come from four other spreadsheets, named North, South, East, and West. Each time you wanted to refer to a national average, you would have to refer to all four. Instead, do this once in the link library, and that figure is available for any other spreadsheets that need it. Not only that, if the formula for the average should change, you only need to modify it once in the link library. All the spreadsheets that refer to it will use the revised figure.

KEEPING SIGHT OF THE SOURCE DATA

Be careful not to move the linked data in the source spreadsheet unless the linking spreadsheet has also been loaded into Quattro Pro. When both spreadsheets are in memory, you can move a cell in one spreadsheet that is referenced in the linking formula, and the formula will follow that data to its new destination. But if the linking spreadsheet is not in memory, the cells will be moved without the formula "knowing" about it. The next time you open that spreadsheet, its linking formulas will still be referring to the same cells, not to the new location where the data was moved.

The problem is compounded by the fact that you will not get an error message because the formulas will still be working as they are supposed to. They will simply be referring to the wrong cells. Make sure you have the linking spreadsheet open when you make changes to any of the spreadsheets it references, or be prepared to rewrite the linking formulas the next time you open that spreadsheet.

You can avoid this problem if the linking formula refers only to named blocks in the source spreadsheet. You can then move the source blocks to a new location even when the linking spreadsheet is not open. When you later open that spreadsheet, the linking formulas will still be referring to the named blocks, which will be found, by name, in the source spreadsheet.

STAYING WITHIN THE 254-CHARACTER LIMIT

A cell entry in a Quattro Pro spreadsheet cannot be longer than 254 characters. You might run into this barrier when writing a linking formula that contains many file links or when the paths to the linked files are very long, such as

[D:\MYDATA\INCOME\JANUARY\SOMESHEET.WQ1].

The more files referenced in your linking formulas, the longer it will take to refresh them when you retrieve the spreadsheet or use the Tools–Update Links–Refresh command. Even simply editing such a formula may produce quite a delay when you press ↵ to place it back in the cell.

Even regular formulas can be cumbersome when they approach the 254-character limit, and the solution is the same for both types of formulas. If you really must refer to 63 other spreadsheets (the most you are allowed to reference), you can break a formula into several pieces, and then write another formula that works with the results of those pieces.

For example, suppose you split a formula among three others, in cells A1..A3. The first formula might refer to files 1 through 20, the second 21 through 40, and so on. A fourth formula could then be placed anywhere in the spreadsheet, and might, for example, total their results, as in @SUM(A1..A3).

AVOIDING LONG PATHS

⊙ A full eight charac-
ters is reserved for
the file name. So even
if you are referencing a
one-character file
name, you are still al-
lowed only 54 charac-
ters for the path
(another character is re-
quired for the period
between the name and
the extension).

Quattro Pro allows a maximum of 63 characters for a file's
name and path. If you try to reference one that exceeds that
maximum in a linking formula, you will see the message

    Path is too long

You probably won't run into this situation unless you are working
on a network or other large disk system where the subdirectories
run many levels deep. Generally, you will find that most computer
users have two or three levels of subdirectories, rarely four.

However, if the path is too long, you may have to copy the
source files to a directory higher up in the subdirectory tree, so
that the path will be shorter.

BRINGING IN LARGE BLOCKS WITHOUT USING LINKS

Linking formulas are so convenient that you may want to use
them under all conditions. But there are a few occasions on
which you might want to take another approach.

Formulas take up more memory than the values in which they
result, and they also require recalculation time. If you need to
reference a very large block of data in another spreadsheet, you
might consider bringing it in as a single block instead of writing
hundreds of linking formulas. There are two ways to do so:

▪ If the incoming
data contains for-
mulas that you do not
want evaluated in the
new spreadsheet, turn
those formulas into
values by using the
Edit–Values com-
mand, as discussed
in Chapter 5.

- Import the block using the Tools–Combine command,
  which generally is faster than using linking formulas to
  bring in the data. Furthermore, once the command is
  finished, it takes up no further recalculation time. The
  command lets you bring in a block from another file
  or the entire file.

- If you only need the data once and will not be updating
  it in the future, you can simply open the second file and
  copy the data that you want into the current spreadsheet.

If you find it both easy and convenient to write linking formulas, you can still use them even when the data will be brought in only once and will not need to be updated. Write the formulas so they capture the data you want, and then use the Edit–Values command to turn those formulas into values. Just specify the source block as the block of formulas and the destination as the upper-left cell of that same block, and the formulas will be replaced by their values.

Spreadsheet formulas allow you to access data in any other cell in the worksheet; linking formulas let you do the same for any other spreadsheet file. As with so many features of Quattro Pro, you never have to use linking formulas, but when you do, the horizons of the program are greatly extended.

In the next chapter, you will learn how to build graphs with your spreadsheet data. The process is easy, but the options are extensive (the Graph menu has the most levels of any of the menu commands).

Putting Your Data into Graphs

Fast
Track

YOU CAN USE QUATTRO PRO'S EXTENSIVE GRAPHICS capabilities to create graphs of your spreadsheet data. A graph can fulfill two essential purposes; it can both inform and dazzle.

This chapter covers the Graph menu commands and options. This is the largest menu in Quattro Pro, and it extends many levels deep. But don't feel as though you must learn everything on the menu before you can actually create a graph. Most of the choices are optional ones, which you can use to fine tune your graph.

A QUICK TOUR

This section takes you on a step-by-step tour of building a graph. It introduces Quattro Pro graphing in the same way that Chapter 2 introduced the process of building a spreadsheet.

We will create a pie graph using a single set of data. First, you must enter the data in a spreadsheet. Then you can use the Graph menu commands to plot the data.

1. On a blank spreadsheet, type the following entries:

CELL	ENTRY
A2	**Quarter**
A3	Fill the cell with a dashed line, \-
A4	**1st Qtr.**
A5	**2nd Qtr.**
A6	**3rd Qtr.**
A7	**4th Qtr.**
B2	**Data**
B3	Fill the cell with a dashed line, \-
B4	**301**
B5	**235**
B6	**365**
B7	**458**

Many of the Graph commands have their counterparts in Quattro 1, but the Graph–Annotate command is unique to Quattro Pro. With it, you can add many more enhancements to your graphs. The Graph Annotator is covered separately in the next chapter.

Your screen should look like the one shown in Figure 12.1.

2. Invoke the Graph–Graph Type command and choose Pie. (If you do not specify a graph type, Quattro Pro will automatically create a stacked-bar graph.)

3. Choose Quit from the Graph menu to return to Ready mode.

From this point, the graph you define will be drawn as a pie chart. But you can choose another graph type at any time and, with a few exceptions, Quattro Pro will simply incorporate all the current graph settings into that new graph type.

4. With the cell selector in cell B4, the first data cell, invoke the Graph command and select Series. On this menu you can specify any of six data blocks to be graphed. We will specify only one.

5. Choose 1st Series, and you will be prompted to specify the block of data.

6. Press the period key to anchor the block at cell B4.

7. Highlight the block B4..B7 and press ↲.

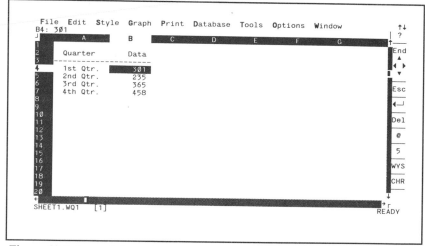

Figure 12.1: Spreadsheet data to be graphed

The address of the block you defined is now shown to the right of the 1st Series command. Now we are ready to view the graph.

8. Choose Quit from the Graph–Series menu.

9. Choose View from the Graph menu.

There are four wedges in the pie graph displayed on your screen; each one represents the amount in one of the cells. Quattro Pro identifies the percent that each wedge is of the whole. The graph is helpful, but the wedges should be identified.

10. Press any key to return to the spreadsheet. The Graph menu is still active. Select Series.

11. Choose X-Axis Series from the Series menu. This is the set of data that describes each of the wedges in the pie chart.

12. Specify the block A4..A7 and press ↵.

13. Choose Quit from the Series menu.

14. Choose View from the Graph menu.

Your graph should look like the one in Figure 12.2. The x-axis series serves to identify each of the data points in the graph, so that each wedge of the pie is now labeled with the text found in the adjoining cell in column A.

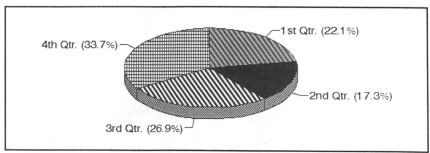

Figure 12.2: The pie chart after defining the data and x-axis

15. When you are finished viewing the graph, press any key to return to the Graph menu.

ADDING DESCRIPTIVE TEXT

There are many options for adding text to a graph. For our example, we'll add two title lines above the pie chart.

1. From the Graph menu, select Text.

2. Choose 1st Line.

3. Type the text to appear as a title at the top of the graph. If your imagination is running slowly, type **This is the First Line**, and then press ⏎.

4. Choose 2nd Line

5. Enter some text, such as **And Here is a Second Line**, and then press ⏎.

6. Choose Quit from the Text menu.

7. Choose View from the Graph menu.

Now your graph has two title lines, as shown in Figure 12.3. The first title is by default always in a larger font size than the second line. Because this is a pie chart, there are no other standard text categories available.

8. Press any key to return to the spreadsheet, and then choose Quit from the Graph menu to return to Ready mode.

ENHANCING THE GRAPH

The graph can be enhanced in many ways at this point, but do you want to spend minutes, hours, or days in the process? For this quick tour, we will be conservative and add just a few features. We will enclose the graph and its title in boxes and explode one of the pie wedges.

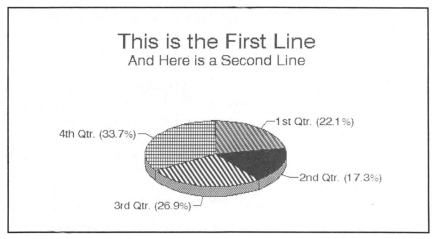

Figure 12.3: The graph with titles

1. Choose the Graph–Overall–Outlines–Graph command. You will see a list of different types of boxes.

2. Choose Rnd Rectangle to enclose the entire graph in a rectangle with rounded corners.

3. Choose Titles from the Outlines menu.

4. Choose Shadow to enclose the graph titles in a rectangle that has a shadow.

5. Select Quit from the Outlines menu.

6. Choose the Customize Series–Pies–Explode command from the Graph menu. You are offered a list of nine pie slices.

7. Choose 2nd Slice.

8. Choose Explode, so that this wedge will be separated from the rest of the pie.

9. Without leaving the Explode menu, press F10 to draw the graph. (You can press F10 at any time to draw the graph, you don't have to use the Graph–View command.)

10. When you are finished viewing the graph, press any key, and then press Ctrl-Break to return to Ready mode in one step.

Your graph should now look like the one in Figure 12.4, which is informative but not cluttered. Some of the many other enhancements we could have made include adjusting the font sizes in the titles, changing the colors used in the graph, and changing the cross-hatching used in the wedges.

SAVING AND PREVIEWING THE GRAPH

After you create a graph, you won't want to lose it. If you save the spreadsheet, the graph settings will all be remembered, so that the next time you retrieve the spreadsheet, you can again draw the graph.

You can run into a problem, however, if you want to define another graph, because there can be only one current graph at a time. But Quattro Pro offers a simple solution: you can give a

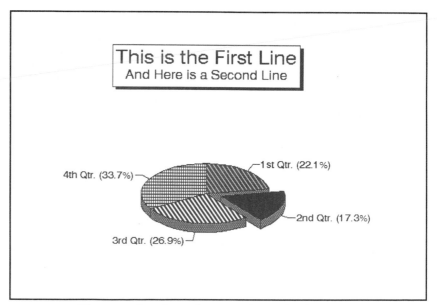

Figure 12.4: The completed graph: attractive and informative

graph a name, and then later recall that graph by its name. You can therefore store an unlimited number of graphs in each spreadsheet.

Now we will name the pie chart.

1. From Ready mode, invoke the Graph–Name–Create command.

2. Type the name **MYGRAPH** and press ↵.

3. Choose Quit to return to Ready mode.

You can create other graphs, and always return to the named graph by using the Graph–Name–Display command, which makes the named graph the current graph.

Now we will preview the graph by printing it to the screen.

4. Use the Print–Graph Print–Destination–Screen Preview command.

5. Choose Go from the Graph Print menu.

The screen preview shows you how the graph will look on the printed page, saving you both time and paper.

SELECTING A GRAPH TYPE

The type of graph you choose to create depends mainly on the type of data you will be graphing. Quattro Pro provides a wide variety of graph types, plus the ability to combine two graph types in one graph. You can also create text graphs, which do not plot data but allow you to create graphic presentation material from text, drawings, and pictures.

If you have created one type of graph, you can turn it into another type simply by selecting the option from the Graph–Graph Type menu. All the settings for the original graph will be relevant to the new type.

GRAPH COMPONENTS

The features of a line graph are quite representative of those in most of the other graphs, so we'll review the components of this type of graph. Figure 12.5 shows a line graph that plots two sets of data.

The *x-axis* is the horizontal line at the bottom of the graph, along which the various categories are laid out, such as the four quarters in Figure 12.5. The position of each category on the axis is identified with a *tick mark*. The *y-axis* is the vertical line on the left, to which the value of each data point is plotted. In the figure, the y-axis *scale* runs from 200 to 500.

There are four data points on each of the two graph lines in Figure 12.5, and each point represents one cell in the blocks that are being graphed. Data points may appear in any of the ten different styles available in Quattro Pro.

Text *titles* appear at the top of the screen, and there is also a title below the x-axis and to the left of the y-axis. Below the x-axis title is the graph *legend*, which is used to identify each of the two sets of data points (you can plot as many as six different sets of

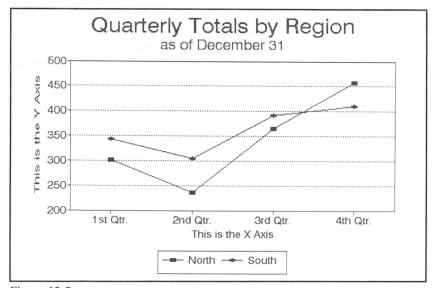

Figure 12.5: A line graph

data). Running from each number on the y-axis are the *grid* lines. These simply make it easier to identify the value of each data point within the graph.

The graph in Figure 12.5 is a simple one, with just a few of the many optional enhancements and features that are available. The other components your graphs may have are covered later in the chapter.

GRAPH TYPE SELECTIONS

You can choose from the following types of graphs:

Although a bar and line graph are interchangeable, when you are plotting several different data sets, a bar graph can become overcrowded. Try both types to see which looks best.

- Bar: A bar graph is built from bars that represent the data. Figure 12.6 shows the data for the line graph in Figure 12.5 as a bar graph. Because the bars are drawn from the lowest end of the y-axis (where it meets the x-axis), the y-axis scale usually starts at zero. A bar graph does not show trends as well as a line graph, but it does show the peaks and valleys along the x-axis.

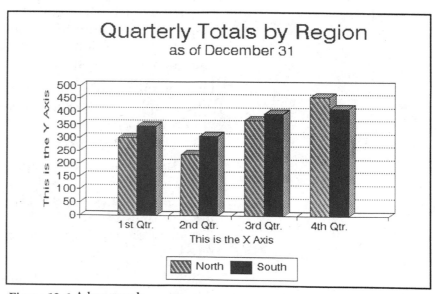

Figure 12.6: A bar graph

- Line: On a line graph, the x-axis consists of text labels, and the tick marks are laid out evenly along the axis. Points are plotted between the x- and y-axes and connected with a line.

- XY: An XY graph is similar to a line graph, but the x-axis consists of numbers, and the tick marks are spaced according to their value. Figure 12.7 shows both an XY graph (above) and a line graph (below) that plot temperature readings throughout the day. The line graph's data points are spaced evenly, even though the readings were not taken at regular intervals. The XY graph takes the actual time of each point into account and better represents the trend of the temperature.

- Stacked-bar: A stacked-bar graph is similar to a bar graph, but instead of a separate bar for each series, the data for each one is stacked on the other to build the bar. The total is represented by the height of the bar, and you also can see how much each series contributed to each bar. Figure 12.8 shows a stacked-bar graph that plots household energy consumption for four years. The height of each bar represents the total, and the bars are subdivided by energy type.

- Pie: The main difference between a pie chart and the other graph types (except a column graph) is that it graphs just one data series. Each value is represented by a wedge that is a percent of the whole data series.

- Area: Like a stacked-bar graph, an area graph accumulates a total for the series. But it is drawn in the style of a line graph. Figure 12.9 shows the data used for Figure 12.8 drawn as an area chart. When you need to plot many data series, an area graph is much less cluttered than a stacked-bar graph.

- Rotated-bar: A rotated-bar graph is a bar graph that has been rotated 90 degrees, so that the bars run from left to right. The positions of the two axes are switched; the x-axis is the vertical line on the left, and the y-axis is the horizontal line at the bottom of the graph. Figure 12.10 shows a rotated-bar graph that plots the production of various assembly plants. The graph is scaled so that the maximum value on the y-axis is the goal for the current year.

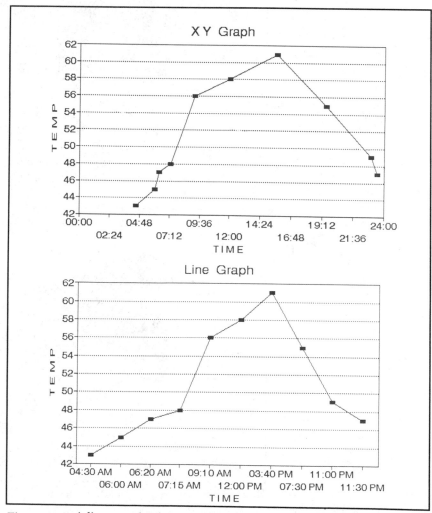

Figure 12.7: A line graph plots a value against a label, but an XY graph plots one value (temperature) against another (time)

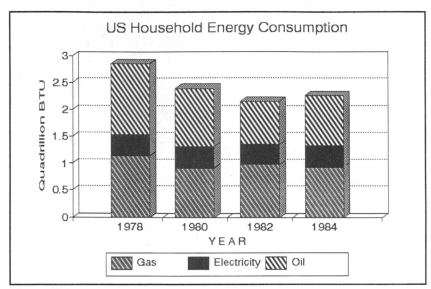

Figure 12.8: A stacked-bar graph shows total energy consumption as the
contribution of each energy source

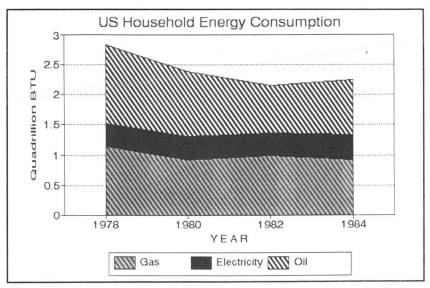

Figure 12.9: An area graph shows total energy consumption as well as
the contribution made by each energy source

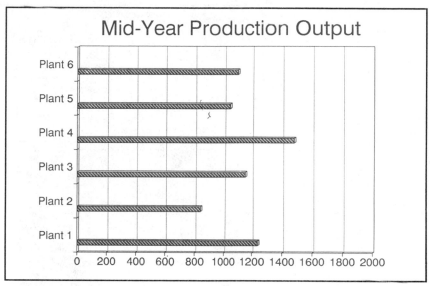

Figure 12.10: A rotated-bar graph

- Column: A column graph is the same as a pie graph except that the values in the single data series are arranged as blocks in a column. Figure 12.11 shows the pie graph you built in the beginning of this chapter (Figure 12.4) switched to a column graph.

- High-Low: In a high-low graph, the data series are plotted in pairs. Each pair of data points (the low and high) are plotted as a single vertical line, with the line's bottom the low value and its top the high value. A high-low graph is suited to tracking pairs of data that mark a high and a low or a beginning and ending value (such as the price of stocks). Figure 12.12 shows a spreadsheet that has a table of temperature readings made over five days. Below it is a high-low graph of the data.

- Text: Quattro Pro's Graph Annotator has some powerful tools for enhancing graphs. You can do so many things with these tools that you may want to create a "graph" that has no graph! That's when you specify a

As described in the next chapter, with the Graph Annotator, you can add line drawing, boxes and polygons, arrows, and text, as well as graphic images from other programs. You can enhance an existing graph or choose Text graph and start from scratch. You do not have to specify a Text graph in order to use the Annotator; it is just another way to access it.

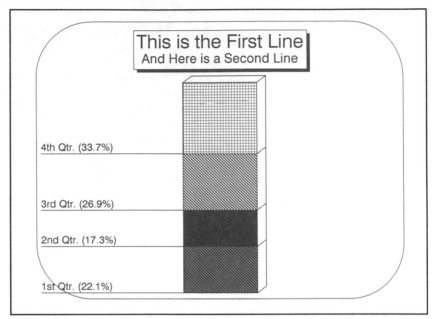

Figure 12.11: A column graph

text graph. All the usual graph settings are ignored for a text graph, and only the features you add via the Graph Annotator are shown.

THREE-DIMENSIONAL GRAPHS

The Graph Type menu includes the 3-D Graphs option, which offers four three-dimensional graph types: bar, ribbon, step, and area. The primary difference between a three-dimensional graph and the other Quattro Pro graph types (such as line, bar, and area) is that a three-dimensional graph has three axes: the x-axis, y-axis, and z-axis.

Figure 12.13 shows a three-dimensional bar graph. This graph uses the same data that was represented in Figures 12.8 and 12.9 (type of energy, year, and quantity used), but by showing the series one behind the other, it presents a bolder and more descriptive image.

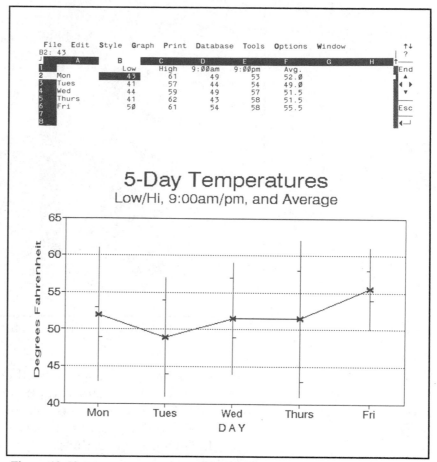

Figure 12.12: A high-low graph that plots temperature readings over five days and the spreadsheet containing the data

The other three-dimensional graph types—ribbon, step, and area—can be used to represent the same type of data as a three-dimensional bar graph. Just choose the style that best suits the trends or comparisons that you are trying to show. For a different effect, you can combine two-dimensional bars or lines in a three-dimensional graph by selecting the Graph–Overall–Three-D–No command.

Don't confuse the third axis of a three-dimensional graph (the axis labeled Oil, Gas, and Electricity in Figure 12.13) with

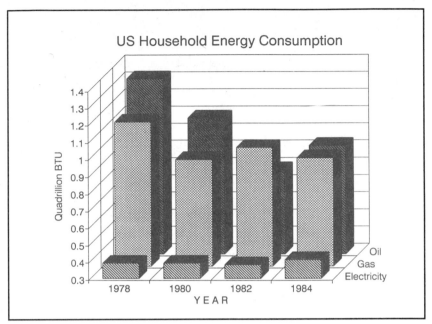

Figure 12.13: A three-dimensional bar graph

the secondary y-axis that is discussed later in this chapter. The z-axis of a three-dimensional graph actually represents a third type of data. The secondary y-axis simply provides a second scale for the y-axis, so that sets of data series that vary widely in scale can be shown together on the same graph without one dwarfing the other.

Because each series of a three-dimensional graph is arranged along the z-axis, there is the risk of a tall series blocking a shorter series behind it. You may have to experiment when you are assigning each spreadsheet data block to a graph series, keeping in mind that the first series is at the back of the graph, the second series in front of the first, and so on.

For example, in Figure 12.13 the first data series is labeled Oil, the second is Gas, and the third is Electricity. You can see that if Oil were placed first, it would partially block the other two series.

SELECTING THE DATA TO BE GRAPHED

It does not matter which series you choose for a block of data, although you normally start with one and work through six.

No matter which graph type you have specified (other than a text graph), you must define the data that is to be graphed by using the Graph–Series command. You can specify from one to six series of data for all graphs except pie or column charts, which plot only one series.

In the graph, each series appears as a different color or style of bar, line, or marker. You can use the Graph–Customize Series command to change any of these attributes for each series.

You can also specify the x-axis labels (the block of text or value cells that appears along the x-axis in the graph) while you are defining the data series. You can adjust the x-axis labels by using options on the Graph–X-Axis menu.

The data you choose for the graph series can be in the current spreadsheet or in another spreadsheet that is active or on disk.

When you graph more than one series, the cells of each one do not have to be adjacent. However, each series should have the same number of cells, or the graph may be misleading. For example, if one series contained 12 cells for each month of the year, but the second series had only 11 cells, your graph would not be comparing the same month in each series.

Any blank or text cells included in your data series will be plotted as zeros in the graph.

Figure 12.14 shows the spreadsheet that was used to create the graphs in Figures 12.8, 12.9 and 12.13. There are three data series defined: the first is the first row of data, B3..E3; the second is B4..E4; and the third is B5..E5.

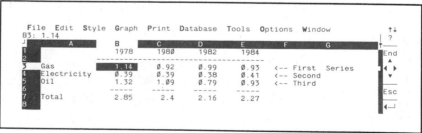

Figure 12.14: Three rows of data used for the graph series

CHOOSING THE SERIES IN ONE STEP

When the data series reside in a single block, you can use the Graph–Series–Group command to specify all of them. You can define as many as six separate series in one step.

The Group command first prompts you to specify whether the data is laid out in columns or rows. To use the data in Figure 12.14, you would choose Rows, and then specify the block B3..E5. Quattro Pro would automatically assign each row to a series.

CREATING A GRAPH IN ONE STEP

By using the Graph–Fast Graph command, you can not only specify all the data series at one time, but you can also include the x-axis labels and the cells for the legend.

When you use this command, Quattro Pro makes a few assumptions about the data in the block you specify. If the data has more rows than columns, it assumes the graph series should be arranged by columns. If there are more columns than rows, the series will be arranged by rows.

The x-axis labels are taken from either the column on the left or the row at the top of the block, depending on whether the series are being arranged by columns or rows. The legends will be taken from either the first column or row—whichever the x-axis is not.

ADDING TEXT TO GRAPHS

By using the options on the Graph–Text menu, you can add text to several key parts of your graph: a two-line title at the top, titles for the x- and y-axes, and legends for the data series. You can also select the font and style for the text.

In Figure 12.12, the following text items appear on the graph:

- 1st Line: 5-Day Temperatures
- 2nd Line: Low/Hi, 9:00am/pm, and Average

All the rules pertaining to creating graphs still apply when you are using the Fast Graph command. Remember to first reset all graph settings with the Graph–Customize Series–Reset command if you are starting a new graph (don't forget to name the current graph if you want to save it). Otherwise, you might end up with one or many titles, colors, or scaling factors that you had not intended to include in the graph.

You can add as much text as you want to any portion of your graph with the Graph Annotator, as described in the next chapter.

- X-Title: D A Y
- Y-Title: Degrees Fahrenheit

ENTERING THE GRAPH AND AXES TITLES

To enter text for the graph titles, use the Graph–Text–1st Line command for the top title, and the 2nd Line command for the second title. Use the X-Title and Y-Title commands to add axes titles. You can use the Secondary Y-Axis command if you are drawing a graph with two y-axes (which will be discussed later).

After invoking one of these commands, you can enter a title as long as 39 characters at the prompt. The text is always centered in its area of the graph.

Another way to enter title text is to reference a cell in the spreadsheet. Instead of typing the text into the command's prompt, you can type a cell address or block name, preceded by a backslash. For example, if you enter \B19 for the first-line title, whatever text is in cell B19 will be used for the top title. The cell to which you refer can have more than 39 characters, and they will all be displayed in your graph.

Another advantage to this method is that the cell to which you refer can be a formula linking to another spreadsheet. This could prove convenient if you want a series of graphs in different spreadsheets to share the same titles.

The address you type in the title prompt will not adjust to cell movement in the spreadsheet. If the entry is \B19 and you later insert a row above cell B19, the text in that cell will now be in cell B20, but your Graph–1st Title command will still be referring to cell B19. You can solve this problem in one of two ways:

- Ensure that the text never moves from its cell, perhaps by entering the graph information in the upper-left portion of your spreadsheet. In that location, you will be less likely to inadvertently insert or delete rows or columns.

- Instead of referring to a cell address, use a block name. For example, you could name the cell that contains the

⊙ Don't get carried away with the possibility of titles that are longer than 39 characters. Generally, 39 is more than enough for a description, and if you use more than that, you risk cluttering your graph.

first title in your first graph GRAPH1_TITLE1. Then when you invoke the Graph–Text–1st Title command, you would enter \GRAPH1_TITLE1.

To clear the text from a title, invoke the command, press Escape, and then press ↵.

ENHANCING THE TEXT

By default, the first title is 36 points, the second title is 24 points, and the other text is 18 points. By using the Graph–Text–Fonts command, you can change the font and style of any of the text in the graph. This command has all the choices that you see when you choose the Style–Font–Edit command (see Chapter 6), including Typeface, Point Size, Style, and Color. It also provides the Drop Shadow option, which is just for graph text. This option is a toggle, as are the other choices on the Style menu. Applying a drop shadow to text displays a "shadow" of the text behind it in a different color. You can adjust the color of the shadow with the Graph–Overall–Drop Shadow Color command.

Whether you adjust the size, style, and color of text in the graph depends on both the purpose and layout of the graph. For example, if there are many tick marks along the x-axis, you may want to switch the x-axis labels to a smaller typeface to avoid crowding.

Any changes you make with the Fonts command pertain only to the current graph. When you reset the graph options with the Graph–Customize Series–Reset command (discussed shortly), the default font and style will return.

You can also include bullets in a graph's first and second titles, the x-axis title, and in the legend by using the bullet codes discussed in Chapter 6. For example, to insert bullet number 2 in a graph title, you would include the text \bullet 2\. When you view or print the graph, the bullet would appear in the title.

Here is an instance where the 39-character maximum may become a hurdle, because the bullet character alone requires

10 characters. You can circumvent this by referring to a cell address for the text of the title, including the bullet.

USING LEGENDS TO IDENTIFY THE DATA

Each of the six series you can plot is identified by a different style than the other series. On a bar, stacked-bar, rotated-bar, pie, area, or column chart, each series will have a unique color or cross-hatching. A line or XY graph will have different markers or line types for the series.

Each series will therefore be distinct from the others, but to identify what data each series represents, you need to include a legend. In Figure 12.9, the legend is below the graph. It identifies the three data series as Gas, Electricity, and Oil.

To create a legend, invoke the Graph–Text–Legends command and enter the text for each data series. Just as with the other graph titles, you can either type the text or refer to a cell. For example, the legends for Figures 12.8 and 12.9 were taken directly from the spreadsheet shown in Figure 12.14 (cells A3, A4, and A5).

The Graph–Text–Legends–Position command allows you to place the legends either at the bottom of the graph (the default) or to the right side of the graph.

The Graph Annotator allows you to reposition the legends and the top titles anywhere in the graph.

INCLUDING INTERIOR LABELS FOR DATA POINTS

Interior labels are text that identifies one or more data points within the graph. You can add them to your graph by using the Graph–Customize Series–Interior Labels command.

With this command, you specify a block in the spreadsheet for each data series for which you want to show interior labels. The block can contain either text or numbers, and it should have the same number of cells as the data series that it will identify. For line and XY graphs, you can choose to place the labels above, left, right, below, or centered on the data points.

For example, you can identify each point on the graph for a series by specifying the same block as the series itself. In other words, the number that is used to plot each point will also appear next to that point. Figure 12.15 shows interior labels added to a graph. This is the same data that is plotted in the energy consumption graph shown in Figure 12.9, from the data in Figure 12.14.

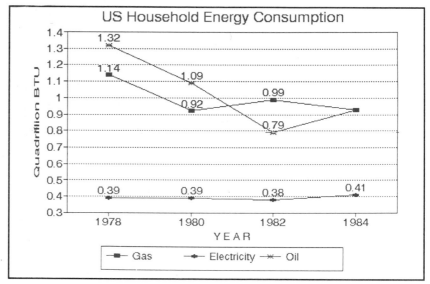

Figure 12.15: Interior labels identify data points in a series

You should use discretion when including interior labels; a graph can easily become cluttered with excess data when every point is identified. However, you can set up a block of cells to identify just a few key points in the graph. Select a block that has the same number of cells as the data series you want to label. In that block, enter text or numbers only in those cells that correspond to the cells in the data series that you wish to label. Leave the rest of the block empty, and then specify that block when you use the Interior Labels command. Only the contents of the occupied cells will appear as labels on the graph.

Interior labels for bar or rotated-bar graphs always appear just above or to the right of each bar. On a stacked-bar graph, the label above each bar represents just the top data series in the bar.

Interior labels do not appear on pie, column, or area graphs.

To turn off the labels for a series, select that series from the Interior Labels menu and then choose None for the position.

RESETTING OR RETAINING GRAPH OPTIONS

When you want to start a new graph that is not built on any previous settings, use the Graph–Customize Series–Reset command. This command allows you to undefine any or all of the six data series, including their associated interior labels. You can also reset all graph settings back to their defaults. Invoke the Reset command to ensure that you will not be surprised by a mysterious title, interior label, or other graph setting that was left over from the previous graph.

The changes you make to the graph series are only active for the current session of Quattro Pro or until you use the Series–Reset command. If you want to retain all the changes you make as the graphing defaults for all future sessions of Quattro Pro, use the Graph–Customize Series–Update command. The current settings of all the graph options will be saved as the defaults.

Note that this command is the same as the Options–Update command, which saves all the spreadsheet system options as the system defaults. Be careful not to accidentally save all the current system settings when you just want to save your current graph settings. As always, when you want to save new default settings, it is a good idea to do so soon after you have loaded Quattro Pro. That way, you should know precisely what settings you have changed since first entering the program.

CUSTOMIZING THE GRAPH SERIES

The first four options on the Graph–Customize Series menu are Colors, Fill Patterns, Markers & Lines, and Bar Width. They allow you to change the attributes of each series on the graph, such as the bars, lines, and markers that represent each data series. All these options have default settings, and you will need to access them only when you want to fine tune your graph, either for clarity or just to enhance its appearance.

Other choices on the Graph–Customize Series menu let you adjust the width of the bars in a bar graph, combine two different graph types in one, add a second y-axis to the graph, and customize pie and column charts.

CHANGING COLORS AND FILL PATTERNS

Be careful not to choose a color or pattern that is already being used by another data series in the graph.

You can change the color of each series in the graph by using the Graph–Customize Series–Colors command. You will see the current color for each series to its right on the Colors menu. When you select a series, a menu of 16 different colors will appear. It is the same menu that you see when you change the color of a font using the Style–Fonts–Edit Fonts command.

In bar, rotated-bar, stacked-bar, and area charts, a different cross-hatching pattern is used to fill each data series. To choose patterns, use the Graph–Customize Series–Fill Patterns command. The current fill pattern will appear next to each of the six series. Choose any of the series, and you are offered a menu with 16 choices of fill patterns.

Changing the colors for the sections of pie and column charts, which graph only a single data series, is done via the Graph–Customize–Series–Pies command, as described later in the chapter.

CHANGING LINES AND MARKERS

Don't duplicate a marker or line style for two different series, or you will confuse the two on the graph.

For line or XY graphs, each series is identified by a different style of line and data-point markers. The first option on the Graph–Customize Series–Markers & Lines menu is Line Styles. It offers eight line styles, such as Solid, Dashed, or Heavy Dashed.

The Markers option lets you choose a marker style for the data points in a series. There are ten marker styles, such as Filled Square, Filled Triangle, or Empty Square.

With the combination of line styles and markers, you effectively have up to 80 different styles available for the six data series.

On line and XY graphs, by default a line with markers is used to indicate each series. The Graph–Customize Series–Markers & Lines–Formats command allows you to choose to show only Lines, only Symbols (markers), Both, or Neither.

For example, you could create a scatter chart, in which only markers are shown, by choosing Symbols from the Format menu. If you want to include a line in your graph that has no data points shown on it, choose Lines. To hide a series without eliminating it from the graph settings, choose Neither. The series will be plotted, but you won't see it on the graph.

ADJUSTING THE BAR WIDTH

The width of the bars in a bar graph are determined by the number of bars plotted. The more bars that are shown, the narrower each one will be. But no matter what their width, all bars are drawn to a specific proportion, determined by the Graph–Customize Series–Bar Width command.

By default, this command is set to 60. This means that all bars take up about 60 percent of the space allotted to them; each bar will be a little bigger than the space between it and the next bar. You can change the percentage from 20, for skinny bars with lots of space between them, up to 90, for fat bars with very little space between them.

COMBINING TWO GRAPH TYPES

By using the Graph–Customize Series–Override Type command, you can combine bar and line charts in the same graph. The command displays a menu with the options Default, Bar, or Line.

Each series is by default set to Default, which means that the current graph type will be used to plot the series. Choose either Line or Bar for a series, and the series will be plotted in that style.

Figure 12.16 shows the bar graph that appears in Figure 12.6 with the addition of a third data series called Goal. The Goal series is plotted as a line graph, and it stands out clearly from the other two. Because the values in the Goal series are greater than the corresponding values for the other two, the line is not obscured by the bars.

How you mix and match graph types depends on the effect you wish to achieve, as well as the suitability of the current graph for mixed styles. It's all too easy to make a graph look cluttered, and a conservative approach is generally the safest.

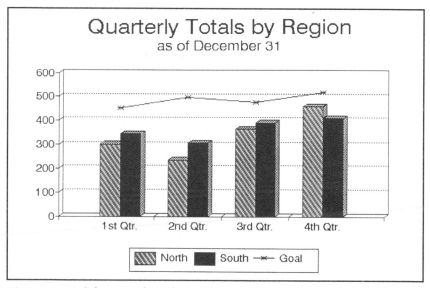

Figure 12.16: A bar graph with the third series shown as a line graph

TAILORING PIE AND COLUMN CHARTS

You can use the Graph–Customize Series–Pies command to modify pie and column charts. This command offers the choices Label Format, Explode, Patterns, Colors, and Tick Marks. All the commands except Explode affect both pie and column charts.

FORMATTING LABELS

By default, each wedge in a pie chart is labeled with the number that represents its percentage of the entire pie. If a pie graph has four slices that are all the same size, each will be labeled 25%. The Graph–Customize Series–Pies–Label Format–Value command allows you to display the actual value associated with each slice instead of its percentage of the whole.

You can also choose $, which prefaces the value with a dollar sign. If you do not want the pie slices labeled, choose None.

EXPLODING WEDGES

By default, all the slices of a pie chart form a complete circle. You can use the Graph–Customize Series–Pies–Explode command to separate, or "explode," one or more slices of the pie from the others and call attention to it.

This command offers a menu of the first nine pie slices. Select one from the list, and then choose Explode to explode it, or select Don't Explode to bring the slice back into the circle.

You can also explode slices of a pie graph by using the same method that is used in Lotus 1-2-3, which involves specifying a second data series. A pie slice will be exploded if the corresponding cell in the second series contains a number greater than or equal to 100. This method also determines the color or pattern used for each slice, as discussed in the next section.

CHOOSING PATTERNS AND COLORS

You can change the pattern or color of each pie slice with the Patterns and Colors commands on the Graph–Customize Series–Pies menu. These are equivalent to the Colors and Fill Patterns commands for the other graphs.

Choosing either command displays the same menu of nine pie slices that is offered by the Explode command. Choose the slice you want to change, and then choose the pattern from the 16 patterns or a color from the 16 colors.

The method used in Lotus 1-2-3 to explode slices from a pie graph can also be used to change their color or fill pattern. There are eight colors and eight fill patterns available in 1-2-3. You specify one for a pie slice by entering a number from 0 to 7 in the corresponding cell in the second series block.

To change the color and also explode the slice, simply add 100 to the number. For example, entering the number 104 in a cell in the second series block will explode the corresponding slice and give it color number 4.

DISPLAYING OR HIDING TICK MARKS

The tick marks on a pie chart point from each pie slice to the label that identifies it. You can use the Graph–Customize Series–Pies–Tick Marks–No command to hide them. Choose Yes to display them.

ADDING A SECOND Y-AXIS

If you want one graph to compare one or more data series that vary widely in scale, you can use the Graph–Customize Series–Y-Axis command to create a second y-axis. You can add a second y-axis to line, bar, and XY graphs.

For example, Figure 12.17 shows a graph that plots the monthly flow of a river and one of its tributaries over a four-month period. The y-axis on the left is for the tributary, and it is scaled from 200 to 500. The y-axis on the right is for the river, and it has a much larger scale, running from 19,000 to 26,000. Each y-axis has been labeled to make it clear exactly what is being shown. Remember that the Graph–Text menu has options for both the y-axis and the second y-axis.

FORMATTING THE X- AND Y-AXES

The appearance of the x- and y-axes is critical to the success of your graphs. Quattro Pro provides quite a few commands that let you tailor the look of the axes. These commands appear on

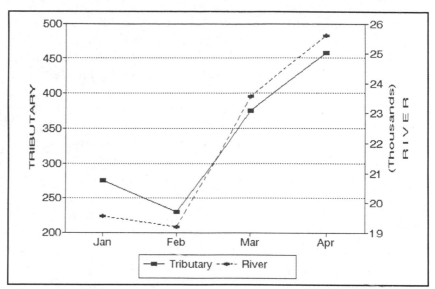

Figure 12.17: A second y-axis serves to compare two widely varying data ranges

the almost identical Graph–X-Axis and Graph–Y-Axis menus. The X-Axis menu has the added command Alternate Ticks, and the Y-Axis menu has the command 2nd Y-Axis. Figure 12.18 illustrates the results of the x- and y-axes formatting described in the following sections.

ADJUSTING THE SCALE

The only time you can scale the x-axis is when you are plotting an XY graph. For all other graphs, the x-axis contains text labels, and scaling is irrelevant.

By default, Quattro Pro automatically scales the y-axis so that the graph data falls comfortably within its minimum and maximum values. For example, in Figure 12.17, the primary y-axis has a minimum of 200 and a maximum of 500. If the graphed data were to change to include a maximum value of 600, the y-axis would automatically increase to a number slightly larger than that.

There may be times when you will want to force the x- or y-axis scale to a specific minimum and maximum. For example, when you are creating a series of graphs that will be compared to one another, it is essential that they all use the same scale on the y-axis. Otherwise, the rise and fall of the plotted lines or bars will be meaningless; you will have to compare the scale of each to see how the numbers in the two graphs relate.

In a case such as this, you can use the Graph–Y-Axis–Scale–Manual command to manually set the scale of the y-axis. From the Y-Axis menu, choose Low, and enter the number that will serve as the minimum value on the y-axis. Then choose High and enter the maximum value on the y-axis. In Figure 12.18, the scale has been manually set to a low of 100 and a high of 900.

Any data points that fall outside the range you set will not appear on the graph. This can be a benefit if you want to "zoom in" on one portion of the graph. You can force the scale to a range that will cover the portion that you want to see, and the rest of the data will not appear on the graph.

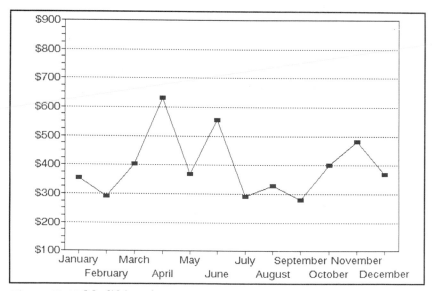

Figure 12.18: Modifying the axes

MODIFYING THE TICK MARKS

Several commands on the X-Axis and Y-Axis menus affect the tick marks along the axes:

- Increment: Specifies how you want the axis divided into ticks. You are prompted to enter a number, which will be used to increment the tick marks. For example, the axis runs from 100 to 900 and you enter 25 as the increment, the tick marks will appear at 125, 150, 175, 200, and so on, as shown in Figure 12.18.

- Format of Ticks: Gives the numbers along the axes a numeric format, in the same way that a numeric cell is given a format in the spreadsheet. The menu includes the choices Fixed, Scientific, Currency, and so on. Just as in the spreadsheet, by default, the format is set to General. In Figure 12.18, the y-axis has been formatted as Currency with zero decimal places.

- No. of Minor Ticks: Specifies how many ticks appear along the axis. By default, this is set to 0, meaning that Quattro Pro will label every tick along the axis. If you set this option to 3, as in Figure 12.18, there will be three unlabeled tick marks between every labeled one. This enables you to eliminate some of the labels to unclutter the axis.

- Alternate: Creates two rows of text for the x-axis tick marks, as shown in Figure 12.18. Use this command when the tick mark labels become crowded because there are too many of them or because they contain more than a few characters.

- Display Scaling: Provides the choices Yes, for automatic scaling, or No, for no scaling. When the numbers on the axes are too large to display without crowding, Quattro Pro automatically scales them by a factor of ten, as in Figure 12.17. If you want the complete numbers to show (and no scaling to take place), set the Display Scaling command to No.

If the numbers are too large to fit in the space allowed, Quattro Pro will display asterisks, just as when a number is too big to display within the cell's column width in the spreadsheet. In that case, you should either change the format of the axis or reinstate scaling.

SELECTING NORMAL OR LOGARITHMIC MODE

When a graph's scale covers a tremendous range, data points near the bottom of the scale can practically disappear from view at the bottom of the graph. For example, a graph that plots the cumulative national debt from 1870 to 1987 would span from 2.4 billion dollars all the way to 2.4 trillion dollars. That's a factor of one thousand. The first graph in Figure 12.19 shows how this appears. As you can see, the data points before 1940, when the debt was about 2.5 billion dollars, are crowded close to the x-axis and can barely be seen.

If you graph the log values of the national debt numbers instead of the numbers themselves, the scale of the graph is drastically reduced. The log value of a number is the power to which you would raise the value of 10 to produce the original number. The log of 100 is 2, because 10 squared is 100. The log of 1 billion is 9, and the log of 1 trillion is 12.

You can use the Graph–Y-Axis–Mode–Log command to change the y-axis scaling to logarithmic. The result is shown in the bottom graph of Figure 12.19. The second title line of this graph makes it clear that the graph is displaying log values. Without this, the graph could be confusing and misleading.

CUSTOMIZING THE BODY OF THE GRAPH

There are several options on the Graph–Overall menu that let you change the appearance of the entire graph. You can include grid lines through the graph, enclose the graph in a frame, change the color of the graph's background, make the graph's bars three dimensional, and display the graph in either color or black and white.

USING GRID LINES FOR PINPOINT ACCURACY

By default, Quattro Pro draws horizontal grid lines across the graph from each labeled tick mark on the y-axis. These lines help

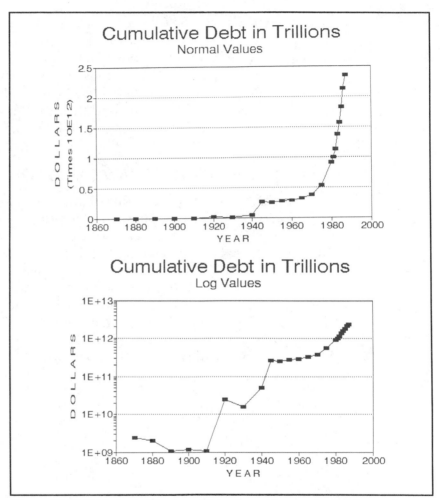

Figure 12.19: With logarithmic scaling along the y-axis, widely varying numbers can be viewed in one graph

to pinpoint the value of the bars or data points on the graph.

You can change the grid with the Graph–Overall–Grid command, which offers the choices Horizontal, Vertical, Both, and Clear. When a line graph has many data points, using both a horizontal and vertical grid can make it easier to determine their values on both the x- and y-axes.

Also on the Grid menu are the options Grid Color, Line Style, and Fill Color. The Grid Color option lets you change the color of the grid lines; choose from the 16 colors offered. The Line Style option lets you choose the line style for the grid lines. By default, the grids are dotted lines. The Fill Color command specifies the color behind the grid lines, within the body of the graph. Again, you can choose from the 16 available colors.

ADDING TEXT AND GRAPH OUTLINES

Another way to enhance a graph is to outline all or a portion of it. The Graph–Overall–Outlines command provides the choices Titles, Legend, and Graph.

In the quick tour in the beginning of this chapter, we used the Titles option to enclose the graph title in a box with a background shadow. We also used the Graph option to enclose the entire graph in a rectangular box with rounded corners. The graph legend is enclosed in a box by default, but you can change its style if you wish.

You can choose from the following box styles:

- Box
- Double-line
- Thick-line
- Shadow
- 3D
- Rnd Rectangle
- None
- Sculpted

USING COLOR AND THREE-DIMENSIONAL OPTIONS

If a graph is too crowded, a two-dimensional graph is often more attractive.

To change the color of the area outside the graph, use the Background Color choice on the Graph–Overall menu.

By default, the components of pie, bar, and column charts are all drawn with a third dimension. You can set the Graph–Over-all-Three-D command to No to draw these graphs as two-dimensional. Note that if a graph is really overcrowded, Quattro Pro will automatically display the graph components in only two dimensions.

To remove all the colors from an entire graph and make it black and white, choose B&W for the Color/B&W option. You can change back to color at any time simply by choosing Color from the menu.

The Graph–Overall–Drop Shadow Color command lets you specify the color of the shadow that will be used for text to which you have assigned a drop shadow. You first choose the color of the text that you want to affect, and then select the color for its drop shadow. For example, you might first choose Green and then Brown, so that any green text will have a brown shadow when you give it the drop shadow attribute.

WORKING WITH GRAPH NAMES

Only one graph in the spreadsheet is the current graph. It is the one you see when you invoke the Graph-View command or press F10. You can modify that graph in any way to create a different graph, but the first graph will be gone, replaced by the new one. To save a graph for future use, you use the commands on the Graph–Name menu: Display, Create, Erase, Reset, and Autosave Edits.

NAMING GRAPHS

You can save a graph to disk as a separate image file by using the Print–Graph Print–Destination–File command, as discussed later in the chapter. This is how you transfer a graph to another program.

The Graph–Name–Create command allows you to name all the graph settings that make up the current graph so you can recall it later.

When you invoke the Graph–Name–Create command, you are prompted to enter a name for the current graph. You can use as many as 15 characters for the name and include any type of characters. The caveats that apply to block names are not applicable to graph names because you use them only when picking a graph to display.

Once a graph is named, you can reset or modify the current graph settings to create a new graph. Later, when you want to view the earlier, named graph, just invoke the Graph–Name–Display command. When prompted, either enter the name of the graph you want to display or pick its name from the list of named graphs that is offered. The graph will immediately be displayed on the screen and become the current graph, replacing the previous current graph.

When you have revised a named graph, you must remember to save the graph settings again under its name. By naming the graph again, you are saving all its settings under a name that already exists; the contents of the current graph replace the contents of that named graph.

For example, suppose you use the Graph–Name–Display command to bring up a graph called Quarter_1. That graph has now become the current graph—the one you see when you press F10. After you make your changes to it, you must use the Graph–Name–Create command and once again specify the name Quarter_1. If you fail to name the graph and then bring up a new graph with the Display command, the changes you made will be lost. The graph named Quarter_1 will be the same as it was before you made the changes.

It can be more than a little frustrating to lose your graph modifications because you forgot to name the current graph. But there's a simple way to avoid the problem: enable the Graph–Name–Autosave Edits command.

By default, this command is set to No, and you must name the current graph before making another graph current. When you set Autosave Edits to Yes, any changes you make to a graph will be saved automatically whenever you call up another graph to replace the current one.

When Autosave Edits is enabled, you still need to use some caution when you work with your named graphs. If you plan to revise the current graph and save it under a new name, you must either turn off Autosave Edits or name the graph before you make any changes.

For example, suppose you are working on a graph named Quarter_1, and you want to revise it and then save it under the new name Quarter_2. If you make changes and then view the graph, the Autosave Edits command will save the graph under the name Quarter_1, which is not what you intended. To avoid saving those changes, be sure to give the current graph its new name, such as Quarter_2, *before* you display it.

In order to retain a graph for a future session in Quattro Pro, you must save the spreadsheet to disk. That may be obvious, but it's easy to overlook. Remember that the graphs you name are part of the current spreadsheet and are saved with it.

The Graph–Name–Erase command removes a named graph from the list. After you erase the graph, you cannot display it again; you would have to rebuild it.

You use the Graph–Name–Reset command to erase all graph names from the spreadsheet. Since this command could cost you hours of work if you invoked it accidentally, it offers a second menu with the choices No and Yes, allowing you to cancel or proceed with the command.

COPYING GRAPHS

After you have taken the time to create and fine tune an informative and eye-catching graph, you may want to use it in another spreadsheet. This way, you can avoid having to duplicate all the specifications in the second spreadsheet. It's easy to do just that when you use the Graph–Name–Graph Copy command to copy graphs. This command is especially helpful when you have created several graphs in one spreadsheet that you would like to include in a slide show (discussed in the next section) in another spreadsheet.

To use the Graph Copy command, you must first assign a graph name to the graph you wish to copy. Follow these steps to duplicate an existing named graph:

1. Open the secondary spreadsheet, the one to which you wish to copy the graph.

2. From the primary spreadsheet, invoke the Graph–Name–Graph Copy command.

3. Select the graph name from the menu of names.

4. Point to the secondary spreadsheet. You can also type in its complete path and name, using the Quattro Pro linking reference, such as [D:\DATA\MYFILE]A1. The cell address is required for proper linking syntax, although nothing is actually copied to that address.

5. Press ↵, and the job is finished.

The graph settings have now been duplicated in the secondary spreadsheet. Be sure to save that spreadsheet if you want to retain this new graph. You should be aware that the series in the new graph are linked to the data in the primary spreadsheet. If you want to use this graph with data in its own spreadsheet (the secondary one), you must select new cells for each data series.

CREATING A SLIDE SHOW

You can design an automated slide show within the spreadsheet with the Graph–Name–Slide command. You specify the block in which you have placed the slide show definition, and the command takes it from there.

The definition block consists of up to five columns, with one row for each slide. You enter the following information in each column, viewing the block from left to right:

The first column, containing the graph names, is required. Each of the other four columns is optional.

- Name of graph: The names of the graphs to display in the order that you want them to appear. Enter each name as it would be shown on the Graph–Name–Display menu.

- Display duration: The time, in seconds, that each graph should be displayed. Leave the cell blank or enter 0 if you want the graph to be displayed until you press any key to continue with the next graph.

- Transition effect: The number, from 1 to 24, of the graph transition effect. If you specify no effect by entering a zero or leaving the cell blank, the default effect is used, which is simply one graphics screen instantly replacing the previous one. It is essentially the same as effect 1, which the Quattro Pro *User's Guide* calls a *cut*. The other effects are variations on five different styles, including the fade (2), sideways and vertical wipes (3–10), spiral (11–17), and dissolves (18–24).

- Transition speed: The speed at which the switch to the next graph happens, with a 0 or blank cell entry as the fastest.

- Sound file: The name of a digitized sound file that will be played during the transition. Several sound files come with Quattro Pro; each has a file name extension of SND. You can also play a sound file via a graph button (discussed in the next chapter) and with the macro command {play}.

Your computer must use a lot of processing power to play a sound file. If you are running Quattro Pro under Windows, or have a memory-resident programming running with it, the sound may not be reproduced very well.

The Quattro Pro *User's Guide* lists all 24 of the slide show transition effects and the range of speeds for each one. Note that you may find the slower transition speeds painfully slow. As you experiment with the slide show feature, always start with a speed of 0, the fastest. You can then try a slower speed, and then one slower, until you find the right speed.

Here is an example of a five-column slide show definition table:

GRAPH	TIME	EFFECT	SPEED	SOUND
INTRO	0	18	1	TRUMPET.SND
QUARTER_1	30	3	3	
QUARTER_2	20	4	3	
QUARTER_3	20	3	3	
QUARTER_4	20	4	3	

GRAPH	TIME	EFFECT	SPEED	SOUND
YEAR_END	40	11	2	AULD.SND
SUMMARY	0	12	2	
Q&A	0	18	1	FIN.SND

You must have an EGA or a VGA video display to use transition effects.

There are eight graphs in this slide show. The first one, INTRO, will be displayed via a dissolve (effect 18) at speed 1. As the graph is being drawn, the sound file, TRUMPET, will be played. Because the entry in the Time column is 0, the graph will remain displayed until the presenter presses a key to continue.

The next graph, QUARTER_1, will be displayed with a wipe-to-right effect at a speed of 3 without any sound effects. It will be displayed for 30 seconds, at which time QUARTER_2 will be drawn via the wipe-to-left effect at a speed of 3. It will be displayed for 20 seconds.

As you can see, there really isn't much to building a slide show. You can experiment with the transition effects and speeds, and reorder the show simply by moving a graph to a different row in the table.

PLANNING A SLIDE SHOW

Although building a slide show is quite easy, designing a *good* slide show requires planning, a knowledge of your audience, and an understanding of the points you wish to make. You also should consider the style, color, and layout of your slides.

If you want to create effective slide shows, be sure to read the Quattro Pro manual entitled *ProView Guide, A Guide to Professional Presentations*, and experiment with the samples and tools in its accompanying spreadsheet files.

The *ProView Guide* contains a wide variety of advice, tips, and techniques to help you design your slide shows. The accompanying spreadsheet files contain the following items:

- Graph templates, in the files named BKG1.WQ1, BKG2.WQ1, and so on. These are sample graphs that give you an attractive and meaningful framework from which to build graphs for your own slide shows.

- A sample slide show, in the file named ALLEN-TWN.WQ1. It demonstrates the techniques for producing a well-designed presentation.

- A macro library, in the file named LIB_MU1.WQ1. It contains practical macros for automating many slide show tasks.

VIEWING A SLIDE SHOW

To see your slide show, simply invoke the Graph–Name–Slide command, and specify the block that contains the definition table. Quattro Pro will run the show, displaying the graphs in the order in which their names appear in the first column of the table.

You can view the previous slide in a slide show by pressing the Backspace key. Also, as explained in the next chapter, you can create graph buttons for your slide shows with the Graph Annotator. These are actually text boxes that you can "push" with your mouse or from the keyboard to select the next graph to view, in any order that you want. You can even use the buttons to invoke spreadsheet macros.

INSERTING A GRAPH INTO A SPREADSHEET

You can view one graph at a time with the Graph–View command (F10), but you can also insert up to eight graphs into the spreadsheet. You can then view the graph and your spreadsheet data at the same time, and watch the graph change as you change the data. You can also print your spreadsheet and graph together.

PLACING THE GRAPH

The Graph–Insert command lets you insert the current graph or any named graph into the spreadsheet. It offers a menu that includes all the named graphs, as well as the one called Current Graph.

The bigger the block that you specify, the larger the graph will be. When Quattro Pro is in text mode, you won't actually see the graph in the spreadsheet. Instead, the block will be highlighted. How you view the graph will be discussed shortly.

An inserted graph will overlay any data in the cells that it occupies. The data will still be there and can be referenced in formulas or copied to other locations, but you won't be able to see it on the display or on the input line.

Instead of showing the cell contents, the input line will show the cell address and the name of the graph. For example, if cell C12 was within the graph's block, you might see this on the input line:

    Graph C12: Quarter_1

When you move the cell selector within an inserted graph in the spreadsheet, that graph also becomes the current graph, at least temporarily. If you press F10, that is the graph you will see displayed. This is very convenient if you do not have the correct hardware for displaying graphs within the spreadsheet. All that graph's settings are reflected within the Graph menus, so you can make changes as necessary. However, as soon as you move the cell selector off the inserted graph's block, the current graph returns to whatever it had been previously.

VIEWING A GRAPH IN A SPREADSHEET

In order to see graphs within the spreadsheet, you must have an EGA or VGA video display. A CGA or Hercules video adapter will not do. You must also put the spreadsheet into graphics mode by using the Options–Display Mode–WYSIWYG command, or by clicking on the mouse button labled WYS. Then the inserted graph will appear in the spreadsheet. If you change the data to which the graph refers, the graph will be updated and you will see the results on the screen.

Figure 12.20 shows the energy consumption graph inserted into the spreadsheet. The entire spreadsheet is in graphics mode, which is why there are more rows displayed than usual.

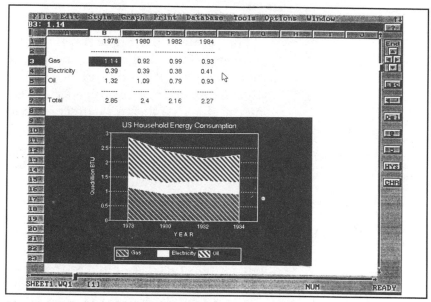

Figure 12.20: An inserted graph will be displayed when the spreadsheet
is in graphics mode

Spreadsheet screen performance will be many times slower
when Quattro Pro is in graphics mode. Unless you have a fast
computer, you will most likely prefer to stay in text mode while
you work. Use the graphics mode when you want to watch a
graph change as you modify its data. The Options–Display
Mode–A:80x25 command returns the spreadsheet to the default
text mode (your graphics adapter may have other text modes).
With a mouse, you can click on the button labeled CHR.

Graphs within the spreadsheet are also affected by the
Options–Graphics Quality command. When it is set to Final, any
Bitstream fonts you have specified for the spreadsheet or a graph
will be used, producing the best printout or display possible.

When Graphics Quality is set to Draft, a Bitstream font will be
used if it is already on disk. If the font has not yet been built, a
Hershey font will appear instead. This produces a lower quality
printout or display, but eliminates the font-building time.

It is a good idea to
leave the Options–
Graphics Quality com-
mand set to Draft. Use
Final only when you are
ready to view the final
result. This allows you
to change font sizes or
rearrange your graphs
without the delays of
font building.

SCALING THE GRAPH

The result of placing a graph within the spreadsheet may be confusing if you don't remember to consider the graph's aspect ratio. The Print–Graph Print–Layout–4:3 Aspect command, which controls how a graph is sized when it is printed (discussed later in this chapter), also affects how a graph appears when it is inserted into a spreadsheet.

By default, the 4:3 Aspect command is set to Yes. This means that Quattro Pro will always maintain a 4 to 3 aspect ratio between a graph's width and its height (4 inches wide by 3 inches tall, for example). No matter what the proportions are of the block you specify when inserting a graph into the spreadsheet, the graph will always appear with a 4 to 3 aspect ratio.

For example, suppose you specify a block that is skinny and tall, such as three columns wide by forty rows deep. In order to maintain the proper aspect ratio, the graph will be three columns wide by only a few rows tall—most of the rows will remain empty. If you really want a tall and skinny graph in the spreadsheet, you must first set the Print–Graph Print–Layout–4:3 Aspect command to No. Quattro Pro will size the graph to fit the size of the block exactly.

When you are inserting a graph into a block of a certain size, you will probably want the 4:3 Aspect command set to No. At other times, when the exact size of the graph is not a critical matter, leave the command set to Yes. Quattro Pro will then proportion the graph to the 4 to 3 ratio.

PRINTING AND SAVING A GRAPH TO DISK

You can print an inserted graph as part of a spreadsheet by sending the output to the Graphics Printer. To print the graph as a separate entity, use the Print–Graph Print command.

The Graph Print menu provides options for specifying another graph to print (equivalent to selecting a block in the spreadsheet), laying out the graph on the page, and choosing the destination for the printout. The Go command is equivalent to Spreadsheet Print.

SELECTING A GRAPH TO PRINT

By default, the current graph (the one you see when you press F10) is printed when you select the Go command from the Print–Graph Print menu. You print one graph at a time and one graph on a page, and there are no headers or footers. If this does not meet your needs, you can place one or more graphs into the spreadsheet, and then print the spreadsheet.

You don't have to resort to the Graph menu's Name–Display command when you want to print a different graph. Instead, you can select another one by using the equivalent command, Print–Graph Print–Name.

You are prompted to enter the name of the graph you want to print. Either type in the name or select one from the list of all named graphs in the spreadsheet.

You can print the selected graph by issuing the Go command, or you can manipulate its placement on the page with the various layout options.

SPECIFYING THE GRAPH LAYOUT

No matter what type of graph you create, each one is enclosed within a rectangular space. You can control the placement of this space on the printed page by using the Print–Graph Print–Layout menu options.

While you are learning about the layout process, you may find it helpful to show the outline of this space around the graph you are printing. Use the Graph–Overall–Outlines–Graph–Box command, and your graph, whatever its shape, will be enclosed in a box. It is that box that you will be laying out on the page.

Like the Layout commands available when you print your spreadsheet, the Layout–Dimensions command allows you to choose either Inches or Centimeters, and the Layout–Orientation command provides the Portrait and Landscape options.

There is no way to tell which graph will be printed when you issue the Go command. All the more reason to test your printout on the screen by setting Destination to Screen Preview.

Some printers, such as laser printers, can't print to the edge of the paper. So even when you have set the margins to 0, there will still be a small margin at the top and left edges of the page.

Setting the margins for your graph is a somewhat different process than that for your spreadsheet. Think of your graph as a picture that you can make any size and place in any position on the page.

Both the Left Edge and Top Edge options are set to 0 inches by default. This means that the left edge of your graph's box will be at the very edge of the paper, and the top edge of the graph will be at the very top of the paper.

Because the graph is a picture that can be sized, you do not specify a right or bottom margin. Instead, you simply specify the width and height of the graph. By default, both the Width and Height options are set to 0, which Quattro Pro interprets as meaning that you want the graph to be as big as possible, given the current page size and the left and top margins. You can set the width and height to any dimension that will fit within the page, although the aspect ratio setting also affects the size of your graph.

As discussed in the section about scaling a graph within a spreadsheet, the Layout–4:3 Aspect command is by default set to Yes. This means that Quattro Pro will always maintain a ratio of 4 to 3 between the graph's width and its height.

Maintaining the 4 to 3 aspect ratio is generally the best way to go. Just remember that you can still size a graph, but its ultimate size will be based on one of two things: either the smallest dimension that you specify for its width and height or the smallest available dimension of the page given the margin settings at the left and top.

There may be times, however, when you want to fit a graph to a specific dimension. In those cases, set 4:3 Aspect to No, which will allow you to size the graph to any dimension.

The last two commands on the Print–Graph Print–Layout menu are Reset and Update. The Reset command here is equivalent to the Reset–All command on the Print–Layout menu. Selecting Reset immediately sets all print options back to their default, including those for spreadsheet printing. You would generally reset all graph settings when you move on to another graph to print, unless it was to be printed in the same style.

The Print–Graph Print–Layout–Update command is equivalent to the Print Layout Update command, and it saves all the Quattro Pro print settings as the defaults for all future sessions.

CHOOSING A GRAPH DESTINATION

You can use the Print–Graph Print–Destination command to send your graph output to a printer, screen, or file. The default destination is the Graph Printer. There is no option for Printer, because, by definition, you cannot print a picture (a graph) on a text printer.

If you want to create a printable file, choose File as the destination. This is equivalent to using the Print–Destination–Binary File command when you print a spreadsheet. The file can later be copied to the printer to produce the graph. By default, Quattro Pro appends the extension PRN to the file name. If you named the file MYGRAPH, you could later use this DOS command to print the file:

```
COPY MYGRAPH.PRN PRN: /B
```

You can also send your graph to the screen by selecting the Screen Preview option on the Destination menu. This produces a graphic reproduction of a printout, just as it does when printing your spreadsheet to the screen. Previewing is a highly valuable means for testing your printouts, especially since graphs can take time to print.

EXPORTING A GRAPH

Another means for exporting a graph in Quattro Pro is by sending it to a graphics file. This is a file that can be read by other graphics programs, not a printable one.

The command Print–Graph Print–Write Graph File offers the following choices:

- EPS File: Encapsulated PostScript file
- PIC File: Lotus 1-2-3 compatible file

- Slide EPS: Encapsulated PostScript file for making 35mm slides
- PCX File: PC Paintbrush compatible file format

By choosing the EPS format, you can transfer the graphics you create in Quattro Pro to a program that imports EPS files.

Lotus 1-2-3 saves its graphs in the PIC format, which is a very common file format. Many graphics programs can import this type of file. For example, if you need to include a few of your Quattro Pro graphs with someone else's 1-2-3 graphs, you can export yours to PIC files. Give them to the person with the Lotus graphs, and they can all be printed together. The startling difference between the Quattro Pro and Lotus 1-2-3 graphs will surely be noticed.

You can select the Slide EPS option to save a graph to a file that you can then send to a slide service to be printed on a 35mm slide. The resulting file is in a PostScript format with an EPS extension. The graph's fonts and the size and colors of its components have been optimized for reproduction on a slide.

To produce the best results, you should choose a PostScript printer as your default printer before writing the graph to an EPS file. You can then select actual PostScript fonts from the Style–Font menu. Then Quattro Pro will not have to translate its Bitstream fonts into PostScript when you create the EPS file.

You can also choose the PCX File option to save the current graph to a PC Paintbrush-compatible file with the PCX file name extension. This is a very popular file format, which can be imported into many drawing, painting, and graphics presentation programs. There are some slide services that will make 35mm slides from PCX files. However, the quality of a slide made from a PCX file is usually not as good as that of a slide made from a PostScript file.

As you have seen in this chapter, the process of graphing in Quattro Pro can be very involved, with dozens of commands coming into play. But you have only seen the tip of the iceberg. The next chapter will introduce you to the Graph Annotator, which will let you make a good-looking graph absolutely outstanding.

Adding Sizzle to Your Graphs

Fast
Track

To resize an object,   **404**

first select it, and then drag any of its handles to a new position. To resize a group of objects, mark the group and then resize any one of the objects. Maintain their proportions by first selecting the group in proportional mode.

To align objects in the drawing pad,   **408**

use the Align command on the Group menu, or use the grid feature accessed through the Visible and Snap-to commands on the Group menu.

To type more than one line of text,   **410**

use the Text command, type a line of text, press Ctrl-↵, and type the next line. When finished, press ↵.

To create a graph button that displays a graph,   **413**

create a text entry in the drawing pad, choose the Graph Button option in the property sheet, and then select one of the named graphs. To use a graph button to run a macro, type the macro code after you select Graph Button.

To import a picture file into the drawing pad,   **421**

use the Clipboard command in the toolbox, choose the Paste From command in the property sheet, and then specify the name of the file you wish to import.

To link an object to a data point in a graph,   **423**

use the Link command in the toolbox.

WITH QUATTRO PRO'S GRAPH ANNOTATOR, YOU CAN embellish and modify your graphs in ways never before available in any spreadsheet program. It provides the following capabilities:

- Modifying graph components by directly manipulating them
- Adding arrows, lines, and shapes in any color or style
- Changing the size of the graph or its components
- Adding text anywhere in the graph
- Creating graph buttons for directing the progress of slide shows
- Inserting portions from other graphs
- Inserting pictures from clip-art files

This chapter describes how to take advantage of the Graph Annotator.

ANNOTATING THE CURRENT GRAPH

You can access the Graph Annotator by either selecting the Graph–Annotate command or, when viewing a graph, by simply pressing the slash key, /.

When you open the Annotator, it automatically displays the current graph. Any changes you make to the graph will remain after you leave the Annotator and return to the spreadsheet; when you use the Graph–View command (F10) to view your graph, the changes will be a part of it.

To create a completely new graph in the Annotator, you should first use the Graph–Customize Series–Reset–Graph command to return all graph settings to their defaults.

If you wish to annotate another graph, you must first use the Graph–Name–Display command to make that graph the current one. When you are finished, be sure to use the Graph–Name–Create command to rename the graph to include these changes.

If you have not defined a graph for the current spreadsheet, the Annotator will display a blank drawing area. Whatever you add here will appear as the current graph in the spreadsheet.

Because you have not specified any data, Quattro Pro will set the graph type to Text. Remember that a text graph is one that shows only what has been added through the Annotator.

When you are working in the Graph Annotator, Quattro Pro is in graphics mode, which allows you to work on the graph itself. The program will run slower than normal, but when you return to the spreadsheet, Quattro Pro will be back in text mode (unless you had previously invoked the Options–Display Mode–WYSIWYG command).

COMPONENTS OF THE GRAPH ANNOTATOR SCREEN

The Annotator screen appears as shown in Figure 13.1, which displays the graph from Figure 12.5, ready to be annotated.

The graph image displayed by the Annotator consists of unique components called *elements*, or *objects*. Each object is either one that you added within the Annotator, such as a line, box, or

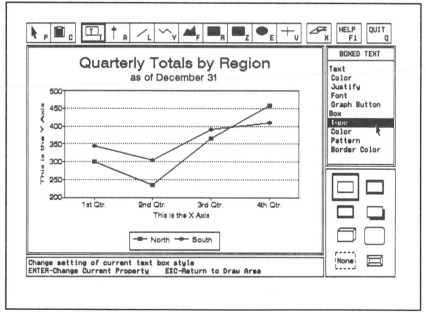

Figure 13.1: The Graph Annotator with a graph to be annotated

picture from another program, or one that came into the Annotator with the current graph.

The graph that you defined within the spreadsheet consists of three distinct objects: the body of the graph, its two-line main titles, and its legend. Within the Annotator, you can create or modify an object without affecting the others.

Each object also has its own set of *attributes*, or *properties*, that you can modify. These include color, pattern, and line style for objects that you draw; or typeface, point size, color, and style for text.

THE DRAWING PAD

The portion of the screen that contains the graph in Figure 13.1 is called the *drawing pad*. The boundaries of this area represent the boundaries created by your screen when you are viewing a graph. The graph in the figure almost fills the drawing pad, and will therefore practically fill the screen when you later view the graph from within the spreadsheet with the Graph–View command.

The arrow below the highlighting in the menu on the right side of the screen is the cursor, or mouse pointer. You don't have to use a mouse in the Annotator, but it is highly recommended. It's much easier to select items from the menus or pick objects in the graph when you use a mouse, and it is almost impossible to draw a curved line without one.

But you can still move the cursor around the Annotator screen without a mouse by using the cursor-control keys. Along with moving the cursor left, right, up, and down with the ←, →, ↑, and ↓ keys, you can also move the cursor diagonally with these keys:

- Home: Up and left
- End: Down and left
- PgUp: Up and right
- PgDn: Down and right

The cursor moves in very tiny increments when you press one of the directional keys. This provides the control you need, such as when you are drawing lines to connect points.

If you need to move the cursor in big leaps across the drawing pad, press and release the Scroll Lock key and then move the cursor, or press and hold down the Shift key as you move the cursor. Either method will take the cursor across the entire width of the drawing pad in about 15 moves.

THE DRAWING TOOLBOX

At the top of the screen in Figure 13.1 are 14 boxes that make up the *toolbox*. Each box contains a symbol that indicates the command that is invoked when you select that box with the mouse. Each one also contains a letter, which is the letter you type to invoke that command from the keyboard.

For example, the box on the far right contains the word QUIT, as well as the letter Q. To select this command, which returns you to the spreadsheet, you can click on the box with your mouse or activate the toolbox (menu bar) by pressing the slash key and then pressing Q.

Table 13.1 summarizes the commands in the toolbox. To deactivate the toolbox or cancel a command, press Escape.

Table 13.1: Graph Annotator Toolbox Commands

COMMAND	FUNCTION
P (Pick)	Allows you to select any component, or object, in the graph for editing.
C (Clipboard)	Provides commands for accessing the Annotator's Clipboard, which you use for copying graph elements or pasting elements from other graphs or pictures into the current graph.
T (Text)	Inserts text in the graph.
A (Vertical Arrow)	Draws arrows to point out important parts of the graph.

Table 13.1: Graph Annotator Toolbox Commands (continued)

COMMAND	FUNCTION
L (Line)	Draws straight lines.
Y (Polyline)	Draws a line between multiple points.
F (Polygon)	Creates a polygon.
R (Rectangle)	Draws a rectangle.
Z (Rounded Rectangle)	Creates a rectangle with rounded corners.
E (Ellipse)	Draws a circle or an ellipse.
V (Vertical/ Horizontal)	Draws perfectly vertical or horizontal lines.
X (Link)	Associates an object in the graph to a data point, so that if the data changes, the object will move with it in the graph.
F1 (Help)	Brings up the Help screen.
Q (Quit)	Leaves the Annotator and returns to the spreadsheet.

THE PROPERTY SHEET, GALLERY, AND STATUS BOX

To the right of the drawing pad, just below the toolbox, is the *property sheet.* This small window displays a list of all properties for either the currently selected object in the drawing pad or the command you have selected. In Figure 13.1, the Text command has been selected, and the list of properties for text appears in the property sheet.

By choosing items from this menu, you can change the properties of the text. Using a mouse, just click on the item you want. With the keyboard, you can use the ↑ or ↓ key to highlight the command you want, and then press ↵.

When you select a command from the toolbox, the drawing pad is still the active area of the screen. To activate the property sheet, you press F3 or use your mouse to click on the property you wish to change. To return from the property sheet to the drawing pad without changing a property, press Escape.

The *gallery* is the small window below the property sheet. It lists all the choices for the currently selected property, such as colors, line styles, or fill patterns. For example, the Box–Type property has been selected in Figure 13.1, and the gallery displays the boxes you can choose to enclose text in the graph.

At the bottom of the Annotator screen is the *status box*, which displays messages and status reports to remind you of the currently active command or property and what you should do next. In Figure 13.1, the status box contains the message

Change setting of current text box style

DRAWING LINES AND ARROWS

Using the Annotator's toolbox commands, you can draw arrows, straight lines, and segmented lines. You can set their attributes before or after drawing them.

DRAWING AN ARROW

An arrow can call attention to an important data point or trend in the graph. You use the Arrow (A) command to draw an arrow in the drawing pad. The properties of an arrow include the color of the arrowhead and the color and style of its shaft.

Use the following steps to create an arrow:

1. Select the Arrow command. Either click on it with your mouse or activate the toolbox by pressing the / key, and then type **A**.

2. Position the cursor where you want the arrow to begin. This will be the end opposite the arrowhead.

3. Press the period key to start the arrow (this is analogous to anchoring the corner of a block when pointing). With a mouse, press and hold down the mouse button.

4. Move the cursor to draw the shaft. If you are using a mouse, just drag to draw the line.

5. When the line is the correct length, press ↵ or release the mouse button. The arrowhead will appear at this end of the line. The color and style of the arrow are determined by the current settings in the property sheet.

To delete an arrow, or any other object in the drawing pad, move the cursor to the object and press the Delete key. You can also delete one or more selected objects, as discussed later in the chapter.

USING ANOTHER ARROW STYLE

You can change an arrow's line style, and if you have a color display, you can also change the color of the line or arrowhead. Here is the procedure for using another line style:

1. Select the Arrow command from the toolbox, but don't draw the arrow yet.

2. If you are not using a mouse, press F3 to activate the property sheet.

3. Select the Style property under the Line option. If you have a mouse, just click on that command. The gallery will now display eight different line styles. The current style is enclosed in a box.

4. Choose the line style you want to use. The property sheet will again be the active portion of the screen.

5. Press Escape to return to the drawing pad and draw the arrow. With a mouse, you can simply select the line style and then immediately go to the drawing pad to draw the arrow.

Figure 13.2 shows the graph from Figure 13.1 with two arrows added: one with a thin shaft and one with a wide shaft. Later in the chapter, you will learn how to select graph objects, such as these arrows, and change their properties.

DRAWING A STRAIGHT LINE

By using the Line (L) command, you can draw a straight line anywhere in the drawing pad. A line has the properties of color and line style.

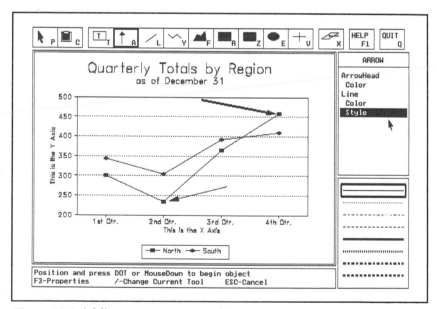

Figure 13.2: Adding arrows to a graph

Drawing a line is the same as drawing an arrow, except that the result does not have an arrowhead. Follow these steps to draw a line of any length:

1. Choose the Line command.

2. Position the cursor where you want the line to begin.

3. Press the period key to anchor that end of the line, or press and hold down the mouse button.

4. Move the cursor to the point where you want the line to end, or drag with your mouse.

5. Press ↵ or release the mouse button.

You can change a line's properties before you draw it, just as you can for an arrow.

DRAWING A SEGMENTED LINE

The Polyline (Y) command allows you to draw a line through multiple points. The process of creating one is a little different from that of drawing a single line.

You start drawing the segmented line just as you draw a straight line: Choose the command from the menu, position the cursor at the beginning of the line, press period (or hold down the mouse button), move to the end point of the line, and press ↵ (or release the mouse button). At this point, however, you can continue the line from point to point. Without pressing period again, move the cursor to the next point you wish to connect with the line, and then press ↵. With a mouse, just move the mouse pointer to the next point and click the mouse.

A line will jump from the cursor or mouse pointer to the previous point on the line. You can continue in this fashion for as many as 1000 points. When you are finished drawing the line, press ↵ a second time, or double-click the mouse.

DRAWING A CURVED LINE

You can also draw a curved line with the Polygon command, which is discussed shortly.

If you have a mouse, you can also draw a curved line with the Polyline command. To do so, either press the Scroll Lock key and then draw the line or hold down the Shift key as you draw the line.

The line that is drawn will curve to match your movements. To finish the curved line, either select the Polyline command again, or release the Scroll Lock or Shift key and then press ↵ or click the mouse.

You can mix curved lines and straight, segmented lines simply by pressing or releasing the Scroll Lock or Shift key at the appropriate point.

DRAWING A VERTICAL OR HORIZONTAL LINE

The Vertical/Horizontal Line (V) command allows you to draw perfectly vertical or horizontal lines, depending on the direction in which you move the cursor. To draw a vertical line, follow these steps:

1. Select the Vertical/Horizontal Line command.

2. Move the cursor to the point where you want the vertical line to begin.

3. Press the period key or hold down the mouse button.

4. Move the cursor vertically, either up or down, but not side to side. As soon as you move the cursor, a line will be drawn in that direction.

5. Extend the vertical line as far as you need it, and then press ↵ or release the mouse button.

To draw a horizontal line, repeat these steps, but move the cursor in a horizontal direction.

DRAWING SHAPES

There are four Annotator commands for drawing shapes. With them, you can draw polygons, rectangles, rounded rectangles, and ellipses (including circles).

DRAWING A POLYGON

With the Polygon (F) command, you can draw multisided figures of any shape or size that can be filled with both a pattern and color. Drawing a polygon is virtually the same as drawing a segmented line, but when you finish the object, the last point is automatically connected with the first one to close the polygon. The inside of the object will be given a color and pattern, which are determined by the current settings in the property sheet.

The property sheet is divided into two categories: Fill and Border. The Fill properties pertain to the inside of the polygon, as follows:

- Color: The color of the fill pattern.

- Pattern: The pattern, or cross-hatching, that will fill the object. You can select No, so that the polygon's interior will be the same color as the underlying color. If you choose the blacked out pattern, the inside will be filled with the pattern color you have selected.

- Background Color: The color that will fill the polygon behind the pattern.

The Border properties of the polygon include the Color and Style choices that all lines have, along with the property Drawn. When Drawn is set to No, the polygon will not have a border. When it is set to Yes, the polygon's outline will appear according to the Color and Style settings.

DRAWING A RECTANGLE
OR ROUNDED RECTANGLE

You can draw rectangles with square or rounded corners by using the Rectangle (R) and Rounded Rectangle (Z) commands, respectively.

Because a rectangle always has two pairs of sides that are parallel to one another, drawing one is a different process than drawing a polygon. Instead of drawing each of the four sides, you anchor one corner of the rectangle and then expand the entire rectangle from that point. Let's draw one, and this time we will set the pattern to a diagonal cross-hatching. First you should erase anything that's in the drawing pad.

1. From the spreadsheet, choose the Graph–Customize Series–Reset–Graph command.

2. Choose the Graph–Annotate command to return to the Annotator.

3. Choose the Rectangle (R) or Rounded Rectangle (Z) command, and you will see the properties for the rectangle appear in the property sheet.

4. Press F3 to activate the property sheet.

5. Select the Pattern command under the Fill option.

6. In the gallery, select the diagonal cross-hatch pattern.

7. Press Escape to return to the drawing pad. Now you are ready to draw the rectangle.

8. Move the cursor to the point where you would like to position one corner of the rectangle (don't worry about exact placement, because you can always move the rectangle later).

9. Press the period key or press and hold down the mouse button to anchor the corner.

10. Move the cursor or the mouse (while holding down the button) toward the point where the opposite corner of the rectangle should be. As you move the

As you highlight each property in the property sheet, the current setting for it will be enclosed in a box in the gallery.

cursor, you will see an expanding rectangle with corners at the beginning point and the cursor.

11. Adjust the size of the rectangle by moving the un-anchored corner at the cursor. When it is properly sized, press ↵ or release the mouse button, and the job is done.

Figure 13.3 shows the resulting rectangle with its fill pattern of diagonal cross-hatching. You can see the mouse pointer at the lower-right corner of the rectangle. Notice the pattern choices in the gallery. The one that is enclosed in the box is the currently selected pattern.

DRAWING AN ELLIPSE

You can draw a circle or an ellipse with the Ellipse (E) command. The attributes for this object are the same as those for the rectangle and polygon. You create an ellipse in the same way

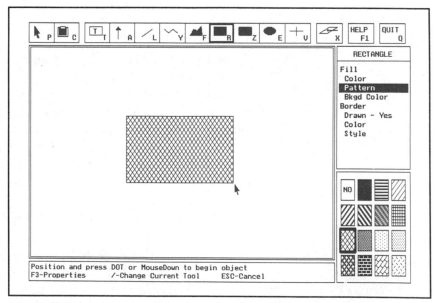

Figure 13.3: A rectangle with a cross-hatching fill pattern

that you create a rectangle. Here is a quick guide to drawing an ellipse:

1. Select the Ellipse command.

2. Move the cursor to the spot where a "corner" of the ellipse should be. You will be drawing a rectangle that defines the outer edges of the ellipse, so you are now anchoring one corner of that rectangle.

3. Press the period key or the mouse button to anchor the corner.

4. Move the cursor away from the centerpoint to expand the ellipse. You will see a rectangle expanding from the point, the edges of which define the size and shape of the ellipse.

5. When you have adjusted the size, press ↵ or release the mouse button. The rectangle will be replaced by an ellipse. The color, line style, and fill pattern will correspond to the current settings in the property sheet.

CREATING A CIRCLE

It is harder to create a circle than an ellipse because you must move the cursor precisely the same distance both vertically and horizontally. Before you finish the command, the rectangle you have expanded should be a true square, equal on all sides. This is one instance in the Annotator when a mouse is not the tool of choice. To create a perfect circle, you should use the cursor-control keys to move the cursor the same number of spaces in both directions. Follow this procedure:

1. Invoke the Ellipse command and anchor one corner as usual.

2. To expand the circle in the vertical plane, count each time you press the ↓ or ↑ key to move the cursor in a vertical direction away from the anchored corner.

Remember to hold down the Shift key to move the cursor in larger jumps.

3. When you have set the diameter of the circle, press the ← or → key the same number of times to expand the circle in the horizontal plane.

4. Press ↵ to complete the circle.

Because you move the cursor the same number of spaces in both planes, the shape will be round and not elliptical.

MANIPULATING OBJECTS

To manipulate existing objects, you must first select them. Then you can delete, edit, size, and move them.

You can use either the mouse or the keyboard to select an object you wish to change. The mouse is generally easier, but the keyboard can prove more effective in certain circumstances.

SELECTING AN OBJECT WITH THE MOUSE

Here is how you select an object with the mouse:

1. Invoke the Pick (P) command, the first command on the left in the toolbox.

2. Point to the object you want to select and click the mouse. That's all there is to it.

You will see eight little black boxes appear along the perimeter of the object. These are called *handles,* and they remind you that the item has been selected and can be used to move and resize the object as well.

If you now select another object, the first object will be unselected. By default, only one object can be selected at a time. But you can select multiple objects, and then edit them all at the same time. There are two ways to select more than one object, or group, when you are using the mouse:

- If the objects are all in the same portion of the drawing pad, position the mouse pointer at one corner of

the area you wish to select, and then press the mouse
button and drag to the diagonally opposite corner. An
expanding rectangle will cover that portion of screen.
When you release the mouse button, the rectangle will
disappear, and any objects within the rectangle will be
selected.

• If the objects are not contiguous, mark each one
separately to create the group. Either press the Scroll
Lock key or hold down the Shift key, and then click on
each object.

Figure 13.4 shows several objects selected on the Annotator
screen.

SELECTING AN OBJECT WITH THE KEYBOARD

To select objects using the keyboard, choose the Pick command,
and then press the Tab key. The first press of the Tab key selects

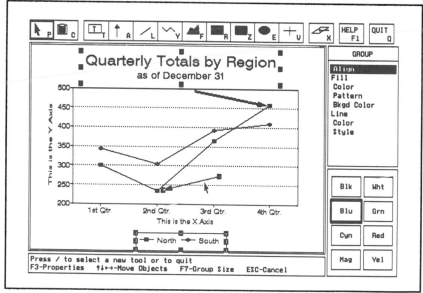

Figure 13.4: Multiple objects selected in the drawing pad

the first object in the drawing pad. The next press unselects the first object and selects the second object, and so on. In this way, you can rotate through the objects, selecting each one in turn. To select multiple objects as a group, select each object and press Shift-F7 before selecting the next one.

Even if you have a mouse, sometimes the keyboard method is a better way to select objects. For example, it may be difficult to tell which images in the drawing pad are separate objects. The only way to determine this is by selecting one image and seeing where the handles appear. It may also be difficult to pick out one object from a complex image. You can use the Tab key to select the object without having to specifically pick it out from the others—just keep pressing Tab until the handles appear on the portion you want.

DELETING AN OBJECT

Use caution when deleting objects because there is no Undo command available in the Annotator.

You can delete any object in the drawing pad, whether it is selected or not, simply by moving the cursor or mouse pointer to the object and then pressing the Delete key.

But if you have selected one or more objects, they will be the ones that are deleted when you press the Delete key. There is also a Delete command on the Clipboard menu that you can use to delete any selected object. The Clipboard's Cut command removes an object which you can later paste back into the drawing pad (the Clipboard will be discussed later in this chapter).

Although you cannot delete the body of the graph in the Annotator, you can delete its main titles and legends. Quattro Pro will automatically reset those options in the Graph menu.

MOVING AND SIZING AN OBJECT

Once you have selected an object, you can change its position or size in the drawing pad. As usual, you will find it easiest to use a mouse to manipulate the objects.

MOVING AN OBJECT

Here are the steps for moving an object with a mouse:

1. Invoke the Pick command and click on the object you want to select. You will see the handles appear along its perimeter.

2. Point to a spot *within* the selected object. Don't point to the handles on its borders, or you will resize the object.

3. Press the mouse button, and you will see a rectangle enclose the object.

4. Drag the rectangle to the new location.

5. Release the mouse button, and the object will be moved to the new location.

To move an object using the keyboard, mark the object, and then move the cursor to the new location. Press ↵, and the job is done.

You can move several related objects in one operation if you first mark them as a group. With a mouse, click anywhere within the group and then drag the objects to a new position. From the keyboard, move the cursor to shift the objects to the new location and press ↵.

Remember that to mark more than one object you can either hold down the Shift key (or press Scroll Lock) as you click on each one with the mouse, or use the Shift-F7 key when you are selecting objects from the keyboard.

RESIZING AN OBJECT

You resize an object with a mouse by selecting it and then dragging any of its handles to expand or contract that side. When you press down the mouse button, the handles will disappear, and a rectangle will appear around the object. You adjust the size of the rectangle and then release the mouse button to complete the resizing.

If you drag one of the corner handles, you can move that corner in any direction, affecting both the vertical and horizontal dimensions of the object. Dragging one of the handles between the corners adjusts the object only in one dimension. For example, if you select the handle on the right side of an object, you can make the rectangle wider or narrower from that side, but not taller or shorter.

To resize an object from the keyboard, first select the object, and then press the period key to activate the handle on the lower-right corner of the object. You can move that corner in any direction by using the cursor-control keys, and thereby resize the object. Remember that you can move the cursor diagonally with the Home, End, PgUp, and PgDn keys, and move it in large jumps by holding down the Shift key. To make another corner the active one, press the period key again. When you are finished sizing the object, press ↵.

RESIZING A GROUP OF OBJECTS

Just as you can move several objects as a unit if you first mark them as a group, you can also resize a group of objects. Simply mark the group and then adjust the size of one of the objects in the group. All the objects will be sized at the same time.

Each object remains anchored in its position in the drawing pad, no matter how you may size it. Expanding the group of objects will cause the space between them to shrink. Contracting the objects will cause the space between them to expand.

If you want to maintain the relative positions of the objects in the group, you can perform a *proportional resize*. You specify the proportional resize mode when you select the group of objects. With a mouse, hold down the Alt key while you drag the rectangle over the objects you wish to select as a group. When you release the mouse button, you will see handles around the outer perimeter of the group, not around each object in it.

Don't release the Alt key before you have released the mouse button; otherwise, the objects will be selected in normal, not proportional, mode.

To select objects in proportional mode from the keyboard, select the objects in the usual way (press Tab and then Shift-F7 to include each object in the group), and then press F7. The objects will lose their individual handles and be enclosed in a rectangle with handles.

As an example, Figure 13.5 shows three squares and two lines that together form one image. You could shrink all these objects by simply selecting them as a group and then resizing one of them, but the result would be as shown in Figure 13.6. Each

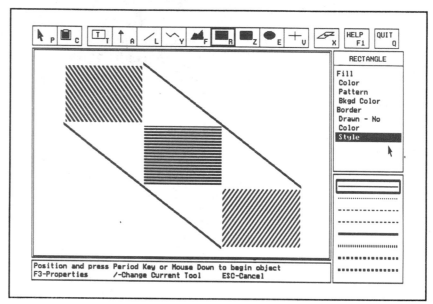

Figure 13.5: Five objects that together create a single design element

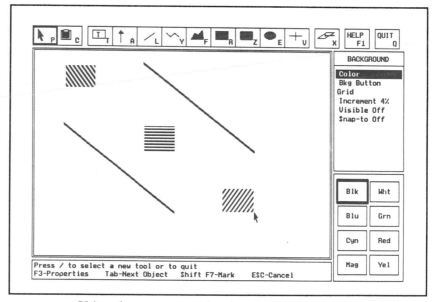

Figure 13.6: Using the nonproportional resize mode creates a very different image

object remains in its original position in the drawing pad, so that the spaces between them all have increased. Figure 13.7 shows the results of resizing the objects in proportional mode.

CHANGING AN OBJECT'S ATTRIBUTES

Once you have selected an object, you can change any of its attributes, just as though you were creating the object for the first time. For example, if you were to select one of the squares in Figure 13.5, the property sheet would list all the properties associated with a rectangle: the Color, Pattern, and Background Color choices for Fill, and the Color and Style choices for Border, and whether it will be drawn or not.

If you press F3 to activate the property sheet, and then change any of these properties, the difference is immediately reflected in the selected object.

You can also modify the attributes of a group of objects. If you were to select all three rectangles in Figure 13.5, all of them

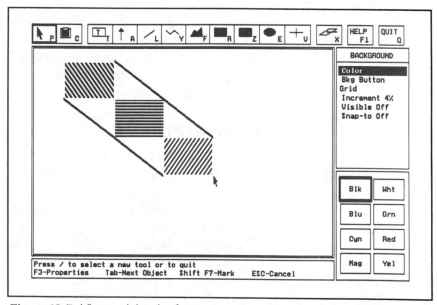

Figure 13.7: After resizing in the proportional mode, the image looks more like the original

would be affected by a change in their attributes.

Note that if you selected all the objects in Figure 13.5, the property sheet would be labeled Group instead of Rectangle because there is more than one type of object in the group: rectangles and lines. Changing the Pattern attribute would affect only the rectangles in the group, but changing the Line Color would affect both the rectangle borders and the lines.

ALIGNING OBJECTS

You will frequently want to line up several objects. The Annotator provides three built-in tools that make object alignment both consistent and effortless: the Group–Align command, and two types of drawing pad grids, Visible and Snap-to.

ALIGNING A GROUP

As mentioned in the previous section, whenever you have selected a group of objects (in the normal or proportional mode), the property sheet displays the Group options. This menu includes the Align command, which gives the choices of aligning the objects along their left or right sides; their tops or bottoms; or through their centers, either vertically or horizontally. As soon as you make your selection from the Align menu, the objects move into perfect alignment.

ALIGNING WITH GRIDS

When you first choose the Pick command in the Graph Annotator, the graph's background is selected by default. The property sheet for the background lists the options Color, Bkg Button, and Grid. There are three choices under Grid: Increment, Visible, and Snap-to. Both the Visible and Snap-to options are toggle commands that are set to No (disabled) by default.

Setting the Visible option to Yes displays a grid of dotted lines in the drawing pad. You can use the grid lines as a guide for aligning objects manually as you create, size, or move them. The grid is simply to help you arrange your work; you can turn it off or on at any time without affecting any of the objects in the drawing pad.

When you enable the Snap-to option, the edges of objects you create or manipulate are automatically "snapped" to the nearest grid lines in the drawing pad. You don't have to line each object up manually. The snap-to effect works with or without the grid displayed. The same grid is used for both the visible and snap-to options. You decide whether you want the grid to be visible, and whether you want objects to snap to its lines.

The Increment option lets you adjust the spacing of the grid lines. This spacing is measured by its percentage of the height and width of the drawing pad. By default, the lines are spaced at intervals of 4 percent of the width and height of the drawing pad, producing 25 lines in each direction. You can make the spacing very tight by setting the increment to a lower number (the minimum is 1), or very loose by setting it to a higher number (the maximum is 25).

ENTERING TEXT

You can enter two types of text in a graph:

- Integral text that is part of the graph
- Free-form text that is entered within the Annotator

Integral text is what you enter via the Graph–Text menu, through the options 1st Line, 2nd Line, X- and Y-Titles, and Legends. You must use the Graph–Text menu to create or make changes to the text of these items; they cannot be changed from within the Annotator. However, you can change attributes that affect the look of the text. For example, you can move or resize the box and the text that it encloses, change the style of the box, or change the font style of the text.

You create free-form text within the Annotator by using the Text (T) command. This text cannot be modified from the Graph–Text menus. It is a separate object in the drawing pad. Using Annotator commands, you can change the typeface, size, style, and color of this text. You can also choose to enclose it in a box, justify it within the box, customize its drop shadow, and apply a color and pattern to the box.

The way that text is presented in the Annotator depends on the Options–Graphics Quality setting. If you change it from Draft to Final, Quattro Pro always uses the Bitstream fonts you specify in the Annotator. If the fonts are not already on disk, they will be built, and that can be a time-consuming process on a slower computer. Therefore, you should generally work in draft mode, and use final-quality mode only for those graphs that require as much accuracy as possible before they are printed.

CREATING AND EDITING TEXT WITHIN THE ANNOTATOR

Within the Annotator, you can create and place text anywhere in the drawing pad, as follows:

1. Select the Text command and position the cursor where you want the text to appear.

2. If you want to change any of the text attributes before you begin, press F3 to activate the property sheet, make your selections, and press Escape to return to the drawing pad.

3. Start typing the text, which appears within a box that expands to surround the text as you type.

4. To type a second line, press Ctrl-↵ and type the text for that line. Proceed in this fashion for as many lines of text as you need.

5. Press ↵, and the text will be placed into the drawing pad. By default, the text will be enclosed in a box.

Just as with text in the spreadsheet, you can create bullets by using the special bullet code, \bullet *n*\, where *n* is a number from 0 through 6 that sets the style of the bullet. Because the Annotator is in a graphics mode, the bullet codes you enter will be displayed as the actual bullet character when you have completed the text entry.

Once you have created text within the Annotator, you can edit that text at any time. Select the text object just as you select other Annotator objects. Then you can type new text that will replace the existing text, or press F2 to edit the existing text. This is similar to working with text within the spreadsheet. When you are finished, press ↵.

MODIFYING TEXT PROPERTIES

You can modify the properties of any text in the Annotator, whether it was created from the Graph–Text menu or from within the Annotator. You can change the properties before creating the text or select one or more existing text objects and then change their attributes.

All text in the Annotator (integral and free-form) has properties that include the text color and font, as well as the box color and type. The text color and font properties offer the same menu of fonts and colors that you see when you use the Graph–Text–Font command. The box color and type properties offer the same boxes that are displayed by the Graph–Overall–Outlines command.

Text that you create within the Annotator also has the justify property, which determines how each line of text in the object will be aligned within the box. The gallery offers left, center, and right justified choices.

The Annotator's Font–Style–Custom Shadow command lets you change the appearance of a text drop shadow. It offers the two choices Right/Left Drop Shadow and Down/Up Drop Shadow. By default, these options are set to 5 and 10, respectively, which place the drop shadow for each letter a bit to the right and below the letter. You can adjust these settings to any value between −100 and 100. A higher number creates a larger offset. A negative value for the Right/Left option places the drop shadow to the left of each letter; a negative number for the Down/Up option places the shadow above the letter.

The interior of the box that encloses any text you create in the Annotator is affected by its pattern and color properties. Be sure to choose a fill pattern that will not make the text in the box difficult to read. You can adjust the colors of both the text and the background pattern to get the most readable result. (Of course, the colors will be meaningless if you are printing the result on a standard black-and-white printer.)

You can move and resize a text object in the same way that you move and resize any other object in the drawing pad. Note that changing the size of the box that encloses the text does not change the size of the text itself. Therefore, you can shrink the box no smaller than the text, and expanding the box will simply leave more room between the box and text within it.

The size of the box surrounding the graph's titles or legends cannot be changed, but you can move these text elements and position them anywhere in the graph. They will remain in their new positions, even if you later change their text from the Graph menu.

DIRECTING YOUR SLIDE SHOWS WITH GRAPH BUTTONS

Any text box you create can be designated as a graph button. However, you cannot make buttons from the default text in graph titles or legends.

Graph buttons offer an exciting new dimension to Quattro Pro. They are easy to implement yet offer tremendous potential for creating dazzling graphics presentations.

A graph button is simply a text box that you add to a graph in the Graph Annotator. You then define the text as a graph button and assign a named graph to it. You can even assign a macro to a graph button.

The dazzle comes later when you display the graph with either the Graph–View command (F10) or as part of a slide show with the Graph–Name–Slide command. When you click on the graph button with your mouse or type the first letter of the text within the box, the graph you assigned to the button will be displayed. Now you can produce more flexible slide shows that anyone else could easily direct.

CREATING A BUTTON TO CALL A GRAPH

Let's create a graph button that calls another graph. Later, we'll create another button that executes a short macro. Our slide show will be small, but it will demonstrate all the steps in creating and using graph buttons.

1. Before you can use a graph button, you must have a named graph in the current spreadsheet. Create a simple graph and view it so you will know how it appears. Then invoke the Graph–Name–Create command, enter the name **Graph1**, and press ↵.

2. Clear all the current graph settings with the Graph–Customize Series–Reset–Graph command.

3. Choose Quit twice to return to Ready mode.

This graph is safely saved in the current spreadsheet under the name Graph1. Now let's create another graph that will eventually contain just two graph buttons.

4. From Ready mode, choose the Graph–Annotate command to enter the Graph Annotator. Because you cleared the graph settings, the drawing pad should be blank.

5. Select the Text command from the toolbox and position the cursor (or mouse pointer) near the center of the screen.

6. Type the text **Graph One**. Don't worry about the position of the text, its style, color, and so on. As explained in the previous section, you can adjust these text attributes after you enter the text. Press ↵ to complete the task.

At this stage, the text box is simply ordinary text. Now we will designate it to be a graph button.

7. Choose the Pick command, and then select the box with your mouse or the Tab key so that its selection handles appear.

8. Press F3 to activate the property sheet, and then choose the Graph Button option.

You will be prompted to select a graph name from the list displayed. The graph you choose is the one that will appear when this button is activated. Figure 13.8 shows the screen at this point.

9. Select Graph1 or type its name into the prompt, and then press ↵.

10. Press Escape to return to the drawing pad.

11. Choose the Quit command from the toolbox to leave the Graph Annotator.

The button is not finished yet; we have one more important step to take. You should be back at the Graph menu.

12. Select the Name–Create command and type **Menu** to name our newly created text graph, and then press ↵.

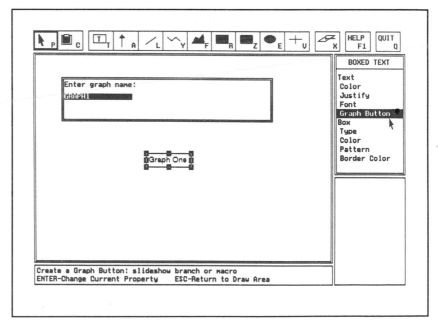

Figure 13.8: Making a text box a graph button

13. Quit the Graph menu and issue the File–Save command to save the spreadsheet, using a name of your choice. Now your work cannot be accidentally lost.

Naming the second graph is a critical step in any graphing procedure. In this case, as soon as you test the graph button, the other graph will be displayed. If you had not named the second graph (Menu), it would be lost. When a graph is named, it can always be recalled. You can also turn on the Graph–Name–Autosave Edits command, so that any changes you make to a graph are automatically saved each time you view it. In this case, it would allow you to edit the Menu graph in the Annotator and immediately test it without losing any of the changes you made.

Now let's test the button.

14. From Ready mode, press F10 to display the current graph, which is the text graph named Menu. You should see the single text box near the center of the screen. There will be no indication that it is a graph button, other than the text you placed in it.

15. If you are using a mouse, click on the box. Or, from the keyboard, type the first letter of the text, **G** (the case is not important).

Immediately, you should see the first graph you created, Graph1, displayed on the screen. Press any key or click the mouse to return to the spreadsheet. It's that easy.

To expand the slide show, the graph that was called from our small menu could also have one or more graph buttons. Some might call other graphs, one might say Quit, but one would certainly say something like Menu, which would recall our graph named Menu.

USING TRANSITION EFFECTS IN GRAPH BUTTONS

In your graph buttons, you can include all the effects that are available for slide shows via the Graph–Name–Slide command, which are described in Chapter 12. To assign various effects,

If you forget to name your graph before testing a button that calls another graph, Quattro Pro may display a message warning that you should save the graph before executing the graph button. But don't take any chances—save your graph after you have revised it.

enter the descriptions after the graph name when you are defining the button. Separate each description with a semicolon.

For example, suppose that you want the button you just created to call Graph1, using transition effect 17 at a speed of 3, and then display the graph for 20 seconds. You would change the button definition to

    Graph1;20;17;3

If you are using a VGA video display, there is one catch to including transition effects in your graph buttons. Because of memory constraints, Quattro Pro cannot display the effects in the normal VGA screen resolution of 640 by 480. When you use effects in your slide shows, Quattro Pro automatically changes from VGA to an EGA resolution of 640 by 350 to show the transition. However, it can't make the switch when you include a transition in a graph button. If Quattro Pro is in a VGA mode, it simply ignores the effect when it displays the graph.

To include the effects in graph buttons, you must first change to an EGA display with the Options–Hardware–Screen–Resolution command. Then you can display your graphs, select the buttons, and see the effects.

PLANNING YOUR GRAPH BUTTONS

Our example only has two graphs and one graph button, but you will most likely want to use many more for your slide presentations. Before you begin to create graph buttons and assign them each a graph name, you should first consider the slides you want to present and the order in which you wish to present them.

As you're mapping the order of the list of slides, consider what other controls you would like to have:

- Will all the slides come from a central menu, or will one slide call another, which in turn calls another, and so on?

Even though the transition effect will be ignored, the graph will be still be displayed for the amount of time you specify.

For valuable tips and techniques, as well as spreadsheet templates, examples, and macros, read the Quattro Pro ProView Guide as discussed in Chapter 12.

- Will each slide have a means of returning to the beginning or main menu?

- Will each slide have a Quit command to leave the slide show?

- If a button invokes a macro, should the macro eventually return to the same graph or should it call another?

This graphic uses the map of the United States that is one of the clip-art picture files that come with Quattro Pro. The USMAP.CLP file can be found in Quattro Pro's subdirectory.

There are many ways to arrange a slide show and countless more ways to design your graphic slides. Figure 13.9 shows one example. Five text boxes point out five states on the map. Each box is a graph button that has another graphic assigned to it. The sixth box, labeled Quit, offers a way to exit the slide show.

When the person viewing the slide clicks on the button labeled CA, for example, a graphic appears showing the state of California, as illustrated in Figure 13.10.

This example presents a need for another graph button feature: the background button. Normally, if the person at the keyboard or mouse presses any key except a graph-button letter, or clicks on a portion of the graph that is not a button, the graph presentation will end, and the the spreadsheet will return to the screen.

You can avoid this potential problem by defining the graph background button. The property sheet for the graph background contains the option Bkg Button. Use it to define the graph that you want displayed whenever the person viewing the presentation selects anything in the graph except a defined button.

When you create an endless loop of graphs such as this, be sure to include a button in the menu graph that serves as the Quit command, as shown in the lower-right corner of Figure 13.9. Otherwise, you would be locked into your graph presentation and might have to restart your compter.

In our earlier example, you could have the background button on the Menu graph display the same graph, Menu. During the slide presentation, selecting any part of the screen except one of the buttons would simply recall the Menu graph. The viewers would not see any change to the screen, and the presenter would have to specifically select one of the buttons to go to another graph or return to the spreadsheet.

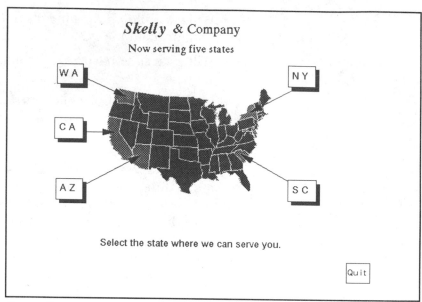

Figure 13.9: The United States map serves as the base for a graph
button menu

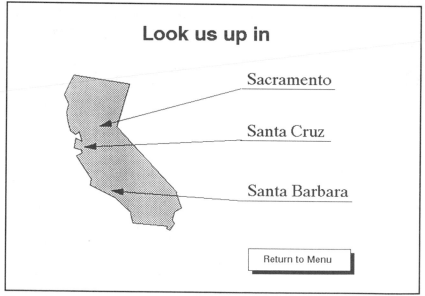

Figure 13.10: A graphic based on the map of California, with a button
that returns to the menu

HIDING A GRAPH BUTTON

For a presentation similar to the one in the above example, you might be tempted to designate each appropriate state as a graph button. That would be a neat idea, but it would also be difficult to implement. Since only text boxes can be buttons, you would have to include a text box within each state that was to serve as a button. Text boxes are always rectangles, so you might be able to make buttons in Wyoming, Colorado, and the Dakotas, but you would have little luck fitting a button in any other states.

However, if the need arises, you can hide a graph button within a graphic object by entering "invisible" text in an invisible box. Follow this procedure to hide a graph button:

1. Because you must enter some text, simply type one letter, backspace over it, type a space character, and then press ↵. You now have some invisible text.

2. Select the text box, size it appropriately, and position it within or surrounding the graphic object.

3. While the box is selected, choose the Graph Button option from the property sheet and assign a graph or macro to the button.

4. Define the Box Type of the text box as None, and the box will disappear. Your graph button is now hidden within the graphic object.

CREATING A BUTTON TO CALL A MACRO

Let's add a second button to our Menu graph. This one will execute a macro. If you're not familiar with macros, just follow along here, and then you can refer to Chapters 16 and 17 for more information about them. Start by retrieving the spreadsheet that contains the graph button graphs you created earlier.

1. Recall the Menu graph by using the Graph–Name–Display command and choosing the name Menu. The

When you type any character other than a slash, the Graph Annotator assumes you want to enter text and automatically goes into that mode.

text graph appears, but don't select the graph button this time.

2. Press the slash key (the menu key) to bring up the Graph Annotator.

3. Position the cursor (or mouse pointer) below the first text box.

4. Type **View Data** and press ↵.

5. Select this text box and choose Graph Button from the property sheet.

6. Don't select a graph. Instead, type the following macro, and then press ↵:

> {goto}M45~{d 3}{r 2}{get A10}{graph}

7. Press Escape to leave the property sheet.

8. Select the Quit command to leave the Graph Annotator, and then any key to return to the Graph menu.

9. From the Graph menu, choose Name–Create and enter **Menu** to rename our revised graph.

10. Choose Quit from the Graph menu to return to Ready mode. We can now test our new button.

11. From Ready mode, press F10, and you will see your two-button menu displayed on the screen.

12. Select the View Data button by clicking on it with your mouse or by pressing V.

You will be returned to the spreadsheet, where the cursor will immediately jump to cell M45 and then move down three rows and right two columns. The {get A10} macro we wrote is pausing (so that you can view data).

13. Press any key. The macro will continue with its next command, which displays the current graph, Menu.

This macro is strictly for testing purposes. A finished macro, whether in a spreadsheet or a graph button, would never contain cell addresses— you would substitute block names for them.

At this point, you could select another button from the menu and continue with the presentation.

There's a major refinement you should make to this macro that will make it much easier to manage, both when you write it and when you later need to revise it. Simply write your macro code in the spreadsheet, not in the Graph Annotator, and invoke it with the graph button. In this example, you could name the spreadsheet macro \VIEW_DATA and enter the command {\VIEW_DATA} into the graph button. This allows you to run a macro that is longer than the 254-character limit in the Graph Annotator. It also will be much easier to view and revise the macro in the future.

WORKING WITH THE CLIPBOARD

The Clipboard (C) command provides the means for importing and exporting objects in the drawing pad, as well as shifting an object to the foreground when it is behind another object. Before you can use most of the commands on the Clipboard menu, you must first select one or more objects.

The Clipboard consists of a file called QUATTRO.CLP that resides in the Quattro Pro subdirectory. It contains the most recently placed item from the drawing pad. Because it is a file, its contents will be available whenever you run Quattro Pro.

The Clipboard is simply a behind-the-scenes storage area for items you select on the drawing pad. You can move (cut) or copy one or more objects to the Clipboard. Later, you can insert (paste) them back into the drawing pad in the current graph, another graph, or even a graph in another spreadsheet.

The Clipboard retains only one set of objects at a time. When you place a new object in the Clipboard, it replaces the previous contents.

The first three commands on the Clipboard menu store and retrieve objects:

- Cut: Copies the selected object or objects to the Clipboard and deletes them from the drawing pad.

- Copy: Same as Cut but leaves the objects in the drawing pad.

- Paste: Copies the contents of the Clipboard into the drawing pad.

The next three commands on the Clipboard menu manipulate objects:

- Delete: Removes the objects from the drawing pad (same as pressing the Delete key).
- To Top: Moves the selected object to the top of the stack of objects, so that it is completely visible.
- To Bottom: Moves the selected object to the bottom of the stack of objects, making another object visible.

The last three commands on the Clipboard menu allow you to create your own files of objects from the drawing pad. You can keep these files for future use and insert them into other graphs in either the current or other spreadsheets.

The Cut To and Copy To commands are equivalent to the Clipboard's Cut and Copy commands, except that you are prompted for a file name before the objects are copied or cut from the drawing pad. The object or objects that you have selected are then saved under that file name. If you do not specify a file name extension, Quattro Pro uses CLP to denote the clip-art file.

The Paste From command is equivalent to the Paste command, but again you are prompted for a file name before the command is carried out. You can specify any clip-art file on your disk.

You can also import graphic files that are in the CGM file format. This means that you can work with the thousands of existing clip-art images that are on the market, as well as graphics exported from other programs. Just include the CGM file extension when you specify the name of the file that you want to bring in with the Paste From command.

Quattro Pro comes with sample clip-art files (CLP and CGM) that you can paste into the drawing pad with the Paste From command. These are all pictures that were created in the Graph Annotator, and they demonstrate not only the versatility of the drawing tools, but also the convenience of saving pictures for future use.

LINKING AN
OBJECT TO A DATA POINT

When you create an object in the drawing pad, the position of that object is fixed. You may be surprised later when you change some data in the graph and find that your enhancements no longer jibe with the bars, lines, or data points in the graph—the graph changed its size or shape, but the objects you added did not.

Figure 13.11 illustrates the problem. The second data point in the North data series has been increased from 235 to 285. You can see where the point used to be; the arrow is still pointing there.

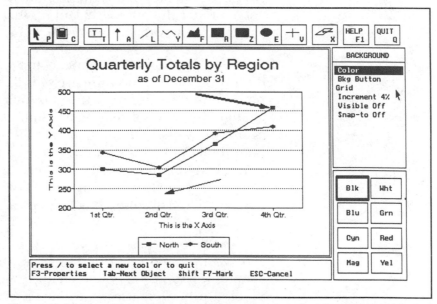

Figure 13.11: An object will no longer be associated with a data point when the value of the data point changes

You could return to the Annotator and move the objects back into position with the graph, but that might be a tedious, never-ending task. To solve this problem, you can use the Annotator's Link (X) command. This command allows you to link an object in the drawing pad to a point in any series of the graph.

Here is how you would link the arrow to the data point:

1. From the Graph Annotator, select the arrow that points to the data mark in the North series above the 2nd Qtr. on the x-axis.

2. Invoke the Link command. The property sheet will offer all six data series, plus the command Unlink.

3. Since the North series is the first data series, select 1st Series. A dialog box will appear, prompting you to enter the link index for this object.

4. This data point is the second in the first data series. Enter the number **2** and press ↵ (or click on the Enter button with your mouse).

The dialog box will disappear, and your graph will look as it did previously. But now the arrow is linked to that second data point in the North series. If you return to the spreadsheet and change the value of that data point, and then view the graph again, you will see that the arrow still points to the data mark, even though that mark has moved.

You can link more than one object to a data point, and you can link a group to a point as well. The Unlink command on the Link menu will dissolve a link between an object and a data mark.

This chapter has introduced you to the effects you can achieve by using Quattro Pro's Graph Annotator. The next chapter will show you how to set up a database within the spreadsheet, a process that can produce some very practical results, even if they are a little mundane compared to the dazzling graphics of the Graph Annotator.

14

Building a
Spreadsheet Database

Fast
Track

THIS CHAPTER DESCRIBES HOW TO SET UP A DATABASE in the spreadsheet. After you have set up your database, you can use the Database–Query commands to find, extract, or delete data from it. You can even access data in external database files, such as those from dBASE or Paradox. If you're a Paradox user, you will be interested in the Paradox Access. With it, you can run Paradox and Quattro Pro at the same time and switch between them as often as necessary.

First, we'll review the basic structure of a Quattro Pro database, and then we'll explore how to manipulate your data, starting with the use of the Database–Sort command.

THE STRUCTURE OF A QUATTRO PRO DATABASE

A *database* is a collection of information that can be arranged and accessed in an orderly manner to produce consistent results. Traditional database programs, such as Borland's Paradox, keep their data in a file. In Quattro Pro, the database is a block in the spreadsheet. A spreadsheet can hold more than one database, although you can work with just one at a time.

In the spreadsheet database, each row of data is a *record* and each column a *field*. Figure 14.1 illustrates a mailing list database. Each record is one person's entry in the list. Each field holds a different type of information: Last Name, First Name, Address, City, State, Zip, and Age. Each cell in the database belongs to just one field and one record.

Here are some guidelines for structuring a Quattro Pro database:

- You cannot spread the data for a single record over several rows; each row is considered to be a separate item. To attach more information to each record, you add more fields. You can have as many as 256 fields and 8191 records in a Quattro Pro database.

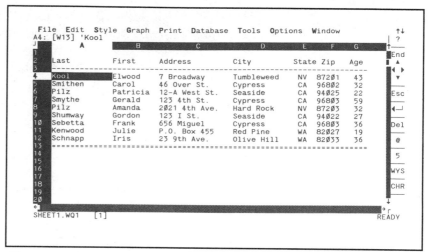

*Figure 14.1:*A spreadsheet database

- A field must contain the same type of data, either numeric or text, in each record. In a mailing list database, a column (field) labeled Zip must contain only zip codes, not names, phone numbers, or addresses. Furthermore, all the zip codes must be of the same type, text or numeric. Never mix the two types in one field.

- Be sure that the data within a field is all of the same scale. For example, you will run into trouble if a field named Distance has some entries measured in feet, others in inches, and still others in miles. When you later wish to select all records where the entry in Distance is greater than 20 meters, you will have a real problem!

- Use consistent spelling for all text entries. For a field labeled State, for example, it would be best to enter the two-letter abbreviations. Don't randomly enter Calif., Cal., CA, or California.

We will be using the mailing list shown in Figure 14.1 in the examples in this chapter. Before proceeding, enter the list in a blank spreadsheet. In row 2 of columns A through G, enter the titles **Last**, **First**, **Address**, **City**, **State**, **Zip**, and **Age**. Then enter the data in the appropriate fields, beginning in cell A4.

Kool, Elwood
7 Broadway
Tumbleweed, NV 87201
Age: 43

Smithen, Carol
46 Over St.
Cypress, CA 96802
Age: 32

Pilz, Patricia
12-A West St.
Seaside, CA 94025
Age: 22

Smythe, Gerald
123 4th St.
Cypress, CA 96803
Age: 59

Pilz, Amanda
2021 4th Ave.
Hard Rock, NV 87203
Age: 32

Shumway, Gordon
123 I St.
Seaside, CA 94022
Age: 27

Sebetta, Frank
656 Miguel
Cypress, CA 96803
Age: 36

Kenwood, Julie
P.O. Box 455
Red Pine, WA 82027
Age: 19

Schnapp, Iris
23 9th Ave.
Olive Hill, WA 82033
Age: 36

SORTING ROWS
IN THE SPREADSHEET

You can sort any block of cells in Quattro Pro; they need not be part of a formally defined database.

Sorting the records in a database is a common task. To sort a block of cells, you must define the block of rows and columns that are to be sorted and the columns that are to be used to determine the sort order. You also select whether the rows should be sorted in ascending or descending order.

Quattro Pro sorts row by row, but not across the columns. In Figure 14.1, for example, you can sort the entries based on last name, so that the rows will be rearranged in the block.

DEFINING THE SORT BLOCK

If you are going to sort a block more than once, give that block a name, such as SORT_BLOCK. This not only helps you in specifying the block, but it ensures that your sort block contains all the relevant rows and columns.

Use the Database–Sort–Block command to specify the rows and columns that are to be sorted. In Figure 14.1, the block would include columns A through G.

Use caution when you are defining the limits of the block to be sorted. If you do not include all the relevant columns, your data will be sorted into disaster. For example, if you sorted the name and address list in Figure 14.1 using only columns A through E, the rows in those columns would be rearranged but the data in columns F and G would not. The Zip and Age entries would no longer line up with the proper records! You would have to retrieve the most recently saved version of your spreadsheet and start over again.

You must also be careful to include only the relevant rows in the block and exclude all rows that you do not want rearranged in the sort. In Figure 14.1, you would include only rows 4 through 12, which contain the actual names and addresses, and leave out the titles in row 2 and the two dashed lines in rows 3 and 13. Therefore, in response to the prompt displayed by the

Database–Sort–Block command, you would specify the block A4..G12 to sort the mailing list shown in Figure 14.1.

DEFINING THE SORT KEY COLUMNS

Before Quattro Pro can sort the rows in the block you have defined, it needs to know which columns to use for ordering the data. For example, in a name and address list, you could sort the records by the Last Name column to arrange them alphabetically or by the Zip column to prepare for a mailing.

You can choose as many as five *key* columns to determine the sort sequence. You use the Database–Sort–1st Key command to define the first key column. If two records could contain exactly the same entry in their key column, you need to define a second key column to define their placement in the sort.

As an example, we'll sort the mailing list by last name. Since there will typically be at least two identical last names in a mailing list (Pilz in this example), we will define a secondary sort key as well. Follow these steps:

1. Before beginning, it is important that you save your spreadsheet database to disk if you have not saved it recently. If you make a mistake while defining the sort block, the data will not be sorted correctly, and you will have to retrieve the spreadsheet on disk.

2. For convenience, move the cell pointer to cell A4, the first cell in the sort block.

3. Before defining the sort, clear any existing settings by using the Database–Sort–Reset command.

4. Choose the Block command from the Sort menu, specify the block A4..G12, and then press ↵.

5. Choose 1st Key from the Sort menu, specify cell A4 (in the Last Name column), and press ↵. (It does not matter which row you specify in that column, as long as it is a valid address.) Next you will see the prompt

    Sort order (A or D)

6. Type **A** to specify ascending order (A through Z). Choosing descending order (D) sorts the list Z through A.

7. Choose 2nd Key, specify cell B4 (in the First Name column), and press ↵.

8. Type **A** for ascending order.

You can choose either ascending or descending order for each of the sort keys you define.

Now we have two key fields defined, and we are ready to sort the rows (did you save your spreadsheet not too long ago?).

9. Issue the Go command on the Sort menu. In an instant, the rows will be sorted.

The rows are now in alphabetical order, based on the entries in the Last Name field, as shown in Figure 14.2. Notice that the sort order for the two identical entries in the Last Name column was determined by their entries in the First Name column.

SPECIFYING SORT ORDER RULES

When sorting in ascending order, Quattro Pro places text entries before numeric ones, so that the word *zebra* would be

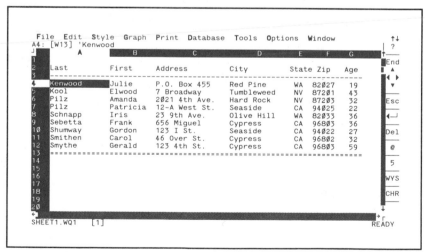

Figure 14.2: Sorting the block A4..G12 by last name and first name

placed above the numbers *1, 2, 1000,* and so on. You can switch this so that a number is sorted before any text by setting the Database–Sort–Sort Rules–Numbers before Labels command to Yes. If you want to retain this new rule for all future sessions of Quattro Pro, you must use the Options–Update command.

Also on the Sort Rules menu is the command Label Order, which has the choices Dictionary and ASCII. By default, entries are sorted in ASCII order, so that uppercase letters (*A, B, C*) come before lowercase ones (*a, b, c*). In ASCII order, the sorting sequence is case-sensitive, so that *Xavier* will be sorted before *alan.* If you do not want the case of the entries in the key column considered, choose Dictionary. Then *alan* will come before *Xavier.* Again, use the Options–Update command to save the new rule as the default for future sessions.

TIPS FOR SAFE AND ACCURATE SORTING

Quattro Pro will sort a block precisely as it has been instructed, but you may get unexpected results. The following sections provide some guidelines that will help you to avoid sorting problems.

WATCH THAT BLOCK

As emphasized earlier, be absolutely sure you are sorting all the columns that belong together in the block. If you leave out one or more columns, the data in them will be left out of the sort, and will no longer belong to the correct records in the block.

Forgetting to include some rows at the top or bottom of the block is not a serious problem. The result will be that the block is not entirely sorted, and you can simply sort again, this time including all the relevant rows.

But if you include rows that do not belong in the sorted block, such as a row of column titles above the block or SUM formulas at the bottom, those extra rows will be sorted with the others. If you do not catch the error right away, it will be too late to use the Undo command. Other than using the Edit–Move command to move each row, there will be no way for you to return the rows to their original order.

PRACTICING SAFE SORTS

As stated earlier, it is always a good idea to save your spreadsheet before sorting. That way, if things should go wrong, you will have a recent copy of your work on disk that you can retrieve. Also, a block name is another primary defense against errors in specifying the block to be sorted.

Of course, if you have enabled the Undo function, you can issue the Edit–Undo (Alt-F5) command after sorting, and the data will return to its original order. After you have sorted a block, therefore, you should take a moment to inspect the results to see if they are satisfactory.

If you will need to sort a block on a regular basis, creating a macro to perform the task will save you time in defining the sort and will also ensure the accuracy of the process. By writing a short macro to sort the block, you get perfect results with the least amount of effort.

Although you never have to use macros, the sooner you do, the better life will become with your spreadsheet. Macros are discussed in Chapters 16 and 17.

ADDING INSURANCE WITH AN INDEX COLUMN

Another way that you can keep tabs on the original order of a database is to create one or two index columns next to or within the sort block. For example, in Figure 14.2, you could insert a column at column A and use it as the index column. Use the Edit–Fill command to fill the column with consecutive numbers, so that each entry in the block has a unique number. When you sort the block, be sure to include this extra column in the sort block so that it is rearranged with the names and addresses.

If you should ever want to return the rows to their original order, just sort the block again using the index column as the first sort key. The rows will be arranged according to the numbers in that column.

If there is an additional source of errors, such as when other people will be using the spreadsheet and sorting the data, you can provide even more insurance by including two index columns: one on either side of the block of data. Each column should be filled with the same numbers, and both should be included in the sort block. No matter how you sort the block, the numbers in each row of the columns should always match, because sorting maintains all the columns in each row.

If the numbers in the index columns do not match, you know that one or both of them was left out of the sort block when the sorting was performed. This is a signal that other columns may also have been excluded from the sorted list.

WATCHING THOSE FORMULAS

There are two effects sorting will have on a formula, depending on where the formula is in relation to the sort block. If there is a formula within the block, it will be referring to cells in either its own row or outside its row. A formula outside the sort block may be referring to cells within the block (if it's not, then we don't need to talk about it).

When a row is rearranged during a sort, a formula in that row will adjust its relative cell references to its new location after sorting, just as it would if it were copied there with the Edit–Copy command. (Absolute cell references, of course, will not adjust.)

If a sorted formula was referring to a cell outside its row, its result will very likely change because it will now be referring to different cells. If the formula was referring to cells in its own row, its result will be the same after the sort because it will still be referring to cells in its row.

A formula outside the sort block will still be referencing the same cell address after the sorting is done; those cells were in a sense copied to a new location, not moved, so the formula did not follow them. However, the result of the formula will very likely be different because other values have been sorted into the cells it references.

DEFINING A DATABASE

A database in Quattro Pro consists of at least two blocks—the data and criteria blocks—and an optional output block. You specify each of these blocks with the commands on the

The last record in
the data block in
Figure 14.3 is a dashed
line. This is not re-
quired, but it delimits
the bottom of the
database, as well as
provides a visual cue to
the user. Any new rows
of data are inserted
above the dashed line.

Database–Query menu. Figure 14.3 shows the database blocks
defined for the mailing list (Figure 14.1).

The *data block* contains the data, where each column is a field,
and each row is a record. In Figure 14.3, the address of the data
block is A2..G13. The very first row of the data block must contain unique *column titles*, which serve as field names. The second
row of the database is always the first record in the database, no
matter what is entered in that row. For example, in Figure 14.3,
a dashed line divides the titles row from the first name in the list.
That dashed line is really the first record, even if it does not contain any useful data.

The *criteria block* (or table as it is called in the Database–Query
command) is where you specify your selection criteria. It consists of at least two cells: a column title from one of the data
fields and a second cell below the title that defines the search.
In Figure 14.3, the criteria table is in the block B17..B18, and it
specifies all entries in the address list who live in the state of
California (CA).

With just these two components, for example, you can search
through your database to find all records with an entry of CA in
the State field or delete all records that match the criterion.

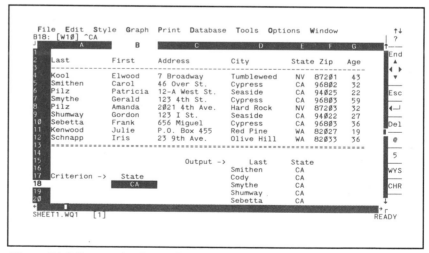

Figure 14.3: Data, criteria, and output blocks

But you can also pull out, or *extract*, all records that match the criteria if you have first specified an *output block*. This is a block of one or more columns, where the title of each column matches one from the data block. In Figure 14.3, the output block has been defined as the block D15..E20. Notice the titles in cells D15 and E15 are duplicates of the titles in cells A2 and E2. Records that match the criteria have been copied to the output block with the Database–Query–Extract command, although only the fields listed in the output block have been filled.

The column titles in each of the three blocks must be spelled exactly the same. If the title of a field in the data block is State, but you spell it ST in the output block, that field will be ignored in the output block. To ensure complete accuracy, use the Edit–Copy command to copy the column titles from the data block to the other blocks as you need them.

DEFINING THE DATA BLOCK

You use the Database–Query–Block command to define the block that contains the data of your database. The most important rule governing this definition is that the first row of this block must contain a unique column title for each column.

In Figure 14.3, you would define the data block as the cells A2..G13. This covers the column titles in row 2 all the way to the last record in row 13 (which happens to be a dashed line). Note that the column titles are a single row, each one is unique, and all are relatively short and therefore easy to type into formulas or commands.

The data block must always begin with the column titles, but there is no rule governing the number of columns or rows that you include in the block. You could use the block E2..F10 in Figure 14.3, for example, if that were the only data you wished to query. The rows below row 10 and the other columns would be ignored by any Query commands you later issue.

USING ANOTHER FILE AS THE DATA BLOCK

The block you define as the data block can be in another
Quattro Pro spreadsheet or in a nonspreadsheet file, such as a
Paradox database. You define the block with the usual linking
syntax (enclose the file name in square brackets and specify the
drive and path when necessary).

For example, if you specified this for the data block:

[C:\DATA\MYFILE]SOMEDATA

the block named SOMEDATA in the file MYFILE in the subdirectory DATA on drive C would be used. Quattro Pro assumes that
this is a spreadsheet file because there was no file name extension
included. That file does not have to be open.

When you want to refer to a database file, be sure to include
the file name extension, including DB for Paradox, RXD or R2D
for Reflex, and DBF for dBASE. You do not need to include the
exact coordinates of the block you wish to query in that file because Quattro Pro will use all its fields and records. Just specify
any valid block, such as A1..A2, to complete the definition. For
example, you could use the file reference

[C:\MOREDATA\NEWDATA.DB]A1..A2

for the Paradox file NEWDATA in the subdirectory MORE-
DATA on drive C.

ASSIGNING NAMES TO THE
FIELDS IN THE FIRST RECORD

When you use the Query commands, you will frequently refer
to the cells in the first record of the data block. In Figure 14.3, this
is row 3, the second row of the data block below the column titles.

To make this repetitive task easier and more accurate, you can
use block names to identify each of the cells in the first record.
You could name each cell after the column title above it, as long
as the titles will serve as effective block names, are no longer

than 15 characters, and do not contain inappropriate characters (such as arithmetic operators, parentheses, and so on).

In Figure 14.3, cell A3 would be named Last, B3 would be First, C3 would be Address, and so on. You could use the Edit–Names–Labels–Down command to name each of the cells in row 3 using the block A2..G2 as the source for the names.

However, the Database–Query–Assign Names command performs exactly the same function, and you do not have to specify the source cells for the names. It simply uses the text in the cells of the first row of the currently defined database to name each cell in the second row of that database.

Once defined, those names can be included in your query criteria; for example, +AGE>30 would find all those who are older than 30.

DEFINING THE OUTPUT BLOCK

The output block can be in another spreadsheet as long as that spreadsheet is open and therefore able to receive data.

You do not have to specify an output block if you are not going to use the Database–Query–Extract and Unique commands. When you will want to extract data, you must define an output block, with the first row containing copies of one or all of the column titles from the data block. In Figure 14.3, the output block titles are in cells D15 and E15.

WHICH COLUMNS TO INCLUDE

When you issue either the Database–Query–Extract or Unique command, Quattro Pro finds each record that matches the search criteria and copies it to the output block. Only those fields that are represented in the output block titles are copied. For example, in Figure 14.3, only two titles were used in the output block, Last and State, and only the last name and state of each matching record were copied.

You can include one or all of the data block's column titles, and they do not have to be in the same order as those in the data block. You can even duplicate column titles in the output block.

Remember that if the title in the output block is not spelled exactly the same as a title in the data block, Quattro Pro will ignore that column and will not copy data to it. Again, the best way to ensure matching titles is by using the Edit–Copy command to copy the titles from the data block to the output block.

THE NUMBER OF ROWS TO INCLUDE

When defining your output block, you can either limit the number of rows in it or let Quattro Pro use as many rows as necessary.

You limit the number of rows by specifying how big the block should be. For example, in Figure 14.3, you might specify the block D15..E20, which would leave just enough rows for the data that was copied there during the Database–Query–Extract command.

If more than five rows in the data block met the search criteria, Quattro Pro would not be able to fit them all in the limited output block and would issue the error message

   Too many records for output block

Usually, you won't know how many records will be found in the data block, so you won't know how large the output block should be. You could specify an overly large number of rows, but instead of limiting the space, you can let Quattro Pro use as many rows as needed.

To do so, just specify the first row of the output block (the column titles), and Quattro Pro will be free to use all the rows to the bottom of the spreadsheet, if necessary. In Figure 14.3, you would specify the block D15..E15, which would give Quattro Pro rows 16 to 8192.

Be very careful to situate the output block so that there are no other data cells below it. Quattro Pro erases all the cells below the output block titles in preparation for the extracted data. Any data in those cells will be erased during the Extract or Unique commands, even if no records from the data block are copied to the output block.

EXTRACTING TO AN EXTERNAL DATABASE

You cannot use a Paradox or dBASE file as the output block because those files cannot be opened in the same sense as a spreadsheet file can be opened. But you can still get your extracted data into them by including a spreadsheet output block in the process.

Specify the output block in the current or another open spreadsheet and proceed with the Database–Query–Extract command as usual. Then use the Tools–Xtract–Values command to save the output block as a database file.

DEFINING THE CRITERIA TABLE

Creating the selection criteria for a database query can be quite simple, but the wide range of selection criteria might make the task rather confusing. You define the criteria block by using the Database–Query–Criteria Table command. There are two different styles of criteria: character and logical formula.

The basic structure of the selection criteria block for each style is the same, and sometimes you can use either style interchange-ably. You can always include both types in the selection criteria. Even though logical formulas are somewhat difficult to understand, you will most likely use them more frequently than character criteria because they can greatly refine the scope of a search.

USING CHARACTER-BASED SELECTION CRITERIA

The selection criterion in Figure 14.3 is as simple as it can possibly be. It consists of the two cells, B17..B18, where the first cell contains one of the column titles, State, from the data block. The second cell contains the text that will be used to select records from the data, CA. In other words, any record where the entry under State is CA will be selected.

If you were to change the text below the column title from CA to WA and then execute the Extract command again, only two records would be selected—those where the State entry is WA in rows 11 and 12 of the data block.

If you now wanted to search for all those who were 32 years of age, you would change the criterion's title to Age and enter 32 below it. Two records would be found—those with the number 32 in their age column, in rows 5 and 8. Or, you could change the title to Last and put Pilz below it, and the two records with the last name of Pilz would be selected, rows 6 and 8.

USING SPECIAL CHARACTERS IN THE CRITERIA

⊙ The three special characters can only be used with a text criterion; they will not work with a numeric one.

When you are using a text criterion and not a numeric one (when you are looking under State and not Age, for example), you can broaden the scope of a search by including the wildcard characters ? and *. These are the same two characters you can use when specifying file names.

Wildcards allow you to find records when you are not sure of the precise spelling, such as Sm* to find both Smithen and Smythe. They also let you find groups of records that all begin with the same characters, such as 95* to find all zip codes in the 95 region (assuming the zip codes were entered into the data block as text, not numbers).

You can also preface the criterion with a tilde, ~, to specify all characters *except* those specified. In other words, using the criterion ~Smith would find all names that are not Smith. Or, you could broaden the exclusion to ~Sm*, which eliminates all names that begin with Sm.

ADJUSTING THE SCOPE WITH MULTIPLE CRITERIA

By using multiple criteria, you can fine tune the search, so that in Figure 14.1, for example, you can find all those who are 32 years old and live in California. To perform this type of search, you use multiple columns in the criteria block, where each column title is one of the titles in the data block. In the example, one column would be Age and the other State.

There are two types of multiple criteria: one selects this AND that, and the other selects this OR that. The example specifies age 32 AND state of California. You could relax the constraints on the search by specifying age 32 OR state of California, which would find more records in the data block.

You specify the condition in the way you arrange the criteria:

- AND: Put all criteria on the same row to narrow the search.

- OR: Put each criterion on a separate row to relax the search.

The following setup specifies an age of 32 AND a state of California:

Age	State
32	CA

This criteria specifies an age of 32 OR a state of California:

Age	State
32	
	CA

To find anyone whose last name begins with an S AND whose first name is not Frank AND who lives in CA, specify this:

First	Last	State
~Frank	S*	CA

You can include as many columns and rows in the criteria block as you need to pinpoint your search.

USING LOGICAL FORMULAS IN SELECTION CRITERIA

Using logical formulas for your criteria allows you to perform searches that could, for example, find people who are older than 30 or all zip codes greater than 80000 but less than 95000. In Chapter 4, you learned that a logical formula is one that

When you use multiple criteria, be sure to include them in the criteria block definition.

returns a result of either 1 (true) or 0 (false). In your query criteria, you can use any of the logical operators listed in Table 4.1.

For example, the logical expression 15>20 would always return false. The formula 3=3 would return true, and +A3>9 would return true only if the entry in A3 were greater than 9.

When you include a logical formula in your search criteria, Quattro Pro will evaluate the formula using the entry from each record in the data block. If the result is true, that record will be selected; if it is false, the record will be ignored.

There are two rules that apply to using a formula in the criteria:

- It does not matter which column title you use, as long as it is one that is found in the data block.

- The formula should refer to the cell in the first row in the column you wish to use to select the records.

Here is a criterion you could use to search for all people over the age of 30 in the database in Figure 14.3:

State

+G3>30

The criterion title is State, which is acceptable because it appears in the data block. The formula below the title refers to cell G3, the first cell below the column title in the Age column. If you had used the Database–Query–Assign Names command in that database, you could write the formula as +AGE>30.

When you invoke a Database–Query command, such as Locate or Extract, Quattro Pro evaluates the formula for each record. The first record is in row 3, but that is simply a dashed line in Figure 14.3, so it would not produce a true result.

The next record is in row 4. Quattro Pro would look at the formula as being +G4>30, and it would select the record if that formula were true. It would evaluate the record in row 5 with the formula +G5>30, and so on. In a sense, Quattro Pro is copying the formula (internally, not literally) so that it adjusts for each row it checks in the data block.

Don't pay too much attention to the result of a logical criterion formula because the result is determined only by the cell to which it actually refers. During the query, the formula will be evaluated for each record in the database.

If you think of the logical formula as being copied down the column during the selection process, you should be able to write a formula to perform any type of query.

If you were to make the reference an absolute one, such as +\$G\$3>30, you would probably not get the result you want. Only the first record would be checked, and if it tested true (were greater than 30), all the records in the data block would be selected—the formula would evaluate as true each time it was checked.

But there are times when an absolute reference can be very helpful, as shown in Figure 14.4. This is the mailing list database with a logical formula in the criterion in cell B16. The formula refers to both the first record in the data block and to cell B18: +AGE>\$B\$18. The number 35 has been entered in cell B18; remember that the name AGE refers to the first cell in the Age column below the column titles, cell G3.

During a query, each cell in column G (the Age column) will be tested against the value in cell B18, and only against that cell, because the reference to B18 in the formula is an absolute one.

The result of the Database–Query–Extract command can be seen in the output block that begins in the block D15..E15 in Figure 14.4. Only those who are older than 35 were selected.

You could also use a logical formula to find any duplicate last names: +A3=A4. Each record would be checked against the record below it, and selected only if the entries were the same.

The output block contains only the First and Last fields, but you can look in the data block for the names that were extracted and see that each has an age over 35. The Age field need not appear in the output block, even though it was used to select the records.

USING MULTIPLE LOGICAL CRITERIA

You can use multiple logical formula criteria in the same way that you use multiple character criteria: place them on the same row for an AND condition or on different rows for an OR condition. You can also include multiple logical statements in a

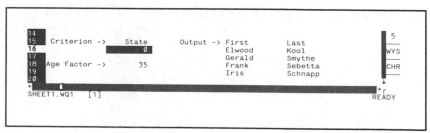

Figure 14.4: An absolute reference in a logical formula criterion

single formula. For example, to find all those who are older than 32 and live in California, you could use this formula:

+AGE>30#AND#STATE="CA"

The formula specifies two different columns in the data block. In this way, you can refer to any column in the data in a single formula. Here is a formula that describes a low and high limit to the age:

+AGE>30#AND#AGE<45

ACCESSING AN EXTERNAL DATABASE

A logical formula in your selection criteria can refer to another spreadsheet or database file. For example, the formula

+[C:\DATA\MYSHEET]C8>40

refers to cell C8 in the spreadsheet named Mysheet.

If the file is a database file, you can also use the column titles in the formula, such as

+[C:\DATA\MYDATA.DB]ZIP="95814"

to find all zip codes that equal 95814.

Remember that if the file to which you are referring is from a different drive or subdirectory than the current spreadsheet, you must specify its path in the reference.

FINDING RECORDS WITH
THE DATA QUERY COMMANDS

After you have defined your database, you can invoke any of these Database–Query commands to select records in the data block that match your search criteria:

- Locate: Highlights each matching record

- Extract: Copies each matching record to the output block

- Unique: Copies each matching record to the output block, but ignore duplicates

- Delete: Removes all matching records from the data block

- Reset: Returns the definitions for the data, output, and criteria blocks to their default settings

The Query command will be executed in the current spreadsheet, even though you may have defined databases in several open spreadsheets. This can be confusing if your database has its data, output, or criteria block in other spreadsheets. If you get lost, just look at the settings on the Database–Query menu next to the Block, Criteria Table, and Output Block commands.

When you have defined your database and invoked one of the Query commands, you can later use the Query key, F7, from Ready mode to execute that command again. This can be convenient if you are performing a variety of searches in your database—just change the criteria and press F7 to proceed with another search.

LOCATING RECORDS

The Database–Query–Locate command does not use an output block. Instead, the mode indicator will display Find, and the cell pointer will jump to the first matching record in the data block. The cell pointer will expand to the width of the database to completely highlight the record, and the blinking cursor will be on the first cell in that row. You have several options at this point:

- Press ↓ to move to the next matching record.

- Press ↑ to move to the previous matching record.

- Press End or Home to jump to the very last or first record in the database, respectively, whether it matches the criteria or not.

If Quattro Pro issues a short beep but does not move the cell selector after you invoke the Locate command, it means that it found no records in the data block that matched your criteria. If that is not the expected result, check your criteria and database definition to see if something needs adjusting.

- Press → or ← to move between the columns of the currently selected record. This allows you to view the contents of each cell, and also to scroll the screen in order to view cells that would otherwise not be visible.

- Type a new entry into a cell.

- Press F2 to edit the contents of the current cell.

- Press Escape or ↵ to cancel the operation. The cell selector will return to the cell it was on before you invoked the Locate command.

- Press F7 to return to Ready mode but leave the cell selector on the selected record.

Dividing a window into panes can greatly facilitate your searches through a database. Frequently, you will want to perform several searches, refining the criteria as you go, editing the records as they are found, and so on. If you split the window with the Windows–Options–Horizontal or Vertical command, you can position one pane of the window over the criteria block and the other over the database.

You can then edit your criteria in one pane, press F6 to jump to the database, press F7 to invoke the Locate command again, and then press F7 once more to return to Ready mode with the cell selector on a selected record. To change the criteria again, just press F6 to return to that pane and repeat the process.

EXTRACTING RECORDS

To use the Database–Query–Extract command, you must have set up and defined an output block. When you invoke the command, Quattro Pro will copy all the selected records to that block.

When you have defined your database, written your criteria, and are ready to extract records to the output block, don't do it. Instead, invoke the Locate command first to get an idea which records will be found given your current Database–Query settings and criteria. When you are sure that only the records you want to find are being selected, you can invoke the Extract command.

The Extract command will copy only those fields that are represented in the output block. You may have included all the fields from the data block or just a few, but only the data from the relevant columns from each extracted record will be shown. The order of the columns in the output block is not important. They do not have to be in the same order as those in the data block.

The Extract command copies all selected records to the output block, but not as the Edit–Copy command does. It actually emulates the Edit–Values command, in that only the results of any formulas in a selected record are copied to the output block. A cell's numeric format, alignment, font, protection status, and shading are copied along with the cell contents (a cell's line drawing will be ignored).

EXTRACTING ONLY UNIQUE RECORDS

The people listed in the name and address list come from many states. How would you find out how many different states were represented? Obviously, you could sort the database by State and then see how many groups of states there were. But there is a much easier method.

When you want to select just one of any duplicates, use the Database–Query–Unique command. This command is similar to the Extract command, in that records are copied from the data block to the output block, and only those fields shown in the output block will be used.

But with the Unique command, each item that ends up in the output block will be different from all the others. In this way, you can create a list of all the unique states in the name and address list, as shown in Figure 14.5.

The input block is the same as in the previous example—the entire database, A2..G13. The selection criterion is shown in cells B15..B16. The State column title is used, and below it are two wildcard characters, ??, that represent any two-character entry in the State column. The output block is the single column that begins with the State title in cell D14. You can see the result of the Unique command in the output block, cells D15..D17.

The uniqueness of each record is determined by the column titles represented in the output block. In Figure 14.5, only the State column was used, so two records were each considered unique if they each had a different entry in the State column.

If you changed the output titles to include both the City and State columns and issued the Unique command, the uniqueness of each record would be based on the entries in both of those fields. The result is shown in Figure 14.6. Now that the scope has been broadened, more records have been copied to the output block. But they are all unique given the fields that were used.

DELETING RECORDS

In the normal maintenance of your database, you may need to delete all records of a certain type. For example, each month

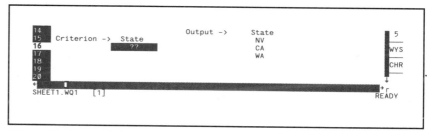

Figure 14.5: The Unique command selects only one of duplicate entries

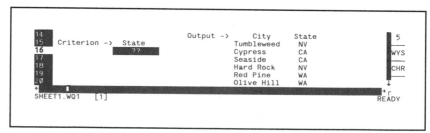

Figure 14.6: The Unique command determines uniqueness by the titles in the output block

you could delete all records from your list of expense accounts that are more than a year old, following these steps:

1. Create the database criteria that will find all records that are older than 365 days from the current date: **+DATE<=@NOW–365**.

2. Use the Database–Query–Extract command to extract all the older records to the output block.

3. Use the Tools–Xtract command to save those older records in the output block to a separate file for record-keeping purposes.

4. Without changing the selection criteria, invoke the Database–Query–Delete command to remove all the older records from the database.

Use caution with the Delete command because the selected records will be eliminated from the spreadsheet. The Edit–Undo (Alt-F5) command will reverse the deletion, but only if you notice the mistake before making any more changes to the spreadsheet.

Therefore, before invoking the Database–Query–Delete command, test your criteria by using the Locate command. Delete the records only when you are sure that the query is working as expected.

Deleting records from a database has almost the same effect as deleting the records with the Edit–Delete–Rows command. Any rows in the database below a deleted record will move up to fill in the gap. But unlike the Delete–Rows command, the Query–Delete command moves up only the cells in the rows within the database. Cells outside the database (left, below, or right) will not be affected. The database will therefore contract, and the definition of the data block will contract along with it.

If the data block has a block name, the named block does not contract with the data block when records are deleted—its coordinates remain unchanged. Keep this in mind because it could create problems for you the next time you perform database operations using the block name.

USING THE PARADOX ACCESS

Quattro has always had a link to Paradox, Borland's highly acclaimed database program. From the very first release, Quattro could retrieve a Paradox database file directly into the spreadsheet, without going through an intermediate translation process. Two years later, Quattro Pro had the added feature of allowing you to use a Paradox database file as the source data for a Database–Query command without first loading the file into the spreadsheet.

But with the release of Quattro Pro version 2 and Paradox version 3.5, an exciting new level of integration was attained with a feature called the Paradox Access. On a computer with an 80286 or higher processor (an AT-style machine or one with an 80386 processor, for example), the two programs can be run at the same time, so that you can switch between them with a single keystroke.

This section describes the Paradox Access and its hardware and software requirements, how to start Paradox in order to have access to Quattro Pro, and how to switch between the two programs.

ADVANTAGES OF THE PARADOX ACCESS

The Paradox Access is created when you run Paradox version 3.5 or later with the special command-line parameter, -qpro (discussed later). Paradox loads and configures itself and leaves memory available for Quattro Pro. After Paradox is up and running, you can immediately switch to Quattro Pro by pressing the hot key, Ctrl-F10.

Your Paradox session will remain in memory while Quattro Pro is brought to the foreground. You can load a spreadsheet and work in Quattro Pro. When you wish to return to Paradox, simply press Ctrl-F10. Quattro Pro will be put into the background, and Paradox comes to the foreground. Your spreadsheet will be safe, and you will find your Paradox work just as you left it.

You can configure Quattro Pro to automatically load a file each time it is invoked from Paradox. By default, it will load the ANSWER.DB file if it is on disk, so that you can produce an answer table in Paradox and immediately load it into Quattro Pro for further analysis, graphing, and so on.

Figure 14.7 shows Paradox with the small address list database that we used in earlier examples. A query was performed using the query form at the top of the screen, and the result appears in the table called ANSWER at the bottom of the screen.

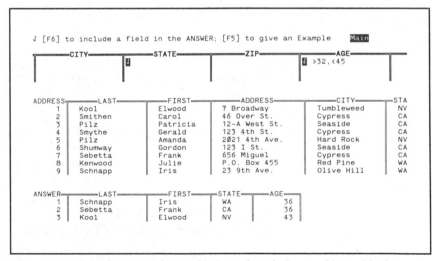

By running both programs together, you can integrate the features of each to provide power that a spreadsheet or database program alone could never offer.

You can work with a spreadsheet database in Quattro Pro, but you are strictly limited by the number of rows in the spreadsheet and the amount of RAM in your computer. Paradox has a wide range of database features, allowing you to perform the following tasks:

- Work with huge databases that have many times more records than a Quattro Pro spreadsheet could hold

In order to use the Paradox Access, your computer must have an 80286 or higher processor. It must also have at least 2 megabytes of memory. Be sure to refer to the hardware and software requirements described later in the chapter.

Figure 14.7: Paradox provides sophisticated tools for working with data

- Link data from multiple tables to create a relational system

- Query multiple tables and produce a single answer table that you can immediately load into Quattro Pro

- Create detailed reports in Paradox's report writer

- Use the Paradox SQL Link to query the data kept on your company's mainframe system and send the result to Quattro Pro

- Work with sophisticated database applications that are far beyond the capabilities of a spreadsheet

On the other hand, Paradox is not a spreadsheet. With the Paradox Access, you can use Quattro Pro's special features:

- Perform mathematical analyses on an imported Paradox table using Quattro Pro's high-powered functions and analysis tools

- Create what-if scenarios using the imported database table

- Create graphs using Quattro Pro's dazzling graphics capabilities

- Print the data in a presentation-quality format

- Save the data as a spreadsheet for further analysis at a later time

The Paradox–Quattro Pro connection means that you no longer have to "overstay" your welcome in either program, nor give up one program's capabilities for the sake of the other.

REQUIREMENTS FOR USING THE PARADOX ACCESS

In order to take advantage of the Paradox Access, your computer system must have adequate hardware, and you must configure its software environment as well.

HARDWARE REQUIREMENTS

Paradox version 3.5 can take advantage of the *protected* mode of operation on a computer running an 80286 (or faster) processor. This is the mode used by OS/2, and it allows Paradox to access up to 16 megabytes of *extended* RAM, giving it ample room for all its program code and the data on which it is working.

In order to use the Paradox Access, you must run Paradox in the protected mode, and your computer must have at least 2 megabytes of RAM, with 640K of conventional memory and extended memory for the rest. If your system has more than 2 megabytes, there will be more RAM available to Quattro Pro. If your system also has *expanded* memory, it can give Quattro Pro even more room for your spreadsheets.

SOFTWARE CONFIGURATION

To ensure that you can run the Paradox Access on your computer, you must adjust the settings of the operating system and configure both Paradox and Quattro Pro appropriately. Make the following revisions to your operating system:

- In your CONFIG.SYS file, include the command **Files=40**, which tells DOS to set aside 40 file handles in memory for use by any programs. In some situations, even this may not be enough, and you will see an error message when you try to switch from Paradox to Quattro Pro. You will have to increase the number and reboot the computer.

- Quattro Pro's subdirectory must be in your DOS path. You can set the path in your AUTOEXEC.BAT file so that it is established each time you boot your computer. For example, your path statement might look like this: **path=C:\DOS;C:\UTIL;E:\QPRO**.

- Run the DOS command SHARE. You only have to run this command once, and the best time to do so is as soon as you boot your computer. Just include the SHARE command in your AUTOEXEC.BAT file.

Even though your computer may seemingly have an ample supply of memory, it may not have enough for the Paradox Access if you run any memory-resident programs. These can include programs such as a disk cache, print spooler, RAM disk, pop-up utility, and an expanded memory manager.

- Quattro Pro and Paradox must each reside in its own subdirectory.

When running with the Paradox Access, Paradox version 3.5 (or later) acts as though it were running on a network. So even if your computer is not connected to a network, you will still need to make adjustments to Paradox.

First, run the NUPDATE.EXE program, which is in your Paradox subdirectory, and use it to set the network type to Other. Specify the location of the PARADOX.NET file, which can be kept in your Paradox subdirectory.

Paradox's working directory and your private directory cannot be the same. The working directory, which anyone can access, is where network database applications would be stored. The private directory is where each user's temporary files would be stored, as well as any files that the user does not want accessed by others. Run the Paradox script called CUSTOM, either from within Paradox or by including it on the command line when you run Paradox:

PARADOX CUSTOM

The Options–
Other–Paradox
menu settings are discussed in more detail
in Chapter 18.

Since Paradox and Quattro Pro are working as though they are on a network, even if you're using a stand-alone computer, you must change the following settings on Quattro Pro's Options–Other–Paradox menu:

- For the Network Type command, choose Other.
- For the Directory command, enter the location of the PARADOX.NET file, as you previously specified in the NUPDATE program.

There are two optional Quattro Pro settings that you can adjust on the Database–Paradox Access menu. These will be discussed shortly.

RUNNING THE PARADOX ACCESS

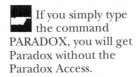 If you simply type the command PARADOX, you will get Paradox without the Paradox Access.

You initiate the Paradox Access by running Paradox with a single command-line parameter. From the Paradox subdirectory, type

    PARADOX -qpro

If your hardware and software are suitable, Paradox will load and be ready to switch to Quattro Pro at the touch of the Ctrl-F10 hot key. However, you can use several other parameters to tune the Paradox Access for its best performance.

USING A BATCH FILE

You can avoid the trouble of remembering the parameters by using the batch file named PXACCESS.BAT that comes with Quattro Pro. It's a two-line batch file:

```
SHARE
PARADOX  -qpro  -leavek 512  -emk 0
```

For most computer systems, this batch file offers the best options for running the Paradox Access (these options are discussed in detail a little later). Also, it's easy to revise if you need to fine tune it for your system.

Where you keep the batch file on your hard disk depends on your subdirectory structure. You could, for example, store it in your Paradox directory and type PXACCESS to start Paradox. Some people have a subdirectory called BATCH or MENU where they keep all their batch files for starting programs. That subdirectory is then included in their DOS path statement.

If you were to place PXACCESS.BAT in a batch file subdirectory, and Paradox was stored on your E drive in a subdirectory called PARADOX, you could revise the batch file in this way:

```
SHARE
E:
cd \PARADOX
PARADOX  -qpro  -leavek 512  -emk 0
```

If the SHARE command is in your AUTOEXEC.BAT file, you can eliminate it from PXACCESS.BAT (but you can also leave it there).

ENTERING COMMAND-LINE PARAMETERS

The three optional parameters that directly affect the Paradox Access are -qpro, -leavek, and -emk.

The first one, -qpro, instructs Paradox to set aside memory for Quattro Pro and run in a multiuser mode, as though it were on a network. This parameter can also take three optional parameters of its own:

The parameters behave the same whether they are used from a batch file or the command line. In general, using a batch file is easier, ensures accuracy, and saves time.

- Use the parameter *filename* to specify the name and location of a spreadsheet, database, or a Quattro Pro workspace file. The first time you switch to Quattro Pro from Paradox, this file will be immediately loaded into Quattro Pro. For example, you might specify D:\DATA\MYFILE.WQ1.

- The *macroname* parameter runs the named macro if it is found in the file name you specified above.

- The parameter */options* refer to one or more of Quattro Pro's regular startup options. But don't use the /X parameter. Because of the need for extended memory to run both Paradox and Quattro Pro at the same time, you can't assign extended memory to Quattro Pro.

These are the same parameters that you can use with Quattro Pro alone. When you include them on the Paradox command line, they must be enclosed in brackets. Use the syntax

-qpro [*filename macroname /options*]

You could, for example, include the following when you start the Paradox Access:

PARADOX -qpro [FILE1 FIRSTMAC]

This tells Paradox to allow switching to Quattro Pro via the Paradox Access. The first time you switch to Quattro Pro, the file named FILE1 will be loaded and the macro named FIRSTMAC will run. Since the file name does not include an extension, Quattro Pro will assume that FILE1 is a Quattro Pro spreadsheet file.

The second parameter used in the batch file example, -leavek 512, instructs Paradox to leave the specified amount of extended memory (512K in this case) unused, so that it can be used by other programs. Specifically, on 80386 machines, this affects extended memory that a memory manager might convert into expanded RAM. The expanded RAM (up to 512K in the example) would then be available to Quattro Pro.

If your computer has more than 2 megabytes of RAM, you might want to set aside more than 512K of extended RAM. Just modify the parameter to a higher number, such as -leavek 1024 to leave 1 megabyte of RAM.

The last parameter, -emk 0, allows Paradox to use only the specified amount of expanded memory (none in this case), and leave the rest untouched. If your system has plenty of extended and expanded RAM, you could specify an amount so that Paradox would also have expanded memory for its own use.

SWITCHING BETWEEN QUATTRO PRO AND PARADOX

Quattro Pro's menu command Database–Paradox Access has three settings that control the switch between Quattro Pro and Paradox:

- Go: You will be switched to Paradox, which will be in exactly the same state as it was when you previously switched to Quattro Pro. You can also use the shortcut Ctrl-F10.

- Load File: Enter the name and, optionally, location of the file that Quattro Pro should load whenever you switch to it from Paradox. The Paradox temporary file

ANSWER.DB is the default. If you don't specify a location, Quattro Pro will look in your Paradox private directory. Whether the file named here is retrieved depends on the next command.

- Autoload: By default, this is set to Yes, which means that Quattro Pro will load the file named in the Load File command each time you switch to it from Paradox.

With these settings, you can perform your database operations in Paradox to produce an answer table as the result. You can then switch to Quattro Pro and have the ANSWER.DB file retrieved automatically.

However, the autoload file does not have to be ANSWER.DB; in fact, it does not have to be a Paradox database. You can specify any file in any valid Quattro Pro format, such as Reflex, Lotus 1-2-3, dBASE, and so on. Just be sure to specify the location, or Quattro Pro will look for the file in either your Paradox private subdirectory or the default Quattro Pro directory.

SAVING YOUR SPREADSHEETS

Before the Paradox Access will load the autoload file into Quattro Pro, it checks to be sure that the current spreadsheet has been saved. If your work has not been saved, you will see the message

Lose changes?

You can choose Yes to replace the current spreadsheet with the incoming autoload file, or No to leave the spreadsheet as is.

On the other hand, if you previously saved the current spreadsheet, the Paradox Access will leave it alone and simply open another spreadsheet for the incoming database file. You might, therefore, have several Quattro Pro files open at the same time as you switch back and forth between the two programs.

When a Paradox table is loaded into Quattro Pro, it becomes essentially a read-only file. You cannot, for example, save

You have encountered a network conflict if you attempt to save a Paradox table in Quattro Pro and get the message *Cannot lock file for writing*. Be sure you have adjusted the operating parameters of both Paradox and Quattro Pro, as discussed earlier.

ANSWER.DB under its original name and location. That would be violating the network file-locking rules under which the Paradox Access is running. You can, however, save the Paradox data under a new file name or location, or as a file type other than Paradox, thereby leaving the original file untouched.

AUTOMATING THE SWITCH

You can use macros in Quattro Pro and PAL scripts in Paradox to automate switching between the programs. In Quattro Pro, use the menu-equivalent command {/ParadoxSwitch-Go}, or the actual keystrokes /dpg. Remember that if there is an autoload file specified in the Database–Paradox Access menu, you might want to have your macro save the current spreadsheet before switching to Paradox.

To switch from Paradox to Quattro Pro, use the PAL command TOQPRO. If you want to switch to Quattro Pro immediately after loading Paradox via the Paradox Access, create the Paradox startup script file named INIT.SC within the Paradox program subdirectory. Include the TOQPRO command in the script.

USING DATABASE FUNCTIONS

Although the same layout is used as the source data for both the database functions and the Database–Query commands, you don't need to define a data block under the Database–Query command in order to use a database function.

The Quattro Pro database functions each begin with @D. A complete list appears in Table 4.10.

All the database functions use exactly the same syntax, as illustrated here for the @DCOUNT function:

@DCOUNT(*data_block*, *column_offset*, *criteria_block*)

Several database functions are illustrated in Figure 14.8 (taken from Figure 14.3). A different one appears in each of the cells F15, F17, and F19. A description of each result is shown to its left. Here are the actual cell contents for each of the formulas:

@DCOUNT($INPUT,4,$CRIT)

@DAVG($INPUT,6,$CRIT)

@DMAX($INPUT,6,$CRIT)

The @DCOUNT function in cell F15 refers to the block names that had been given to both the data block, A2..G13, and the criteria block, B15..B16. By making the references absolute, it was a simple matter to copy one formula to the other two cells and then perform the minor editing to create the other two.

Here is how the first formula would look if block names had not been used (and how the formula looks when it is being edited):

@DCOUNT(A2..G13,4,B15..B16)

The *data_block*, A2..G13, is named INPUT, and is the same data block that was defined in the Database–Query–Block command used in previous examples. The first row of the data block, row 2, contains the unique column titles, and each row below it is a record in the database.

The *column offset*, 4 in the example, refers to the column in the database on which the function should perform the given calculation. This column number is counted from the first column in the data block, which is column 0. In Figure 14.3, column 4 is the State column.

The *criteria block*, B15..B16 is named CRIT, and is again the same criteria block that was used in an earlier example. Its first cell contains a column title, State, and the cell below that contains the criterion, which is NV in Figure 14.8. Just as with the

> The first column in the data block that is specified in the function is the beginning of the block, so it has an offset of 0. The column to its right is *one* column from the beginning of the block, so it has an offset of 1, and so on.

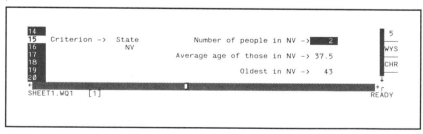

Figure 14.8: Database functions perform arithmetic only on the records selected by the specified criteria

Database–Query commands, a database function can refer to character or logical formula criteria, criteria that use wildcard characters, and multiple criteria of either type.

The @DCOUNT formula in cell F15 is searching through the database named INPUT, using the criterion in the block named CRIT, and counting all occurrences of NV in the State column (the column with an offset of 4). As shown in Figure 14.8, the result is 2, because there are two instances of NV in the State column.

The other two functions in Figure 14.8 use the same data block and the same criterion, but they are looking at the column with an offset of 6, the Age column. The @DAVG function is averaging all the ages for those whose state is NV, which consists of two, 43 and 32, for an average of 37.5.

The @DMAX function returns the largest number in the Age column for those whose state is NV, which happens to be 43.

The database functions will automatically check all the records in the database each time the spreadsheet is recalculated. If you were to change one of the entries in the State column from CA to NV, each of the formulas would be evaluated based on the new entry; the count would now be 3, and there could be a new average and maximum age for those whose state is NV.

Unfortunately, the database functions recalculate rather slowly compared to the other functions. If you use them too liberally in your spreadsheet, recalculation time will increase significantly.

This chapter has described how to structure a spreadsheet database and sort and query the data. The next chapter discusses more data-analysis tools. You will learn how you can combine the Database–Query commands, the database functions, and the Tools–What-If command to produce a simple but powerful reporting tool for your spreadsheet databases.

15

Performing Advanced Data Analysis

Fast
Track

YOU HAVE SEEN HOW THE QUATTRO PRO BUILT-IN functions provide mathematical shortcuts for common spreadsheet applications. Quattro Pro also provides built-in processes that serve as shortcuts for very involved mathematical routines. These include the Frequency, What-If, and Solve For commands on the Tools menu, and the Regression, Optimization, and Matrix commands on the Tools–Advanced Math menu.

You could write your own routines to perform the same steps as these commands, but the process would be long and involved, subject to mistakes, and would run more slowly than the built-in commands. How often you use these advanced data analysis commands really depends on the type of work you do in Quattro Pro.

CALCULATING FREQUENCY DISTRIBUTION

In Lotus 1-2-3, the equivalent command is Data–Distribution.

The Tools–Frequency command provides a fast way to count all the occurrences of values in a block that fall between a given range of values. You specify two blocks for the command:

- *Values*: The cells that contain the values you wish to count.

- *Bin*: A two-column block. The first column contains the numeric categories into which each number in the values block will be counted. The second column contains the count for each category.

The command looks at each value in the values block, finds where it would fall in the bin block, and adds one to the current count in the second column of the bin block. An example will help to clarify this.

Using the name and address list from the previous chapter, we will determine the age grouping of everyone in the list—how many are between the ages of 10 and 20, 20 and 30, and so on.

Our table will look at groups in increments of ten years. We must first create a bin block. (The values block already exists as the Age column.) We can use the Edit–Fill command to create the block in one operation.

1. With the mailing list database on your screen, use the Database–Sort command to sort it by the Age column: Specify A4..G12 for the Block option, G4 for the 1st Key option in ascending order, and then choose Go. This step is not required for the Frequency command, but it makes it easier to verify the results.

2. We will fill the block A14..A20, which will later be the bin block. Move the cell selector to cell A14 before we begin.

3. Invoke the Edit–Fill command. It will prompt you to specify the block to be filled.

4. Press the period key to begin the fill block at cell A14.

5. Press the ↓ key to highlight the block A14..A25 and press ↵. This block is larger than we will need, but we will limit the scope of the fill operation by specifying the stop value.

6. Enter **10** for the start value and press ↵ (our bin block will start with age 10).

7. Enter **10** for the step value and press ↵ (our categories will each span 10 years).

8. Enter **70** for the stop value and press ↵ (this is probably larger than any age in the address list).

The Fill command will enter the numbers from 10 to 70 in the block A14..A20, as shown in Figure 15.1. Now we will count the frequency of occurrence of each age in the Age column.

9. Invoke the Tools–Frequency command. It will prompt you for the values block.

10. Specify the ages in the Age column, G4..G12, and press ↵.

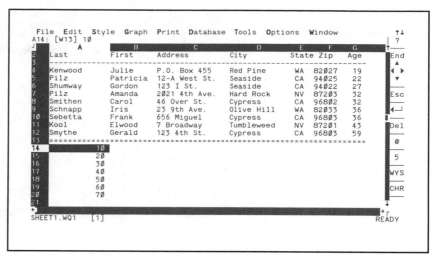

```
    File  Edit  Style  Graph  Print  Database  Tools  Options  Window       ↑↓
    A14: [W13] 1Ø                                                             ?
   ┘         A              B            C            D         E    F    G
   2    Last           First        Address      City       State Zip  Age  End
   3    ------------------------------------------------------------------    ▲
   4    Kenwood        Julie        P.O. Box 455 Red Pine    WA  82Ø27  19   ◄ ►
   5    Pilz           Patricia     12-A West St. Seaside    CA  94Ø25  22    ▼
   6    Shumway        Gordon       123 I St.    Seaside     CA  94Ø22  27
   7    Pilz           Amanda       2Ø21 4th Ave. Hard Rock  NV  872Ø3  32   Esc
   8    Smithen        Carol        46 Over St.  Cypress     CA  968Ø2  32
   9    Schnapp        Iris         23 9th Ave.  Olive Hill  WA  82Ø33  36   ←┘
   10   Sebetta        Frank        656 Miguel   Cypress     CA  968Ø3  36
   11   Kool           Elwood       7 Broadway   Tumbleweed  NV  872Ø1  43   Del
   12   Smythe         Gerald       123 4th St.  Cypress     CA  968Ø3  59
   13   ===================================================================   @
   14               1Ø
   15               2Ø                                                         5
   16               3Ø
   17               4Ø
   18               5Ø                                                        WYS
   19               6Ø
   20               7Ø                                                        CHR
   21
    ←                                                                    →┌
    SHEET1.WQ1    [1]                                               READY
```

Figure 15.1: Using the Edit–Fill command to create an evenly incremented bin block

11. Specify the bin block as the column of numbers you created, plus the blank column to its right, A14..B20. Then press ↵.

In a split second, the right column of the bin block will be filled with the number of ages that fall between each bin number, as shown in Figure 15.2. The Tools–Frequency command checks each age and increments the first cell in the bin block that is greater than or equal to the value. A person who is 30 years old would be counted in the cell next to 30 in the bin block. Someone who is 31 would be counted next to 40 in the bin block.

Notice that there is a zero in cell B21, below the last entry in the bin block. This cell contains the count of any numbers in the values block that are greater than the categories in the bin block. For example, an entry in the Age column of 71, 87, or 91 would have been counted here.

Note that the entries in the second column of the bin block are not formulas. If you were to add new entries to the names and address list or change any of the existing ages, you would have to invoke the Tools–Frequency command again to get an accurate count.

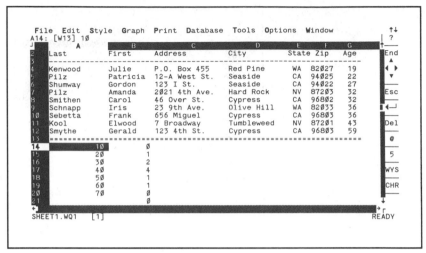

Figure 15.2: The Tools–Frequency command counts the number of occurrences of each value in the values block

CREATING WHAT-IF TABLES

In Lotus 1-2-3, the equivalent command is Data–Table.

The Tools–What-If command provides a convenient means for creating a table of calculations without writing formulas for each cell in the table. It derives its name from its ability to help you create and manipulate "what-if" scenarios with your spreadsheet data.

The command has two options for creating a table: 1 Variable and 2 Variables. With each, you specify a table (block) of spreadsheet data and formulas that are to be used in filling in the interior of the table with the calculated results. The results are based on a single variable cell that you specify for the 1 Variable command, or two cells that you specify for the 2 Variables command.

Once you have set up a table and invoked either of these commands, you can use the F8 key from Ready mode to invoke the command again, just as you can use the Query key, F7, to invoke the most recently used Database–Query command.

The Tools–What-If–Reset command returns all the What-If options to their default settings.

THE STRUCTURE OF THE TABLES

Figure 15.3 shows the structure of a 1-variable table in the block A4..E9. Its cells have been labeled to indicate its general layout, which consists of the following elements:

- Values: In the table's first column, cells A5..A9, are the values that you enter as the basis for the calculations. You can use as many rows as you need for the values, from one to the maximum number of rows in the spreadsheet.

- Formulas: In the table's first row, in cells B4..E4, are the formulas that you enter that will produce the results in the interior of the table, based on the values in the first column. There are four formulas in Figure 15.3, but you can enter just one or as many as you need, as long as they arc all in one row. Each formula can be different, although you can have duplicates if that serves some purpose.

- Variable: The trick to this table is a single cell somewhere else in the spreadsheet, F16 in the figure, that will be used as the variable during calculations. It does

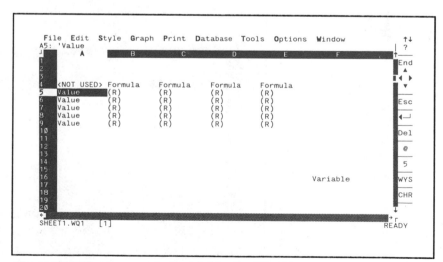

If you are going to be using a what-if table and its variable cell on a regular basis, consider giving them each a block name.

Figure 15.3: The layout of a 1-variable what-if table

not matter what the variable cell contains because its contents will not be used during the calculations. Instead, each value in the first column will be substituted into that cell (not literally, just internally). The formula in each column will then be evaluated, and the result will be placed in each formula's column in the value's row. Therefore, your formulas will generally refer to the variable cell, although this isn't required.

- (R): Under the formulas row are the results that are produced by evaluating each formula when one of the values in the first column has been substituted into the variable cell.

The corner cell, A4 in Figure 15.3, is not used in a 1-variable table. This cell need not necessarily be blank, it just does not play a role in the table.

When you construct a 1-variable table, each value will be placed in the variable cell, each formula evaluated, and each result placed in the appropriate cell.

Figure 15.4 shows the structure of a 2-variable what-if table. As in a 1-variable table, you enter values in the first column. Cells A5..A9 are labeled Value 1 in the figure. But you also enter values in the first row of the table, B4..E4. These are labeled Value 2 in the figure.

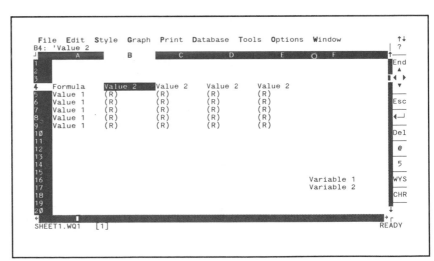

Figure 15.4: The layout of a 2-variable what-if table

Just one formula is used in a 2-variable table, which is always placed in the upper-left corner of the table (cell A4 in the figure).

There are always two variable cells associated with the 2-variable table, shown in cells F16 and F17 in the figure. When the table is calculated, each Value 1 is placed in Variable 1; each Value 2 is placed in Variable 2. The formula is evaluated, and the result is placed in the cell at the junction of the two values.

As with the 1-variable table, you can use as many rows and columns as you need. Just remember that the formula always appears in the first cell of a 2-variable table. Each of the two variable cells can reside anywhere in the spreadsheet, and their contents do not affect the results in the table.

CONSTRUCTING A 1-VARIABLE WHAT-IF TABLE

As an example, we will create a 1-variable table of results that are based on the proposed purchase price of a house. Figure 15.5 shows the shell of this table. Each column of the table will contain the following:

- Proposed purchase price: The first column of the table, the values, will contain a range of proposed house prices, from a low to a high.

- Loan amount: This will be 80 percent of the purchase price.

- Loan payment: The monthly amount determined by the @PMT function, using the loan amount and a constant interest rate and term.

- Property taxes: This is 1.25 percent of the purchase price divided by 12 for the monthly cost.

- House insurance: This is $250 plus 0.5 percent of the purchase price divided by 12 for the monthly cost.

- Monthly total: The total is determined by the @SUM function, using the payment, taxes, and insurance amounts.

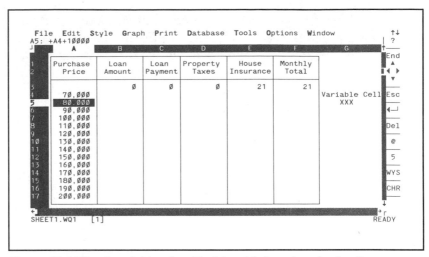

Figure 15.5: The 1-variable what-if table with its values in the first
column and formulas in the first row

Let's start by laying out the table as shown in Figure 15.5. You
don't have to include the line drawings in the table; they are
there simply to make the columns stand out.

1. Label columns A through F as shown in the figure,
   using rows 1 and 2. These rows will not be part of the
   what-if table; they simple serve to identify each column
   for us.

2. Move the cell selector to cell A4 and enter **70000** as
   the low value for the proposed purchase price. You
   can always adjust this value up or down to an amount
   that you feel is reasonable.

You could use the
Edit–Fill com-
mand to create the
range of prices, but a
formula is more
flexible. All you have to
do is change the first
value in cell A5, and all
the other values will ad-
just in relation to it.

3. In cell A5, enter the formula **+A4+10000**, and then
   copy this formula to the rest of the cells in this
   column, A6..A17.

The variable cell for this table is cell G5, although any cell in
the spreadsheet could be used. Now we will enter each formula
for the cells B3..F3. Some of these will refer to the variable cell,
and some will not.

4. In cell B3, enter **+G5*0.8**. This calculates the amount to be borrowed as 80% of the purchase price.

5. In cell C3, enter **@PMT(B3,0.12/12,360)**. The @PMT function calculates the monthly loan payment. It refers to the loan amount in column B, and uses 12% as the annual interest and 360 months as the term. Note that a formula does not have to refer to the variable cell.

6. In cell D3, enter **+G5*0.0125/12**. This calculates a property tax of 1.25% of the purchase price, spread over 12 months.

7. In cell E3, enter **(250+G5*0.005)/12**. This produces a house insurance cost, based on ½% of the purchase price plus a base amount of $250, spread over 12 months.

8. In cell F3, enter **@SUM(C3..E3)** to total each of the monthly costs. Again, this formula does not reference the variable cell.

Your spreadsheet should now look like the one in Figure 15.5 (without the line drawing). Remember that the results of the formulas that are displayed in row 3 won't be used in the table. Now we are ready to issue the Tools–What-If command to calculate the results.

9. For convenience, position the cell selector on cell A3, the first cell in the table.

10. Issue the command Tools–What-If–1 Variable. You will be prompted for the block of cells that should be used as the data table.

11. Specify the block A3..F17 and press ↵. Now you are prompted to specify the input cell (the variable).

12. Indicate cell G5, press ↵, and the table will be evaluated.

13. Choose Quit from the What-If menu.

Remember that you can use the Table key, F8, from Ready mode to invoke the command again. This lets you make adjustments to the values or formulas in the table and play "what-if" with a single keypress.

In the wink of an eye, Quattro Pro will calculate all the formulas for each value and place the results in the appropriate cells, as shown in Figure 15.6. These results are simply numeric values, as you can see on the input line for cell B4 in the figure.

Instead of using the What-If command, you could have copied formulas down each column to produce the desired results, but the results placed in a table by the What-If command use less RAM than formulas do, and they do not require recalculation time once the table has been created.

CONSTRUCTING A 2-VARIABLE WHAT-IF TABLE

Now we will design and execute a 2-variable table. We will build a rate chart that shows the monthly payment required for a loan given its principal and interest rate. The term will be fixed at 30 years (360 months). Figure 15.7 shows the basic layout of our loan payment table (with line drawing added to separate the results from the values).

You enter the values and formulas in the same way that you enter them for a 1-variable table.

File Edit Style Graph Print Database Tools Options Window

B4: 56000

	Purchase Price	Loan Amount	Loan Payment	Property Taxes	House Insurance	Monthly Total	
		Ø	Ø	Ø	21	21	
	70,000	56,000	576	73	50	699	Variable Cell
	80,000	64,000	658	83	54	796	XXX
	90,000	72,000	741	94	58	893	
	100,000	80,000	823	104	63	990	
	110,000	88,000	905	115	67	1,086	
	120,000	96,000	987	125	71	1,183	
	130,000	104,000	1,070	135	75	1,280	
	140,000	112,000	1,152	146	79	1,377	
	150,000	120,000	1,234	156	83	1,474	
	160,000	128,000	1,317	167	88	1,571	
	170,000	136,000	1,399	177	92	1,668	
	180,000	144,000	1,481	188	96	1,765	
	190,000	152,000	1,563	198	100	1,861	
	200,000	160,000	1,646	208	104	1,958	

SHEET1.WQ1   [1]   READY

Figure 15.6: The table after running the Tools–What-If–1 Variable command

1. Enter **50000** in cell A3.

2. In cell A4, enter the formula **+A3+10000** to increment that value by a fixed amount.

3. Copy the formula to the rest of the cells in that column of the table.

4. In cell B2, enter the interest rate, **0.08**.

5. Invoke the Style–Numeric Format command, choose Percent with zero decimal places, and specify the block B2..F2.

6. In cell C2, enter the formula **+B2+0.02** to increment the first rate by 2%.

7. Copy the formula to the block D2..F2.

8. The key to the entire table is the formula. Enter this in cell A2: **@PMT(G4,G7/12,G10)**.

You can see the formula on the input line in Figure 15.7. The @PMT function uses G4 as the principal, G7 as the interest rate (divided by 12 for a monthly rate), and G10 as the term. Again,

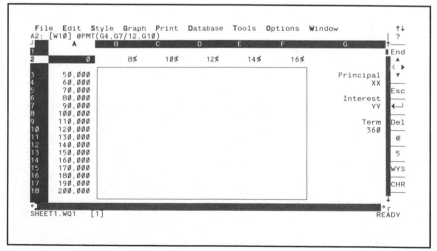

Figure 15.7: The 2-variable what-if table with its values in both the first column and first row and the formula in its first cell

As with the 1-variable table, the two variable cells can be anywhere in the spreadsheet; they need not be adjacent to one another or even related to one another.

note that the contents of G4 and G7, the first and second variable cells, are irrelevant to the table.

In a 2-variable table, the values in the first column are substituted into the first variable cell, while the values from the first row of the table are substituted into the second variable cell. When the table in Figure 15.7 is calculated, the loan amounts in column A will be placed in cell G4 and the interest rates in row 2 will be placed in cell G7. Now we will specify the table and see the results.

9. Start with the cell selector on cell A2, the first cell in the table.

10. Invoke the Tools–What-If–2 Variables command.

11. Specify the block A2..F18 as the cells to use for the table.

12. Specify G4 as the first input (variable) cell.

13. Specify G7 as the second input cell, and the table will be evaluated.

14. Choose Quit from the What-If menu.

The results should appear as they do in Figure 15.8. To produce another set of results, just change the first loan amount and the first interest rate, which would therefore change all the other amounts and rates, and then press F8 to evaluate the table again.

REPORTING ON A DATABASE

The success of your database reporting depends on the accuracy and consistency of the data in your database. If you use a variety of spellings for each state, for example, the list of unique states would be much longer.

One of the most powerful uses for a what-if table is as a reporting tool for your spreadsheet databases. For example, you could build a simple report to compile statistics on the sample mailing list database. Creating a report requires the use of three major tools that we have discussed:

• The Database–Query–Unique command, to extract one of each entry in the category on which you will be reporting.

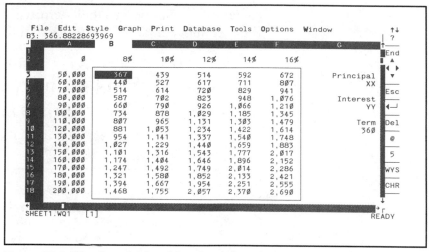

```
 File  Edit  Style  Graph  Print  Database  Tools  Options  Window      ↑↓
B3: 366.88228693969                                                      ?
J┌─────────A────────B────────C────────D────────E────────F────────G──────┤
1                                                                        End
2          Ø        8%       10%      12%      14%      16%              ▲
5       50,000      367      439      514      592      672    Principal  ▼
4       60,000      440      527      617      711      807      XX
5       70,000      514      614      720      829      941              Esc
6       80,000      587      702      823      948    1,076    Interest  ◄┘
7       90,000      660      790      926    1,066    1,210      YY
8      100,000      734      878    1,029    1,185    1,345              Del
9      110,000      807      965    1,131    1,303    1,479      Term
10     120,000      881    1,053    1,234    1,422    1,614      360
11     130,000      954    1,141    1,337    1,540    1,748              @
12     140,000    1,027    1,229    1,440    1,659    1,883
13     150,000    1,101    1,316    1,543    1,777    2,017              5
14     160,000    1,174    1,404    1,646    1,896    2,152
15     170,000    1,247    1,492    1,749    2,014    2,286              WYS
16     180,000    1,321    1,580    1,852    2,133    2,421
17     190,000    1,394    1,667    1,954    2,251    2,555              CHR
18     200,000    1,468    1,755    2,057    2,370    2,690

SHEET1.WQ1   [1]                                                        READY
```

Figure 15.8: The 2-variable table after using the Tools–What-If–2
Variables command

- The database functions to perform arithmetic on each category that you extract.

- The 1- or 2-variable what-if table to simplify and automate the final reporting process.

Figure 15.9 shows the results of using the Unique command to extract states from the mailing list database. Here is a summary of the Database–Query command settings used:

- Data block: A2..G13

- Criteria table: B15..B16

- Output block: C16

Cell C16 is the first cell in the table, but it is not used in the calculations. The fact that it still contains the label State for the database output block has no bearing on the table.

After you have a list of each unique state in the State column, you can write functions to perform the desired calculations. Place these functions next to the extracted states to form the structure of a 1-variable what-if table.

Figure 15.10 shows this what-if table in the block C16..G19. The three state entries serve as the values in the first column, and the four database functions in row 16 will drive the calculations. There is a label identifying each of the functions in the row above it. Here are the actual formulas:

- Cell D16: @DCOUNT(A2..G13,6,B15..B16)
- Cell E16: @DMIN(A2..G13,6,B15..B16)
- Cell F16: @DMAX(A2..G13,6,B15..B16)
- Cell G16: @DAVG(A2..G13,6,B15..B16)

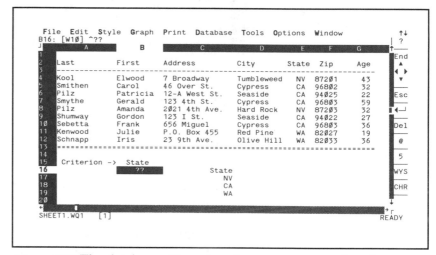

Figure 15.9: The database with each unique state extracted to the output block

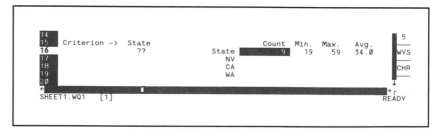

Figure 15.10: The shell of the what-if table with the values (states) in the first column and the formulas (database functions) in the first row

In the example, the @DCOUNT function uses the database in the block A2..G13. It will look in the column that has an offset of 6 from the first column in that database—column G, the Age column. The criteria it will use to select the items in that column is in the block B15..B16, the same criteria block used by the Query–Unique command.

The result of this function is 9 because the criterion it uses contains the wildcard characters ??, which select all two-character entries in the State column, and therefore all the records in the database. Because each record also has an entry in the Age column, the @DCOUNT function returns 9 (if one of the records had no entry in the Age column, the result would be 8).

To calculate the table, you would issue the command Tools–What-If–1 Variable from Ready mode. Then specify C16..G19 as the block for the table and B16 as the input (variable) cell. After you choose Quit from the Tools–What-If menu, the results of the table will be produced, as shown in Figure 15.11.

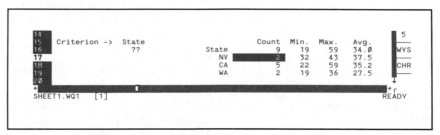

Figure 15.11: The results in the table after issuing the Tools–What-If–1 Variable command

USING ADVANCED MATH COMMANDS

The Tools–Advanced Math menu contains the Regression command, which performs a regression analysis on data in your spreadsheet. This is a commonly used method for calculating unknown data based on measured observations. The Invert and Multiply commands perform matrix arithmetic for solving linear equations. The Optimization command is a powerful tool for optimizing linear problems. You supply the variables and

If you don't have a degree in math or statistics, you may find some of these Advanced Math commands rather esoteric. If you don't have a need for them now, you may just want to familiarize yourself with their options and keep them in reserve.

constraints, and Quattro Pro finds the best solution for optimizing the system.

You should keep in mind that each routine on the Tools–Advanced Math menu is command driven, just like the Database–Query and Sort commands, and will not be updated unless you specifically execute it again. Therefore, whenever you make changes to your spreadsheet, you may have to invoke the command again.

ESTABLISHING A RELATIONSHIP WITH LINEAR REGRESSION

It may often appear that one set of data (variables) fluctuates in rhythm with another set. For example, when you walk faster, your heart rate goes up, and when you drive faster, your car's gas mileage goes down. If you have a sufficient number of data points, you can use regression analysis to determine whether or not there is any significant linear correlation (straight line) between the two sets of data. It will also let you predict an otherwise unknown data point in one set based on a value in the other and the trend of the fluctuations.

The Regression command takes the following input:

The independent variables can consist of more than one column, as long as there are more rows than columns.

- Independent: The block of data, also called the x-axis variables, that you think might be causing the other set of data to fluctuate. For example, a set of measurements of your walking speed.

- Dependent: The column of data (the y-axis variables) that you think are being affected by the independent variables, such as your measured heart rate at each of the measured speeds.

- Output: The cell where the table of results will be created. It will use a block of nine rows and at least four columns. An extra column will be used for each extra column beyond two in the independent block.

• Y Intercept: The calculated point at which the y-axis meets the x-axis. The default is Computed; choose Zero to force the y-axis intercept to zero.

PERFORMING THE REGRESSION ANALYSIS

Those who know their way around a forest or mountain can calculate the air temperature based on how fast the crickets are chirping. Although this appears to be a pretty woodsy ability, it's actually based on regression analysis. If you perform a regression analysis on sample data, you will find that there is a linear relationship between the temperature and how fast the crickets chirp.

You must first collect some data out in the field by counting the number of cricket chirps per second (the dependent data) at various temperatures (the independent data). Of course, to count cricket chirps per second for this method, you might also need a high-quality tape recorder and a stopwatch. Enter the following twelve data pairs and the two-line column titles into the block A1..B14 in your spreadsheet:

Temp.	Chirps/ Second
88.6	17.1
72.3	15.3
70.1	14.4
81.5	17.3
94.2	19.8
76.0	15.5
70.5	15.2
82.8	17.6
81.4	16.7
84.1	16.4
80.4	15.9
85.3	17.2

Now follow these steps to compute the regression table:

1. Invoke the Tools–Advanced Math–Regression–Independent command and specify the block A3..A14, the temperature readings.

2. Choose Dependent from the Regression menu and specify the block B3..B14, the number of chirps per second.

3. Choose Output and specify the cell E3, where the upper-left corner of the output table will be placed.

4. Choose Go, and the table will be created.

Figure 15.12 shows the data (enclosed in line drawing) and the results of the Regression command. The items in the regression table, shown here with their calculated values, contain key information for the regression analysis:

- Constant (2.130069): The corresponding y value if x were zero.

- Std Err of Y Est (0.601974): The standard error of the dependent estimate. The smaller this number, the better

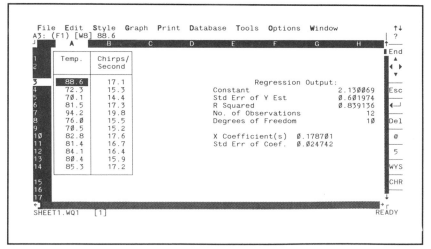

Figure 15.12: The regression output table

the calculated regression values describe the relationship of the data.

- R Squared (0.839136): The coefficient of determination; it will be a value between 0 and 1. The closer it is to 1, the more tightly related are the x and y data.

- No. of Observations (12): The number of rows in either of the two blocks of data.

- Degrees of Freedom (10): The number of observations minus one, minus the number of columns in the independent variables.

- X Coefficient(s) (0.178701): The coefficient of the independent variables. This and the constant allow you to calculate a variable in one data set from an unmeasured variable in the other.

- Std Err of Coef. (0.024742): The error factor built into the x coefficient.

CALCULATING THE REGRESSION

With this information, we can go out into the woods and calculate the temperature just by counting cricket chirps. We can do so in two ways, both of which involve writing the linear regression formula. Before we do, however, let's sort the data to arrange it by temperature.

1. Invoke the Database–Sort–Block command and specify the block A3.. B14.

2. Choose 1st Key, specify A3 as the first sort key, and press ↵.

3. Type **A** and press ↵ to choose ascending order.

4. Choose Go. The data will be sorted by temperature, and you will be back in Ready mode.

Just by sorting our data, it appears that there is a relationship between the temperatures and the chirps: as the temperature increases, so do the chirps.

The regression formula will show us the straight-line path through the sample data. To determine how fast the crickets will be chirping (dependent variable) at a given temperature (independent variable), the formula simply multiplies a temperature by the x coefficient in the regression table and adds the constant:

Chirps = Constant + X Coefficient * Temp.

Figure 15.13 shows the data with the regression formula in each cell of column C (formatted as Fixed with two decimal places). Here is the formula in the first cell, C3 (shown on the input line in the figure):

+$H$4+$G$10*A3

Each formula's result represents the precise number that is needed to produce a straight-line relationship between the independent and dependent variables.

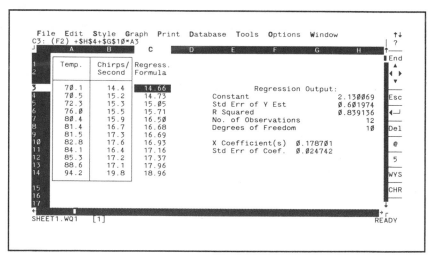

Figure 15.13: The linear regression formulas calculate the straight-line relationship between the independent and dependent variables

GRAPHING THE REGRESSION

Now we can draw a graph with our calculated regression formulas. This will not only illustrate the relationship between the data and the calculated line, but will also provide a means of determining the temperature when we have counted the crickets' chirps per second.

1. Invoke the Graph–Graph Type command and choose XY (the graph wouldn't work as a line graph).

2. Invoke the Series–X-Series command and specify the temperatures (independent variables), A3..A14, which will serve as the x-axis of the graph.

3. Choose 1st Series and specify the chirps per second (dependent variables), B3..B14. We will plot our data to show how it relates to the calculated regression line.

4. Choose 2nd Series, and specify the regression formulas, C3..C14.

5. Choose Quit from the Series menu.

6. From the Graph menu, choose Customize Series– Markers & Lines–Formats.

7. Choose 1st Series and select Symbols, so that the actual data will be represented only by symbols.

8. Choose 2nd Series and select Lines, so that the regression line will be a plain line with no data points on it.

9. Choose Quit three times to return to the Graph menu.

10. Choose Overall–Grid–Both to set both horizontal and vertical grid lines.

11. Choose Quit to return to the Graph menu.

12. Choose Text–Legends–1st Series and enter **Observed**.

13. Choose 2nd Series and enter **Linear Regression**. The legends will identify the symbols and line on the graph.

14. Choose Quit to return to the Graph–Text menu.

15. Select X-Title and enter **Temperature**.

16. Select Y-Title and enter **Cricket Chirps per Second**.

17. Choose Quit twice to return to Ready mode.

18. Press F10 to view your graph.

The graph should look like the one in Figure 15.14. The straight line is the regression line, and the points around it are the observed dependent data, the chirp count.

You can include this graph in your knapsack the next time you go camping and use it to determine the temperature when you have counted the crickets' chirps. If you estimate they are chirping about 16 times per second, you can look on the graph for 16 on the y-axis and follow that line across until it meets the regression line. Then go straight down to the x-axis, and you will see that the temperature is about 77 degrees.

Or you can leave the graph at home and take your slide rule. With a little algebra, we can write the regression formula to calculate a temperature given the chirp count:

$$\text{Temp.} = (\text{Chirps} - \text{Constant})/\text{X Coefficient}$$

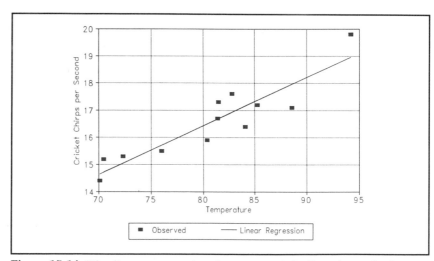

Figure 15.14: The linear regression forms a straight line through the observed data points

Therefore, given a chirp count of 16, you can use the formula

Temp. = (16–2.13)/0.1787

to discover that the calculated temperature is 77.6. This would be the method you would use within Quattro Pro.

Regression analysis has the best results when you use it to determine a value that falls within the range of observed data. In the example above, we counted 16 chirps per second and found that that equated to about 77 degrees, well within the scope of the data.

It is also too easy to jump to the conclusion that the independent variables are *causing* the dependent variables to fluctuate. That may often be the case, as with our crickets, but it is not the linear regression that proves that. It simply shows that both sets of variables fluctuate together, which in itself is quite worthwhile. By measuring just one value, either dependent or independent, you can determine the corresponding value in the other data set.

PERFORMING MATRIX OPERATIONS

The Multiply command on the Advanced Math menu lets you multiply two matrices to solve for one or more unknowns in a set of equations. The Invert command lets you invert a matrix. You can then multiply one matrix by the result of the inverted matrix, thereby effectively dividing one matrix by another.

MULTIPLYING MATRICES

A typical use for matrix multiplication is calculating the cost of a product based on its components. Suppose you run a bakery and want to determine the costs for several of your baked goods. Each of them uses the same ingredients, although in different proportions.

The baked goods we want to price are cake, bread, cookies, and fudge. For this example, we are going to make up the quantities for each ingredient so that the operation of the matrix will be simple and self-evident. The ingredients and their prices per unit are as follows: Flour (2), Eggs (3), Sugar (4), and Milk (5). Here are the recipes for each item:

- $1F + 2E + 2S + 1M$ = Cake
- $3F + 3E + 3S + 3M$ = Bread
- $4F + 4E + 4S + 0M$ = Cookies
- $4F + 0E + 4S + 2M$ = Fudge

The spreadsheet in Figure 15.15 shows the layout for our matrix calculations. The first matrix, B3..E6, contains the coefficients of the recipes, which are the quantities of each ingredient. Notice that there is no milk in the cookies recipe and no eggs in the fudge; each is represented by a zero. The second matrix, B9..B12, is the constant matrix, and contains the cost for each ingredient.

In order to multiply matrices, the first matrix must have the same number of columns as the second matrix has rows. In this case, there are four columns in the first matrix and four rows in the second.

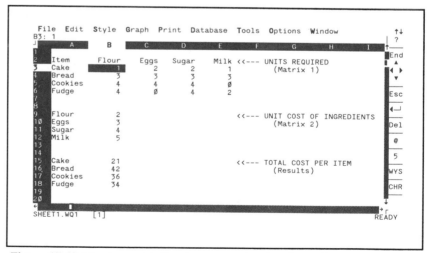

Figure 15.15: Matrix multiplication can solve for the unknowns in linear equations

We can now perform the multiplication to produce the result matrix. It will have as many rows as the first matrix and as many columns as the second: four rows by one column.

1. Invoke the Tools–Advanced Math–Multiply command, specify the block B3..E6 as the first matrix, and press ↵.

2. Specify the block B9..B12 as the second matrix and press ↵.

3. Specify cell B15 as the destination cell and press ↵.

The results will appear in the four cells, B15..B18, as follows:

- Cake: 21

- Bread: 42

- Cookies: 36

- Fudge: 34

By looking at these results, you can see how the multiplication was performed. Here is the equivalent formula for the first result, the cost of cake:

$$+B3*B9 + C3*B10 + D3*B11 + E3*B12$$

INVERTING A MATRIX

Inverting a matrix is equivalent to inverting a number. The inverse of the number 4 is ¼. If you multiply 8 by ¼, the result is 2, the same result as dividing 8 by 4.

You can invert a square matrix (equal number of rows and columns) by using the Invert command. The result of inverting a matrix can be used to multiply another matrix, thereby effectively dividing that matrix by the first one.

By including a matrix inversion with matrix multiplication, we can work our recipe problem from the other end. If we know the total cost for each recipe and how much of each ingredient goes into the recipe, we can calculate the cost per ingredient. Here are the recipes from before, but this time with the total cost included:

- 1F + 2E + 2S + 1M = 21

- 3F + 3E + 3S + 3M = 42

- 4F + 4E + 4S + 0M = 36
- 4F + 0E + 4S + 2M = 34

Figure 15.16 shows the spreadsheet that performs the calculations. The first matrix, B3..E6, is inverted to the block C9..F12. That block is then multiplied by the total cost block, B15..B18, and the result placed in cell B9.

Follow these steps to perform the matrix calculations:

1. Invoke the Tools–Advanced Math–Invert command, specify the block B3..E6 as the matrix to be inverted, and press ↵.

2. Specify cell C9 as the destination and press ↵. The result of the inversion will be placed in cell C9, and you will be back in Ready mode.

3. Invoke the Tools–Advanced Math–Multiply command, specify the block C9..F12 as the first matrix, and press ↵.

4. Specify the block B15..B18, the total costs, as the second matrix, and press ↵.

5. Specify the cell B9 as the destination and press ↵.

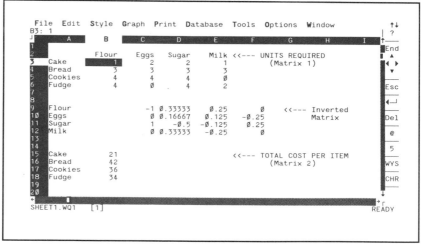

*Figure 15.16:*By first inverting a matrix, you can perform matrix division

You will recognize the results in cells B9 through B12:

- Flour: 2
- Eggs: 3
- Sugar: 4
- Milk: 5

USING LINEAR OPTIMIZATION

Optimization is the process of finding the optimum results based on a set of variables, and it provides a means for allocating resources among a set of related activities. Quattro Pro's Tools–Advanced Math–Optimization command is perhaps the most powerful analytical tool in the program; it is certainly the most complex.

For those who work in operations research, build models based on linear programming, or use the Simplex method of optimization, Quattro Pro's Optimization command will be the perfect spreadsheet tool. But even without tapping the complete scope of linear programming, you can use the Optimization command to great effect in a wide variety of spreadsheets. We will use an example that demonstrates the core of the process and the command's options.

Our bakery from the earlier examples is supposed to be a money-making business. The question is: How many of each bakery item should we produce to maximize our profits? Do we make an equal number of each, or do we put all our efforts into one item that seems to make the most profit? With the Optimization command, the answer is close at hand.

Figure 15.17 shows the spreadsheet that will produce the result. You should recognize the numbers in the block B4..E8 as the recipe quantities used in earlier examples. There is an extra row, called Labor, that represents the amount of time that it takes to bake a quantity of each item.

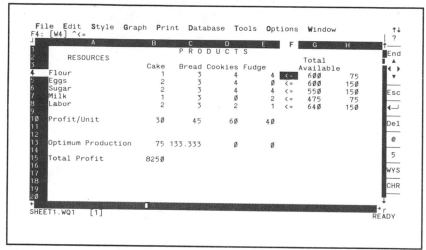

Figure 15.17: The spreadsheet optimization model

The following settings on the Optimization menu are needed to define the model:

The Reset command on the Optimization menu resets all options back to their defaults; there is no way to reset just one of them. Therefore, you should consider writing a short macro that sets all the options. Then you could easily modify the settings by simply editing the macro and executing it again. Remember to start the macro with the Optimization–Reset command. See the next chapter for information about macros.

- Linear constraint coefficients: The first block to note is the numbers in cells B4..E8. These are the quantities of each ingredient (labeled in column A) that are required to bake each item (labeled in row 3).

- Inequality/equality relations: The block F4..F8 contains the operators that define the relationship between each ingredient and how much of it is available. You enter them as text. In the first row, for example, all the flour that is used to bake the items must be less than or equal to 600.

- Constant constraint terms: The block G4..G8 contains the numbers that absolutely limit our glorious plans to make a profit. In this example, the ingredients that go into all the baked goods cannot exceed these constraint terms.

- Objective function: The profit we make on each item is shown in the block B10..E10. The profit we make from bread, for example, is 30. The larger a number in this row, the more likely that item will be favored in our optimization.

- Extremum: This is the only command on the Optimization menu that does not require a cell input. Choose either Smallest or Largest to minimize the results or maximize them. In this case, we choose Largest, because we want to find the largest profit of all the different scenarios.

Once we have specified all of the above options, we can specify the cells where the results should be placed:

- Solution: This single cell, B15, receives the total profit for our model.
- Variables: This block, B13..E13, labeled Optimum Production in the figure, receives the number of each baked good that we should produce in order to maximize our profits.

In this case, the total profit (the solution) could also be calculated by multiplying the number of each item that we bake (row 13) by its profit, which will be calculated and shown in row 10, and then summing those results. Therefore, instead of specifying the solution cell, you could use the formula @SUMPRODUCT(B13..E13, B10..E10).

After you have set these options, invoke the Go command on the Optimization menu. The solution will be placed in cell B15, and the variables will be in cells B13..E13. As shown in Figure 15.17, here are the results:

- Cell B13: 75
- Cell C13: 133.33
- Cell D13: 0
- Cell E13: 0
- Cell B15: 8250 (solution)

These results tell us that the best way to use our limited supplies (column G), based on the ingredients in each recipe (B4..E8) and the profit we make for each baked good (row 10), is to bake 75 cakes and 133 loaves of bread, which will produce a maximum profit of 8250.

These results are based only on the given values. If we change any of the three parameters (recipe, inventory, or profit) and invoke the Go command again, the results could be drastically different.

The other commands on the Optimization menu allow you to further refine the parameters of the model.

The Bounds for Variables option lets you specify a lower and an upper value between which each of the result variables must fall. You use a two-row block with the same number of columns as the variables block. In the first row, enter the lowest value that you will accept for each variable; use the second row for the highest value. For example, if your bread chef was working under a contract that guaranteed at least 30 loaves per period, but no more than 100, the lower bound would be 30 and the upper 100. To specify only that the variable be greater than zero, enter a 0 for the lower bound and any text entry for the upper-bound cell.

With the Formula Constraints option, you can specify a block of formulas instead of the blocks containing the linear constraint coefficients, inequality/equality relations, and constant constraint terms. One formula substitutes for each row of constraint coefficients.

For example, the formulas for flour and labor in Figure 15.17, respectively, would look like this:

```
600-(1*$B$13+3*$C$13+4*$D$13+4*$E$13)
640-(2*$B$13+3*$C$13+2*$D$13+1*$E$13)
```

In the first formula, the 600 is the constant constraint term, the values 1, 3, 4, and 4 are the linear constraint coefficients, and the cell addresses refer to the variables for which Quattro Pro will solve. It will use this formula but keep the result positive, in effect providing the less-than-or-equal-to relationship.

The Dual Values option allows you to have a column containing as many cells as there are constraints in the input portion of the model. When the model is evaluated, a number will be placed in each cell in this column that represents the amount by which the solution cell will change for each increment of 1 to the corresponding constant constraint value. For example, if a cell in the Dual Values column is 15, you could change the constant constraint by 3, which would increase the solution by 45.

The Additional Dual Values option provides for a row containing as many cells as there are variable cells in the output portion of the model. When the model is evaluated, a number will be placed into each cell in this row that represents the amount by which the solution cell will change for each increment of 1 to either the lower or upper bound for the corresponding variable. This applies only to the bound that is limiting the resulting variable. For example, suppose a variable is 50, its lower bound is 0, its upper bound is 50, and the corresponding dual value for that variable is 12. If you increase the upper bound from 50 to 53, the solution cell will increase by 36.

WORKING BACKWARDS WITH THE SOLVE FOR COMMAND

The Tools–Solve For command lets you solve a mathematical formula "backwards," in the sense that you use the command after you have already set up a mathematical relationship in the spreadsheet.

The Solve For command has three settings that define the problem to be solved:

- Formula Cell: A cell address or block name for a cell that contains a formula.

- Target Value: The value, or cell address or block name that contains a value, in which you would like the formula to result. This value can be either positive or negative.

- Variable Cell: A cell address or block name to which the formula refers.

After specifying these three settings, you can issue the Tools–Solve For–Go command. It will then find a value for the variable cell that causes the formula cell to result in your target value. To use this command, you must heed a few restrictions:

- The formula in the formula cell cannot contain any string arguments, nor can it evaluate to a date number.

- The variable cell must contain a numeric value—not text, a date function, or a formula.

- If you will have protection enabled when the Solve For command is doing its job, the variable cell must be unprotected.

You could also rewrite the formula to solve for degrees Celsius when the degrees Fahrenheit are known. But the example illustrates how the Solve For command lets you avoid what could be a tremendous amount of work in a large spreadsheet model.

As a bare-bones example, consider this formula in cell A1, which converts degrees Celsius into degrees Fahrenheit:

(A2*9/5)+32

Cell A2 contains the value 70, so that the formula in cell A1 results in 158. Now suppose that you would like the Solve For command to find what value in cell A2 (degrees Celsius) is equivalent to 212 degrees Fahrenheit. You would specify the three Solve For command options in this way:

1. Issue the Tools–Solve For command.
2. Specify cell **A1** as the Formula Cell.
3. Enter a Target Value of **212**, our desired result.
4. Specify cell **A2** as the Variable Cell, the cell to which the formula refers.
5. Issue the Go command.

The command will quickly come to a conclusion and place the value 100 in cell A2, which causes the formula in cell A1 to result in 212.

Actually, you will find that the number in cell A2 is not quite 212, but some tiny fraction greater or less than that amount. This is because the Solve For command makes a series of "guesses" (*iterations*) by changing the number in the variable cell and then checking the effect of each iteration on the formula cell. When it gets close enough to your target value, it considers the job done. There are two other options under the Tools–Solve For–Parameters command that control the iteration process:

- Max Iterations: The number of guesses the command should make before it stops, even if it has not come close to an answer. You can specify from 1 to 99; the default is 5.

- Accuracy: This number specifies how close you want the command to get to the target value before it considers the job completed. By default, the amount is 0.005.

For example, you might see a result such as 99.999999621286 in the variable cell. This shows that the Solve For command reached a solution within five iterations that was within 0.005 of the target value.

The solution in the variable cell will be either slightly higher or slightly lower than the precise solution, depending on whether or not the value already in the variable cell is higher or lower than the solution. You can assist the Solve For command by first placing a value in the variable cell which produces a result that is "in the ballpark" of your desired result.

You could also enter a smaller number for the Accuracy option to force the command to get closer to the exact answer, but this shouldn't be necessary for most day-to-day problems.

Let's use the Solve For command in conjunction with the example from Figures 15.5 and 15.6, in which we built a what-if table that produced a table of monthly payments, given certain variables associated with buying a house. Suppose that we now want to know exactly how expensive a house we could buy and still keep our payments down to just $1,200 per month. We'll build a new spreadsheet and then use the Solve For command to find the answer.

Figure 15.18 shows our new layout in the block B1..C8. The first four rows contain our known amounts: purchase price, loan amount (80 percent of the purchase price), loan period, and interest rate. The next three rows contain formulas that calculate the payments which contribute to the total monthly payment. In the last row is a formula that sums the three payments to produce the total. The numbers used in this example are the same as those in row 4 of Figures 15.5 and 15.6, resulting in a monthly payment of 699.

Here are the actual cell contents in Figure 15.18:

CELL	ENTRY
C1	70000
C2	+C1*0.8
C3	30

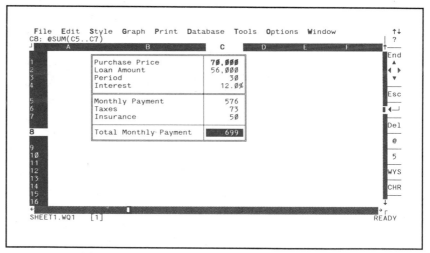

Figure 15.18: The Tools–Solve For command will be used to find a purchase price that will produce a specified total monthly payment

CELL	ENTRY
C4	0.12
C5	@PMT(C2,C4/12,C3*12)
C6	+C1*0.0125/12
C7	(250+C1*0.005)/12
C8	@SUM(C5..C7)

We want the Solve For command to tell us what number in the Purchase Price cell, C1, will cause the Total Monthly Payment cell, C8, to result in 1200.

1. Invoke the Tools–Solve For command.
2. Specify cell **C8**, the total monthly payment, as the Formula Cell.
3. Enter a Target Value of **1200**.
4. Specify cell **C1**, the purchase price, as the Variable Cell.
5. Choose the Go command.

In an instant, the Solve For command will enter the value 121723.77 in cell C1, and the formula in cell C8 now evaluates to 1200 (actually 1199.9999). This example gives you an idea of how valuable this command would be in a large spreadsheet model.

This chapter has introduced you to the power of Quattro Pro's advanced analytical tools. The next chapter is the first of two on the subject of macros, one of the most potent tools in Quattro Pro and often one of the most underused.

Macros: the Ultimate Spreadsheet Tool

Fast
Track

IN THE LANGUAGE OF COMPUTERS, A *MACRO* IS A SERIES of actions that can be executed with a single keystroke. In Quattro Pro, a macro can consist of keystrokes that you could otherwise type from the keyboard, as well as special commands from the macro command language. This chapter will introduce you to the basics of writing macros.

ADVANTAGES OF MACROS

All too frequently, spreadsheet users think that macros are only for programmers. In fact, that is far from the truth. The sooner you begin to experiment with macros and include them in your spreadsheets, the sooner you will master the power of Quattro Pro. Here are some of the tremendous advantages of using macros:

- Consistency: A macro will always execute in the same way.

- Accuracy: Once you have tested the macro and know that it works correctly, it will always produce accurate results.

- Speed: Macros execute many times faster than you can type.

- Simplicity and convenience: Once you have written a macro to perform a spreadsheet task, you no longer have to concern yourself with that task, because the macro does all the work for you.

- Power: Macros can be as long and involved as you care to make them, and they can handle complex tasks that might otherwise be almost impossible to perform manually.

- Documentation: Believe it or not, a set of macros can serve as excellent documentation for your spreadsheet. By examining each macro routine, you can understand the purpose and normal use of the spreadsheet.

A QUICK TOUR

A macro in Quattro Pro consists of nothing more than text in one or more cells in a block in a column. The text is the macro code. As an example, we will build a *keyboard macro*, which will simply play back as keystrokes the characters you enter as the macro code.

CREATING A MACRO

Start with a blank spreadsheet and follow these steps to create the macro:

1. Move the cell selector to cell B2, which will be the *location* of your macro. (Any other cell could be used.)

2. Type the label **Quattro Pro has columns and rows**, and then press ↵ to enter it into the cell. This will be the *text* of your macro.

3. Give this cell a block name: Invoke the Edit–Names–Create command, enter the name **\Z** (the name is back-slash Z), and press ↵. Don't include spaces in the name.

4. Press ↵ again to specify cell B2 as the cell to be named.

You now have a macro in cell B2 that is named \Z. But it doesn't look very special, does it? A macro is just text that you execute as a macro. Whether that text does anything useful, or even correctly, is up to your macro-writing capabilities.

EXECUTING THE MACRO

Let's get some use out of your new macro. Follow these steps to execute it:

1. Move the cell selector to any blank cell except the one directly under the macro (B3).

2. Hold down the Alt key and press Z.

If your macro didn't work, you may have named the wrong cell \Z, or you may have entered the text in a cell other than B2. Be sure that the text and the name are both for the same cell.

If you wrote the macro correctly, the text in cell B2 should appear on the input line, just as though you had typed the phrase yourself. Figure 16.1 shows the spreadsheet with the macro code in cell B2 and the result of the macro's execution on the input line.

The macro simply read each character and executed it as a keystroke. Note that the text was not entered into the current cell—the macro did not press ⏎ for you. You could press ⏎ now, type more text after the phrase, or just press Escape to clear the input line.

You could even invoke the macro again. It would repeat the text on the input line as many times as you pressed Alt-Z (up to the 254-character cell maximum, of course).

EDITING A MACRO

Now that we have tested our macro, let's go back and edit it so that it will write the phrase and then enter it into a cell.

1. Move the cell selector back to the macro in cell B2.

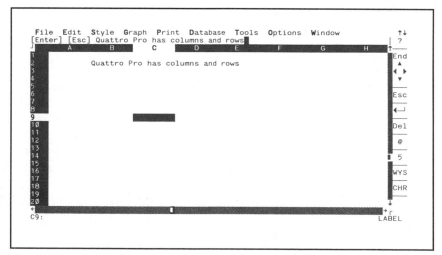

Figure 16.1: A macro is simply text in a named cell

2. Press F2 to edit the cell.

3. Type a single tilde, ~, at the end of the phrase.

4. Press ↵ to complete the edit and return to Ready mode.

5. Move the cell selector to a blank cell (not B3) and invoke the macro again by pressing Alt-Z.

This time, you should see the phrase entered into the current cell, just as though you had typed it and pressed ↵. As you might have guessed, when Quattro Pro is executing a macro, it interprets the tilde as a press of the ↵ key. Just about every key on the keyboard has a code that can be used in a macro.

MACRO BASICS

The short exercise in the previous section introduced just about every aspect of writing and using macros.

- Macros are simply text that you type into a cell.

- There are really only two parts to a macro: the text and the named location.

- By giving the macro cell a name, you can invoke it from the keyboard.

- When a keyboard macro executes, it produces the same result as typing the characters from the keyboard.

- Some characters, such as letters and numbers, are taken literally in the macro. Others, like the ↵, have a special code that must be used.

This is why you should test the macro in a cell other than the one below the macro text itself. If the macro were to write any text into that cell, it would then have more text to execute!

Once you have invoked a macro, it executes every character in the cell you specified (such as by pressing Alt-Z), and then looks in the cell below it for more. If it finds more text there, it will execute it, and then look in the cell below that for more. In this way, it will continue executing down a column until one of four things occurs:

- It encounters a blank or nontext cell.
- It encounters a macro {quit} command (as explained in the next chapter).
- An error occurs in the macro.
- The user presses Ctrl-Break.

Because macros must always be text, a blank or nontext cell will cause the macro to stop, and the spreadsheet will return to Ready mode.

Don't confuse a cell with a numeric value with the appearance of numerals within a text string. You can write a macro that enters numbers into a cell, but the macro itself must be a text entry. For example, to enter the number 987 into a cell, you would preface the macro with a label prefix, like this:

'987~

Then it would be a text entry. When you invoke the macro, however, the first thing it would type is a 9, so that it would be creating a numeric entry.

It's all too easy to write a macro that misfires, and a programming error on your part will sometimes cause the macro to stop and display an error message, at which point you will have to press Escape to return to Ready mode.

Finally, you can press Ctrl-Break to stop the macro, in the same way that Ctrl-Break will cancel a print job.

LAYING OUT YOUR MACROS

In the next chapter, you will see how you can store your macros in one spreadsheet and run them in another. But frequently, you will want your macros and data all in the same spreadsheet, and in that case, you must exercise care in how you lay them out.

DETERMINING LINE LENGTH

Because a macro is just text in a cell, you can enter as many as 254 characters. But this would be much too long for easy reading on the screen when you want to review or edit the macro. In general, you should try to keep the length of each macro line to less than 75 characters. That way, you can view the entire macro without scrolling the screen.

When macro lines are too short, they take up many rows and can be difficult (or tiring) to read and edit. On the other hand, if a macro is complex and will be difficult to interpret, you may want to keep the lines shorter than usual.

You will typically determine a macro's line length by the number of logical steps on that line. For example, if a macro formats a block of cells, prints the block, and then saves the block to a separate file, you would use at least three macro lines—one for each process. Because print routines can require many steps, you might also break down the printing portion of the macro into two or more lines.

PLACING THE MACRO

You can write a macro in any cell in the spreadsheet, but there are a few guidelines you can follow to make them more convenient to manage, easier to interpret, and less prone to damage.

You should keep all your macros together in the same area of the spreadsheet, so that the only time you go to that area is when you want to write, edit, or inspect one of your macros. You can also include any variable cells in a portion of that area, so that they, too, will be easy to find and maintain.

Figure 16.2 shows a convenient arrangement for storing both your macros and variable cells. Three columns are involved.

The code for the macros is in column C, below the list of variables in that column. Between each macro is a blank cell, so that there is no chance of one macro running into another.

Column B contains the name of the macro or variable (the block name) in the cell to the right.

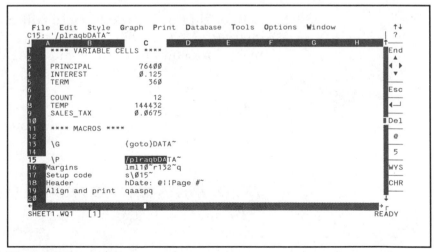

Column A has been narrowed to only one space wide. It is used for comments or other explanatory text that will help you to decipher the macros when you return to revise them in the future. Comments will overhang into column B when there is nothing in that column, but you can always see the full text of a comment by highlighting its cell and reading its contents on the input line.

Columns A, B, and C would be reserved for macros and variables. The spreadsheet data could start in column D and extend into any columns to the right. Also, spreadsheet data would not be placed in rows 1 through 20, but would instead start anywhere below row 20.

By structuring your spreadsheet in this manner, you can delete a row or column in the data or macro area without the possibility of damaging information in the other area. In this way,

You can take advantage of the names you enter in column B when you are first setting up your macros by using the Edit–Names–Labels–Right command to name each cell in column C.

Figure 16.2: Segregate your macros and variable cells in their own portion of the spreadsheet

your spreadsheet will grow diagonally downwards, block by block, starting with variables and macros in the upper-left corner of the spreadsheet.

NAMING AND RUNNING A MACRO

In the earlier example, you saw how you can invoke a macro from the keyboard. But that method is just one of seven ways to invoke a macro:

- From the keyboard
- Using the Execute command
- Replaying a recorded macro with the Instant Replay command
- From another macro
- Creating an autoexecuting macro
- Specifying a named macro when you load Quattro Pro
- Replaying a block within the Transcript utility

Replaying a recorded macro will be explained later in the chapter when we discuss how to record macros. Invoking a macro from another macro and using the Transcript utility are covered in the next chapter. The other methods are described in the following sections.

Remember that once you have written and named a macro, you must save your spreadsheet if you want to keep that macro for future sessions.

INVOKING A MACRO FROM THE KEYBOARD

To invoke a macro from the keyboard, you must give the macro a special name that consists of the backslash and a single letter, such as \A, \B, or \M. Then you can invoke the macro by holding down the Alt key and pressing the letter, such as Alt-A, Alt-B, or Alt-M.

This method gives you quick access to as many as 26 different macros, but no more than that. This may be more than enough for you, but you may find it difficult to remember the purpose of a macro with just a single-letter name.

You can name or rename a macro with the Tools–Macros–Name command, which has the choices Create and Delete. These commands have no unique connection to macros. They are identical to the commands of the same name on the Edit–Names menu. In fact, it should be emphasized that a macro name is just another block name.

INVOKING A MACRO WITH THE EXECUTE COMMAND

The Execute command will let you invoke a macro in any cell in the spreadsheet, whether you had intended that cell to be a macro or not. You should therefore verify that the cell you are choosing is the one you want.

By using the Tools–Macro–Execute (Alt-F2) command, you can invoke the text in any block as a macro. The Execute command prompts you for the address of the macro you wish to run. You can type in an address, point to the cell, or type in the block name of the macro. You can also press F3 after you invoke the Execute command to bring up the usual list of block names. After you specify the cell and press ↵, Quattro Pro will execute the macro at that location, just as though you had invoked it from the keyboard.

One advantage of this method is that the macro does not have to be named, which can be a convenience during the macro-testing phase. Another advantage is that you can use longer, more descriptive names for your macros, so that it will be easy to pick the one you want from the list of block names.

Once you are no longer bound to a one-character macro name, you should consider following a simple naming convention that makes it very easy to pick your macros from the list of block names. Because the list of names is alphabetized, you can group all your macro names together on the list by starting each name with the same character. An obvious character to use is the backslash, \. You might create macro names such as \PRINT_TOTALS to print a block and \SAVE_BLOCK to save a block of the spreadsheet to disk. When you later press F3 to select a macro for the Execute command, all your macro names will be grouped together at the end of the names list.

RUNNING THE AUTOEXECUTING MACRO

One way to execute a macro involves no action on your part. Each spreadsheet can have one named macro that will automatically be executed whenever that spreadsheet is opened. By default, the name that is used is \0 (backslash zero).

If you name a macro \0, save the spreadsheet, and then later retrieve that spreadsheet, whatever code is in the cell named \0 will be executed as soon as the spreadsheet appears on the screen.

You can change the default name to another by using the Options–Startup–Startup Macro command. Just type in another block name and press ⏎, and then use the Options–Update command to retain this change for future sessions.

The autoexecuting macro is a very powerful feature that can serve as the gateway to all your spreadsheets. At the least, it lets you conveniently set up your spreadsheet each time it is retrieved. It might move the cell selector to a specific location based on the current date, import a file of current data that is renewed on your disk each day, or provide you with a summary of the spreadsheet as it currently stands.

But you can go much farther with this feature. Simply by having a macro that starts automatically, you can completely automate the functioning of a spreadsheet from the moment it is retrieved. When you couple the autoexecuting macro with the autoloading spreadsheet (discussed in Chapter 8), you can build a Quattro Pro session that is automated right from the DOS prompt. This might be hard to imagine so early in the learning process, but the possibilities are immense.

SPECIFYING A MACRO AT STARTUP

When you are loading Quattro Pro from the DOS prompt, you can specify the name of a spreadsheet to load and a macro to run in that spreadsheet. For example, to load a spreadsheet named Mysheet and run a macro called START, you would type this command at the DOS prompt:

Q MYSHEET START

If there is an autoexecuting macro in Mysheet, it will be ignored in deference to your request to run the START macro.

INCLUDING SPECIAL KEYS IN MACRO CODES

You have already seen how the tilde (~) serves as the ↵ key in a macro. There are also codes for most of the other keys on your keyboard, including the function keys. Your macros can really do exactly what you could do from the keyboard.

Most of these codes are enclosed in braces, and because they are computer commands, you must spell them precisely with no extra spaces or other characters. Here are a few examples of these codes and their keyboard counterparts:

{right}	→
{pgup}	PgUp
{home}	Home
{esc}	Escape
{goto}	F5, the Goto key
{calc}	F9, the Calculate key

A list of all the keys and their macro codes appears in the inside cover of this book.

You can include multiple commands by adding a space and then a number after the command. For example, {up 3} will move the cell selector up three cells, as though you had pressed ↑ three times. The command {pgdn 5} is equivalent to pressing the

The commands {right}, {left}, {up}, and {down} can be abbreviated to a one-letter code, such as {r}. In the early stages of learning to use macros, however, you might want to use the longer command to make the code easier to interpret.

PgDn key five times. You can use any valid number, such as a formula that returns a number or a cell address that contains one.

Suppose that you are entering a lot of data into the spreadsheet, and each time you enter data into a cell in one particular column, you must also enter data in the cell 30 rows below that cell. You could write a simple macro to move the cell selector down to the next cell: {down 30}. Give the macro a name such as \D for down, and when you want to move down to the lower cell, just press Alt-D. To return to the top, you could have another macro named \U, for up: {up 30}.

ACCESSING THE MENU WITH KEYSTROKE OR LOGICAL MACROS

Perhaps the most important key you can include in your macros is the Quattro Pro menu key. You can activate the menu within your macros by including either the slash key, /, or the command {menu}. Once you have activated the menu, you can perform any spreadsheet task that you could otherwise do manually. Now the power of macros really begins to take off.

Remember that a macro is simply emulating what you could be doing from the keyboard, so in order to activate the menu the spreadsheet must be in Ready mode. Also, don't forget that when you are writing a macro that begins with the slash key, you will have to preface it with a label prefix in order to avoid actually bringing up the menu.

You can use two different styles of keyboard macros to access the menus in Quattro Pro: keystroke and logical. A *keystroke macro* consists of exactly the same keystrokes that you would use were you to type the commands from the keyboard. A *logical macro* uses what are known as menu-equivalent commands instead of keystrokes. Logical macros require more text than keystroke macros, but they are more descriptive and therefore easier to interpret.

WRITING KEYSTROKE MACROS

Here is a simple keystroke macro that applies a numeric format of Currency with two decimal places to the current cell:

/snc2~~

The macro starts with the slash key to activate the menu (although you could also use the {menu} command). The three letters *snc* invoke the Style–Numeric Format–Currency command. The macro then enters 2 as the number of decimals required and presses ↵ twice to complete the command and format the current cell. You can type those keystrokes by hand to verify that this is what the macro will do.

Keystroke macros tend to be very short, and therefore take up little room in the spreadsheet or in your printed documentation. But this also makes them difficult to decipher if you are not familiar with the Quattro Pro menu structure.

A problem arises when you load a worksheet from Lotus 1-2-3 that contains macros that access the Quattro Pro menu. The macro shown above would be written like this in 1-2-3 to invoke the Range–Format–Currency command:

/rfc2~~

But this macro would fail miserably under the default menus of Quattro Pro; in fact, it would try to issue the File–Close command. There are two ways around this problem.

The first solution is simply to change to the Lotus 1-2-3 menu tree before you run 1-2-3 macros, using the Options–Startup–Menu Tree–123 command (discussed in Chapter 18). Your Lotus 1-2-3 macros will work because they will be accessing a Lotus-compatible menu. You could even revise the macro so that it changed the menu tree at the start and reset the menu tree when it was finished.

Another solution is provided by the Tools–Macro–Key Reader command. By default, this is set to No, which means that a Lotus

1-2-3 macro that accesses the menu will fail when run under Quattro Pro's default menu system. When it is set to Yes, however, 1-2-3 macros will be interpreted as they execute, so they will successfully access the Quattro Pro menus. You don't have to change to the 1-2-3 menu tree first.

The Key Reader command translates Lotus 1-2-3 macros when they are run under the Quattro Pro menu system, but it doesn't work for any other macro styles or menu trees. If you run your Quattro Pro keystroke macros while using a different menu tree, such as the 1-2-3 or original Quattro tree, another problem can arise.

For example, suppose you wrote a macro to run under the standard Quattro Pro menu tree, such as the one shown above. Later, you decide to use the original Quattro menu tree (or the Lotus 1-2-3 menu tree), and then run your macro. The macro will execute the same keystrokes as it always did, but those keystrokes will now be activating different menu commands. The results could be disastrous. The solution is to use logical macros.

WRITING LOGICAL MACROS

Quattro Pro's logical macros use what are known as menu-equivalent commands, which execute a specific menu command no matter which menu tree you might be using.

For example, here is a logical macro that performs exactly the same task as the macro that was used to illustrate keystroke macros:

The *@ Functions and Macros* reference manual that comes with Quattro Pro has a complete list of menu-equivalent commands, as do the Quattro Pro Help screens.

{/ Block;Format}c2~~

This macro would work correctly no matter which menu tree you were using. For example, the menu-equivalent command, {/ Block;Format}, replaces the three keystrokes /sn.

Menu-equivalent commands never really access the menus—you won't see the menus pull down as each command is executed. This allows you to execute some commands without having to quit the appropriate menu. For example, you can specify the block named MY_BLOCK for the Graph–1st Series command by using {/ 1Series;Block}MY_BLOCK~. If you were to execute just that single macro, Quattro Pro would be in Ready mode when the macro finished.

If you used the equivalent keystroke macro, when the macro finished, it would still be in the Graph–Series menu. The macro would have to invoke the Quit command twice to return to Ready mode: /gs1MY_BLOCK~qq.

Logical macros are always enclosed in braces and begin with a / and a space. The actual command is broken down into two pieces, such as Block and Format in the example above. The second command is simply a subcommand of the first one. A print macro in the logical style might have the following commands:

{/ Print;Block}MY_DATA~

{/ Print;LeftMargin}12~

{/ Print;RightMargin}110~

With keystroke macros, you must know the menu structure of Quattro Pro in order to write a macro that accesses the menu. With logical macros, you not only must know the menu structure, you must also know the menu-equivalent command for the command you wish to invoke.

Fortunately, Quattro Pro has two built-in features that will help you get going, as well as prove to be valuable aids no matter what your skill level.

AIDS TO WRITING MACROS

There are two tools that greatly ease the process of writing macros:

- Instead of pondering over the exact spelling of a macro command, you can select it from the Macros menu and include it in your macro as you are writing the macro.

- Instead of writing the macro code, you can simply type the commands that you want in the macro and have Quattro Pro record your keystrokes as a macro.

USING THE MACROS KEY, SHIFT-F3

In Chapter 4, you learned that when you are writing a formula, you can select a function from the list that is displayed by pressing the Functions key, Alt-F3. There is a similar key that will help you write macros. It is appropriately called the Macros key, and you access its list by pressing Shift-F3.

Because there are so many macro commands, the Macros list divides them into submenus in the categories of Keyboard, Screen, Interactive, Program Flow, Cells, File, and / Commands. All you have to do is flip through these menus to find the macro command you want, highlight it on the list, and press ↵ to insert the command into the input line.

The first category, Keyboard, has all the keyboard commands that we discussed earlier, such as {right} and {home}. The category called / Commands has all the menu-equivalent commands that you use when writing logical macros. In order to limit each menu-equivalent command to only two commands, there are several categories that do not actually appear on the Quattro Pro menus.

For example, there is no Block command on the Quattro Pro menus that would correspond to the command we used earlier, {/ Block;Format}. There are also commands called {/ Basics; }, {/ Titles; }, and {/ ValueColors; }. The Quattro Pro @ *Functions and Macros* reference manual has a complete list of all the menu-equivalent commands, which are cross-referenced for Quattro Pro and Lotus 1-2-3 commands.

RECORDING YOUR MACROS

You can cut down on a lot of the work of writing macros by taking advantage of the Tools–Macro–Record command (Alt-F2 R). This toggle command switches the spreadsheet in and out of Record mode. When the Rec indicator appears at the bottom of the screen, your keystrokes are being recorded behind the scenes as you type. By default, your keystrokes are recorded using menu-equivalent commands.

You can use the Tools–Macro–Paste command (Alt-F2 P) to copy those recorded keystrokes into your spreadsheet in the form of a macro, ready to be executed.

You can also use the Tools–Macro–Instant Replay (Alt-F2 I) command to play back the most recently recorded macro without actually copying it into the spreadsheet. This is a handy feature when you want to test the results of your recorded macro or use a macro for just a single task.

Let's record a simple macro to see how it works. Start with a blank spreadsheet and follow these steps:

1. Invoke the Tools–Macro–Record (Alt-F2 R) command. You should see the Rec indicator appear in the status line at the bottom of the screen. From now on, Quattro Pro will record your keystrokes as you type them.

2. Wherever the cell selector may be in your spreadsheet, press the Goto key F5, specify cell A5, and press ↵.

3. Move the cell selector right five cells to cell F5.

4. Invoke the Print–Block command and specify the block F5..H10 as the block to be printed.

5. Choose Layout–Margins–Left from the Print menu and specify **10** as the left margin.

6. Choose Right from the Margins menu and specify **130** as the right margin.

7. Choose Quit from the Margins menu.

8. Choose Setup String from the Layout menu and enter **\014** as the setup string. Whoops, make that **\015**, and then press ↵.

9. Choose Quit from the Layout menu.

10. Choose Adjust Printer–Align from the Print menu.

11. Choose Quit to return to Ready mode.

12. Turn off macro recording by invoking the Tools–
    Macro–Record command again. The Rec indicator
    should disappear from the bottom of the screen.

Your keystrokes have been recorded, and we can now paste
them back into the spreadsheet as a macro.

13. Move the cursor to cell C2, a convenient place to start
    our macro.

14. Invoke the Tools–Macro-Paste (Alt-F2 P) command.
    You are prompted for the name of the macro.

15. Type the name **\P**, followed by ↵, to give this macro a
    keyboard-invocable block name. Now you are
    prompted for the block in which the macro should be
    pasted (copied).

16. Specify C2..D2 and press ↵. Quattro Pro will try to for-
    mat the macro so that it is no wider than these two
    columns.

⊙ This macro is not
quite ready to use.
See the discussion of
macro etiquette later in
the chapter.

The macro will be pasted into the cells, just as though you had
typed the cell entries:

```
{GOTO}A5~{RIGHT 5}
{/ Print;Block}.
{RIGHT 2}{DOWN 5}~
{/ Print;LeftMargin}10~
{/ Print;RightMargin}130~
{/ Print;Setup}\014
{BACKSPACE}5~
{/ Print;Align}
```

Notice the sequence of keystrokes in the seventh line, where
the Backspace key and the numeral 5 were entered to correct the
setup code. Each keystroke was recorded as it was typed. You
could now edit the sixth line of the macro to correct the setup
code, and then delete the seventh line.

You can also add code to the macro, either by recording and pasting or by writing it directly into the spreadsheet.

RECORDING KEYSTROKE MACROS

By default, macros are recorded in the logical, menu-equivalent style. If you prefer keystroke macros, you can use the Tools–Macro–Macro Recording (Alt-F2 M) command and choose Keystroke from the menu. Now your macros will be recorded in the keystroke style. Here is how the macro we recorded in the previous example would look:

```
{GOTO}A5~{RIGHT 5}
/pb.
{RIGHT 2}{DOWN 5}~
lml10~r130~q
s\014
{BACKSPACE}5~qaaq
```

Remember, keystroke macros will work only when run under the same menu tree in which they were created. You cannot record a keystroke macro within the original Quattro menus and expect the macro to execute properly under the Quattro Pro menus. However, you can use the Tools–Macro–Key Reader command to translate Lotus 1-2-3 keystroke macros.

APPLYING A MACRO TO A COMMON TASK

If you are looking for a routine chore to automate in a macro, start with your print jobs, which take place entirely within the context of the Quattro Pro menu. Because a print macro consists only of keystrokes (and not command language macros), it is a simple matter to record the entire macro. Just turn on the macro recorder and manually run through the print routine, and then paste your macro into the spreadsheet.

All the advantages of using macros are aptly suited for printing spreadsheets:

- The macro can execute all the print commands in an instant.

- The printout will always have the same look because the macro is always consistent.

- If your spreadsheet has multiple print routines, you can write a macro for each one, which greatly justifies the time involved in writing the macros.

- You won't have to remember all the print options; you will only need to invoke the macro.

- If you ever want to change the print options, you can easily make adjustments to the macro.

Look back at Figure 16.2. There is a print macro in the block C15..C19. Its first cell, C15, has been named \P, as you can see in cell B15. This is a keystroke macro, and it may look confusing at first, but the descriptive text in column A next to each line of the macro provides some clarification. Here is each character from the first line of the macro:

/plraqbDATA~

and here are the results of each keystroke:

/	Activates the Quattro Pro menu
p	Invokes the Print command
lra	Chooses the Layout–Reset–All command
q	Chooses Quit from the Print–Layout menu
b	Chooses Block from the main Print menu
DATA	Specifies the block named DATA as the print block
~	Presses ↵ to enter the block name

If you prefer to use logical, menu-equivalent macros, the line from above would look like this:

        {/ Print;ResetAll}
        {/ Print;Block}DATA~

You can see how this would be much more readable than the keystroke style, although more characters are needed. Here is the complete print macro from Figure 16.2, shown in the logical style:

        {/ Print;ResetAll}
        {/ Print;Block}DATA~
        {/ Print;LeftMargin}10~
        {/ Print;RightMargin}132~
        {/ Print;Setup}\015~
        {/ Print;Header}Date: @||Page #~
        {/ Print;Align}
        {/ Print;Go}
        {/ Print;FormFeed}

Once you have automated a few print routines, you will begin to reap the rewards of learning this new language of macros.

PRACTICING GOOD MACRO ETIQUETTE

The more you write macros, the more you will realize macros are really just another way to program a computer. As with any programming language, the success of your macros depends to a large degree on the care you take when writing them. It's wonderfully easy to write a "quick-and-dirty" macro to handle an immediate chore in the spreadsheet. But it's another matter to write macros that automate the daily routines of using the spreadsheet. They must be absolutely accurate, efficient, reliable, easy to run, and easy to maintain.

That's a grand set of requirements, but your use of macros will grow as you learn about them, and simple macros have fewer hurdles to overcome. There are many rules of etiquette that will help you write successful macros; this section will introduce some of the more important ones.

USING BLOCK NAMES

You can reference a cell by using its address in a macro, but this can create a big problem. Here is a macro that jumps the cell selector to B10:

{goto}B10~

On the surface, this macro seems perfectly reasonable. But a macro is just unchanging text in the spreadsheet. The macro shown above will not perform as you expected if you insert 15 new rows at row 5. It will still jump the cell selector to B10, but what had been cell B10 will now be cell B25. To avoid this problem when referencing cells in the spreadsheet, your macros should always refer to block names, such as:

{goto}THAT_CELL~

Now the macro will work as planned no matter how you alter the spreadsheet.

You don't have to name every cell a macro might need to reference. Frequently, you can use a single cell as a point of reference for the macro; once it finds that cell, it can perform whatever duties are required in the vicinity of that cell. Here's a macro that jumps the cell selector to a named cell, and then erases the cells in a block three rows below it:

{goto}SOME_CELL~

```
{down 3}

/ee{right 2}~
```

It's quite acceptable to reference cell addresses while you are writing and testing a macro, but when the macro nears completion, you should eliminate those cell addresses and use block names instead.

SPECIFYING ALL MENU SETTINGS

When you save your spreadsheet, all the current settings for the various spreadsheet commands are saved with it. These include the options for the Graph, Print, Database–Query, and Edit–Search commands, for example. The next time you retrieve your spreadsheet, you can immediately print the same block with the same settings as you used in the previous session.

This implies that once you have specified all the print settings, a macro to print that block in the spreadsheet would be a rather simple one, such as {/ Print;Go}. But life is rarely so simple, and you are just courting danger if you take this approach.

If you are going to take the time to encapsulate a spreadsheet routine into a macro, then you should take a little extra time to specify all the options for the particular routine if these options are different from the defaults. For a print macro, specify the block, margins, page length, header, and whatever else you might include in the printout, as in the earlier print macro example. Each time you run the macro, you can be sure that precisely the right settings are being used.

There is a very important preliminary step you should take when you are going to specify all the options for a particular command. In order to ensure that every option on the menu you are using is set correctly, you should first reset all the options to their defaults. All commands that retain their settings when you save the spreadsheet have a reset option, such as the following:

- Printing: Print–Layout–Reset–All
- Graphing: Graph–Customize Series–Reset–Graph

- Database Sort: Database–Sort–Reset
- Database Query: Database–Query–Reset
- Searching: Edit–Search–Options Reset

Therefore, your print macros should always begin with the {/ Print;ResetAll} command (or /plra in the keystroke style). Then your macro can go on to specify all the necessary settings.

WRITING WITH A CONSISTENT STYLE

Quattro Pro will execute your macros no matter how you make them look. You can write short lines of code that take up many rows, or very wide lines that take up just a few rows. You can use all uppercase or lowercase letters for macro commands, or mix the two.

But remember that someday you will come back to the macro in order to make changes. The changes might be needed to expand the scope of the macro, to fix a bug, or because the spreadsheet has been altered and the macro no longer works.

You should develop a consistent writing style for your macros and stick with it. The style you use is less important than the fact that you have a style at all. If you review the macros in this chapter, you will see examples of some rules of style:

- All macros are in one section of the spreadsheet.
- Where possible, each macro line is a related set of operations.
- Overly short or long lines are avoided.
- Macros are separated with a blank row.
- All macro commands are lowercase, such as {goto}, /p, and {right}.
- All references to cell addresses or block names are uppercase, such as A5, MY_DATA, and PRINT_TOTALS.

One difficulty with using lowercase letters for macro commands is that Quattro Pro records commands in uppercase. You may therefore want to reverse the style so that commands are uppercase, {RIGHT}, and block names and addresses are lowercase, such as some_block. The important thing is that you maintain a consistent style.

The importance of macros cannot be overstated. The more you integrate macros into your spreadsheets, the faster and farther you will go with Quattro Pro.

What you have seen of macros in this chapter is only the beginning. In the next chapter, you will learn about the macro command language, which allows you to write macro programs that automate your spreadsheets.

17

Advanced Macro Topics

Fast
Track

IN THIS CHAPTER, YOU WILL LEARN HOW TO ENHANCE keyboard macros with the macro command language and turn your spreadsheets into powerful programming tools. You will also learn about the process of testing and debugging macros, the Transcript utility, and how to create a macro library.

WRITING MACROS WITH THE COMMAND LANGUAGE

If you are still using the /x macros from Lotus 1-2-3 version 1A, you can continue to use them in Quattro Pro. But you should try to shift your macro writing to include the command language keywords, which generally execute faster and are more flexible.

The Quattro Pro macro command language consists of a set of macro keywords, or commands, and an orderly system of stringing them together into what are essentially programs. You use the command language in conjunction with your keyboard macros.

STRUCTURE OF THE COMMAND LANGUAGE

In the last chapter, you learned about the macro commands that represent keys on your keyboard, such as {right}, {left}, and {home}. The command language keywords are an extension of this set of commands, and in some ways, are similar to @ functions. For example, macro keywords must be spelled precisely (although it does not matter whether you use uppercase or lowercase) and follow syntax rules. Many of them require one or more parameters. Unlike @ functions, however, you cannot enclose one macro command within another.

For example, when you want your macro to alert the user, you can use the macro command {beep} to issue a short beep. Like all keywords, this one is enclosed in braces and there are no spaces before or after the command and the braces.

By default, this command issues the same beep that Quattro Pro issues when an error occurs. But you can specify a different tone by including a number, from 1 to 4, as a parameter in the command (using the command without a parameter produces the same beep as the number 1). There is always a space between the command and the first parameter. As with any Quattro Pro command or function, you can use a number, a formula that produces a number, or a reference to a cell that contains a number.

For example, if cell G5 contains the number 2 and is named THAT_CELL, all the following commands are equivalent and would issue the same tone:

{beep 2}

{beep 16/8}

{beep G5}

{beep THAT_CELL}

Some macro commands can take multiple parameters, each separated with a comma. For example, you specify four parameters for the keyword {message}, using the syntax

{message *cell, col, row, time*}

Here is how this macro would look if you wanted to display the message contained in the block named NOTE1 in a message window that starts at column 20 and row 10 for 10 seconds:

{message NOTE1,20,10,@NOW+@TIME(0,0,10)}

The only space in this command is between the keyword, message, and the first parameter, NOTE1. There are three parameters that are numeric, and one that must be a cell reference. Other commands may use text as one or more of their parameters.

Unlike keyboard macros, a command language keyword must be entered in one cell only. You cannot divide it among cells in the column. With this exception, all the rules that were discussed in the last chapter apply to your macros, whether or not they include command language keywords.

INVOKING ANOTHER MACRO

One of the advantages of the command language is its ability to invoke other macros. Your macro can do this by branching to the second macro or by calling it as a subroutine.

BRANCHING TO ANOTHER MACRO

You use the macro command {branch} within one macro to invoke and give control to another macro. It is equivalent to the GOTO command in the BASIC programming language.

This command takes just one parameter: the name of the macro that will be invoked. For example, {branch \PRINT_JOB} gives control to the macro in the cell named \PRINT_JOB. You can also branch to a cell address, but as explained in the previous chapter, it is never a good idea to do so.

RUNNING ANOTHER MACRO AS A SUBROUTINE

You can call another macro as a subroutine, and when that second macro is finished, control will return to the calling macro. To make the call, just place the name of the macro within braces, such as {\PRINT_JOB}. This is equivalent to the GOSUB command in BASIC.

The called subroutine will remain in control until it encounters either a blank cell or a {return} command. The {return} command is not required at the end of the subroutine, but it is a good idea to use this command to absolutely delimit the end of the macro.

Processing will continue in the first macro with the command that follows the call to the second macro. For example, this macro formats a block, calls a print macro, and then moves the cell selector:

> {Block,Format}f0~NEW_DATA~
>
> {\PRINT_JOB}
>
> {goto}SOME_DATA~

The print macro will be invoked, and when it is finished, control will return to this macro, which will continue with the {goto} command.

There are two major advantages to using subroutines in your macros:

- It is much less difficult to interpret or revise a relatively short primary macro that makes calls to subroutines.

Although you can use a cell address instead of a name, you not only risk all the disadvantages of using cell addresses in macros, but you will also make your macro incompatible with Lotus 1-2-3. That program requires that a subroutine call refer only to a block name.

- A subroutine macro can be shared by many primary macros, so you do not need to duplicate the same code in different macros.

In the example, the primary macro calls \PRINT_JOB, which may contain hundreds of lines or just a few. If you want to inspect that macro, you can view it in the spreadsheet; otherwise, that code is out of the way and not cluttering up the primary macro. Once the print macro has been written as a separate subroutine, it is a simple matter for another macro to refer to it.

One difference between branching and calling a subroutine is that you can pass parameters to the secondary macro when it is called as a subroutine. You simply include one or more parameters within the braces, as you would for any other macro command parameters.

For example, suppose you have four blocks in the spreadsheet named QTR1, QTR2, QTR3, and QTR4, and they all have the same layout. Instead of writing four separate print macros, you could write just one. When the primary macro invokes the print subroutine, it would pass it the name of the block that should be printed. The following, therefore, would print the block named QTR1.

    {\PRINT_JOB QTR1}

When you include parameters in a call to a subroutine, the first command in the first line of the subroutine must be a {define} command. This command specifies where the parameters are to be stored and whether they are to be considered as text or numeric data.

For example, the print macro that is called in the above example would need to define the parameter (QTR1), so that its first line might look like this:

    {define PRINT_CELL}

It places the parameter (the text QTR1) in the cell named PRINT_CELL. The macro would continue, and when it wanted to access the parameter, it would refer to the cell named PRINT_CELL. It could do so as many times as necessary.

The following short exercise will give you a hands-on example of using subroutines and parameters.

1. In a blank spreadsheet, move the cell selector to cell C1.

2. Use the Edit–Names–Create command to name that cell **TEMPVALUE**.

3. Move the cell selector to cell C3, and name that cell **\Z**.

4. Enter this macro into cell C3: **{MYBEEP 2} {quit}**.

5. Move the cell selector to cell C5, and name that cell **MYBEEP**.

6. Enter this macro into cell C5: **{define TEMPVALUE:value}**.

7. Below it, in cell C6, enter this macro: **{beep TEMPVALUE}**.

8. In cell C7, enter the macro command that returns control to the calling macro: **{return}**.

The \Z macro calls the macro named MYBEEP (in cell C5) as a subroutine and passes it the parameter 2. The first line in MYBEEP places the parameter it receives into TEMPVALUE (cell C1). The second line then issues the {beep} command and sets the tone of the beep according to the number it finds in TEMPVALUE.

Invoke the \Z macro and hear the results. The parameter, 2, will be treated as a value and placed in cell C1, TEMPVALUE. The screen should look like the one in Figure 17.1 (although each named cell has been labeled in column B). You can change the 2 in \Z to a 3 and invoke the macro again. The new parameter will be passed when the macro is run.

ADDING COMMENTS AND PLACE HOLDERS

You can include a comment anywhere within your macros by prefacing it with a semicolon and enclosing it within braces, as in

{;This is a comment and will not be executed}

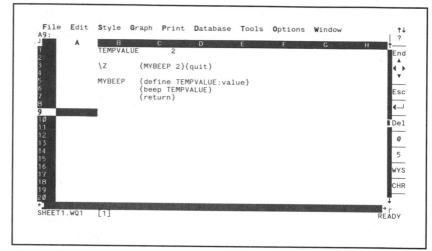

Figure 17.1: Passing a parameter to a subroutine

The braces indicate it is a macro command, and the semicolon signifies that it is just a comment that should not be executed.

A comment can serve many purposes:

- Explain the macro code that lies below it
- Serve as a title that divides one portion of a macro from another
- Cross reference the names of other macro routines to help you interpret the flow of the program
- Make clear your intentions for any future macro writers

You can also take advantage of comments when you are testing your macros. During the testing phase, you will not want to run certain routines, such as those that print or save your spreadsheet. You can exclude them from the macro simply by prefacing them with a semicolon, and if necessary, enclosing them in braces. For example, to skip over a macro command that would start a print job, just add a semicolon:

    {;/ Print;Go}

Lotus 1-2-3 does not have the comment macro, but it does handle the twin brace place holder, { }.

If you do not include any text within a comment, it can still serve as a place holder in your macros. Simply enter an opening and closing brace, { }. You can even leave off the semicolon when you have just the two braces. Just be sure not to include any characters within the braces if you don't preface them with a semicolon. When the macro executes, the braces will be ignored, and the macro will continue with the next step.

You can use a place holder to serve as a visual break between two sections of a macro or to reserve a line for future use. You can always insert a comment or place holder in a macro simply by inserting a new row for it. It is also easy to eliminate one—just delete the row.

CREATING YOUR OWN MACRO MENUS

One of the benefits of Quattro Pro is its easy-to-use menu system that accommodates both new and expert users. With the macro command language, you can create the same system of menus for your macro commands and reap the same benefits.

Most of your spreadsheets will have some sort of normal working routine, so that you follow the same steps each time you use them. In an ideal spreadsheet, all those steps would be included in a macro menu. You or other users could use the menu to make the choices necessary to complete the spreadsheet.

To create a macro menu, you must first structure the menu code in the spreadsheet, and then invoke that code with either the {menubranch} or {menucall} macro command.

THE STRUCTURE OF A MACRO MENU

Each choice in a macro menu always consists of three cells in a column:

- Top cell: The text that will appear on the menu as the selection item.

- Middle cell: The description, or help text, of the selection item.

- Bottom cell: The actual macro code that will be executed if that item is selected from the menu.

For example, the first choice in a macro menu might look like this (in three cells in a column):

Month_End

Run the update routine to compile monthly figures

{UPDATE}

The text of the menu can overhang its cell; it need not fit within the column width. When the menu is invoked, it will be displayed so that all the text is visible.

A macro menu can have as many as 256 choices, as many as there are columns in the spreadsheet. Enter each new choice in the next trio of cells in the column to the right.

In order to access the menu from a macro, you should give its first cell a descriptive block name (although a name is not required). You might name a menu of print choices \MENU_PRINT or give the name \MENU_VIEW to a menu that offers various spreadsheet blocks that you can view.

If you are going to run a Quattro Pro spreadsheet under Lotus 1-2-3, never use more than eight choices in a menu, which is the most that program can handle.

INVOKING A MENU

You cannot invoke a menu macro directly from the keyboard; it can only be called from another macro. You can use the {menubranch} command to call a macro menu and give control to it, just as the {branch} command gives control to another macro. You include the address or block name of the macro menu as a parameter, as in

{menubranch \MENU_SORT}

This macro would give control to the macro menu named \MENU_SORT.

You can also call a macro menu as a subroutine with the {menucall} command. This is equivalent to calling a macro as a subroutine by enclosing its name in braces. When the macro you select from the menu is finished, control will return to the first command after the {menucall} statement.

An example of a macro menu is shown in Figure 17.2. The menu starts with its first choice in cell C3, \Data_Entry. Two other choices are visible in columns D and E, and there are others that are off the screen. The macro named \M has been used to invoke the menu, which appears in the upper-left corner of the spreadsheet. You can see that there are actually six choices on the menu: Data_Entry, Print, Save, Consolidate, Import, and Exit.

Just as with a Quattro Pro menu, you can select an item from the active macro menu by either highlighting it and pressing ↵, clicking on it with your mouse, or by pressing its first letter, such as S for Save.

As you move the highlighter through the menu, the description line for the highlighted choice appears at the bottom of the screen, just as it does for Quattro Pro menus.

The third line of the macro menu code contains the beginning of the code that will be executed for the selection you make from the menu. You can place as many lines of macro code as you want below each choice, but there is really no need to do so.

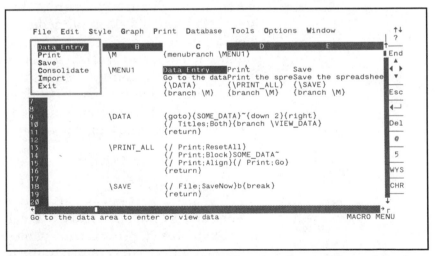

Figure 17.2: A macro menu, the subroutines it calls, and the activated menu

In order for the first-letter method to work correctly, you should ensure that each item begins with a different letter. If you simply cannot structure the menu that way, use numbers or letters to preface each choice, such as 1)Data_Entry, 2)Data_Combine, and so on.

In this example, each choice has just two lines of code below it. The first is a call to a macro subroutine, such as {\DATA} for the first choice. By calling another macro from the menu, you can place the main body of the code in another location where it will be easier to read and maintain.

You can see the macro named \DATA in cell C9. It occupies three cells of macro code and ends with the {return} command, which sends control back to the menu.

The second line of the macro code under each item on the menu contains {branch \M}, which sends control to the macro named \M in cell C1. As you can see, that macro simply calls the menu again.

In other words, when you select a choice from the menu, a subroutine macro is called. When that macro is finished, the menu will be called once again.

USING THE ESCAPE KEY IN A MENU

Menus that you create with macros follow the same convention as Quattro Pro menus: when you press Escape, the menu is canceled and control returns to the previous command or menu. In the Quattro Pro menus, this generally means you will step back through a chain of menus each time you press the Escape key, until you reach Ready mode. But when you press Escape within a macro menu, you can sometimes get unexpected results.

This is because control returns to the next command after the one that called the macro (it does not matter whether the {menubranch} or {menucall} command was used). Suppose you had invoked the following macro:

{menucall \MYMENU}

{goto}THEDATA~

The first command makes a call to the menu named \MYMENU. If you press Escape while that menu is active, control would immediately return to the {goto} command. This can be quite useful if you have structured your commands so that a press of the Escape key gives the user a convenient way to cancel a menu.

Figure 17.3 provides an example. This spreadsheet consists of the macro \M in cell C1, which invokes the menu \MENU1 in cell C4. There is just one choice on this sample menu, which calls a second menu in cell C9, \MENU2. That menu also lists a single choice, which calls a third menu, \MENU3, in cell C15.

This layering of menus is just like the multilayered menus of Quattro Pro. Now look at the macro code in \M, \MENU1, and \MENU2 that calls each of the menus. All of them are written so that if you press the Escape key, the previous menu is called.

Notice that the final command in \MENU1 and \MENU2 calls the \M macro. In this way, the final press of the Escape key will not return you to Ready mode, but will instead invoke \M, which in turn calls \MENU1. In other words, there is no way to return to Ready mode from this menu system.

Don't worry, you can press Ctrl-Break to cancel the macro, as usual. But providing a secure system such as this allows you to write macros that maintain control of the spreadsheet and offer the user the choices required for the normal completion of the spreadsheet.

Depending on the use of your menu-driven spreadsheet application, you can offer a menu item that lets the user return to Ready mode. The command might be called Ready, for example, and would use the single macro command {quit}.

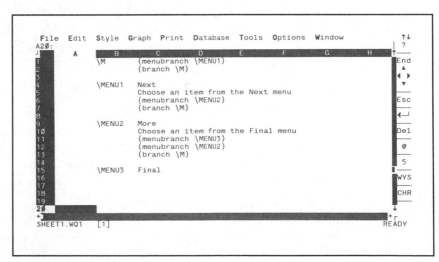

Figure 17.3: You can write your macro menus so that the Escape key always recalls the previous menu

USING THE COMMAND LANGUAGE KEYWORDS

The Quattro Pro macro command language has a variety of keywords. They are presented here in the same categories that are listed when you press the Macros key, Shift-F3.

Many of the macro commands take parameters, as described in the following list:

Remember that whether you are writing a simple keyboard macro or a complex macro program, your macros should refer only to block names, never to cell addresses.

condition	A logical expression that is evaluated as either true or false
col	A column number, usually of a block
item	A number, string, value, cell address, or block name
location	A cell address or block name
n	A numeric value or a cell address or block name that contains a numeric value
prompt	A text message or a cell address or block name that contains text
row	A row number, generally of a block
s	A string or a string value or a cell address or block name that contains a string or string value
t	The data type, either Value or String
time	A time of day, most often expressed as the current time plus a certain amount of time, such as @NOW+@TIME(0,0,10) to specify 10 seconds from now

CONTROLLING THE SCREEN

Some macro commands let you control the screen effects during macro execution. The {windowsoff} command freezes the display in the spreadsheet window, and the {paneloff} command

The {windowsof} and {paneloff} commands are essentially only for Lotus 1-2-3 compatibility; Quattro Pro normally disables the display to speed macro execution.

has the same effect on the menus, input, and status line portions of the screen. Macros execute so quickly that the screen
can become blurred while they are running. You can use one or
both of these commands to save the user from this distraction.

Because they freeze the screen, these commands can make it
very difficult to test your macros. Therefore, you should generally include them only when you are in the final stages of writing
the macro.

Table 17.1 summarizes the macro keywords for controlling
the screen.

INTERACTING WITH THE USER

You can use keywords to allow your macros to interact with
the person behind the keyboard. They can serve to prompt the

Table 17.1: Macro Keywords for Controlling the Screen

KEYWORD	FUNCTION
{beep *n*}	Computer beeps using tone *n* (1–4).
{indicate *s*}	Sets the mode indicator to the string *s*, to a maximum of five characters. You should enclose the text in quotation marks. Use this command without a parameter to return the mode indicator to its default status.
{paneloff}–{panelon}	Freezes the display of the menus, input line, and status line until the macro is finished or they are turned back on with the {panelon} command.
{windowsoff}–{windowson}	Freezes the display of the spreadsheet until the macro is finished or the screen is turned on again with the {windowson} command.

user to enter information, offer a menu, display a message, and insert a timed pause into a macro.

For example, the {?} command pauses macro execution until the user presses ↵. All features of Quattro Pro are accessible while the macro pauses. Caution is advised, however, because as soon as ↵ is pressed, the macro will continue, and there is no way to ensure that Quattro Pro is in a mode that will not conflict with the macro.

Note that if you want the user to select something, such as a file name for the File–Open command, you must insert a tilde after the pause, as in {?}~. When the user presses ↵, it will be intercepted by the macro as a signal to continue, but will not be accepted as a ↵ for selecting the file.

Table 17.2 lists the macro keywords for interacting with the user.

CONTROLLING THE PROGRAM FLOW

The macro commands that control program flow contain the basic elements of any programming language. They provide the

Table 17.2: Macro Keywords for Interacting with the User

KEYWORD	FUNCTION
{?}	Macro execution pauses until the user presses ↵. The only indication that the macro is still active (although waiting) is the Macro indicator on the status line.
{breakoff}–{breakon}	Disables the functioning of the Ctrl-Break key. Use extreme caution with this command—you can write a macro that is impossible to cancel.
{get *loc*}	Pauses and waits for any key to be pressed. The keystroke is stored as a character in *loc*. Keys such as ↓ and Home are stored as their macro equivalents, {down} and {home}.

Table 17.2: Macro Keywords for Interacting with the User (continued)

KEYWORD	FUNCTION
{getlabel *prompt, loc*}	Pauses and displays *prompt* in the input line. Waits for user to type a response and press ↵. The entry is stored as text in *loc*. *Prompt* can be up to 70 characters, and it should be enclosed in quotation marks. You can also use a string formula to refer to a cell address or block name that contains the message.
{getnumber *prompt, loc*}	Same as {getlabel}, but the user input is stored as a numeric value. If a nonnumeric entry is made, the result will be ERR in *loc*.
{graphchar *loc*}	When viewing a graph or a message via the {graph} or {message} macro, this command captures the keystroke that the user presses to return to the spreadsheet.
{look *loc*}	Checks for keyboard activity during macro execution by looking for keystrokes in the computer's keyboard buffer. If a key was pressed, the macro-equivalent character is entered in *loc*. The keyboard buffer is not cleared, and the macro takes no action on the keystroke.
{menubranch *loc*}	Gives control to the macro menu at *loc*. That menu must be structured as a menu or problems will result.
{menucall *loc*}	Same as {menubranch}, except that the menu is called as a subroutine. When the macros associated with the menu are finished, control will be returned to the first command after {menucall}.

Table 17.2: Macro Keywords for Interacting with the User (continued)

KEYWORD	FUNCTION
{message *loc, col, row, time*}	Displays the contents of *loc* as a message in a box, whose upper-left corner begins at screen position *col* and *row*. The message is displayed until *time*, so enter the time as a time value, such as @NOW+@TIME(0,0,5) to display the message for 5 seconds. A *time* of 0 seconds displays the message until the user presses a key. The width of the message box is determined by the width of *loc's* column.
{play *file-name*}	Plays the digitized sound file specified by *file-name*.
{stepoff}–{stepon}	Turns off or on the macro debugger's single-step mode. This has the same effect as the Tools–Macro–Debugger–No or Yes command. You can run the macro at normal speed, and it will go into single-step mode when it reaches the {stepon} command. It will proceed step by step until the macro finishes or a {stepoff} is encountered.
{wait *time*}	Pauses the macro until *time*. No keystrokes will be processed during the pause. Enter *time* as a value for a specific point in time, not as a number of minutes or seconds. To pause for 10 seconds, enter the command {wait @NOW+@TIME(0,0,10)}.

tools that turn your keyboard macros into full-fledged programs.

For example, the {branch} command passes control to another macro. The {for} command calls another macro for a specified number of iterations (looping). The {if} command branches to another macro only if a logical condition is met. The {onerror} command catches a system error without halting the macro.

Table 17.3 summarizes the macro keywords for controlling program flow.

MANIPULATING THE CONTENTS OF CELLS

Some macro commands let your macros manipulate spreadsheet cells. For example, you can use the {blank} command to erase cells and the {recalc} command to recalculate cells.

Table 17.4 lists the macro commands for manipulating the contents of cells.

Table 17.3: Macro Keywords for Controlling the Flow of Macro Programs

KEYWORD	FUNCTION
{branch *loc*}	Passes control to macro at *loc*.
{define *loc1:t,loc2:t...*}	Denotes locations for storing arguments passed when another macro calls it as a subroutine. The type *t* can be Value or String.
{dispatch *loc*}	Branches to the macro whose address or block name is entered into the cell at *loc*. It is similar to the @@ function in that it makes an indirect reference to the macro via the intermediate cell.
{for *counter,start,stop,step,loc*}	Invokes the subroutine at the cell *loc* and repeats it for each *step* between *start* and *stop*. The current count is stored in the cell *counter*. The macro {for VAR,1,10,1,\LOOP} executes the macro named \LOOP 10 times (the count runs from 1 to 10 and steps 1 for each loop). The number of each loop, starting with 1, is stored in the cell named VAR.
{forbreak}	Cancels the looping of the {for} macro and returns control to the next command after the {for} statement.

Table 17.3: Macro Keywords for Controlling the Flow of Macro Programs (continued)

KEYWORD	FUNCTION
{if *cond*}	Similar to the @IF function. The *cond* is a logical expression that the macro evaluates. If the expression is false, execution continues in the next cell below, skipping any other commands in the same cell as the {if} command. If the expression is true, macro execution continues in the same cell. If the true statement does not branch to another macro, the macro in the cell below (the false statement) will also be executed. For example, {if VAR>10}{branch \CONTINUE} checks a cell named VAR. If the contents of that cell are greater than 10, the macro will branch to \CONTINUE.
{onerror *macro-loc,[message-loc]*}	Traps a system error (which would normally halt macro execution) and branches to the macro in *macro-loc.* You can place the generated error message into *message-loc.* For example, above a macro that brings in another file, you could insert the command {onerror \CATCH_ERR,SHOW_ERR}. If an error occurs, macro execution will branch to \CATCH_ERR. The error message that is generated, such as "File not found," will be placed in SHOW_ERR.
{quit}	Stops macro execution and returns to Ready mode.

Table 17.3: Macro Keywords for Controlling the Flow of Macro Programs (continued)

KEYWORD	FUNCTION
{restart}	Clears all subroutine layers (subroutines can call other subroutines to as many as 32 layers deep) and resets the hierarchy to its default status. Use it to break out of a subroutine or {for} statement and cancel the tie to the calling macro. Execution continues immediately after the {restart} statement.
{return}	In a subroutine, returns control to the calling macro. Although it is not required (control is returned when the subroutine is finished), including {return} provides a visual end to the macro subroutine and ensures that the macro will not inadvertently run into another.

READING AND WRITING TEXT FILES

You will probably use the text file manipulation commands rarely, because most of your work will deal directly with the spreadsheet. These commands are quite similar to the file commands found in BASIC and other programming languages.

You can manipulate just one text file at a time, and you specify that file with the {open} command. Once a file is open, all the other file commands will act only on that file. To work on a second file, you must use the {close} command to close the file that is currently open, and then open the other one.

Table 17.5 lists the macro keywords for working with text files.

Table 17.4: Macro Keywords for Manipulating Cells

KEYWORD	FUNCTION
{blank *loc*}	Erases the block *loc.* The {blank} command can be accessed from any mode (unlike the Edit–Erase command), such as while editing a cell or selecting items from the Quattro Pro menus.
{contents *target,source,[w],[f]*}	Places the contents of *source* cell in *target* cell, but always as a string. You can optionally specify a width, *w,* and a format style, *f,* to make the resulting string look like the source number with a numeric format. For example, {contents OTHERCELL,FIRSTCELL,9,120} places the contents of FIRSTCELL in OTHERCELL as text, using a cell width of 9 and a format number of 120. See the Quattro Pro *@ Functions and Macros* reference manual for the numbers of the numeric format styles.
{let *loc,item[:t]*}	Places *item* in *loc.* You can optionally specify the type *t* as either String or Value. If *item* is a cell address or name, the {let} command places only the contents of that cell in the cell at *loc,* unlike the Edit–Copy command, which copies all cell attributes to the destination.
{put *loc,col,row,item:t*}	Places *item* in the cell at the column and row offset in the block named in *loc,* as optional type *t.* For example, {put A1..D10,2,3,16+5} places the value 21 (the result of the formula) in cell C4. The column and row numbers are counted as offsets from the first column in the block named in *loc.* In the example, column C has an offset of 2 from the first column in the block (A), and row 4 has an offset of 3 from the first row in the block (1).

Table 17.4: Macro Keywords for Manipulating Cells (continued)

KEYWORD	FUNCTION
{recalc *loc,[cond],[n]*}	Recalculates the cells in *loc* row by row. If the two optional arguments are not included, just one recalculation will occur. With the options, it repeats the recalculation up to *n* times or as long as *cond* is true. Use {recalc} to update the formulas in a block without having to recalculate the entire spreadsheet.
{recalccol *loc,[cond],[n]*}	Same as the {recalc} command, except that recalculation occurs column by column instead of row by row.

Table 17.5: Macro Keywords for Working with Text Files

KEYWORD	FUNCTION
{close}	Closes the currently opened text file.
{filesize *loc*}	Enters the file size (in bytes) in the cell at *loc*.
{getpos *loc*}	Enters the current file pointer position (in bytes) in the cell at *loc*.
{open *file-name,access-mode*}	Opens the text file *file-name* for future manipulation by the other file macro commands. The *access-mode* can be Write, Read, Modify, or Append (not available in Lotus 1-2-3), which can be abbreviated to W, R, M, or A. If the command fails (if you misspelled the file name, for example), macro execution continues in the same cell. Otherwise, execution continues in the next cell below.

Table 17.5: Macro Keywords for Working with Text Files (continued)

KEYWORD	FUNCTION
{read *n,loc*}	Reads *n* number of bytes from the currently open file and places the text in the cell at *loc*. The bytes that are read are those that begin at the current pointer location in the file (as indicated by the {getpos} command).
{readln *loc*}	Same as {read}, except that you do not specify a number of bytes. Instead, all the bytes from the file pointer's position in the file to the end of the current line are read and placed in the cell at *loc*.
{setpos *n*}	Positions the file pointer on byte number *n*, where byte 0 is the first byte in the file.
{write *s1,s2...*}	Writes the string *s1* into the currently opened file at the file pointer's position in that file. To write more than one string, separate each from the next with a comma, up to a maximum of 254 characters.
{writeln *s1,s2...*}	Same as {write}, except that the characters for a carriage return and line feed are entered after the text.

DEBUGGING YOUR MACROS

Getting a macro to work perfectly can often be a frustrating job. A single out of place keystroke can cause the macro to fail miserably, as can a misreference to a cell or block. Fortunately, Quattro Pro has the macro debugger, an excellent tool that can help you work the bugs out of your macros.

The debugger lets you execute your macros one step at a time while you view the macro code, instead of the usual flash-and-it's-done performance. You can also set breakpoints within your macros to halt execution at those specified points. You can view any cells in the spreadsheet and see how their contents change as the macro executes.

RUNNING A MACRO IN STEP MODE

When you are ready to test a macro, use the command Tools–Macro–Debugger–Yes (Alt-F2 DY) to invoke the debugger. Until you run a macro, the only change you will notice in the spreadsheet is the Debug indicator on the status line.

When the spreadsheet is in Debug mode, as soon as you invoke a macro (by pressing Alt-P for a print macro, for example), the Debug window opens in the lower portion of the screen, and macro execution goes into single-step mode. Figure 17.4 shows a macro as it executes in single-step mode.

The upper pane of the Debug window is where you see the macro code that is being executed. The lower pane is where you can watch trace cells as the macro executes.

Figure 17.4: The macro debugger as a macro executes in single-step mode

In Debug mode, the macro executes each step when you press the spacebar. This gives you complete control over the speed of execution. You can also press ↵ to let the macro finish at normal speeds, although the spreadsheet will still be in Debug mode.

As you can see in Figure 17.4, the upper pane of the Debug window shows three lines of macro code. The macro code currently being executed is on the second line, with the previous macro code shown above and the next macro code to execute shown below. Each line has its source file name and cell address to the left, so you can pinpoint the sequence of events. As you press the spacebar, each command or keystroke in the macro on the second line is executed, and it is also highlighted in the code to show you just where you are in the macro.

Because the Debug window simply overlays the spreadsheet, action continues as usual in the spreadsheet as the macro executes. You can temporarily hide the Debug window by pressing Escape.

Being able to see the macro as it executes step by step is in itself a great advantage, but the debugger offers other useful features. The Debug menu, available while you are executing a macro in Debug mode, lists the commands Breakpoints, Conditional, Trace Cells, Abort, Edit a Cell, Reset, and Quit.

The Abort command stops the macro as though you had pressed Ctrl-Break to cancel it. The Edit a Cell command lets you change a cell in the middle of macro execution. The macro is temporarily stopped, and you are prompted to specify the cell you wish to edit. When you are finished editing that cell, choose Quit from the Debug menu, and the macro will continue. In this way, you can revise your macro as it is executing.

SETTING BREAKPOINTS

A *breakpoint* is a special code in a program that causes the macro to break (pause or stop), allowing you to view the code and its results up to that point. The debugger allows you to set four regular and four conditional breakpoints in your macros.

After you set either type of breakpoint in a macro, you can invoke the macro in Debug mode, and then press ↵ to let it execute at full speed. When the macro breakpoint is reached, it will stop and go into single-step mode. You can now press the spacebar to step through the macro or press ↵ to continue at full speed. In this way, you can speed by the code that you know is correct and quickly reach a line where you would like to inspect the current state of the spreadsheet or code.

SETTING REGULAR BREAKPOINTS

As an example, suppose you wanted a breakpoint in the macro shown in Figure 17.4 (which builds a small table), at the line containing the {/ Block;Copy} command, cell C3. You would follow these steps to set the breakpoint:

1. Invoke the Tools–Macro–Debugger–Yes command to put the spreadsheet in Debug mode.

2. Invoke the macro (Alt-Z in the figure). The Debug window will appear.

3. Press the slash key to display the Debug menu.

4. Choose the Breakpoints command and specify which of the four available breakpoints you wish to define. You are then offered a menu with two choices, Block and Pass Count.

5. Choose Block and specify C3 as the cell at which the macro should pause and continue in single-step mode. If you specify more than one cell, the first cell in the block will be the breakpoint.

6. Choose Quit three times to return to the Debug window and continue with your macro.

7. Press ↵ to let the macro execute at full speed.

Breakpoints are not shown in your code; they are stored internally.

The code will execute in an instant, until it hits cell C3, the breakpoint. It will then pause and go into single-step mode, allowing you to view the spreadsheet (press Escape to view the entire screen) or the macro code.

If the macro you are debugging is a looping macro, such as one that uses the {for} command, you may want to specify a number for the Pass Count command for the breakpoint. If you enter 5 as the pass count, for example, the breakpoint will not stop the macro until the macro has executed that code five times.

SETTING CONDITIONAL BREAKPOINTS

A conditional breakpoint will only stop macro execution when a specified condition is true. Instead of specifying a line in the macro code as the breakpoint cell, you use any cell in the spreadsheet that contains a logical formula.

For example, you could specify a cell that contained the formula +D21>1400 as the conditional breakpoint. When you then execute the macro at full speed in Debug mode, Quattro Pro will watch that cell. When its result is true (cell D21 contains a value greater than 1400), the macro will pause and go into single-step mode, no matter which line of code was being executed.

CLEARING BREAKPOINTS

You can change the definition of any breakpoint simply by specifying a new cell. But when you have been debugging one macro and want to move on to another, you will probably want to reset all the regular and conditional breakpoints.

From within the debugger, you can use the Reset command to clear all breakpoints. From within the spreadsheet, you can use the Tools–Macro–Clear Breakpoints command.

SETTING TRACE CELLS

An executing macro takes control of the spreadsheet. You may find that the macro has taken the cell selector off to some corner of the spreadsheet to do its work, while you must sit by and wonder just how these changes are affecting other cells in the spreadsheet.

This is such a common situation that the debugger has a tool to handle it. The Trace Cells command on the Debug menu lets you specify up to four *trace cells*, which are cells you wish to trace during macro execution.

Each cell you specify will appear in the lower portion of the Debug window, with its spreadsheet file name and cell address to its left. As the macro executes, the results in the trace cells will be updated in the window, so you know just how your macro is affecting those cells. The Debug menu's Reset command or the spreadsheet command Tools–Macro–Clear Breakpoints will clear all trace cells as well as breakpoints.

FINDING YOUR WAY WITH TRANSCRIPT

The Transcript utility is essentially a macro-recording tool that is constantly recording your keystrokes in Quattro Pro. It is quite unobtrusive, and you may not have even noticed that it was active. It saves all your keystrokes to a file named QUATTRO-.LOG in the Quattro Pro subdirectory. You can view the contents of that file by issuing the Tools–Macro–Transcript command (Alt-F2 T).

Transcript serves both as a macro recorder and a file-recovery utility. Because it captures all your keystrokes, it provides a history of all your actions in Quattro Pro. With that history and the commands on the Transcript menu, you can rebuild a damaged spreadsheet from any point in the recorded history. Because it records your keystrokes as macros, it is a convenient way to record macros without using the Tools–Macro–Record command.

When you invoke the Tools–Macro–Transcript command, the Transcript window appears, as shown in Figure 17.5. As you can see, each line in the window looks just like a recorded macro. By default, your keystrokes are recorded in the logical style, as set by the Tools–Macro–Macro Recording command.

You can move the highlighter up and down the rows to scroll through the window. The key to this code is the *check point*, or

Transcript does not keep an infinitely long QUATTRO.LOG file! It saves only a specified number of keystrokes and then starts a new log file. It still provides more than enough protection, but don't get too relaxed with your file-saving habits.

the point at which you started fresh by using either the File–Retrieve, File–Save, or File–Erase command. A vertical line joins all the rows from the check point to your most recent keystrokes. Those rows represent all the work you have done on the spreadsheet in this session.

FIXING BROKEN SPREADSHEETS

Since Transcript creates one long macro of all your actions in Quattro Pro, you can use it to rebuild the spreadsheet from the point at which you started with it—the last check point. If you accidentally erase a block, for example, you can use Transcript to rebuild your spreadsheet to the point just before you made the mistake.

Transcript will replay all the keystrokes you entered between the time you started and the point where you erased the block. The starting point is the File–Erase command if you started from a blank spreadsheet, or the File–Retrieve command if you loaded an existing spreadsheet.

You can use the Transcript command Undo Last Command just as you would use the Undo (Alt-F5) command. It simply

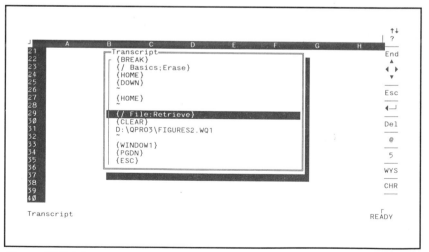

Figure 17.5: The Transcript window showing your keystroke history

replays all your keystrokes from the last check point up to, but not including, your most recent keystroke (the one you want to undo). This can be a real life saver if you have forgotten to enable the Undo command (with the Options–Other–Undo–Enable command).

You can also rebuild your spreadsheet to any point you specify in the Transcript history. Highlight that line in the Transcript window and choose the Restore to Here command. The spreadsheet will be rebuilt up to that point.

If you are not happy with the version of your spreadsheet that you last saved to disk, you can't use the Restore to Here command to fix that. You must instead use the Playback Block command, as described shortly.

CREATING MACROS FROM YOUR KEYSTROKE HISTORY

There is really no difference between the code that Transcript creates and that created by the macro recorder. The macro recorder simply makes it a step or two easier to access the recorded code.

You can access the code in Transcript either by playing it back immediately or by copying it to the spreadsheet, where you can later use it as a macro.

PLAYING BACK YOUR RECORDED KEYSTROKES

Before executing a block of code in Transcript, be sure the cell selector is on an appropriate cell in the spreadsheet. Otherwise, the keystrokes that are played back may end up in the wrong place at the wrong time.

Transcript's Playback Block command allows you to execute a block of code in the Transcript window. It is equivalent to the Tools–Macro–Execute command, which lets you run spreadsheet macros.

In order to play back a block of code, you must first mark that block. In the Transcript window, move the highlighter to the first row you want to execute, press the slash key to display the Transcript menu, and choose Begin Block. The current row will be flagged with a pointer at its left. Move the highlighter to the last row you want to execute and select End Block from the

Transcript menu. All the rows between the beginning and end will be flagged.

Now you can invoke the Playback Block command, and all those keystrokes will be executed as though they were a macro. And just as with a macro, you can press Ctrl-Break to cancel the routine.

You can also choose the Transcript command Single Step, which is quite similar to the macro debugger's single-step mode. By default, this command is set to No, so that Transcript code is played back at full speed. If you choose Yes, the code is executed a step at a time as you press the spacebar. Another Transcript command is Timed, which inserts a short pause after each keystroke is played before executing the next one.

USING YOUR RECORDED
KEYSTROKES IN THE SPREADSHEET

Just as with the macro recorder, you can copy the Transcript history to the spreadsheet, where it can be named and used as a spreadsheet macro. Use the Begin Block and End Block commands to mark the block you wish to bring into the spreadsheet. Select the Copy Block command and specify the name of the block where you want the macro copied. Then specify its location, and the recorded macro will be copied into the spreadsheet.

ADJUSTING THE RECORDING PROCESS

By default, Transcript saves no more than 2000 keystrokes to the QUATTRO.LOG file. When that limit is reached, the file is renamed QUATTRO.BAK, and a new log file is started. You always have at least two log files available, containing up to 4000 keystrokes.

You can use Transcript's Max History Length command to change the number of keystrokes retained in the log file. You can set this number anywhere between 0 and 25000. If you find that Transcript is slowing down your computer when it saves your keystrokes to disk, you can turn Transcript off by setting this command to zero. If you do, remember to save your spreadsheets on a regular and relatively frequent basis.

Transcript does not write each keystroke to disk, but instead saves it in a buffer area in memory. By default, Transcript keeps no more than 100 keystrokes in the buffer. When the buffer fills, the keystrokes are written to the QUATTRO.LOG file, so that every 100 keystrokes, Transcript will write to disk. If you should lose your spreadsheet due to some disaster, you can rebuild it with Transcript and never lose more than 100 keystrokes.

You can use the Failure Protection command to change this number from 1 to 25000. Using a value of 1 would have Transcript constantly writing to disk. This would degrade your computer's performance and be an annoyance, but you would be guaranteed that every keystroke was safely stored on disk. You could make the number larger, so that Transcript will write to disk less frequently, although there will be fewer recent keystrokes on disk if you later need to rebuild your spreadsheet.

MANAGING YOUR MACRO LIBRARIES

Because macros are simply text in a spreadsheet that you execute as a macro, they are quite portable and can be used in any spreadsheet. As you integrate more and more macros into your daily spreadsheet work, you will begin to see some of the disadvantages inherent in this system:

- Macro code takes up space in the spreadsheet, and therefore in your computer's limited amount of RAM and disk space.

- Macros are vulnerable to damage in many ways, such as by deletion, by insertion of a row that splits two macro lines, or by deletion of a block name.

- If you have several spreadsheets that all use the same macro routines, that code will be duplicated among them. Duplication takes up even more RAM and disk space.

- Changing a macro in one of the spreadsheets requires that you change it in all of them.

Quattro Pro's multispreadsheet environment makes the problem of duplication even more evident, because you will frequently work with several spreadsheets that are all similar in structure and use identical macros.

CREATING A MACRO LIBRARY

To circumvent these drawbacks and accommodate multiple spreadsheet use, Quattro Pro has a simple solution. You can designate any spreadsheet as a *macro library*, so that macros in it can be accessed by any other active spreadsheet.

To make the current spreadsheet a macro library, simply invoke the Tools–Macro–Library–Yes command, and the job is done. You won't see any difference in the spreadsheet. In fact, the only way you can tell that a spreadsheet has been designated as a library is by looking on the Tools–Macro menu and seeing if the Library choice has a Yes or No to its right.

If you have two or more spreadsheets active, and one of them is a macro library, you can invoke macros either in the current spreadsheet or in the library. If the macro name you invoke is not in the current spreadsheet, Quattro Pro will then search the library for the named macro and execute it.

If you have more than one library open, each will be searched until the named macro is found. For that reason, you should avoid duplication of macro block names among active macro libraries.

Although any spreadsheet can be named as a macro library, you will most likely keep only macros in it. You can then easily maintain your macros, which will ensure their well-being and longevity.

WORKING WITH MULTIPLE SPREADSHEETS AND LIBRARIES

When a macro is executed from a library, it can affect the spreadsheet either directly, by moving the cell selector for example, or indirectly, such as by using the {let} command to make a cell entry.

LIBRARY MACROS THAT PRODUCE DIRECT EFFECTS

Direct manipulation by a macro can be straightforward, whether a macro is in a library or not. For example, the macro

{home}Jan~{right}Feb~{right}Mar~

moves the cell selector to cell A1 and enters three labels in the block A1..C1. If this macro were executed from a library, it would affect the active spreadsheet—the one in which the cell selector resides. You could switch to any open spreadsheet and execute the macro there, and the text would be entered into the first row of that spreadsheet.

On the other hand, a macro that refers to a block name (as it should), such as

{goto}SOMECELL~Jan~

{right}Feb~

{right}Mar~

would move the cell selector to the specific named block. However, if that block name does not exist in the current spreadsheet, the macro would fail.

LIBRARY MACROS THAT PRODUCE INDIRECT EFFECTS

Macro command keywords generally affect the spreadsheet without moving the cell selector, and in that sense, they affect the spreadsheet indirectly. This is one of their advantages; filling a cell with the {let} command, for example, is faster than moving the cell selector to that cell, typing the entry, and then pressing ⏎. The cell selector need not be moved, so that many operations can take place without changing the screen.

Here is an indirect macro that produces the same effect as the one shown earlier:

Yes, this indirect macro goes against the rules and refers to cell addresses, but consider it a test macro.

{let A1,"Jan"}

{let B1,"Feb"}

{let C1,"Mar"}

Because this macro takes an indirect action on the cells A1..C1, the results will not be the same as in the previous macro, which used the {goto} command. No matter which spreadsheet is active when you invoke this macro, it is the macro library spreadsheet that will be affected.

Therefore, command language keywords will always affect the spreadsheet in which they reside. Unfortunately, that is probably just what you do not want to happen, and it would tend to defeat the flexibility and portability of a macro library. But once again there is a simple solution to the problem:

- When you want a macro command to affect the active spreadsheet, include a linking syntax in the command's cell reference.

The trick is that you do not have to specify a particular spreadsheet by name, which in itself would defeat the use of a macro library. Instead, you can use a special file reference in the form of two brackets with no file name: []. The macro will interpret this as meaning "act on the specified cell in whichever spreadsheet is active."

You could rewrite the indirect macro example so that it will affect only the active spreadsheet:

{let []A1,"Jan"}

{let []B1,"Feb"}

{let []C1,"Mar"}

You can include the paired brackets in any macro, even if it is not part of a library, and they will not interfere with the workings of the macro. In fact, the only time you would not want to use the linking symbols is when a macro in a library specifically needs to affect its own spreadsheet.

This would be the case in the following macro, which sets cell A1 in the active spreadsheet to the value in a variable cell, B44, in the library spreadsheet:

{let []A1,B44}

The reference to A1 includes the brackets, so that only the cell in the active spreadsheet is affected. But the reference to B44 does not include the brackets, so that only B44 in the library spreadsheet will be used.

Of course, in the real world, you would use block names, so that the macro might ultimately look like this:

{let []SOMECELL,VAR1}

The rule for using the brackets applies to all command language keywords. If the macro command

{put []SOMEBLOCK,0,0,MYCELL}

were in a library, it would place the contents of MYCELL, which would be referenced in the library spreadsheet, into the first cell of the block named SOMEBLOCK in the active spreadsheet.

The menu command

{menubranch []\MENU3}

would branch to a menu in the active spreadsheet. If the macros in that menu made other branches, those branches would be to macros in that spreadsheet, not the originating macro library.

On the other hand, a library macro that makes a subroutine call to a macro in the active spreadsheet will have control returned to it when the subroutine has finished. For example, the macro

{[]\MY_MACRO}{branch \NEXT_MACRO}

calls the subroutine named \MY_MACRO in the active spreadsheet. When that macro has finished, control will return to the library spreadsheet, and execution will continue with the branch to \NEXT_MACRO.

You can see why you should exercise a little caution and do plenty of testing when you create a macro library that includes macro command keywords.

With a little practice, you will find that macros complement just about any spreadsheet you create, whether it is a simple keyboard macro that automates a print routine or a huge macro library that automates a complete accounting system.

This chapter completes the discussion of Quattro Pro's spreadsheet tools. In the final chapter, you will learn about the many configuration options you have for tailoring Quattro Pro to your own needs and taste.

Configuring
Quattro Pro

Fast
Track

THIS CHAPTER EXPLAINS HOW TO USE THE COMMANDS on the Options menu to tailor Quattro Pro to your needs. That menu is divided into two groups: system and global. You adjust the system commands to change the program-wide defaults for Quattro Pro, and you change the global commands to change the defaults for any spreadsheet. The global settings have been discussed in detail in previous chapters.

Following is a list of the global commands that appear on the Options menu, with the chapter in which each was discussed:

Formats–Numeric Format	Chapter 6
Formats–Align Labels	Chapter 3
Formats–Hide Zeros	Chapter 6
Formats–Global Width	Chapter 6
Recalculation	Chapter 4
Protection	Chapter 3

The only system command that will not be covered here is the Options–Graphics Quality command. It was discussed extensively in both Chapters 6 and 7.

APPLYING SYSTEM AND GLOBAL SETTINGS

You can save the current settings for the system commands by using the Options–Update command. This makes them the settings for future sessions of Quattro Pro.

The current global settings, however, are saved only with the spreadsheet that was active when the changes were made (assuming you save the spreadsheet to disk). No other spreadsheets are affected by the changes. When you later retrieve that spreadsheet, those global settings will once again be in effect for it and it alone.

As discussed in Chapter 6, you can use the global command Options–Formats–Numeric Format to specify the format that will be used for all cells in the current spreadsheet. You might change it from the default, which is General, to Fixed with two decimal places.

However, you can use the local command Style–Numeric Format to apply a format, such as Currency with zero decimal places, to a block of cells. The Currency format would override the Fixed format that was specified in the global command. When you save the spreadsheet, both the global format style for the entire spreadsheet (Fixed) and the local format for the block of cells (Currency) will be saved as well.

By default, a number in a cell that has the Currency format will be displayed with a preceding dollar sign, such as $45. You can use the system command Options–International–Currency to change the dollar sign to another character. You might choose the British pound sign (£45), for example. This change will affect the Currency format in all active spreadsheets. If you retrieve a spreadsheet from disk, any cells with the Currency format will be displayed with the pound sign instead of the dollar sign.

The changes you make with the local and global commands are saved with the spreadsheet that contains them. The system command settings, however, are retained only for the current Quattro Pro session, unless you save the current system settings with the Options–Update command.

> To enter an upper ASCII character, such as the British pound sign, hold down the Alt key and type the decimal equivalent using the numeric keypad. Type 156 for the pound sign.

SAVING SYSTEM DEFAULTS

> The Print–Layout–Values command displays a list of current print settings.

The system defaults are stored in the Quattro Pro program files QUATTRO.MU and RSC.RF. Each time you load Quattro Pro, it configures itself based on the information stored in those files.

It has been noted more than once in this book that because the Update command saves all system settings, you should invoke it only when you know exactly which settings you have changed since loading the program. Before you issue the Update command, you can invoke the Options–Values command to see a list of most of the system options and their current settings. However, the list is not complete. For example, it does not show the settings for the Options–Display Mode or Options–International–LICS Conversion commands.

Therefore, the best way to save your system settings is to load Quattro Pro, make the adjustments, and then issue the Options–Update command. This is a wise course of action, even if it means that you will first have to save your spreadsheet, exit to DOS, and then reload Quattro Pro.

To provide yourself with a little insurance, you should make backup copies of the two original program configuration files before you save any new defaults. Simply copy them under new names within the Quattro Pro subdirectory. For example, you could use the Edit–Duplicate command in the File Manager or the COPY command from the DOS prompt and change their names to QUATTRO.MU1 and RSC.RF1.

If you save your Quattro Pro system defaults and then realize that you inadvertently saved many that you did not want, you can copy your backup files back to their original names. Again, use the Edit–Duplicate command in the File Manager or the COPY command from the DOS prompt.

SPECIFYING YOUR HARDWARE

A math coprocessor is a secondary computer processor that handles only mathematical calculations. Because it is specialized, it calculates many times faster than the main processor in your computer. Math chips are not inexpensive, but they may be worthwhile for those who do intensive math or vector graphics work on their computers.

Quattro Pro can usually detect the hardware environment in which it exists. In most cases, it knows how much conventional and expanded memory your computer has, whether there is a math coprocessor installed, the type of video adapter it is using, and whether a mouse is being used. However, there are some devices, such as your printer, that cannot be detected. Quattro Pro therefore must be told the brand and model of printer you are using.

The Options–Hardware menu offers three commands, Screen, Printers, and Mouse Button, which you will access only occasionally because those devices do not change once you have installed and defined them for Quattro Pro. It also has three displays that tell you how much memory is available in your computer and whether or not it has a math coprocessor.

WATCHING THE MEMORY DISPLAYS

You will frequently refer to the two memory displays on the Hardware menu: Normal Memory and EMS. Normal Memory refers to the 640K (maximum) of conventional memory that all DOS computers have. It is the memory in which all standard DOS programs are run. Invoke the Options–Hardware command, and you will see the amount currently available in your system, the total amount available for spreadsheets, and the percent of the total that is still available. If your computer has the usual 640K of normal RAM, you will probably have about 350K left for spreadsheets after you load Quattro Pro.

The EMS display shows how much expanded (EMS) memory your system currently has available, the total amount available for spreadsheets, and the percent that is still available. This type of memory goes beyond the normal 640K that can be accessed by DOS. Quattro Pro can use EMS memory for storing your active spreadsheets, but it cannot run its own program code there.

SETTING THE SCREEN PARAMETERS

The Options–Hardware–Screen command offers several selections for adjusting the Quattro Pro display. On a standard computer, you may never have to access this menu because Quattro Pro can detect the type of display adapter. But there will be occasions when it will be necessary to make manual adjustments. For example, your portable computer may be using a standard video adapter, such as CGA or EGA, with a nonstandard display. Quattro Pro will detect the adapter but not the display itself.

The Screen Type command offers a menu of the available video drivers with which Quattro Pro can work. The first item on the list is Autodetect Driver, which is the one you will use unless you are having a problem with Quattro Pro and your monitor.

For example, you might have a video card that is supposed to be Hercules compatible, but that Quattro Pro detects as a plain

Later in this chapter, expanded and conventional memory are discussed in relation to the Options–Other–Expanded Memory command. That command lets you allocate different types of spreadsheet data to expanded memory so that you can fine tune Quattro Pro and balance its capacity against its speed of operation.

monochrome card (nongraphics). It will therefore not allow you to display graphs on your screen. In that case, you could select Hercules from the Screen Type menu to tell Quattro Pro that your video card acts like a Hercules card. If that takes care of the problem, you will want to save this new setting for all future sessions of Quattro Pro.

Some video cards offer more than one resolution setting, and you can use the Options–Hardware–Screen–Resolution command to adjust your display. You will usually not need to adjust this because Quattro Pro picks the best resolution for the job.

The Options–Hardware–Screen–Aspect Ratio command lets you adjust the screen aspect ratio (the scale of its width to its height) that Quattro Pro uses when it works in graphics mode. You may need to use this command if you have a portable computer that has a screen that is proportionally wider than normal, and your pie graphs look more like football graphs.

Invoke the Aspect Ratio command, and the screen will be put into graphics mode with a circle in the center. If Quattro Pro is working well with your video system, the circle will be round. If it is not round, use the ↑ or ↓ key to adjust the circle's aspect ratio. When it looks round, press ↵ to return to the spreadsheet. Then use the Update command to save this change as the system default.

The last command on the Screen menu is CGA Snow Suppression, which by default is set to Off. Try changing this to On if you have a CGA video adapter and the screen flickers noticeably when you scroll in Quattro Pro.

DEFINING YOUR PRINTERS

When you installed Quattro Pro, you answered questions about your computer's printer, and that information was used to set the options on the Printers menu. If you change printers or need to refine your selections, choose the Options–Hardware–Printers command to adjust the printer options.

To select a new printer or change the settings for your current printer, choose either the 1st Printer or 2nd Printer command.

As mentioned in Chapter 13, in order to include transition effects in graph buttons, first use the Options–Hardware–Screen–Resolution command to switch from VGA to EGA mode.

Don't confuse the two printers listed on the Printers menu with the text and graphics printers that you can access on the Print menu. The Print command always sends your output to the same physical printer—it just uses one of two different modes, text or graphics.

Both options offer a menu with the following choices:

- Type of Printer: Choose the printer's brand and model. You can also select the graphics resolution, but keep in mind that the higher the resolution (more dots per inch, dpi), the slower the printing process will be.

- Device: The port to which the printer is connected. This is generally either Parallel-1 (your parallel printer port) or Serial-1 (your first serial port).

- Baud Rate, Parity, and Stop Bits: If you are using a serial printer, you can specify the serial communications parameters of baud rate, parity, and stop bits. Usually, you will not have to adjust these, but if you are having printing problems, refer to your printer manual to see what these settings should be. Then adjust them accordingly in Quattro Pro.

Once you have defined a printer, choose Quit from the menu to return to the Printers menu. If you have two printers selected, you can use the Default command to select one of them as the default printer. You may change the default printer frequently if you use each of the two printers for different types of printouts. For example, if your second printer is a color printer, you might make it the default when you print graphs.

The other choices on the Printers menu allow you to fine tune your selections:

- Plotter Speed: If you are using a plotter, this command specifies the speed at which Quattro Pro will print. By default this is set to 0, meaning that no adjustments will be made, and the plotter will run at its preset speed. Change this setting from 1 (slow) to 9 (fast) to allow for printing to different types of media or with different types of pens.

- Fonts: Specify the type of font cartridge in your laser printer and whether or not Bitstream fonts should be scaled in your graphs (see below).

- Auto LF: By default this is set to No. Change it to Yes only if you are having problems printing. Refer to your printer manual.

- Single Sheet: If your printer does not use continuous feed paper, change this setting to Yes. When printing, Quattro Pro will prompt you to insert a new piece of paper after every form feed.

The Fonts option on the Printers menu offers the two choices LaserJet Fonts and Autoscale Fonts. Laser printers can use font cartridges, which provide several different fonts from which to choose. To tell Quattro Pro which cartridge your printer is using, follow these steps:

1. Choose the Options–Hardware–Printers–Fonts– LaserJet Fonts command.

2. Choose either Left or Right to specify which cartridge you will be defining for your laser printer.

3. Select the cartridge from the list that is offered. You will be returned to the Printers menu.

Another setting on the LaserJet Fonts menu is Shading Level. You can adjust this setting to specify the darkness of gray shading in LaserJet printouts, such as shading applied with the Style– Shading–Grey command. By default, Shading Level is set to 30 percent. Increase this number to darken gray shading; lower it to lighten shaded areas.

The Autoscale Fonts option on the Printers–Fonts menu determines how Quattro Pro treats Bitstream fonts in your graphs when you change the size of the graph. Remember that you select fonts by size, such as 8 points for a small font or 18 points for a large one.

But a graph has no absolute dimensions. You can change its size in the Graph Annotator or when you are printing it (by specifying how large the graph should be on the page). In order to give you this flexibility, Quattro Pro automatically scales the fonts you have included to match the size of the graph.

By default, the Autoscale Fonts option is set to Yes. If you specify an 18-point font for a graph's title, and then print the graph so that it is only 4 inches wide by 3 inches tall, Quattro Pro will automatically reduce the size of the font in the title to keep it in proportion to the graph.

If you want to retain precisely the font size that you choose for graph text, set the Autoscale Fonts option to No.

SETTING YOUR MOUSE BUTTONS

By default, the left button on your mouse is the active one—the button you click to make a selection. If you operate the mouse with your left hand, you might prefer to use the right mouse button.

The Mouse Button command on the Options–Hardware menu lets you designate either the left or right button as the active one. If you want to retain the new mouse button designation for future sessions with Quattro Pro, remember to use the Options–Update command.

SETTING COLORS

If you are using a color video display, Quattro Pro offers a range of colors for many of its screen components, which can be changed with the choices on the Options–Colors menu. This menu lists all the structural components of Quattro Pro: Menu, Desktop, Spreadsheet, Conditional, Help, and File Manager (you can also change the colors of the File Manager with its own Options–Colors command). Each choice brings up another menu that lists all the components of the item.

On the Options–Colors–Spreadsheet menu, the WYSIWYG Colors command lets you adjust the colors that are used for the spreadsheet when you are working in WYSIWYG (graphics) mode. Next to each component is its current color setting. For example, you might see White on Blue next to Spreadsheet–Frame, or Black on White for Menu–Text.

If you have a monochrome system, your choices will be limited. All the Color commands will be available, but your choices of colors will consist only of Normal, Bold, Underline, Inverse, and Empty.

Follow these steps to change the color of the input line (we won't save this change with the Update command, however). If you have a monochrome system, your color choices will be limited to the five attributes listed above.

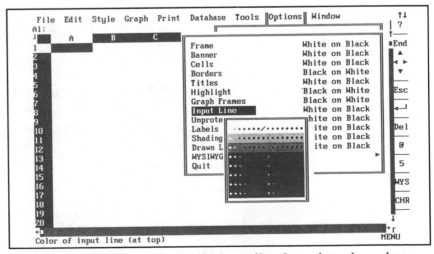

Don't try to select the Input Line option from the Spreadsheet menu by typing its first letter, I. Many items on the Color menus share the same first letter. You could easily end up changing the colors for the wrong portion of the screen.

1. Invoke the Options–Colors–Spreadsheet command.

2. Move the highlighter to the Input Line option and press ⏎, or click on that choice with your mouse.

You will see a color palette from which you can choose the color you want for the input line. This is the same palette that appears when you are changing any of the colors in Quattro Pro. The current color of the input line is indicated by a small rotating line.

Figure 18.1, although not in color, shows the layout of the menus and color palette. You can see the rotating line near the center of the top row of the palette, indicating that the input line is currently white on black, as you can also see in the menus to the right of the Input Line choice.

*Figure 18.1:*Selecting a color for the input line from the color palette

3. Use the arrow keys to highlight the second color in the bottom row of the palette, and then press ↵ (or click on that color with your mouse).

The palette will disappear, and the Input Line choice on the Spreadsheet menu now shows that its current color is Blue on White. If you wanted to retain this color for all future sessions of Quattro Pro, you would now use the Options–Update command.

GUIDING YOUR WAY WITH CONDITIONAL COLORS

Besides being able to create pleasing displays by changing the colors of Quattro Pro's various components, you can also use colors as signals.

The Options–Colors–Conditional menu offers some very interesting color choices that let you identify numeric values in the spreadsheet. For example, you can specify a range between a low and a high value, and any numbers that fall outside this range will be given a different color. Before these colors take effect, however, you must first enable the conditional colors with the Conditional–On/Off command. By default they are disabled.

The following options appear on the Conditional menu:

- On/Off: By default, all the options on the Conditional menu are turned off. Set this to Enable in order to have them take effect.

- ERR: Cells with results equivalent to @ERR. By default, these are red on black.

- Smallest Normal Value: The lowest value in the acceptable range.

- Greatest Normal Value: The highest value in the acceptable range.

- Below Normal Color: The color for cells whose contents fall below the smallest normal value.

- Normal Cell Color: The color for cells whose contents fall between the smallest and greatest normal values.

- Above Normal Color: The color for cells whose contents fall above the greatest normal value.

The numbers you enter for the smallest and greatest normal values are saved with the current spreadsheet, and in that sense are more like global settings. The colors you select for numbers that fall outside the normal range, however, are saved as system defaults, not with the spreadsheet.

Three options on the Colors–Spreadsheet menu can also help you find your way about the spreadsheet:

- Titles: Cells that are locked as titles with the Window–Options–Locked Titles command.

- Unprotected: Cells that you have unprotected with the Style–Protection–Unprotect command.

- Labels: Cells that contain labels. Change this from its default color to differentiate labels from numeric value cells.

RESETTING THE COLOR PALETTE

When you have adjusted, revised, and played with Quattro Pro's colors so that the spreadsheet now looks like an interior decorator's nightmare, don't worry. You can change all the colors back to their factory defaults by using the Options–Colors–Palettes command. This command has four choices; use the one appropriate to your computer's video adapter and monitor:

- Color: Both your video adapter and monitor are color.

- Monochrome: The video adapter is either standard monochrome or a Hercules graphics card.

- Black & White: The video adapter is color with a black-and-white display; this is often needed on portable or Compaq computers.

Even if your lap-
top computer uses
a shades-of-gray display,
you may find that the
Color command works
best for resetting Quat-
tro Pro's colors.

• Gray Scale: The video adapter is color with a display that shows shades of gray in place of colors; this may be needed on some laptop computers.

If you reset the colors to their defaults, you can then save them for future sessions with the Options–Update command.

CHANGING THE INTERNATIONAL SETTINGS

Quattro Pro's Options–International command offers the choices Currency, Punctuation, Date, Time, Use Sort Table, LICS Conversion, and Overstrike Print.

In the beginning of this chapter, the Currency command was used to demonstrate the effect of system settings on the local and global settings within a spreadsheet. Changing the Currency option, or any of the other options on the International menu, will affect all spreadsheets in Quattro Pro.

The Options–International–Currency command changes the character that is displayed for a cell that you have formatted as Currency with the Style–Numeric Format command. You specify one or more characters (the $ is the default) and whether the characters should precede or follow the number in the display.

This style would
require a much
wider column than the
default style that uses
the dollar sign.

For example, you could specify the word *Dollars* (with a preceding space) as the text and Suffix for its position in the display. The number 245 would appear as:

245.00 Dollars

The Options–International–Punctuation command offers a list of eight choices, which let you specify the character used as the decimal point (a period by default), the separator between thousands in a numeric display (comma), and the separator between arguments in @ functions and macro commands (comma, period, or semicolon).

For example, here are the first three items on the Punctuation menu (the separator used in @ functions is illustrated within the parentheses):

A. 1,234.56 (a1,a2)

B. 1.234,56 (a1.a2)

C. 1,234.56 (a1;a2)

Option A is the default. Keep in mind that the only time the separator between thousands appears in the display is when you have formatted a cell with either the Currency or Comma formats.

On the other hand, the character you select for the decimal point is the one you must use when you enter a decimal fraction. If you use a different character, Quattro Pro will beep and reject your entry.

The Date and Time choices on the International menu determine the style that will be used for the International numeric formats. There are two such formats on the Style–Numeric Format–Date menu: one is called Long International and the other is called Short International.

By default, the two International date formats look like this for the date January 31, 1992:

01/31/92

01/31

The Style–Numeric Format–Date–Time menu also has these two styles, although they describe a time, not date, format. The Long and Short styles look like this for the time 2:30 and 10 seconds in the afternoon:

14:30:10

14:30

The Options–International–Use Sort Table command allows you to change the order in which Quattro Pro sorts your data

The Database–
Sort–Sort Rules–
Label Order command
offers the two choices
Dictionary and ASCII.
Choosing Dictionary
produces the same sort-
ing order as using the
International sort table.

when you use the Database–Sort command. This command accesses what are known as sort table files, which have an SOR file
extension. Borland's database program, Paradox, also uses SOR
files to determine its sorting order.

The Use Sort Table menu lists all the SOR files that are found
in the Quattro Pro subdirectory. The ASCII.SOR file is the
default sort table. When you sort a block with the Database–Sort
command, the text entries in it will be arranged according to
their ASCII value. In that order, numerals come before letters
and uppercase letters precede lowercase ones.

The sort table file INTL.SOR (International) causes data to
be sorted in a dictionary fashion where, for example, uppercase
A and lowercase A are sorted next to one another. Numerals still
precede the letters of the alphabet. This provides a more appropriate order for data that contains characters beyond those
used in the English alphabet.

The two other sort table files offered on the Use Sort Table
menu are NORDAN.SOR (Norwegian and Danish) and SWED-
FIN.SOR (Swedish and Finnish). Each provides an order that is
similar to the effects of the International sort table, but is also
proper for those characters unique to the language.

The LICS Conversion option on the Options–International
menu allows you to specify how Quattro Pro should handle
characters from the Lotus International Character Set, known
as LICS, when you retrieve a Lotus 1-2-3 spreadsheet.

LICS consists of 256 characters, each of which is identified by
a unique number, just as ASCII characters are. In fact, the first
128 LICS and ASCII characters are identical. But the second 128
characters, which make up the extended character set, are not
always identical.

Quattro Pro normally works with the ASCII character set.
By default, the LICS Conversion option is set to No, so that when
you retrieve a WK1 file into Quattro Pro, any LICS characters are
translated into their equivalent ASCII character. If you set the
LICS Conversion option to Yes, any incoming LICS characters
from a 1-2-3 file are displayed as they would appear in Lotus 1-2-3.

It does not matter how the LICS Conversion option is set when you save your spreadsheet in the WK1 format. The characters are always saved as the proper LICS characters.

The last option on the Options–International menu is Overstrike Print. Some printers (generally older ones) can print only standard alphanumeric characters. They cannot print accented letters, for example. Set the Overstrike Print option to Yes, and Quattro Pro will be able to print many of the otherwise unprintable characters. It does so by printing both the letter and accent in the space of a single character.

CHANGING THE DISPLAY MODE

If you are using a CGA or Hercules graphics card, you will have only one option, 80x25.

Depending on the capabilities of your video adapter, you can change the output of your display with the Options–Display Mode command. For example, on a computer with a VGA video card, the Display Mode command offers these standard choices:

A: 80x25

B: WYSIWYG

C: EGA: 80x43

D: VGA: 80x50

Unless you made WYSIWYG mode the default during installation or with the Options–Update command, Quattro Pro uses the 80x25 mode, which is the standard display on DOS computers. This provides 80 characters across the screen and 25 lines.

The EGA and VGA options are also text modes, but they use a smaller font and therefore fit more lines on the screen. If you find yourself getting lost in your spreadsheet, it may be helpful to use one of these extended screen modes.

USING EXTENDED DISPLAY MODES

Many specialized VGA display adapter cards are supported by Quattro Pro. They are listed on the Options–Display Mode menu under their brand name. For example, you will see ATI VGA Wonder, STB PowerGraph VGA, Video-7 VRAM VGA, and others. If your computer has one of these video cards, or a card that can emulate one of them, you can choose from several other display modes.

For example, if you have a Video-7 VGA card, select it from the Options–Display Mode menu. You will be offered a second menu with a list of specialized text display modes. These include 80x60, 100x60, 132x25, 132x28, and 132x43. You can choose one of them to set a new display mode for your screen. Figure 18.2 shows the screen when it is running in the 132x43 mode.

In this mode, more than three times as many cells are visible than in the normal 80x25 mode. Whether you prefer this display depends somewhat on the quality of your monitor and the resiliency of your eyes. Nonetheless, using one of the extended modes will give you a broad overview of your spreadsheet.

Note that this and the other extended modes are *text*, not graphics, even though the tiny fonts and huge expanse of screen may seem far from what you consider a text display. There are two ways to tell that the screen is still in a text mode:

- If you have inserted any graphs into the spreadsheet, they will not be visible, but will appear as highlighted

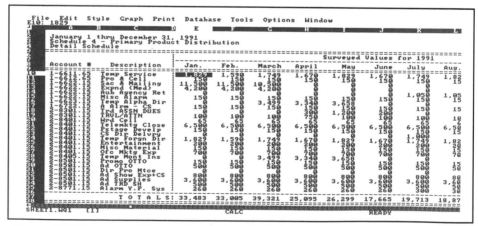

Figure 18.2: The spreadsheet when using the VGA 132x43 text mode display

boxes, as they do in the standard 80x25 mode.

- The screen response is still very fast when you move the cursor and scroll the screen.

The type of video adapter that Quattro Pro automatically detects determines the options that appear on the Display Mode menu. Therefore, if you are using a VGA video card, for example, and you do not see the four choices shown at the beginning of this section, Quattro Pro may be having difficulty detecting your video adapter. In that case, try using the Options–Hardware–Screen–Screen Type command and change it from Autodetect to VGA (or whatever style of card you are using). Reissue the Options–Display Mode command, and you should see the four VGA choices.

USING WYSIWYG MODE

There may be several text modes available on your video display, but there is only graphics mode, called WYSIWYG on the Display Mode menu. (You can also click on the WYS mouse button to change to WYSIWYG mode.) The acronym WYSIWYG stands for *what you see is what you get*, and it refers to the fact that what you see on the screen looks just like what you will get when you print your spreadsheet. However, you must have an EGA or a VGA video adapter to use WYSIWYG mode.

Running Quattro Pro in graphics mode helps you to make your spreadsheets more attractive and informative. You have seen the benefits of WYSIWYG mode throughout this book:

- When adjusting the height of rows (Chapter 4)
- When applying fonts to cells (Chapter 6)
- Instead of test printing in Screen Preview mode (Chapter 7)
- To display or hide the spreadsheet grid lines (Chapter 10)
- To display graphs within your spreadsheet (Chapter 12)

All programs run slower in graphics mode than they do in standard text mode. In general, you should choose one of the text modes for the bulk of your work in Quattro Pro.

One more advantage of WYSIWYG mode is that characters can be displayed in any size. The Options–WYSIWYG Zoom % command lets you either reduce the Quattro Pro display to show more cells in a smaller font, or enlarge the display to show fewer cells in a larger, more readable font.

By default, WYSIWYG Zoom % is set to 100 percent, so that fonts appear very similar to how they will look when printed. You can set this option as low as 25 percent to reduce fonts to a quarter of their original size, or as high as 200 percent to double the size of all fonts on the screen.

Realize that when a 12-point font is reduced to 25 percent, it will be nothing more than an unreadable squiggle on the screen. But seeing more than 50 columns and 200 rows at the same time can give you a broad overview of the spreadsheet, somewhat like the results of the Window–Options–Map View command.

Enlarging the display allows you to zoom in on smaller fonts without straining your eyes. Showing fewer but larger cells can be useful when you are presenting your spreadsheet to others.

Note that enlarging or reducing the spreadsheet display with the Options–WYSIWYG Zoom % command has no effect on your printed output. On the printed spreadsheet, the fonts will appear in the size you selected with the Style–Font command.

Another point to remember is that if you are running Quattro Pro with the Options–Graphics Quality command set to Final, it will need to access a different screen font each time you adjust the size of the display with the Options–WYSIWYG Zoom % command. If the font does not already exist on disk, Quattro Pro will have to build it. Therefore, even when you want the best screen font, you should work in Draft mode as you experiment with different zoom factors. Change to Final mode only after you have found a satisfactory setting for the zoom percent.

SETTING THE STARTUP OPTIONS

There are several startup configuration settings that you can adjust and save as the defaults. In Chapter 8, you learned that Quattro Pro will automatically load a spreadsheet with a specified name when the program is first loaded. In Chapter 16, you learned about the autoexecuting macro, which Quattro Pro will automatically run each time it loads a spreadsheet that contains the specially named macro.

To configure Quattro Pro's startup options, you adjust the items on the Options–Startup menu. One command on this menu is of particular importance, especially if you are working in close quarters with others. You can use the Options–Startup–Beep command to turn off any beeps, chirps, or buzzes that Quattro Pro sounds when you make an error, select a file in the File Manager, and so on. Once these signals are silenced, however, you must pay closer attention to the screen and be on the alert for error messages; otherwise, you may find yourself in for difficulties.

Another command on the Startup menu, Edit Menus, may not be of importance to you unless you were a user of the Menu Builder add-in in the original Quattro. The command was included in Quattro Pro to retain compatibility with Quattro, but it is not a documented or supported feature in Quattro Pro.

SPECIFYING THE FILE OPTIONS

All the file-related commands on the Options–Startup menu have been mentioned in Chapters 8 and 16. We will briefly review them here.

SETTING THE DEFAULT DIRECTORY FOR YOUR SPREADSHEETS

Each time you load Quattro Pro, it uses the same subdirectory as its default for your spreadsheet files. You can specify which directory this should be by using the Options–Startup–Directory command, which prompts you for a drive and subdirectory. You must specify a valid location, and then use the Options–Update command if you want this directory to be retained as the default for future sessions with Quattro Pro.

The global counterpart to this command is the File–Directory command, which you can use to change the default directory for the current session of Quattro Pro.

Instead of naming a specific directory for Quattro Pro to use each time it loads, you can have it always look to the directory that was current at the time it was loaded. You do this by entering a single period as the directory to use in the Options–Startup–Directory command.

Later, from the DOS prompt, you can make a data directory that contains your spreadsheets the default DOS directory, and then load Quattro Pro simply by typing Q. Quattro Pro will load and use the current data directory as its default.

In order to load Quattro Pro from any directory on your hard disk, you must include the Quattro Pro subdirectory in your DOS path. If your path is already too long and you don't want to add Quattro Pro to it, you can still load the program without first changing to its subdirectory by including Quattro Pro's location within the command to run it. For example, if it is located on your C drive in a subdirectory named QPRO, you would type this at the DOS prompt:

C:\QPRO\Q

NAMING THE AUTOLOAD FILE

Chapter 8 discussed Quattro Pro's autoload spreadsheet name. Each time you load the program, it looks in the default directory for a spreadsheet with the special autoload name. If it finds that name there, it immediately loads the spreadsheet.

By default, Quattro Pro searches for a spreadsheet named QUATTRO.WQ1, but you can change the search name with the Options–Startup–Autoload File command.

NAMING THE STARTUP MACRO

Chapter 16 demonstrated the use of the autoload macro. Each time you load a spreadsheet, Quattro Pro checks to see if the spreadsheet contains a macro with the special autoload block name. If it finds such a name, it will then run the macro. By default, this name is \0 (backslash zero), but you can change it with the Options–Startup–Startup Macro command.

■ If you are running Quattro Pro via the Paradox Access, the Autoload File command is ignored. This is true whether or not you have enabled the Database–Paradox Access–Autoload command.

NAMING THE DEFAULT FILE EXTENSION

If you don't specify a file extension when you are saving a spreadsheet, Quattro Pro will append the extension WQ1 to the file name. You can change this default extension with the Options–Startup–File Extension command.

You would normally not want to change the WQ1 extension because it serves to identify a spreadsheet as having been created by Quattro Pro. But you may find occasions where a another default extension will be a great convenience.

For example, if you are creating many spreadsheets in Quattro Pro that will later be imported into Lotus 1-2-3, you could change the file extension to WK1. You could then save each spreadsheet without specifying the extension, and let Quattro Pro do it for you. But even in a case such as this, you would probably not use the Options–Update command to save this extension as the system default.

CHOOSING A MENU SYSTEM

Quattro Pro is a very accommodating program, and perhaps its most flexible feature is its menu interface. When you load Quattro Pro, it configures its menus by loading the menu file QUATTRO.MU. This file contains all the menus in the program, as well as some of the system defaults.

Quattro Pro comes with two other menu files that emulate two popular spreadsheets. The file 123.MU contains the Lotus 1-2-3 menu tree, and Q1.MU contains the menu tree for the original Quattro.

You can change to any menu tree by using the Options–Startup–Menu Tree command. The command reads the disk and offers you a list of all the menu files it finds (those with an MU extension). You simply pick the one you want, and in an instant you will be using those menus.

When you load another menu tree, the system defaults from its MU file are also loaded. If you later change a system setting in Quattro Pro, and then use the Options–Update command, the current settings will be saved to the current MU file. If you want that change to affect more than one menu tree, you will have to make the same change while using each of the menu trees.

Quattro and Lotus 1-2-3 share many commands with Quattro Pro although they may be worded differently. For example, the Block–Names–Create command in Quattro Pro is invoked under the Range–Name–Create command within the Lotus 1-2-3 menu tree. In the Quattro menu tree, however, the equivalent command is Block–Advanced–Create.

You can see why recording or writing macros in the logical style is so much more effective than using keystroke macros. Otherwise, you would have to contend with three keystroke macros to perform the same task in Quattro Pro, Lotus 1-2-3, and Quattro:

    /bnc

    /rnc

    /bac

Using the 123.MU menus, the command is Worksheet–Global–Default–Files–Menu Tree. On the Q1.MU menus, the command is the same as that in Quattro 1: Default–Startup–Menu Tree.

In fact, before you start experimenting with other menu trees, you might write the following logical macro as a simple safety net:

    {/ Startup;Menus}

No matter which menu tree you are using, this macro calls up the list of available menu files. Without it, you might have trouble finding the appropriate command on the 1-2-3 or Quattro menus to return the menu tree to the Quattro Pro default.

PROGRAMMING THE MOUSE PALETTE

If you have installed your mouse software and mouse, when you load Quattro Pro, you will see the mouse palette along the right side of the spreadsheet. As mentioned in Chapter 1, you can program the buttons on this mouse palette.

The mouse palette consists of the nine icons, or buttons, on the right side of the screen below the two-arrow zoom icon. The first two buttons on the palette are not programmable:

- The question mark (?) calls the Quattro Pro Help system, just as though you had pressed F1.

- In the button with the four arrows and the word End, you can click on one of the arrows, and the cell selector will be moved as though you had pressed End and the corresponding arrow key.

You can program each of the other seven buttons to type any keystrokes or invoke any Quattro Pro menu or macro command. Buttons one through four and six and seven are already programmed:

- Esc: Escape key
- ↵: Enter key
- Del: Delete key
- @: Functions key, Alt-F3
- WYS: Options–Display Mode–WYSIWYG command
- CHR: Options–Display Mode–80x25 command

As an example, let's change the meaning of the fifth button to perform what could be a frequent task: split the screen horizontally, unsynchronize the panes, and move the cell selector to the lower pane. Follow these steps:

1. Invoke the Options–Mouse Palette command.
2. From the list of the seven buttons that is offered, choose 5th Button.
3. Choose Text from the menu that is offered.
4. Press Escape to clear the existing text (the numeral 5 with a preceding and following space). You are allowed

to enter up to three characters, which will be used as the text on the mouse button in the palette.

5. Type **WIN** and press ↵ to signify that this is the window button.

6. Choose Macro from the menu.

7. Press Escape to clear the existing macro, the {beep} command. You can enter up to 25 characters that will be executed as a macro when this button is clicked.

8. Enter the macro /**woh**/**wou{window}** and press ↵.

9. Choose Quit three times to return to Ready mode.

We are using a keystroke macro because the equivalent logical macro would require 49 characters.

You will notice that the fifth mouse button now displays the WIN label. It is ready to be used.

10. Move the cell selector to one of the rows near the middle of the screen.

11. Move the mouse pointer to the WIN button and click on it.

In a flash, the window will split horizontally, the panes will be unsynchronized, and the cell selector will jump to the bottom pane.

As with all the other system commands, you must use the Options–Update command to retain the changes you make to the mouse palette.

SETTING THE CHOICES ON THE OPTIONS–OTHER MENU

The items on the Options–Other menu include Undo, Macro, Expanded Memory, Clock, and Paradox. You use the Undo command to enable or disable the Edit–Undo command (Alt-F5), discussed in Chapter 3.

TURNING OFF THE DISPLAY FOR MACROS

Macros execute so quickly that the screen can become a confusing blur of activity. This constant rewriting of the screen not only tends to distract the user, but it also slows down the macro.

The Options–Other–Macro command lets you choose which areas of the screen should not be rewritten during macro execution. The choices are Both, Panel, Window, and None. The default setting is Both, so that Quattro Pro freezes the entire screen while a macro is executing.

If you select None, the entire screen is rewritten whenever a macro command induces any activity on it, such as selecting a menu or moving the cell selector.

The other two commands, Panel and Window, have equivalent macro commands. During macro execution, the macro command {paneloff} freezes the display of the input line, menus, and status line; and {windowsoff} freezes the main body of the screen. Therefore, these two macro commands are not really needed because the screen is frozen by default.

You may at times want the screen refreshed during macro execution, perhaps so that it behaves like a Lotus 1-2-3 macro. In that case, use the Options–Other–Macro command to disable only that portion of the screen that you do not want refreshed. For example, choosing Window will disable the display for the window but allow the display of the menus, input line, and status line.

ALLOCATING THE SPREADSHEET TO EXPANDED MEMORY

If your computer has EMS memory, Quattro Pro will use it for storing all or part of each open spreadsheet. By default, it stores only spreadsheet data in EMS memory; the formatting components are kept in normal (conventional) memory. Because accessing data in EMS memory is slower than retrieving the same data from normal memory, splitting a spreadsheet between the two types of memory provides a reasonable balance between speed and capacity.

Quattro Pro does not refresh the screen during macro execution, but when you are using the macro debugger, all screen activity is shown. If it were not, the debugger would not be very practical.

If you're not sure whether Quattro Pro is successfully accessing your computer's expanded memory, run the program named EMSTEST.COM, which is located in the Quattro Pro program subdirectory.

The Options–Other–Expanded Memory command is by default set to Spreadsheet Data. If you are working on many spreadsheets at the same time, or one or more very large spreadsheets, you may want to set this command to Both. Thereafter, both the spreadsheet data and formatting information will be stored in EMS memory.

You can also choose Format from the Expanded Memory menu to store just the spreadsheet formatting, but not its data, in EMS memory. You can choose None to store everything in normal RAM, but this will produce only a minor increase in Quattro Pro's speed.

Once you have changed the Expanded Memory setting, in order for the change to take effect, you must close all open spreadsheets and then load them again.

SETTING THE CLOCK

Remember that any display of the current date or time on your computer is driven by your computer's internal clock. If that clock is not accurate, the display will not be accurate.

Quattro Pro shows the current spreadsheet's file name in the status line at the bottom of the screen. With the Options–Other–Clock command, you can choose to display the current date and time in the status line, as well.

The options are Standard and International, which refer to the format that will be used to display the date and time. If you want to turn off the display, choose None.

DEFINING NETWORK
PARAMETERS FOR PARADOX FILES

You can open a Paradox database file as a spreadsheet, either directly with the File–Retrieve or Open command or via the Paradox Access (as discussed in Chapter 14). You can also query a database file by using the Quattro Pro Database–Query commands. If you are working on a stand-alone computer without the Paradox Access, there is nothing more to consider.

If you are working on a network, talk to the network administrator, who can give you the information you need for the Options–Other–Paradox settings.

If you are working on a network or using the Paradox Access, you must provide some additional information on the Quattro Pro Options–Other–Paradox menu:

- Network Type: By default, this is set to Disabled. If you are working on a network, specify the type (brand) of network you are using. If you are not on a network but will be using the Paradox Access, specify Other as the type.

- Directory: Specify the drive and directory where the PARADOX.NET file is located.

- Retries: Enter the number of seconds that Quattro Pro should wait before it again tries to access a previously locked database file. The default is 300 seconds.

Once you have set these options, be sure to use the Options–Update command to save them as the system defaults.

Although this is the final chapter, it may be just the beginning of your partnership with Quattro Pro. The appendix that follows covers the installation of Quattro Pro.

A

Installing
Quattro Pro

INSTALLING QUATTRO PRO IS A SIMPLE PROCESS IN most cases. There are a few decisions you will have to make during the installation routine, but you will most likely find the questions understandable and the choices self-evident.

The first section of this appendix provides a quick overview of the installation process, which should be more than enough for normal installation. If you are unsure of some of the steps in the Install program, you have had trouble installing Quattro Pro previously, or you simply prefer to follow a more detailed approach, you can refer to the second section, which provides step-by-step guidance.

QUICK INSTALLATION

From the DOS prompt, follow these steps to start the automated installation routine:

1. Insert the Quattro Pro Disk 1 in drive A.

2. Change to drive A by typing **A:** and pressing ↵.

3. Start the Install program by typing **INSTALL** and pressing ↵.

4. Follow the instructions on the screen and, when prompted by the program, replace the disk in drive A with the next one of the set.

5. Before the installation routine is finished, you must respond to questions about Quattro Pro configuration for your system.

You will then be returned to the DOS prompt, ready to run Quattro Pro. If you want to use a mouse with Quattro Pro but have not already installed it for other software on your system, refer to the section about installing your mouse, later in this appendix.

Important! You cannot simply copy each of the Quattro Pro disks to your hard disk. You must run the Install program that is on the first disk. Many of the files are in a compressed format, and the Install program decompresses them during installation.

STEP-BY-STEP INSTALLATION

For this discussion, we will assume that you are installing Quattro Pro on your hard disk C, and that your floppy disk is drive A. Just substitute another letter for either if you will be using another drive.

Before you begin, make sure that you have all the Quattro Pro floppy disks at the ready, as you will need them all for the installation. You should also check to be sure that you have at least 5 megabytes of free disk space. To do so, at the DOS prompt, issue the command **DIR C:**.

If the last line of the directory listing indicates that you have more than 5 megabytes available, then you're ready to go. If you have less than that, you will have to delete some of the files on your hard disk to make room for Quattro Pro.

On some computers, such as some laptops and portables, you may find it difficult to read the screens of the Install program. Try running it again, but this time use the parameter /B, for black and white: **INSTALL /B**.

1. Make drive A the default by typing **A:** and pressing ↵.

2. Place the first Quattro Pro disk in drive A.

3. Run the Install program by typing **INSTALL** and pressing ↵. An introductory screen will appear, followed by a prompt that asks you to enter the source drive to use. The default will be A (or whatever floppy disk drive you started from).

4. Type in a different drive letter if appropriate, or press ↵ to accept the default entry. Next you will be asked for the name of the subdirectory in which you want to install Quattro Pro. The default will be C:\QPRO.

5. To change the drive or subdirectory name, move the cursor down to that item on the screen, press ↵, type in the new destination, and press ↵. For example, specifying E:\QUATTRO will install the program on your E drive in a subdirectory named QUATTRO.

6. Position the cursor on the first item, Start Installation, and press ↵.

7. The Install program will begin copying files to the destination on your hard disk. After the files on each disk are copied, the program will prompt you to insert the next disk, until all the disks have been copied.

When the files on all the disks have been copied, you will be asked the following questions about your system configuration:

Even if you have a laptop computer that emulates color by using shades of gray, the Color setting for the Monitor Type option works best in most cases. You can later change to Gray Scale or Black and White from within Quattro Pro by using the Options–Colors–Palettes command.

- *Monitor Type:* The Install program detects the type of video card you are using, but it can't detect the type of monitor that is connected to that card. If you have a color video card, you will need to specify whether your monitor is Color (the default), Black and White, or Gray Scale.

- *Company Name:* Press F2 and enter your company name. It will appear in Quattro Pro's log-on screen when you start the program. If this is your personal copy, you can simply enter Personal.

- *Name:* Press F2 and enter your name. This will appear with your company name on Quattro Pro's log-on screen.

- *Serial #:* Press F2 and enter the serial number from Disk 1 of the Quattro Pro disks. The number should look something like AB123C45678901.

- *Are you installing Quattro Pro on a network server?:* If you are installing Quattro Pro on a computer that is not connected to a network, choose No. Otherwise, you will need to answer a few questions about your network. Do not choose this option until you have spoken with the network administrator, who should take responsibility for all software installation on the network.

The more subdirectories that you include in your DOS PATH command, the slower your system will operate whenever DOS is searching for a program file to run.

- *Edit AUTOEXEC.BAT file?:* Install is asking if you want it to edit your AUTOEXEC.BAT file and include your new Quattro Pro subdirectory in a PATH command. Although this allows you to invoke Quattro Pro from any subdirectory on your hard disk, in most cases, it really

APP. A

You can always change to any available menu tree from within Quattro Pro by using the Options–Startup–Menu Tree Command.

isn't necessary. Instead, you should choose No for this option. To do this, press F2 to edit the entry, and then select No from the menu of choices that is offered. Then press ↵ to record your choice.

- *User Interface:* Instead of using Quattro Pro's default menu system, you can choose the original Quattro menus. It is recommended that you stick with the Quattro Pro menus for now, as these are logical and easy to use. If you want to try the Quattro or Lotus 1-2-3 interface, you can choose it from within Quattro Pro at any time.

- *Printer Manufacturer:* Press F2 and select your printer's manufacturer from the list that is offered.

- *Printer Model:* Press F2 and choose your printer's model from the list.

- *Printer Mode:* Depending on the printer you have selected, you may be offered a choice of print resolution, such as 100x100, 200x200, and so on. These are for graphics printouts, not ordinary text. You can choose the highest density for now. Your graphics-mode printouts will look their best, although they will take longer to print than at lower resolutions. You can later choose a lower density from within Quattro Pro.

In order to run Quattro Pro in WYSIWYG mode, your computer must have either an EGA video adapter capable of 640x350 resolution or a VGA adapter.

- *WYSIWYG Mode:* You can choose to have Quattro Pro loaded in either text or WYSIWYG (graphics) mode. Because running in WYSIWYG mode slows down the program, it is recommended that you choose No and run Quattro Pro in standard text mode. You can later switch to WYSIWYG mode from within the program by using the Options–Display Mode–WYSIWYG command.

If you choose to run Quattro Pro in WYSIWYG mode, when you first use the program, you may want to change its Options–Graphics Quality setting to Draft. This will reduce the quality of your screen display and printouts, but it will avoid font-building delays while you are familiarizing yourself with the program. You can retain this setting for future sessions by using the Options–Update command. Fonts and font building are discussed in Chapter 6.

- *Install Quattro Pro for Windows?*: If you have Microsoft Windows (version 3.0 or higher) installed on your hard disk, you can choose Yes to have the Install program create a Windows program group and icon for Quattro Pro. When you are prompted for the location of your Windows program, enter the drive and path, such as C:\WIN, and press ↵.

If you choose to install Quattro Pro for Windows, the next time you run Windows, you will find a new program group called QPRO, with a program icon for Quattro Pro. When you click on, or run, the icon, it runs the program information file Q.PIF, which is in your Quattro Pro subdirectory. The settings in Q.PIF should be acceptable for most computer systems. You can also run Quattro Pro by using the Windows Program Manager's Run command. Just specify the drive, path, and either the Quattro Pro PIF file or its program name, such as C:\Q\Q.EXE.

- *Bitstream Character Set:* Quattro Pro uses Bitstream downloadable fonts when you print to your graphics printer (high-quality output). Choose whether you want to use the Standard U.S. or Standard European character set for your fonts. The European character set contains more characters, so its font files are about 20 percent larger than those containing the U.S. character set.

- *Fonts to Build:* You can create a set of soft fonts that will be stored on disk in your Quattro Pro subdirectory. You can skip this step for now by choosing None. When you are printing in Final quality mode in Quattro Pro, it will build any fonts that are needed and store them on disk. On the other hand, it can take as long as a minute to build a single font on an 8088 computer, so you may want to build some fonts now. Having the fonts already available on disk will save printing time.

After you have responded to the fonts prompt, you will be returned to the DOS prompt, ready to run Quattro Pro.

SAVING YOUR CONFIGURATION FILES

Quattro Pro saves all its system resources and defaults in two files named QUATTRO.MU and RSC.RF. When you are running Quattro Pro, it updates these files as you make changes to the configuration and default settings of the program. There may be times when you have made changes to Quattro Pro that you later realize are not only unwanted but will be difficult to revise.

To avoid the inconvenience of reconstructing Quattro Pro's default configuration, you can provide yourself with a little insurance by making backup copies of QUATTRO.MU and RSC.RF. Just copy each of them under a new name, such as QUATTRO.MU1 and RSC.RF1, in the Quattro Pro subdirectory. From the DOS prompt, use the following commands:

        COPY QUATTRO.MU QUATTRO.MU1

        COPY RSC.RF RSC.RF1

To return Quattro Pro to the same system configuration that was established when you installed the program, just copy the two backup files to their original names. Use the following two commands from the DOS prompt:

        COPY QUATTRO.MU1 QUATTRO.MU

        COPY RSC.RF1 RSC.RF

INSTALLING YOUR MOUSE

If you plan to use a mouse with Quattro Pro, you must first install it, which involves two steps:

1. Physically connect the mouse to your computer. It may plug into a serial port on the back of your computer,

or it may have its own interface card that you must first plug into an available slot inside your computer. Use care, and follow the manufacturer's instructions.

2. Install the mouse software, or driver. Again, refer to the instructions that came with your mouse, and copy the necessary files to a subdirectory on your hard disk, such as one that you use for utility programs.

Once your mouse is physically installed and the software is copied to your hard disk, you are ready to load the mouse software. There are two different types of mouse software. One type is a program file, which might be called MOUSE.COM, that you run from the DOS prompt. The other type is a device driver that can only be invoked from within your CONFIG.SYS file when the computer boots up. If the driver is called MOUSE.SYS and is stored in the UTIL directory on your C drive, for example, you would include the following command in your CONFIG.SYS file:

device=C:\UTIL\MOUSE.SYS

A mouse driver such as this is loaded every time you turn on your computer. The first variety (program file) can also be loaded each time you turn on your computer if you include a command to call it within your AUTOEXEC.BAT file. For example, if the software is named MOUSE.COM and is stored in C:\UTIL, you would include the following command in your AUTOEXEC.BAT file:

C:\UTIL\MOUSE

If your mouse does not seem to be working properly with Quattro Pro, you may have to adjust the mouse program parameters. For example, on some computers that use the mouse software driver from Microsoft, the mouse pointer will disappear in the Quattro Pro Graph Annotator and reappear in the spreadsheet. In that case, try using the /Y parameter after the MOUSE command.

To read the most recent tips on mouse driver compatibility, import the README file from the Quattro Pro subdirectory into a blank Quattro Pro spreadsheet. Use the Tools–Import–ASCII Text File command and specify the file name **README.** (be sure to include the period at the end of the name).

If you are using the MOUSE.COM driver, at the DOS prompt, you would simply type

MOUSE /Y

You can use this command even after you have already loaded your mouse, and the parameter will be passed to it. This is one of the advantages of using the mouse program. Another is that you can remove the mouse from memory with the command

MOUSE OFF

Consult the documentation that came with your mouse for other command-line parameters.

Once the mouse software is loaded, it remains available until you either turn off the computer or run the mouse program with a switch that unloads it from memory. When you run Quattro Pro, it will automatically detect the presence of the mouse, and you will see the mouse pointer on the screen.

Index

? (question mark), on mouse
  palette, 19
{?} command (macros), 554
" (quotation mark)
as label prefix, 37, 59
    for text values, 63–64, 99, 100
' (apostrophe) as label prefix,
  57, 58
/ (slash key)
    to access Graph Annotator,
      387
    to access menus, 22, 522
$ (dollar sign), 61
    for absolute cell reference,
      87
** (asterisks)
    on graphs, 365
    in place of numeric display,
      66, 171
^ (caret) for centering text, 58,
  168
% (percent sign), 62
# (pound sign)
    in header or footer, 209–210
    for logical operators, 61
& (ampersand), for joining text
  strings, 98
@ (at sign)
    for functions, 92
    in header or footer, 209–210
@ functions, separator for, 592
@ *Functions and Macros* reference
  manual, 524, 526
@ functions list (Alt@=F3), on
  mouse palette, 20
\ (backslash)
    in macro name, 518
    as repeating label prefix, 35,
      59, 179
    in setup codes, 216
| (broken vertical bar)
    in header or footer, 209–210

as label prefix, 59, 217, 260
|:: (vertical bar, double colons)
  print code, 185
~ (tilde)
    for exclusive search, 444
    in macros, 514
123.MU menu file, 601
3-D linking, 319
35mm slides, 382
80286 processor, 457

Abort command, in macro
  debugger, 564
@ABS function, 94
absolute cell references, 61, 86–89, 120
    function key F4 for, 88–89
    in linking formulas, 320–321
    in query, 447
    vs. relative, 44, 123
absolute value of number, 94
Accuracy option (Solve For
  command), 503
@ACOS function, 94
active cell, 7
active corner, for anchoring, 138
active spreadsheets, command
  language keywords and, 574
active window, 296, 299–300
Add option (Tools–Combine
  command), 247–249
Additional Dual Values option
  (Optimization menu), 501
address, of cell, 6
Adjust Printer–Form Feed
  command, 50, 200
Advanced Math commands,
  485–501
Align option (Adjust Printer
  command), 220
alignment
    changing for block
    of cells, 59–60

of numbers, 64–65
of text, 411
Alt key
    for macros, 518
    and resizing objects, 405
ampersand (&), for joining text
  strings, 98
anchor, rotating, 137–138
anchoring block corner, 85
AND search criteria, 444–448
ANSWER table, 455
apostrophe (') as label prefix,
  57–58
arc cosine, 94
arc sine, 94
arc tangent, 94
area graph, 344, 346
arrow keys, 12, 14
Arrow command (Graph
  Annotator), 392–394
ASCII characters, 101, 582
ASCII code
    for Escape, 216
    sorting by, 435
ASCII files. *See* text files
ASCII.SOR file, 594
@ASIN function, 94
asterisks (**)
    on graphs, 365
    in place of numeric display,
      66, 171
at sign (@)
    for functions, 92
    in header or footer, 209–210
@ATAN function, 94
@ATAN2 function, 94
attributes
    of graph object, 389
    of spreadsheet information
      functions, 96–97
Auto LF (Printer menu), 587

for files in Control pane, 278
for records, with data query
commands, 448–453
search criteria
logical formulas in, 445–447
multiple, 444–445
special characters in, 444
@SECOND function, 103
segmented lines, from Graph
Annotator, 395
Select key (Shift-F7), 137
serial #, in install program, 613
serial printers, defining settings
for, 586
Series–Reset command, 357
{setpos} command (macros), 562
settings, local, global, and system,
168–169
setup codes for printer, 207,
216–218
.SFO file name extensions, 236
shading attributes
adding, 184
and copying, 132
shapes, from Graph Annotator,
397–401
SHARE command (DOS), 457,
459–460
shell of spreadsheet, creating,
34–37
Shift-Tab key, 13
Short International date format,
593
shortcuts
for entering dates, 105–106
for menus, 23–25
user-defined, 23–25
@SIN function, 95
sine, 95
Single Sheet (Printer menu), 587
Single Step (Transcript utility),
570
sizing objects, 404–407
Skip Line option (Adjust Printer
command), 220
slash key (/) to access menus, 22,
522
Slide EPS files, 382

slide shows, 372–375
arranging, 416–418
graph buttons for, 412–421
@SLN function, 108
software, for mouse, 617
Solution (Optimization menu),
499
.SOR file name extension, 594
sort key columns, defining,
433–434
sorting
avoiding problems in,
435–437
block of cells for, 435
File List, 281
in File Manager, 275
and formulas, 437
index column for, 436–437
order for Database-Sort
command, 593–594
rows in spreadsheet, 432–437
rules for order of, 434–435
sound files, 373, 556
source block of cells, 131
spreadsheet information
functions, 96–99
spreadsheets, 6. *See also* multiple
spreadsheet files; shell of
spreadsheet
closing, 240–241
color of, 588
combining vs. linking, 249
compression of, 265–267
creating, 278
expanding and contracting,
158–160
fixing broken, 568–569
linking, 43–45
maximum size of, 81
recalculation of, 113–115
retrieving, 241–243
save process for, 462–463
sorting rows in, 432–437
working with portions of,
245–249
@SQRT function, 95
square matrix, inverting, 495
square root, 95

SQZ! file-compression utility,
265–267
stacked-bar graphs, 344, 346, 356
stacking windows, 298–299
standard deviation
population, 112
sample, 112
start value, for Edit–Fill
command, 156
starting Quattro Pro, 5
from any directory, 600
options for, 598–602
specifying macro when,
520–521, 600
statistical functions, 95–97
status box (Graph Annotator), 392
status line, 8–11
Std Err of Coef, for regression
analysis, 489
Std Err of Y Est, for regression
analysis, 488–489
@STD function, 97
@STDS function, 97
step mode, for macro debugging,
563–564
step value, for Edit-Fill command,
156
{stepoff} command (macros), 556
stop bits, for defining printers, 586
stop value, for Edit-Fill command,
156
Storage of Values option, in SQZ!
utility, 266
straight-line depreciation, 108
string. *See* text entry
@STRING function, 100, 102
string functions, 98–102
Style–Alignment command, 59,
64, 168
Style–Block Size command, 173
Style–Column Width command,
66, 172
Style–Font command, 192
Style–Hide Column command
Expose, 176
Hide, 175–176
Style–Insert Break command, 185

FREE CATALOG!

SYBEX ®

Mail us this form today, and we'll send you a full-color catalog of Sybex books.

Name _____

Street _____

City/State/Zip _____

Phone _____

Please supply the name of the Sybex book purchased.

_____

How would you rate it?

_____ Excellent   _____ Very Good   _____ Average   _____ Poor

Why did you select this particular book?

_____ Recommended to me by a friend

_____ Recommended to me by store personnel

_____ Saw an advertisement in _____

_____ Author's reputation

_____ Saw in Sybex catalog

_____ Required textbook

_____ Sybex reputation

_____ Read book review in _____

_____ In-store display

_____ Other _____

Where did you buy it?

_____ Bookstore

_____ Computer Store or Software Store

_____ Catalog (name: _____)

_____ Direct from Sybex

_____ Other: _____

Did you buy this book with your personal funds?

_____ Yes   _____ No

About how many computer books do you buy each year?

_____ 1-3   _____ 3-5   _____ 5-7   _____ 7-9   _____ 10+

About how many Sybex books do you own?

_____ 1-3   _____ 3-5   _____ 5-7   _____ 7-9   _____ 10+

Please indicate your level of experience with the software covered in this book:

_____ Beginner   _____ Intermediate   _____ Advanced

Which types of software packages do you use regularly?

_____ Accounting	_____ Databases	_____ Networks
_____ Amiga	_____ Desktop Publishing	_____ Operating Systems
_____ Apple/Mac	_____ File Utilities	_____ Spreadsheets
_____ CAD	_____ Money Management	_____ Word Processing
_____ Communications	_____ Languages	_____ Other _____

(please specify)

Which of the following best describes your job title?

_____ Administrative/Secretarial	_____ President/CEO
_____ Director	_____ Manager/Supervisor
_____ Engineer/Technician	_____ Other _____

(please specify)

Comments on the weaknesses/strengths of this book: _____

_____

_____

_____

_____

PLEASE FOLD, SEAL, AND MAIL TO SYBEX

SYBEX, INC.
Department M
2021 CHALLENGER DR.
ALAMEDA, CALIFORNIA USA
94501

SYBEX ®

Quattro Pro Quick Keys and Their Macro Equivalents

F: File Manager window only
G: Graph Annotator window only
*: Not available in Lotus 1-2-3

Cursor-Control Keys	Macro Equivalent
←	{left} or {l}
→	{right} or {r}
↑	{up} or {u}
↓	{down} or {d}
Ctrl-← or Shift-Tab	{bigleft} or {backtab}
Ctrl-→ or Tab	{bigright} or {tab}
End	{end}
Home	{home}
PgDn	{pgdn}
PgUp	{pgup}

Program-Control Keys	
/	{menu} or /
Alt-*n*	{window*n*}
Backspace	{bs} or {backspace}
* Caps Lock off–on	{capoff}–{capon}
* Ctrl-\ (backslash)	{deleol}
* Ctrl-Backspace	{clear}
Ctrl-Break	{break}
* Ctrl-D	{date}
Del	{del} or {delete}
Enter	~ (tilde) or {cr}
Esc	{esc} or {escape}
Ins	{ins} or {insert}
* Ins off–on	{insoff}–{inson}
* Num Lock off–on	{numoff}–{numon}
* Scroll Lock off–on	{scrolloff}–{scrollon}